ILLUSTRATED DICTIONARY OF MICROCOMPUTER TERMINOLOGY

by Michael Hordeski

TAB BOOKS
BLUE RIDGE SUMMIT, PA. 17214

FIRST EDITION

FIRST PRINTING—OCTOBER 1978

Printed in the United States of America

Library of Congress Cataloging in Publication Data

Hordeski, Michael.
Illustrated dictionary of microcomputer terminology.

1. Microcomputers—Dictionaries. I. Title.
TK7885.A2H67 001.6'4'03 78-10421
ISBN 0-8306-9875-2
ISBN 0-8306-1088-X pbk.

Preface

Microcomputers have been hailed as the most important development in the history of electronics. Since the inception of digital logic, computer designers have been driven towards methods and machine configurations which would produce the lowest cost per gate, or logical function, and require the least amount of auxiliary equipment for a complete computing system. The first promise of microcomputer feasibility appeared in the fifties with the introduction of mass-produced transistors; the semiconductor industry was born. This radical change in the method and nature of electronic devices not only affected the computer and communications industries, but also changed the lives and lifestyles of many of us throughout the world. This development spawned a number of new companies and industries with the vision and management necessary to succeed using this new technology. Older companies which elected to participate and diligently pursue this technology also prospered.

The second great period of change occurred in the sixties, when mass-produced integrated circuits appeared. The first circuits, which contained one or two gates per chip and sold for as much as $125, created an impact which may have been greater than the introduction of the transistor itself. These first integrated circuits allowed the complexity and size of equipment to be reduced by a factor of ten, while simultaneously lowering the overall cost of the finished equipment to one-tenth of the transistor equivalent. Also, the original equipment manufacturer became a logic designer and system architect rather than a designer of circuits. Again, many new companies prospered, as well as the older firms that grasped the concept of the new integrated-circuit technology.

Similar events have taken place in the seventies as the development of microprocessors and related circuits necessary for microcomputer systems proceeded. Order-of-magnitude improvements even now are being achieved by those manufacturers with the vision and knowledge necessary to employ the new microcomputer technology. The end-item manufacturer must now place a greater emphasis on programming and other software-related activities than in the past.

A major problem with any new revolutionary technology is the nomenclature. In a fast-moving explosive field such as microcomputers, terms and concepts develop with the technology, and the field soon has its own unique language.

This book was written to reflect the current usage of all terms related to the microcomputer industry. Both hardware and software terms are included, with particular emphasis on software concepts. These concepts are the forces that will shape the products of tomorrow. Hardware and manufacturing concepts are discussed in all cases where these concepts are important to the developers and users of microcomputer systems. This dictionary draws heavily upon the current literature from industry periodicals, product manuals, and conference presentations; and for all those who have aided in the dissemination of microcomputer knowledge, I am indebted.

All acronyms and terms in this dictionary appear in alphabetic sequence, ignoring hyphens, which are used sparingly and only to avoid ambiguity where the term is a single concept and common usage is dictated by the hyphenated form. Many concepts appear more than once due to the common use of acronyms in the electronics industry. The reader is directed to review related definitions and terms to obtain a fuller understanding of key concepts in microcomputer technology. These key concepts are treated in depth, while many other terms are related to microcomputers and computer development and are included to provide the broader understanding required for this complex and evolving field. Many examples are given to illustrate key concepts and to avoid confusion with similar or related terms. Cross references are included for similar terms as an aid to the reader.

I wish to thank all of those who encouraged me through this project and especially my good friend Ken Sessions, who reviewed the entire manuscript and offered many helpful suggestions. My appreciation is extended to all of those in the electronics industry who have contributed to microcomputer literature and terminology, with a special thanks to Rockwell International and the Fairchild Camera and Instrument Corporation for permission to use the many excellent illustrations from their product manuals.

To become knowledgeable during this truly revolutionary period in the history of electronics technology, one must read technical articles and books, attend the specialized seminars and short courses, employ independent experts for consultation, and constantly keep up with new developments. Without a firsthand grasp of the language and terminology of microcomputers, all of these efforts would be futile. If this book can aid in the understanding of any portion of this required knowledge, then it will have fulfilled its purpose.

Michael F. Hordeski

Contents and Thumb Index

A

absolute address—An identification for an exact location where information is stored in a computer system.

absolute code—A code which specifies the memory location where an instruction operand is stored; thus, a code that uses absolute addressing and lists the exact location where the operand is to be found.

absolute error—The amount or value of an off-tolerance state, expressed in the same unit of measure as the quantity being monitored or measured.

absolute maximum ratings—The published limiting values for the operation and environmental conditions for electronic equipment. Absolute maximum ratings should not be exceeded in order to maintain the expected reliability of the equipment.

absolute-value machine—A computer that processes all data using full values of all variables at all times. Absolute-value machines operate in a contrasting mode to incremental machines.

absolute-value transducer—A device that produces an output proportional to the input, but always of the same polarity. The output does not change polarity and remains at the absolute value of the input proportion.

acceleration time—The total elapsed time between application of a read or write instruction, and transfer of the acted-upon information to its storage medium.

acceptance test—A test to show compliance of purchased equipment or services with the purchaser's stated requirements, specifications, or conditions of purchase.

access—The ability to obtain data from, or place data into, a storage device or register.

access time—The total time required to deliver data after initiation of a command to retrieve it from its storage medium. Internal data storage usually provides the fastest access time, but tends to increase system costs. Processing with internal storage can be done in less than a microsecond, while external random access processing is typically in terms of milliseconds. The ideal access time would of course be zero, and for many purposes the nanosecond speeds of some internal storage units appear to be virtually zero. When this is the case, it is called *immediate access* on *simultaneous access*.

accounting machine—See *tabulator*.

accumulator—A temporary storage register in a processing unit, where the results of arithmetic or logic operations are stored. The accumulator may operate on one word length, one word and one character, two words, or two words and two characters. Sometimes the accumulator is made up of two registers which function at a double word length.

accumulator address—An address used when the operand is in an accumulator. For example, the 6800 uses two accumulators, a primary (A) and a secondary (B); the instruction

```
ASL   A   ; (shift A left)
```

shifts the contents of register A to the left by one bit length.

A C dump—The removal of alternating current from a unit either intentionally, accidentally, or conditionally. An AC dump results in the removal of all power from a unit unless special provisions are made for a backup system.

ACIA—Abbreviation for *asynchronous communications interface adapter,* a unit which provides the data formatting and control to interface asynchronous communications data to organized systems. The interface can include such functions as: select, enable, read/write, interrupt, and the logic for data transfer. The parallel data from the bus is transmitted in the serial mode using the ACIA. Error checking and variable word lengths are allowed with this adapter.

ACK—Abbreviation for *affirmative acknowledgement.* ACK as used in block data transmission signifies that a previous transmission block has been accepted by the receiver and the receiver is now ready to accept the next block of data.

A/D—Abbreviation for *analog-to-digital.*

adapter—A device which allows operation between different parts of a microcomputer system.

ADC—Abbreviation for *analog-to-digital converter.*

A/D converter—See *analog-to-digital converter.*

add—1. The mathematical operation of summing. 2. The command to perform a summing operation.

addend—In a summing operation, the contents of a storage register addressed for addition to the augend. The resultant is the sum.

adder—A device which outputs the sum of two or more numbers presented as inputs. The adder is the main arithmetic element of the arithmetic and logic unit in some computers. The adder can perform addition, subtraction, multiplication, and division with the help of the accumulator and other storage registers.

addition—The summing of two or more numbers. Addition is always performed in a microcomputer by summing two numbers at a time—the augend and the addend. The augend is usually the contents of the accumulator, and the addend is the contents of a storage register which is addressed. A typical microprocessor like the 8080 contains several data registers. One of these registers functions as the accumulator with all arithmetic and logic operations being performed in it; the other registers hold temporary results and provide the operands of instructions to control the accumulator. In the case where the operand is stored (for example) in register D, the instruction

```
ADD   D     ; (A= A + D)
```

adds the contents of the register D to the accumulator and stores the result in the accumulator.

Another microprocessor, the Motorola 6800, uses one register (A) as a primary accumulator and another (B) as a secondary accumulator; in this case the operand is likely to be stored in memory. To add the contents of the memory location to the accumulator, we can use the extended addressing of the 6800 and write the following instruction:

```
ADD  B   $212   ; (add the
       contents of M (212) to B)
```

The symbol $ indicates that 212 is a

hexadecimal number to the assembler.

address—A label identifying a location where information is stored. An address can be represented by characters or bits that name, label, or number a location, a part of storage, a data source, or a destination. Also, an address can be that part of an instruction that identifies the location of the operand of that instruction.

A location in a city can be located if one knows the street address; similarly, if one knows the computer storage medium's address for a desired amount of information, then this information can be located in the storage unit. When the information is put into the storage unit, an address is assigned to each word; then when a word is desired, the address is used to find that particular word.

Storage locations in a microcomputer can be thought of as being similar to a set of post office boxes, message boxes at hotel front desks, stock room bins, and the storage bins of hat-check services like this:

00	01	02	03
04	05	06	07
08	09	10	11
12	13	14	15

Storage Assignments

All the storage locations are identified by a specific label and the locations are capable of holding various items. The contents of the locations change, but the locations and the location numbers remain the same. While the storage locations of the examples given can hold many different items at any one time, an address in a computer unit stores only one unit of data at a time.

If the storage unit had 2000 locations, then the address would be numbered from 0000 to 1999. Each of these numbers signifies only a unique location; it says nothing about the contents of the location. Instructions deal only with address numbers; for example, let $144 be stored in address 1888. If it is desired to have the machine print this amount, the instructions will indicate that 1888 be printed. The microcomputer will interpret this to mean that the contents of 1888 be displayed, resulting in the printout of $144.

A simple payroll program might have the following English instructions:

(1) Start the machine.

(2) Read the employee's payroll data into storage for processing.

(3) Multiply hours worked by the hourly rate to find gross earnings.

(4) Multiply gross earnings by the withholding percentage to find the tax deduction.

(5) Add the hospitalization insurance deduction to (4) to compute the total deduction.

(6) Subtract the total deduction from the gross earnings to find the take-home pay.

(7) Print a check for the amount of the take-home pay with the employee's name and identification.

(8) Stop the machine at the end of processing for the last employee.

The storage locations for such a program can be assigned as shown in the accompanying pigeon-hole layout.

In this example the payroll data is stored in locations 00 to 04; location 05 is used for temporary storage, and the

00 STORE EMPLOYEE NAME	01 STORE HOURS WORKED	02 STORE HOURLY RATE	03 STORE WITHHOLDING PERCENTAGE	04 STORE HOSPITALI-ZATION DEDUCTION	05 TEMPORARY STORAGE AREA
06 READ DATA INTO 00, 01, 02, 03, 04.	07 WRITE CONTENTS OF 01 INTO ARITHMETIC UNIT	08 MULTIPLY CONTENTS OF ARITHMETIC UNIT BY CONTENTS OF 02	09 STORE RESULT OF 08 IN 05	10 MULTIPLY RESULT OF 08 BY CONTENTS OF 03	11 ADD RESULT OF 10 TO CONTENTS OF 04
12 SUBTRACT RESULT OF 11 FROM CONTENTS OF 05	13 STORE RESULT OF 12 IN 18	14 PRINT CHECK FOR CONTENTS OF 18	15 MAKE CHECK PAYABLE TO CONTENTS OF 00	16 IF 00 EMPTY STOP	17 GO TO 06
18 STORE TAKE-HOME PAY	STORAGE ASSIGNMENTS				

instructions are assigned to locations 06 to 17 (which become the program storage areas)! The first instruction sets the location of the payroll data 00 to 04. The location of this data is arbitrary; it could have been placed after the instruction set.

address field—The instruction segment that stipulates a specific memory location where an information element may be accessed.

address modification—An alteration to the address portion of a program instruction that results in an internal transfer to a new memory location when the original address is called for after the first time in an iterative routine.

add/subtract time—The time required for a circuit, system, or machine to perform addition or subtraction operations. The add/subtract time does not include those times required to obtain the numbers from storage, nor does it include the time involved in placing the answers into storage. Add time includes the total elapsed time required to fetch and execute one fixed-point add instruction using any machine instructions (such as overlapped memory, lookahead, and parallel operation). The add operation is done for a full word from memory to register, or from memory to memory—not from register to register.

algebra—Mathematical operations in which letters and other nonnumeral characters are used to represent variables and constants.

ALGOL—Acronym for *algorithmic language*. With a few exceptions, this language is not being implemented on microcomputers. It is an arithmetic language designed for scientific applications and involves computer processing of numerical procedures (algorithms). ALGOL is used more extensively in Europe than in the U.S.

algorithm—A precisely defined set of rules or a structured procedure which provides the solution to a problem in a finite number of steps. An example of an algorithm follows:

Suppose that it is desired to compute the value of a polynomial of the form

$$f(x) = ax^n + bx^{n-1} + cx^{n-2} \ldots$$

For $n = 5$ we can write the following algorithm:

$$f(x) = (((((a)\,x + b)\,x + c)\,x + d)\,x + e)\,x + f$$

This algorithm indicates that the computation can be done by repeating a multiply-and-add step five times.

alphabet—An ordered set of unique representations usually called characters; the 26 letters of the Roman alphabet and 0 and 1.

alphabet code—A set of letter-character abbreviations for computer instructions, which a computer can interpret as the instructions themselves.

alphabetic-numeric—Alphanumeric.

alphameric—A contraction sometimes used for *alphanumeric*.

alphanumeric—Characters which include the letters of the alphabet, numerals, and other symbols used for punctuation and mathematical operations.

alphanumeric instruction—An instruction containing both letters and numbers.

ALU—Abbreviation for *arithmetic and logic unit*.

analog—A continuous DC level of voltage or current, the magnitude of which is usually proportional to an unrelated parameter or function being monitored or measured.

analog computer—A computer that uses variables represented by voltages, currents, or other parameters whose values are analogous to the quantitative magnitude of the variables.

analog-to-digital conversion—The process of representing precisely a varying voltage or current by a series of discrete pulses when the varying voltage or current itself is an analog of some other form of information. Analog-to-digital conversion techniques are required to convert any information that is in analog form into the digital form required by the microcomputer. Analog data is frequently encountered in data acquisition as voltage from a transducer, potentiometer, or other sensor of physical data.

Most methods of conversion involve division of the signal conversion device into two sections. The analog section contains all analog functions of the converter, and the digital section contains the digital functions of the converter. A major part of the digital portion can be done with the microcomputer software, if software is available for this purpose. The software can control the analog section, determine the digital value of the input of the analog section, and perform calculations with the data. If a multiplexer is used in the data acquisition system, the software can perform the function of a controller for channel selection, end-of-conversion flags, and error checking.

Successive-approximation conversion is widely used and can provide both serial and parallel outputs. The conversion system uses a digital-to-analog converter in a feedback loop which generates a known analog signal. The unknown input is compared with this signal and then sensed by the digital section.

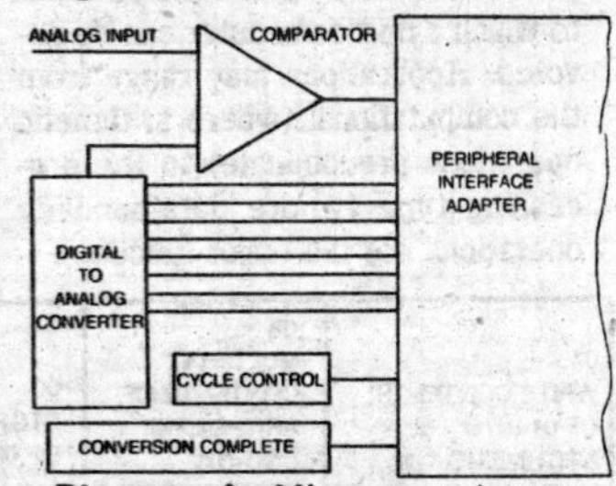

Diagram of a Microcomputer.

The successive-approximation register is implemented in the software of the microprocessor. Successive approximation provides medium conversion speeds when used in this arrangement.

analyzer—A routine to analyze a program. The routine usually consists of summarizing references to storage locations and tracing jump sequences.

AND—A logic operation that states that if A and B are both statements, then A AND B is true if both statements are true, but it is false if either is false or both are false. Truth is usually expressed by the value 1, while 0 is used to indicate a false state. The AND operator is usually represented by a centered dot

A • B

or by no sign

AB

An inverted *u* is sometimes used to denote the logical product

A ∩ B

Finally, the standard multiplication sign may be used to express the AND function

A × B

AND circuit—A circuit that performs the AND function.

AND gate—A gate that performs the AND function.

anticoincidence circuit—An electronic network that outputs a signal if and only if two different input signals are received.

application—The system or problem to which a microcomputer can be devoted. Applications may range from the computational (where arithmetic operations predominate) to the processing type (where data-handling operations are the major function).

application study—The detailed process of determining the system and set of procedures for using the microcomputer in a particular application. This involves establishing the definite functions and operations of the machine along with specification development and machine and peripheral selection criteria.

APT—Abbreviation for *automatically programmed tools,* a special computer language for programming the operation of numerically controlled machine tools.

argument—The independent variable which identifies the location of a number in a mathematical operation. The argument can result in the value of a mathematical function when substituted, or it may be the operand in operations on one or more variables.

arithmetic and logic unit—That part of the microcomputer that performs arithmetic, logic, and related operations. It is the arithmetic and logic unit that performs the major part of the actual data processing. Calculations are performed and logic comparisons are made in this part of the chip set.

In a program involving a simple series of payroll calculations, we might have the following instructions:

07 WRITE CONTENTS OF 01 INTO ARITHMETIC UNIT	08 MULTIPLY CONTENTS OF ARITHMETIC UNIT BY CONTENTS OF 02	09 STORE RESULT OF 08 IN 05	10 MULTIPLY RESULT OF 08 BY CONTENTS OF 03	11 ADD RESULT OF 10 TO CONTENTS OF 04

application note—A published paper, usually from a product or device manufacturer, which offers suggestions, recommendations, or instructions for using the manufacturer's product or device in a specific manner or for a specific purpose.

application program—The ordered set of programmed instructions by which a computer performs an intended task or series of tasks, as opposed to a microprogram.

The first instruction requires that the contents of address 07 be written into the arithmetic and logic unit. The ALU must have the capability to store temporarily the data contained in address 01. Typically, registers would be used to store this data. The number of registers and the data flow pattern vary among microcomputers and this results in differences between arithmetic and logic units, but typical operations might take place as follows.

Instructions are coded in a more convenient form as shown below. The first instruction tells the microcomputer to CLear the contents of Address 01 to the register known as the accumulator. The contents of address 01 are now held in both address location 01 and the accumulator. The second instruction means that the contents of address 02 are to be MULtiplied by the contents in the accumulator. Execution of this instruction might take the form shown below.

(1) Read the contents of 02 into a storage register.

(2) Transfer the contents of the accumulator and the storage register to the adder, which performs the multiplication.

(3) Store the product of the multiplication in the accumulator.

The next instruction states that the contents of the accumulator are to be STOred in address 05. The read-in to address 05 will erase any information that may have been there.

The next instruction is another multiplication and can be handled the same as the second instruction. The last instruction states that the contents of address 04 are to be ADDed to the contents of the accumulator. The contents of 04 are read into the storage register, erasing the previous contents; the adder then totals the contents of the accumulator and the storage register. The sum is stored in the accumulator.

Every arithmetic operation requires two numbers and results in an answer. Multiplication requires a multipicand and a multiplier to produce a product, for example, and subtraction uses a minuend and a subtrahend to find the difference. On this basis, at least three registers are always required: two to store the two numbers temporarily and one to store the result. Sometimes the accumulator is used for more than one function; in this case, the number can first be stored and then the result.

arithmetic mean—The arithmetic mean is found by summing the items of interest and then dividing by the number of items in the series.

arithmetic operation—A mathematical manipulation of numbers or symbols performed for the purpose of solving a problem as stated by a prescribed formula using numbers and/or symbols.

arithmetic progression—Any sequence of numbers in which the difference between two adjacent numbers is constant (as 5, 10, 15, 20...).

arithmetic section—The portion of a machine where the arithmetic and logic operations are performed; hence, the ALU.

arithmetic shift—Any shift that does not affect the sign position. An arithmetic shift results in the multiplication of a number by an integral power of the radix.

arithmetic unit—The part of a computer system that performs arithmetic operations; an arithmetic and logic unit.

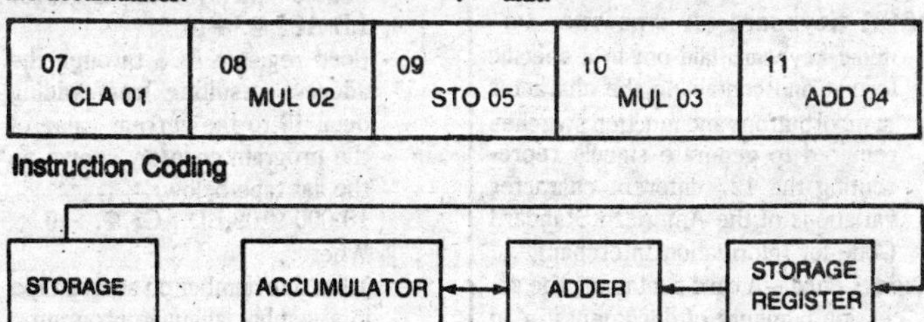

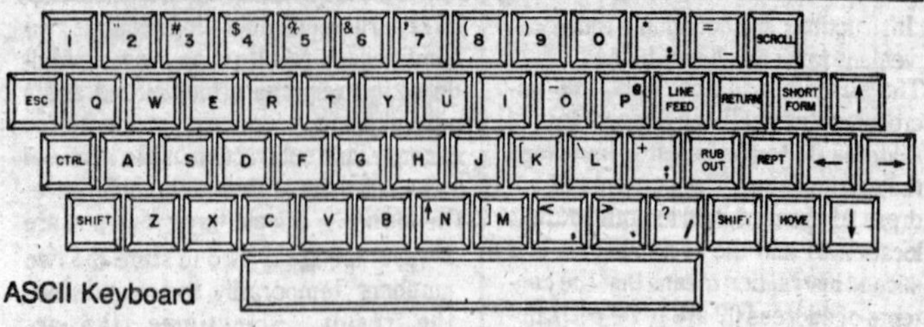

ASCII Keyboard

armed interrupt—An interrupt which can accept and hold the interrupt signal. A *disarmed* interrupt ignores the signal.

array—1. A group of devices, components, or numbers arranged in a logical or meaningful pattern. 2. A matrix.

artificial intelligence—The study of computer techniques to supplement the intellectual capabilities of humans. Artificial intelligence is concerned with the more effective use of digital computers through improved programming methods.

artificial language—A language designed for a particular application area that has not evolved through long usage to a natural language.

ARU—Abbreviation for *audio response unit*, a device which connects a computer system to a telephone to provide a verbal response to inquiries.

ASCII—Abbreviation for *American Standard Code for Information Interchange*, an eight-level code (seven bits plus parity check) widely used for information interchange in data processing systems, communication systems, and associated equipment.

ASCII keyboard—A typewriter terminal keyboard laid out in a specific format and containing the character symbol buttons and function switches required to generate signals representing the 127 different character variations of the American Standard Code for Information Interchange.

aspect card—A card containing the accession numbers of documents in an information retrieval system.

assemble—To integrate subroutines by adapting or changing relative or symbolic addresses to absolute addresses, thereby performing the functions of an assembler or assembly program. See *assembler*.

assembler—A computer program that is used to translate symbolic language into machine language. A typical program supplied by a microcomputer manufacturer is loaded using PROM or ROM chips and then executed using the same type of microcomputer to perform the assembly operation. In contrast to these "hardware assemblers" in which the program is run on the same hardware, the program can be written in FORTRAN language which can be adapted to run on any machine capable of compiling FORTRAN programs. A source program written in FORTRAN is then used to obtain an object tape for the microcomputer. Machines which function as FORTRAN assemblers are available though time-sharing computer service firms. The following is an example of an assembler program:

> Source tape (symbolic language)
> LD AC$,@. +10
> (load register AC$ through the address resulting from adding octal 10 to the current value of the program counter, shown on the list tape below)
> 10 000 9109 LD AC$,@.+10
> Where:
> 10 = line number on source tape in assembly language program.
> 000 = location of instruction.

CHARACTER OR SYMBOL	PARITY BIT	ASCII CODE	DECIMAL EQUIV
NUL	0000	0000	0
SOH	1000	0001	1
STX	1000	0010	2
ETX	0000	0011	3
EOT	1000	0100	4
ENQ	0000	0101	5
ACK	0000	0110	6
BEL	1000	0111	7
BS	1000	1000	8
HT	0000	1001	9
LF	0000	1010	10
VT	1000	1011	11
FF	0000	1100	12
CR	1000	1101	13
SO	1000	1110	14
SI	0000	1111	15
DLE	1001	0000	16
DC1	0001	0001	17
DC2	0001	0010	18
DC3	1001	0011	19
DC4	0001	0100	20
NAK	1001	0101	21
SYN	1001	0110	22
ETB	0001	0111	23
CAN	0001	1000	24
EM	1001	1001	25
SUB	1001	1010	26
ESC	0001	1011	27
FS	1001	1100	28
GS	0001	1101	29
RS	0001	1110	30
US	1001	1111	31
Sp	1010	0000	32
!	0010	0001	33
"	0010	0010	34
#	1010	0011	35
$	0010	0100	36
%	1010	0101	37
&	1010	0110	38
	0010	0111	39
(	0010	1000	40
)	1010	1001	41
*	1010	1010	42
+	0010	1011	43
, (COMMA)	1010	1100	44
–	0010	1101	45
. (PERIOD)	0010	1110	46
/	1010	1111	47
0	0011	0000	48
1	1011	0001	49
2	1011	0010	50
3	0011	0011	51
4	1011	0100	52
5	0011	0101	53
6	0011	0110	54
7	1011	0111	55
8	1011	1000	56
9	0011	1001	57
:	0011	1010	58
;	1011	1011	59
	0011	1100	60
=	1011	1101	61
	1011	1110	62
?	0011	1111	63

CHARACTER OR SYMBOL	PARITY BIT	ASCII CODE	DECIMAL EQUIV
	1100	0000	64
A	0100	0001	65
B	0100	0010	66
C	1100	0011	67
D	0100	0100	68
E	1100	0101	69
F	1100	0110	70
G	0100	0111	71
H	0100	1000	72
I	1100	1001	73
J	1100	1010	74
K	0100	1011	75
L	1100	1100	76
M	0100	1101	77
N	0100	1110	78
O	1100	1111	79
P	0101	0000	80
Q	1101	0001	81
R	1101	0010	82
S	0101	0011	83
T	1101	0100	84
U	0101	0101	85
V	0101	0110	86
W	1101	0111	87
X	1101	1000	88
Y	0101	1001	89
Z	0101	1010	90
[	1101	1011	91
\	0101	1100	92
]	1101	1101	93
^	1101	1110	94
_	0101	1111	95
`	0110	0000	96
a	1110	0001	97
b	1110	0010	98
c	0110	0011	99
d	1110	0100	100
e	0110	0101	101
f	0110	0110	102
g	1110	0111	103
h	1110	1000	104
i	0110	1001	105
j	0110	1010	106
k	1110	1011	107
l	0110	1100	108
m	1110	1101	109
n	1110	1110	110
o	0110	1111	111
p	1111	0000	112
q	0111	0001	113
r	0111	0010	114
s	1111	0011	115
t	0111	0100	116
u	1111	0101	117
v	1111	0110	118
w	0111	0111	119
x	0111	1000	120
y	1111	1001	121
z	1111	1010	122
{	0111	1011	123
¦	1111	1100	124
}	0111	1101	125
	0111	1110	126
DELete	1111	1111	127

9109 = hexadecimal equivalent of 16-bit machine language word.
LD AC$, @.+10 = the statement in assembly language written by the programmer.
Object tape (machine language)
1001 0001 0000 1001

Assemblers also provide instructions that control the assembly of instructions into machine language. These assembler instructions can save programming time and reduce errors while allowing modifications to be processed more easily. Typical areas that assembler instructions can help in are:

numbering—For example, B can be used to signify that literals in operand fields be interpreted as binary numbers and 0 and D can be used to signify octal and decimal values.

origins—To store the next instruction at location 112 decimal, the statement ORIGIN 112D can be used; consecutive locations follow 112 until a new origin statement appears.

comments—To add comments in English in the source file, use symbols such as the solidus (/), comma (,), semicolon (;), or colon (:). The assembler can ignore symbols following this symbol on each line of the source text, at the same time reproducing the comments for the final list file.

equals—For labeling registers, equal signs (=) can be used, which means that either the original label or a more descriptive term can be used interchangeably as names for the register. Equal signs can also be used to set the contents of a register in either binary, decimal, or octal.

tables and other sets of data—By using a statement such as TABLE D 23, 37, 41, three data words (in decimal) can be stored in successive locations in memory starting at a location labeled TABLE.

Another feature of assemblers is the ability to detect and flag errors. Syntactic errors—those errors that result from misuse of the language—are the only type that can be detected unless special routines are used; logic errors and errors of intent will be passed by. Statements containing errors are printed in the list file with flags (code letters signifying the error) or an entire error message. Errors that are easily detected include duplicate address labels, undefined address labels, undefined instruction mnemonics (misspelled operation codes), undefined operand field labels, incomplete number of operands, and invalid numbers of wrong number system.

An example of an error message from an assembler:

Program with errors:

		NUMBERS OCTAL
		ORIGIN 0
	ENTRY 1	LOAD R1, MEM 1
		LOAD R2, MEM 2
error	*	'LOAD' IS UNDEFINED OP-CODE *
	ENTRY 1	COMPARE R1, R2
error	*	DUPLICATE ADDRESS LABEL *
		JCOND PLACE

```
error             *   'PLACE' IS UNDEFINED ADDRESS
                          LABEL *
error             *   OPERAND MISSING *
                      JUMP FINISH
                      STORE R1, MEM; IF R1 GREATER
                          THAN R2, EXCHANGE
error             *   'MEM' UNDEFINED *
                      STORE R2, MEM 1
          FINISH      HLT
error             *   'HLT' IS UNDEFINED OPERATION *
          MEM 1       = 1732
          MEM 2       = 1840
                  *
error                 NUMBER IS INVALID OCTAL *
                  *
                      END
```

Program with corrections:

```
NUMBERS OCTAL         ORIGIN 0
ENTRY 1               LOAD R1, MEM 1
                      LOAD R2, MEM 2
          ENTRY 2     COMPARE R1, R2
                      JCOND GREATER, PLACE
                      JUMP FINISH
          PLACE       STORE R1, MEM 2; IF R1 GREATER
                          THAN R2, EXCHANGE
                      STORE R2, MEM 1
          FINISH      HALT
          MEM 1       = 1732
          MEM 2       = 2040
                      END
```

Macro capability, a feature sometimes found in assemblers, can be very useful when similar but slightly different sections of coding are used over and over again. The differences in the coding do not allow the use of conventional subroutines for repeating.

The macro is defined in parameters such as data values, addresses, labels, or instructions. Once the macro is defined for the assembler, a single statement produces an expansion of the macro for all the parameters. The statement begins at the location the expansion is desired and contains a listing of the values of the exercised.

assembly language—A language that uses words, statements, and phrases to produce machine instructions. Most microprocessor programs are written as a series of source statements that are then translated using an assembly language into machine code.

assembly list—A printed list that occurs as a by-product of the assembly procedure. The assembly list shows the instruction sequence with all details of the routine using coded and symbolic notations. The list is very useful during debugging operations.

assembly unit—Any device which performs the function of assembly, or a portion of a program which is capable of being assembled into a larger program.

astable multivibrator—An oscillator usually composed of one or two flipflops that produces a square-wave output as a result of self-triggering. See *bistable multivibrator.*

asynchronous—A system in which each event or operation starts as a result of a signal that the previous operation is complete and the microcomputer is now ready for the next operation. Synchronous machines have a master clock which sends pulses for timing to all critical circuits. Asynchronous machines do not use a master clock system for overall control; some timing circuits may be used for local control, but overall control is provided by the completion of a switching operation which serves to initiate the next operation.

asynchronous computer—A computer that operates primarily in the asynchronous mode.

audit—A systematic examination of records, documents, and other evidence for determining the following:

(1) The legality of transactions
(2) If all transactions have been recorded
(3) If transactions are reflected accurately
(4) Assets and liabilities
(5) Compliance set procedures
(6) The effectiveness of accounting system

The audit can be an effective means of examining new procedures and systems in an organization.

audit trail—A system for tracing items of data step by step. The audit trail begins with the recording of the transaction, follows through the processing steps and any intermediate records that may exist, and ends with the production of output reports and other generated records. A representative sample is chosen of previously processed source documents and an audit trail is traced through the system to test the adequacy of procedures and controls.

In manual systems, transactions are usually recorded in books of original entry, then they are connected to the final output by ledgers, summary books, and other documents. A visual and easily traceable path is left for the audit trail.

In automatic systems, steps in the processing function which were previously visible are now stored in reels of magnetic tape, disks, and other storage media. In many of these systems, an approach that circumvents the computer processing is

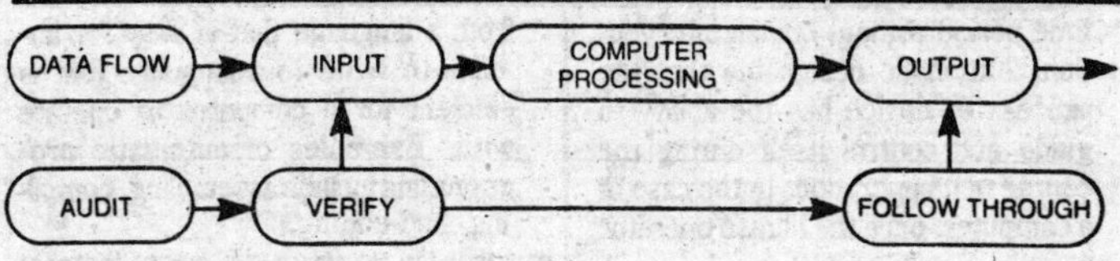

Around-the-Computer Audit Trial

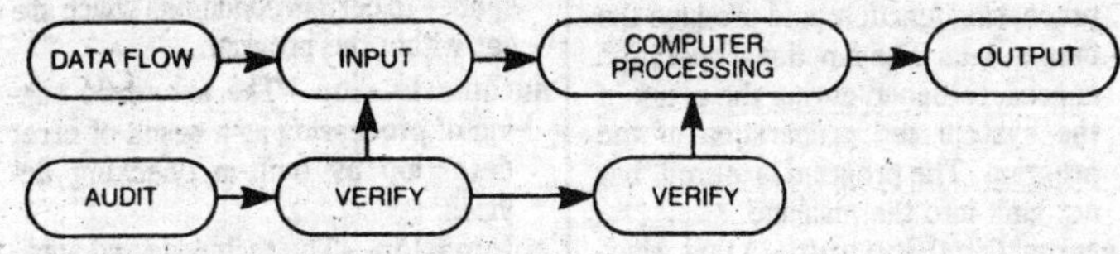

Through-the-Computer Audit Trial

used, the assumption being that if the input data is correct and the output is handled properly, then the processing *must* be correct.

An alternative method verifies that if the input is correct and the internal processing is properly conducted, the output is then assumed to be correct. The around-the-computer approach is usually suitable for many systems during the initial phases of construction or modification of a system. It is sometimes adequate for simple low-volume systems, but the through-the-computer approach is desirable for most larger systems. A combination of methods can allow cross checks in many applications.

augend—The numerical value to which an addend is added to obtain a sum.

automatic—Used to indicate that a process or device functions for a finite

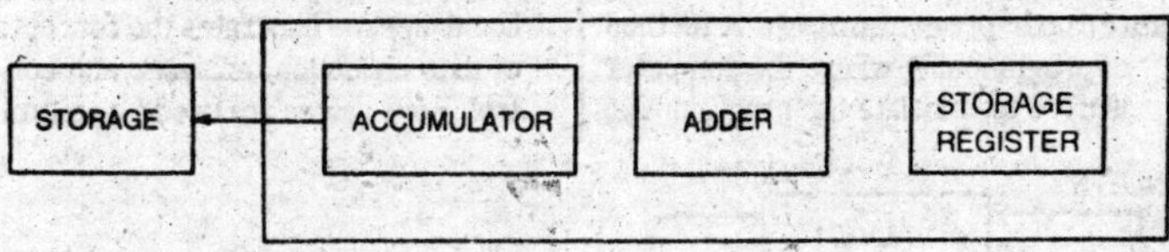

Around-the-Computer Audit Trail

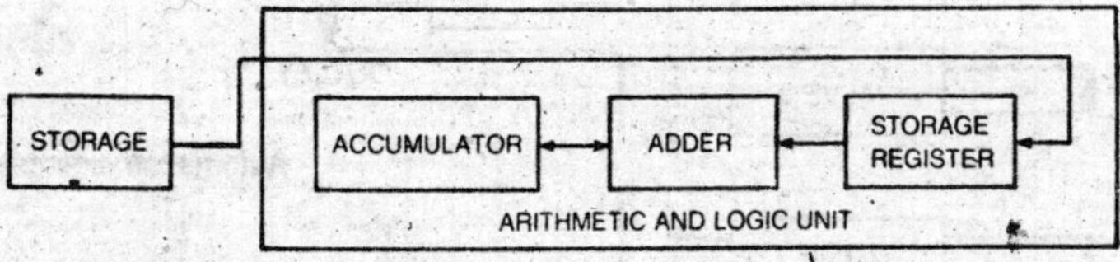

Through-the-Computer Audit Trail

time period without human intervention. Automatic designates that the process or device has the ability to guide and control itself during the course of its operation. In the case of a computer, once the human operator has set up the machine to operate, it will function by itself within definite prescribed limits. The machine will digest the input data, perform the processing function, and produce the output data. The functional operation is predetermined during the setup of the system and preparation of the program. The program is stored, but not built into the machine.

automatic calling unit—A unit which allows a business machine to dial calls automatically.

automatic code—A code which allows a machine to translate symbolic language into machine language.

automatic dictionary—A translating device that provides word-for-word substitution from one language to another. An automatic dictionary is used in automatic searching systems for substituting codes for words and phrases during encoding.

automatic feed punch—A card punch that incorporates an integral hopper, a track, and a stacker for the automatic movement of cards through the machine.

automatic programming—A method of programming where the computer is used to translate the programming from a language that is easy for humans to write to a language that is efficient for a computer to operate with. Examples of automatic programming include assembling, compiling, and editing.

automatic routine—A set of instructions that is executed independently of any manual operations. An automatic routine is usually triggered in response to certain conditions which are set within the program.

automatic stop—The automatic halting of processing as a result of error detection by built-in checking devices.

automation—The technique and application of implementing a process such that human intervention is minimized. The microcomputer can be a useful tool in the automation of manufacturing and inspection of almost any product. The microcomputer can be programmed to operate milling and drilling machines, turret latches, and other machine tools with more speed and accuracy than is possible with human operators. A part or process can be inspected using suitable transducers; data from the transducers can be used by the microcomputer to control and adjust the machine tool or valve.

An example of automation on a liquid pipeline illustrates the concepts of data collection, analysis, and control. Four valves are used for control-

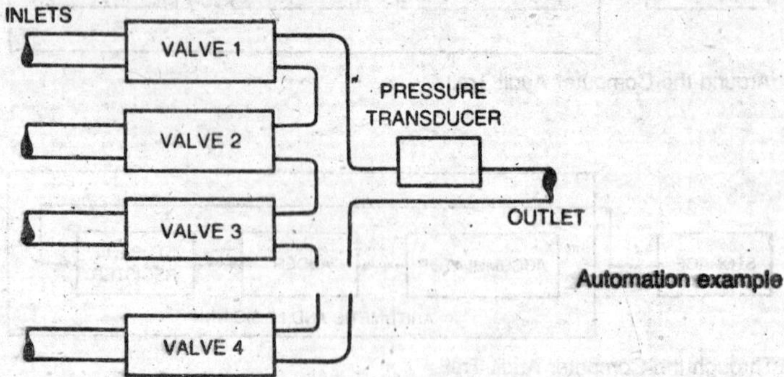

Automation example

ling the flow rate within the pipeline, and pressure transducers are used to monitor the liquid pressure on the pipeline walls. Data from the pressure transducers is used by the microcomputer to control the inlet valve openings. The desired pressure on the pipeline walls is 90 psi. The flow chart for the microcomputer program might be:

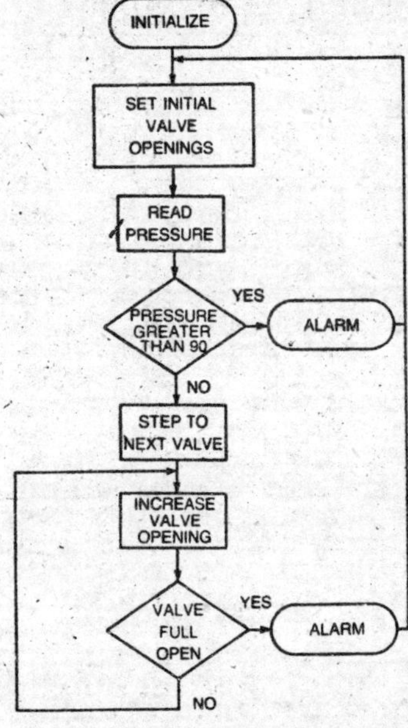

automaton—A robot-like machine designed to simulate the operation of high-order living beings.

automonitor—A microcomputer's record of its functions; also, a program or routine written for this purpose.

auxiliary equipment—The peripheral equipment not in direct communication with the central processing unit. All auxiliary equipment must be interfaced with the CPU through a peripheral interface adapter.

auxiliary storage—A storage device which is used in addition to the main storage method. Auxiliary storage usually holds much more information than main storage, and the information is not as rapidly accessible as main storage.

available machine time—The number of hours the computing machine is available for use. The available machine time is the time the machine is under power, when no maintenance is being performed and the machine is known or believed to be operating correctly.

available time—Available machine time.

average—1. The typical value representative of any one of a group of values related to the same source; also called the median or median value. 2. The sum of a group of numbers divided by the quantity of numbers summed.

average effectiveness level—A percentage computed by subtracting the total machine down time from the total performance hours and dividing this difference by the total performance period hours. Down time is usually measured from the time the defect has been reported to maintenance to the time the equipment is returned to the user in proper operating condition.

average transfer rate—The transfer of blocks of data over a long enough time to include gaps between the blocks, words, or records. Regeneration time and other items not subject to program control are included. Programmed control items such as starting, stopping, and searching are not included.

B

babble—The crosstalk from a large number of channels in a system. Also, the disturbing sounds in system operation resulting from such crosstalk.

background processing—Automatic execution of lower priority programs when higher priority programs are not using the machine. Some batch processing such as inventory control, bookkeeping, and housekeeping operations is often allowed to be interrupted on orders from remote units.

band—1. A range of frequencies or the frequency spectrum between two limits. 2. A continuous recording track on a storage device such as a magnetic drum or disk. The surface of the drum or disk is divided into more or less equally spaced rings which are called bands, each with its own read/write head for reading in or writing out data (or both).

bandwidth—A frequency range between minimum and maximum frequency point of stated attenuation. The attenuation limit is usually 3 dB (half power) at the bandwidth limits.

base—See *radix*.

base address—The number in an address which serves as the reference for subsequent address numbers.

base notation—A notation consisting of a decimal number, written as a subscript with its value indicating the base or radix of the number. For example, 10_2 indicates the number 10 has a binary base, and 11_8 indicates the number 11 has a base of 8.

base number—The radix of a counting system which indicates the quantity of characters for use in each of the digital positions. With a binary number, only the characters 0 and 1 are used and the base number is two.

BASIC—An algebraic programming code developed at Dartmouth College. The name is an acronym formed from the initial letters of *beginners' all-purpose symbolic instruction code.* BASIC is a conversational type of programming language using English-like statements and mathematical notation. A BASIC program is made up of lines of statements which contain instructions for the compiler. Each line starts with a number that identifies the line as a statement and indicates the order of statement execution in relation to the other lines of the program.

The program is entered into the system, and it can be saved, listed, retrieved, or executed using the commands available in BASIC. When the user enters a program, the system does not store the program as entered but translates it into an intermediate form that can be used in two different ways. The intermediate code can be used to produce an ASCII program or interpreted to execute a program in the operating system.

In the *immediate* mode it is not necessary to write a complete program in order to use BASIC. This mode is useful for debugging and desk calculation problems. Program loops are allowed, as shown in the following calculation of a table of square roots:

```
FOR L = 1 TO
9 / PRINT
L, SQR (L) / NEXT L

1   1
2   1.41421
3   1.73205
4   2
5   2.23607
6   2.44949
7   2.64575
8   2.82843
9   3
```

batch—An assortment of data items that may be processed during a single computer program run.

batch processing—A method of processing in which a number of items are grouped for processing during the same machine run. Batch processing systems usually do not require immediate updating of files, as data is gathered up to a specific cutoff time and then processed.

batch total—The sum of certain quantities, related to batches of unit records which is used to verify the accuracy for a particular batch. For example, in a payroll calculation, the batches could be employees and the batch totals the number of employee hours per each employee, or the total pay per each employee.

batten—See *cordonnier*.

baud—A unit of signaling speed derived from the length of the shortest code element. The speed in baud is equal to the number of code elements per second transmitted. It is also the unit of modulation rate, with one baud equal to a rate of one unit interval per second and the modulation rate equal to the reciprocal of the duration in seconds of the unit interval. The modulation rate for a unit interval of 20 milliseconds is 50 baud.

Baudot code—A communications code which contains five binary symbols. The correct interpretation depends on knowing the previous history of the message; for example, whether a capital or lowercase character was last struck. If a sixth bit is used, called the case bit, the Baudot code can be uniquely identified. Some examples of the code are shown below:

	CASE	1	2	3	4	5
A	0	1	1	0	0	0
B	0	1	0	0	1	1
S	0	1	0	1	0	0
Y	0	1	0	1	0	0
4	1	0	1	0	1	0
&	1	0	1	0	1	1
8	1	0	1	1	0	0
0	1	0	1	1	0	1
:	1	0	1	1	1	0
;	1	0	1	1	1	1

B-box—A register which contains a quantity used to modify addresses; an index register.

BCD—Abbreviation for *binary-coded decimal*, a method of coding in which each decimal digit is coded into a separate 4-bit word. BCD is also known as the 8421 code due to the weight assigned to each 4-bit word.

DECIMAL	BCD	
	8 4 2 1—	WEIGHT
0	0 0 0 0	
1	0 0 0 1	
2	0 0 1 0	
3	0 0 1 1	
4	0 1 0 0	
5	0 1 0 1	
6	0 1 1 0	
7	0 1 1 1	
8	1 0 0 0	
9	1 0 0 1	
10	0 0 0 1	0 0 0 0
11	0 0 0 1	0 0 0 1
12	0 0 0 1	0 0 1 0

benchmark—A test criterion used for measuring the performance of a product. Microprocessors, for example, can be evaluated using a benchmark program to compare different types. A flow chart in assembly language can be used to test each type with respect to execution time, accuracy, and other critical parameters for a particular application.

benchmark problem—A routine used to evaluate the performance of computing machines and software. A typical problem might be to perform nine complete additions and one complete multiplication and measure the time to complete all operations, which include (1) operation acquisition from storage, (2) performance of the operation (3) storage of the result, (4) selection of the next instruction, and (5) instruction execution.

benchmark task—Benchmark problem.

bidirectional—Capable of operation in two directions; for example, toward the input and toward the output.

bidirectional bus—A bus that accepts both input and output signals on a single line.

bidirectional bus driver—A power driver which can operate with bidirectional signals.

bidirectional data bus—A bus that accepts both input and output data signals on a single line.

binary—Countable using two digits, zeros and ones. The basic requirement of a computer is its ability to represent numbers and to perform operations on the numbers represented; and since any number can be represented by an ordered arrangement of ones and zeros, most computers use this system of counting. In the binary number system, the carry is used with the two digits. The numbers used to count to ten are as follows:

DECIMAL	BINARY
0	0
1	1

BINARY	DECIMAL
10	2
11	3
100	4
101	5
110	6
111	7
1000	8
1001	9
1010	10

A weighting table can be used to convert any binary number to its decimal equivalent. Each digit is multiplied by its position coefficient and the results added to obtain the decimal number:

2^3	2^2	2^1	2^0	BINARY WEIGHT
1	0	1	0	BINARY NUMBER
8	0	2	0	DECIMAL EQUIVALENTS

DECIMAL NUMBER $= 8 + 0 + 2 + 0 = 10$

The table can be extended to the left as far as desired. The 1 in the far left position is always called the most significant bit, abbreviated MSB. The digit in the far right position is called the least significant bit, LSB.

binary arithmetic—Mathematical operations performed using the binary digits of 1 and 0. In the binary number system, there are four addition rules:

$0 + 0 = 0$
$1 + 0 = 1$
$0 + 1 = 1$
$1 + 1 = 0$ and carry a 1

These rules are demonstrated in the following example of adding the binary equivalents of 10 and 14.

```
carries ——► 111
            1010 = 10
          + 1110 = 14
          ---------
           11000 = 24
```

The microcomputer could add these numbers by using three registers (A,

B, and C). The program could have the following steps:

(1) Load numbers to be added, 1010 and 1110, into registers A and B.
(2) Clear C to remove any bits stored there.
(3) Transfer the contents of A to C (they now hold the same value).
(4) Add the contents of B to C, using the addition rules, and store in C.

The sum is now stored in C for transfer to another location or readout. Multiplication has a similar set of rules:

$$0 \times 0 = 0$$
$$0 \times 1 = 0$$
$$1 \times 0 = 0$$
$$1 \times 1 = 1$$

An example of a multiplication follows:

```
    1010 = 10
  ×  101 = 5
    1010
  1010
  110010 = 50
```

Multiplication can be done in a microcomputer by multiple additions, multiple shifts, or a combination of both. A shift to the left results in a multiplication by two. In the above example, 1010 is shifted left twice for a multiplication of four and then 1010 is added to the result to give a multiplication by five.

Subtraction is usually done by *complementing*, which involves changing all ones to zeros and all zeros to ones in a binary system. To perform binary subtraction:

(1) Complement the subtrahend.
(2) Add it to the minuend.
(3) Move the digit from the most significant position and add it to the value of the least significant position, performing the end-around carry.

For example, to subtract 1011 from 1100:

(1) Complement 1011 = 0100
(2) Add to the minuend:

```
   1100
 + 0100
  10000
```

(3) Perform the end-around carry:

10000

00001

Division is accomplished with binary numbers by repeated shifts and subtractions. For example:

```
        101
101 ⟌ 11010
       101
        110
        101
          1 ← remainder
```

binary cell—An elementary unit of storage which can be placed in either one of two possible stable states.

binary code—A code in which every element has only one of two possible values, which may be the presence or absence of a pulse, a one or a zero, or a high or a low condition for a voltage or current.

binary coded decimal—See BCD.

binary coded decimal number—The representation using the binary coded decimal system. For example, the binary coded decimal number for 9 is 1001.

binary counter—A counting circuit which produces an output for every two input pulses, producing a division by two. Also called a *flip-flop* and sometimes a *toggle circuit*.

binary digit—A numeral in the binary system of notation. Usually known as a *bit*, the digit may be a one or a zero.

binary dump—A portion of a program that allows for printing, displaying, or punching a binary copy of a portion of memory.

binary loader—A device used to load a binary format, such as that required by a binary dump program, link editor, or assembler. In a binary tape loader, object tapes from the assembler can be loaded for debugging. The loader reads the tape using a teletypewriter reader and processes each record, which contains address, object and checksum data, by placing the object data into the locations specified by the address data.

binary point—A point located half the distance between the integral powers of two in a binary number.

binary row—A method of representing binary numbers on a punched card using rows instead of columns. This system is convenient for computer systems using words of less than 40 bits long; the card can then be used to store up to twelve words on each half.

binary search—A method for locating an item in an ordered set of items by repeatedly dividing in half the set of items until only the desired item remains.

binary signaling—A method of communications where information is transferred by the presence or absence of the two state variations of the signal.

binary-to-decimal conversion—The process of converting a binary number to its equivalent in decimal form.

bionics—The application of biological techniques to the design of electronic hardware and systems. Bionics uses the knowledge gained from the study of living systems to create hardware that functions in a manner analogous to the biological systems being studied. The result sometimes creates hardware which strongly resembles the characteristics as well as the functions of living systems.

bipolar—Having two polarity levels. Bipolar transistors are configured as npn or pnp "sandwiches," as opposed to the controlled channel construction of field-effect devices such as MOS (metal-oxide semiconductor) transistors and integrated circuits. Since bipolar devices have low capacitance, switching time (the time required to turn them on and off) can be very short, resulting in very fast computer operations.

Bipolar IC devices tend to have a higher surface area per unit volume compared to MOS, which tends to keep the cost of fabrication high for complex chips. Another disadvantage of bipolar IC construction is the requirement of isolation barriers between adjacent devices, which adds to fabrication costs. Bipolar devices also dissipate more power than MOS, since they operate on current rather than voltage.

Bipolar-device fabrication usually requires about 12 masking steps and four diffusion steps; MOS requires five masking steps and one diffusion. Bipolar processing can be complex because of the number of alternating diffusion steps required to produce the isolating barriers on the chip.

The first bipolar microprocessor chips to appear were 10 times faster than the MOS microprocessor available at the time. With a machine cycle time of 200 ns, the architecture of the bipolar chips was a two-bit slice approach and the instruction set was microprogrammable. The device was designed for products in which it would be tailored for a specific application.

Later bit-slice bipolar chips used sets of 4-bit chips, each chip consisting of a register file read by two address multipliers. Data in the registers passes through a set of latches. One of the chips contains the arithmetic logic unit and provides data routing control. An internal register is used for temporary storage of results and double-precision arithmetic storage. Bit-slice microprocessors are now being produced with Schottky-TTL logic, integrated injection logic (I^2L), and emitter-coupled logic (ECL), all of which are bipolar in form.

Schottky microcomputer chip sets have two major components—the microprogram control unit (MCU), and the central processing element (CPE). These can be combined with a bipolar memory to construct controller– processors using a minimum of auxiliary logic.

A programmable microcontroller can provide the best features of both stores program controllers and microprocessors. These systems can be used in high-speed instruments, control systems, and data processing acquisition systems. A unit can be put on a single circuit board and can perform 8-bit binary or 4-bit BCD arithmetic; it can test individual bits and perform data manipulation. A typical unit might have:

(1) A 32-word × 8-bit register file.

(2) A last-in, first-out (LIFO) stack of 16 levels for nesting subroutines.

(3) High-speed multilevel interrupt capability.

(4) Parallel and serial input/output.

(5) Field-programmable ROM of 1000 words for program memory, expandable to 4000 words.

Available development aids include a control console for program development with high-speed paper tape reader and time-sharing cross assembler. A typical central processing element can be used in an array of eight to construct a 16–bit controller-processor.

Bipolar read-only-memories are typically set up as 512 eight-bit words with an access time of 70 nanoseconds and are used as lookup tables, microprogram storage, code conversion, and function and character generation. For subroutine programming, the ROM can cover a particular area of the main memory with a window into the core at each ROM location containing a zero data word. Then a read or write operation allows an operand to be extracted from or entered into the core or main memory. The subroutines can then be programmed in ROM knowing that return addresses will be stored in and retrieved when the first location of the subroutine has a zero data word.

Bipolar random-access memories can be used as high-speed buffer memories or replacements for high-speed core memories. These can be organized as 256 words of one bit with eight-bit binary addressing and usually have separate address and input/output lines. The eight address inputs select the proper bit location and a write enable line is used to determine if a read or write mode is being used at any particular time. A series of chip enable inputs determine both the logic and impedance state of the output. Logical 1 or 0 is controlled by the chip enable along with an off or high impedance state. These states are used when connecting the output to a common bus.

Bipolar microprocessors offer a building-block approach from which complex processing systems can be constructed, using various hierarchies or levels of control memory. Both microinstruction and macroinstruction programming can be used in these systems.

Many bipolar chip sets that use the slice approach do not have fixed instruction sets. The user must develop these and store them in microprogram memory. Then the various peripherals including additional memory can be connected with the chip set to form a microcomputer, and additional programs are developed and stored as the design proceeds.

A typical chip set includes microprogram control units, central processing elements, and programmable read-only memories (PROMs).

biquinary—A method of coding which uses two parts of a binary code to represent a decimal number, one of which has the value of decimal zero or five, and the other the value of zero through four, as shown below:

DECIMAL	BIQUINARY	DECIMAL INTERPRETATION
0	0 000	0 + 0
1	0 001	0 + 1
2	0 010	0 + 2
3	0 011	0 + 3
4	0 100	0 + 4
5	1 000	5 + 0
6	1 001	5 + 1
7	1 010	5 + 2
8	1 011	5 + 3
9	1 100	5 + 4

This system is used in the hand-manipulated abacus and soroban. A modified biquinary system has been used in some early computers such as the IBM-650. The modified system uses seven bits with the following weights from left to right: 5, 0, 4, 3, 2, 1 and 0. Since every decimal number is represented by two ones and five zeros, it is very easy to make a code check by counting the ones and zeros. Some arithmetic operations are difficult to mechanize with this system, which also requires a large amount of memory compared to other systems. More than 100 characters are required to represent just the first ten decimal numbers as shown:

DECIMAL	BIQUINARY (7 bit)
0	0100001
1	0100010
2	0100100
3	0101000
4	0110000
5	1000001
6	1000010
7	1000100
8	1001000
9	1010000

bistable—Having the capability of assuming either of two stable states in a circuit or circuit element. A typical bistable circuit is a flip-flop or bistable multivibrator, which can store one bit of data. All computer operations are carried out by setting and resetting bistable elements. The action of bistable elements is such that if the circuit is in a stable state with a zero output, a change of the input produces a change of the output to a one state; and if it is in a stable state with a one output, then a change of the input produces a change in the output to a zero state. The change in the input can be a pulse of limited duration which allows a series of bistable elements to function as a counter or register.

bistable multivibrator—Flip-flop.

bit—A blend word formed from *binary digit*, a unit of information equal to one binary decision. It can be a single character in a binary number, a single pulse in a coded group of pulses, or a unit of information capacity.

When used as a unit of information capacity, the capacity in bits is equal to the logarithm to the base two of the number of possible states available. In a memory, for example, each element is capable of representing a zero or a one at any instant, and the total number of ones and zeros at any instant is the capacity of the memory.

bit-bender—A computer hobbyist.

bit check—A manual or machine-conducted examination of a word or bit group to verify presence of a parity bit in its prescribed position.

bit density—The number of bits of digital data that can occupy a given volume or area of storage medium.

bit location—1. A storage position capable of storing one bit. 2. The position of a specific digit in a binary number.

bit parity—The condition of an output group of bits when a check bit is used to parity-balance the total value for the purpose of error checking. A specific bit is used to indicate if the sum of ones in a series of bits is odd or even. The series of bits can be a word or a series of words and the check bit must be separated from the counting operation. In a typical system, if a one parity bit indicates an odd number of ones in a series, then a zero parity bit indicates an even number of ones. If the total number of ones, including the parity bit, is always even, the system is called an even-parity system. If the total number of ones is odd, the system becomes an odd-parity system.

bit rate—The number of individual data bits processed in a given period of time (usually in one second).

bit sign—The value of a binary digit used to indicate the polarity of data representing a number or quantity, such as an angle. The binary digit carrying this value is called the *sign bit*.

bit-slice—An approach in structuring microprocessors such that the resulting microcomputers are put together using a building block technique. A typical processor using bit-slice chips might use four 4-bit microprocessor chips. Some other bit-slice microprocessors (like the early 3000 series) are only two bits wide. The bit-slice approach lets the user configure the microprocessor and requires the development of a specialized instruction set during the initial design phase. A 16-bit processor can be built up with two dozen or less chips that will handle programs designed for popular minicomputers at similar speeds. The processor consumes only about 10W of power with an instruction time of about 1 ns and a cycle time of 300 ns.

blank—1. A location in a storage medium (character or space) which is used to provide a method of checking the accuracy of the operations. 2. A quartz plate.

blank, switching—Dead band.

blank transmission—A feature which allows checking of the data field for all blank positions. Used as a control measure, a blank transmission can (1) prevent destruction of existing records in storage, (2) indicate when the last item on a card has been processed, and (3) instruct the computer to skip a calculation when a blank is encountered.

block—1. A group of words considered as a unit. On magnetic tape, a block is considered to be any group of words recorded in the serial mode which is separated by intervening blank spaces. Each block is considered to be made up of one or more records. The records can be reduced to blocks to decrease acceleration and deceleration times of the tape machine. Blocks are ten or more words in length and separated by enough blank spaces to allow the tape to start and stop accurately before read or write operations are attempted. 2. Geometric figures in block diagrams to show basic functional relationships, such as a part of a circuit or a part of a program.

block diagram—A graphic representation of any operational circuit or system when each functional element is presented as a box or block, and the relationship of each element to other elements is depicted by connected lines depicting hierarchy.

block input—A group of words to be transferred from external storage to internal storage (input).

block length—The number of characters, bits, or words comprising a defined unit word or character group.

block output—A group of words to be transferred from internal storage to an external destination.

block sort—A sort of one or more of the most significant characters of a key to serve as a means of making workable-sized groups from a large volume of records to be sorted.

block transfer—The conveyance of a word or character grouping from one register or device to another.

blockette—A subdivision of a block, which is treated as a unit, particularly during input and output transfer.

blocking—The combining of two or more records into one block.

blue-ribbon—Adjective used to describe a program which is handwritten and designed to run properly the first time. The blue-ribbon program is carefully written and debugged to remove all program errors before running (also known as a *star* program).

board—1. A panel that can be changed by adding or deleting wires or corrections. Also called a jumper board, plugboard, or panel. 2. A circuit board.

bode plot—A method of plotting control-element transfer functions which uses logarithms of gain or phase angles versus the logarithm of the frequency of the plotted function. For closed-loop system control, it is desirable to obtain the maximum gain while retaining control loop stability. The higher the gain of the system, the faster the system response and the better the control of the controlled variable.

Analysis of a closed-loop control system usually begins with an assessment of the frequency response of each component in the system. If this information is not known, frequency response tests are conducted. From the characteristics of the frequency response, the maximum gain for loop stability can be calculated using a bode plot.

In the bode plot, the gain and phase of the control component are plotted as a function of the log frequency as shown:

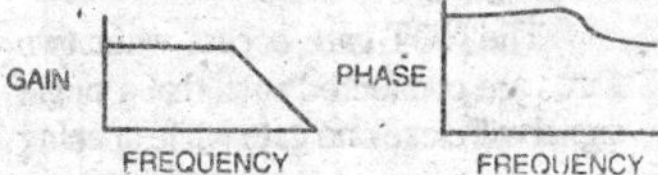

The frequency at which the phase is −180 degrees is called the critical frequency and the gain at this frequency must be less than one for loop stability.

Bode plots have the following advantages for control system analysis:

(1) Since logarithms are used, the expressions for gain are additive.
(2) For many electronic elements, the shape allows representation of the exact plot by straight line asymptotes.
(3) Since the bode plot is easy to construct, it provides a convenient starting point for more complex methods of control analysis.

bookkeeping—Maintenance of accounting ledgers, either manually or by machine. Bookkeeping represents an application area for microcomputers which involves variations of inventory control and general accounting. Generally the first stage in inventory control requires information collection, which is the recording in symbolic form the level of inventory presently available, as indicated in various source documents. Following the collection stage, the information from the source documents is combined with information regarding the available balances of stock left in the processing stage. Next comes a comparison of the available balances with either the reorder point figures or the maximum allowable stock amounts. The final stage involves some form of output such as a listing of the stock numbers and quantities on purchase order forms for the purchasing department.

For a general accounting operation, the typical primary end products are income statements and balance sheets with supporting documents.

Boolean algebra—A deductive system or process of reasoning named after George Boole, an English mathematician who lived from 1815 to 1864. A system of theorems which uses symbolic logic to denote classes of elements, true or false propositions, and on-off logic circuit elements. Symbols are used to represent operators such as AND, OR, NOT, EXCEPT, IF...THEN, etc. When Boole introduced his system in 1847, one purpose was to provide a shorthand notation for the system of logic originally set up by Aristotle. Aristotle's theorems dealt with statements that were either true or false, never partially true or partially false. Boolean algebra likewise consists of single-valued functions with only two possible output states.

For a long time Boole's system lay dormant, almost forgotten; however, it is now recognized as an effective method of handling single-valued functions with two possible output states. When Boolean algebra is applied to binary arithmetic, the two states become 0 and 1; when applied to switching theory, the two states become open and closed, as shown in the following analogy:

0 =   1 =

The convention normally used is 0 for an open or low state, and 1 for a closed or high state.

The AND function occurs if two or more gates are placed in series, and the resulting configuration is called an AND gate. This arrangement will transmit information if and only if all series gates are closed. This is shown above in the next column.
The equivalent equation in Boolean algebra is:

AB = C   (A and B equals C)

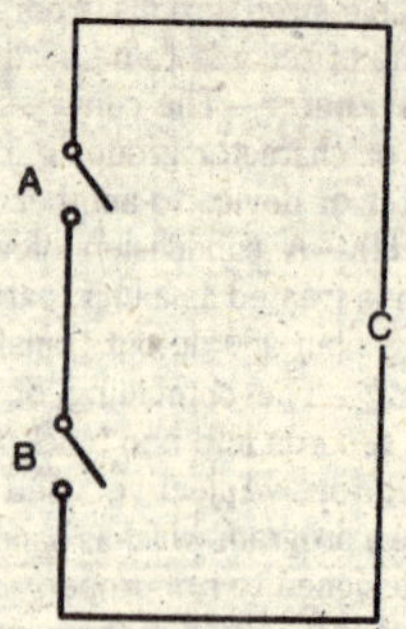

Also, the following truth table can be written:

A	B	C
0	0	0
0	1	0
1	0	0
1	1	1

The OR function occurs if two or more gates are placed in parallel. The result is called an OR gate, and transmission occurs when one or more gates are closed. This is shown in the following circuit:

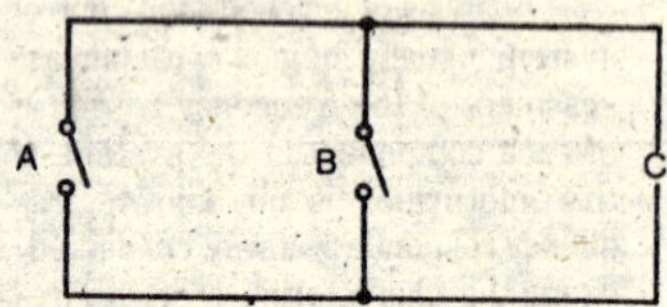

The equivalent equation in Boolean form is:

A + B = C   (A or B equals C)

and the truth table is shown on the following page.

The NOT gate occurs when two gates are connected such that a single signal will close one gate while opening

A	B	C
0	0	0
0	1	1
1	0	1
1	1	1

the other. The NOT gate forms the complement of its input, thus a 1 on the input to the gate results in a 0 on the output and a 0 on the input results in a 1 on the output. If the input is labeled A, the output is labeled $\bar{A}$ ($\bar{A}$ not, or not A). An entire function can be complemented. For example, if:

$$A = B(C + D)$$

Then:

$$\bar{A} = \overline{B(C + D)}$$

The commutative and associative laws apply in Boolean algebra:

$$AB = BA$$

$$A(BC) = (AB)C = ABC$$

Some other identities are:

$$1 + A = 1 \qquad 0 + A = A$$

$$1A = A \qquad 0A = 0$$

$$A(B + C) = AB + AC$$

$$A + A = A \quad A + \bar{A} = 1 \quad \bar{\bar{A}} = A$$

$$AA = A \qquad A\bar{A} = 0$$

Also, De Morgan's laws, which only apply to Boolean algebra, can be verified as:

$$\overline{A + B + C + \ldots N} = \bar{A}\bar{B}\bar{C}\ldots\bar{N}$$

$$\overline{ABC\ldots N} = \bar{A} + \bar{B} + \bar{C}\ldots\bar{N}$$

bootstrap—A technique designed to cause a circuit, stage, or operation to bring itself into a desired state by means of its own action. The name is taken from the impossible situation of a person lifting himself off the ground by pulling on his bootstraps. Used as a machine routine, the bootstrap technique involves loading the first few instructions into storage, following which these instructions are used to bring in the rest of the routine—usually by the entering of a few manual instructions or the use of a special key function.

A bootstrap is also that part of a program which is used to establish another version of the program. A bootstrap loader is used when there is no loader available in the main memory. The bootstrap is used to read into memory any series of bytes (usually without error checks) and is keyed into the console or implemented in ROM, where it is permanent. The bootstrap loader should contain as few instructions as possible in case it has to be keyed in via the console. The bootstrap is also sometimes used to load an absolute loader into the main memory.

In microprocessor systems, a bootstrap loader can allow the user to enter data and program into RAMs from a teletypewriter, keyboard, or paper tape and execute the program from the RAMs. The loader usually is a PROM that plugs into the prototype board.

In tape operations, a bootstrap is used as a subroutine which loads a binary loader when other loaders are not available (as in systems having no automatic loader). Bootstrap loaders are available for most input devices, and for paper tape systems require only about eight words for manual keying.

borrow—The negative carry which occurs in direct subtraction. In the direct subtraction of *(continued overleaf)*

```
  10110
-   101
  10001
```

the subtraction operation begins in the rightmost column, where a 1 is borrowed from the next-left column to convert the rightmost 0 to a 10. The process is repeated as the operations move leftward column by column.

boundary—A special register which selects the upper and lower addresses for each user's memory block in a multiprogrammed system.

box—1. Any block or enclosed area that is used to represent a function, circuit, stage, or element graphically. 2. The symbol used in flow charting to indicate a choice or branch in the path of the flow.

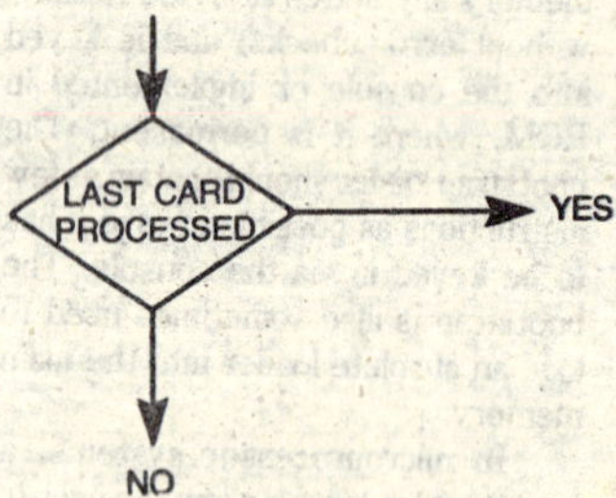

The diamond-shaped decision box always has one entrance line and two exit lines, or branches. The exit paths are determined by a yes or no, or other comparison test. In the example given, the condition to be determined is if the last card of a stack or deck has been processed. If the answer is yes, the program is allowed to branch away from the loop that it has been following. If the answer is no, then the processing of the cards continues until completion.

bps—Abbreviation for *b*its *p*er *s*econd. For serial transmission, bps is equal to the speed at which a device or channel transmits characters. See also *baud*.

branch—The selection of one or more paths in the flow of data or signals through a system or stage. Selection of a path is based upon some criterion to allow a decision to be reached. The instructions used to mechanize the selection are sometimes called *branch instructions.* Transfer of control and jump operations are also used in this context. In a microprocessor program, branching is done on the basis of computed results causing modification of the function or program sequence. The usual modification can be classed as (1) a change of the program direction, or (2) a departure from the normal sequence.

Very few programs do not take advantage of the microcomputer's ability to determine the direction that a program should take based upon intermediate results. For testing a condition and providing alternative paths for the program, microinstructions which are sometimes called *conditional skip instructions* are used.

A transfer of control can be handled in the 8080 as follows:

```
AAA:      .     ; (stack address)

      JMP BBB   ; (go to BBB,
                  then return)
```

Control is transferred in this sequence to BBB, then when that routine is completed, control goes back to AAA, the address at the top of the stack.

branch-on—A term used to mark indicators or switches on a control console to indicate when branching is taking place. A branch-on indicator is used to show that conditions for a particular group of registers are such that branching will occur for the next block of data. Branch-on switches are used to control the use of certain memory locations or index registers. The setting of the switch determines if the program is to branch at that location.

branch point—The location in the program where one or more choices is selected, depending upon the character of the most recent data processed.

breadboard—An initial or experimental model of a process, program, or device. Temporary arrangements of early electronic circuits used modifications of kitchen breadboards. These evolved to the many types of boards available for prototype work today, but the name held up and is still used today. Specialized breadboards are available for designing custom microcomputer interfaces. A typical board allows for data transfer over the data line using program control with or without interrupts. Board area is allowed for 14-, 16-, 24-, 36-, and 40-pin integrated circuits along with discrete components. Power and ground buses are provided as well as edge connectors for input/output cables or card interconnections.

break—Used to refer to an open circuit or an interruption which usually allows transmission from the other end of the transmission system.

breakpoint—A point in a program which allows a conditional interruption to permit visual checking, printouts, or other analysis. Breakpoints permit debugging and are usually indicated by a breakpoint flag or controlled by a breakpoint switch on the console. With a breakpoint in the program, the user has an opportunity to check, correct, and modify the program before continuing its execution.

breakpoint instruction—An instruction which causes the machine to either transfer control or stop and take some special action. The breakpoint instruction is usually triggered by some specific conditions placed into the program.

b-register—A register which can store words used to change an instruction before it is executed by the program. The b-register (also called index register or b-box) is sometimes used to extend the operation of the accumulator during multiply and divide operations.

Some machines use many index registers, their basic function being to add a number to part of an instruction after the instruction leaves storage on its way to the control unit and before it goes into the instruction register. The instruction entering the instruction register does not have to be identical with the one read from storage, since the contents of the index register may be added to it before it reaches the instruction register. B-registers allow changes to be made in the program just before program execution.

bridge—1. An inadvertent solder connection on a circuit board between two conductive paths. 2. A full-wave rectifier composed of four diode legs. 3. A circuit used in some data acquisition transducers to compensate for temperature and other errors. The system is derived from the Wheatstone bridge, a widely used method for the precision measurement of resistance. In strain gage transducers used for pressure or stress measurement, a bridge circuit is required to display the small resistance change that occurs. The strain gage is placed in one or more arms of the bridge as shown below:

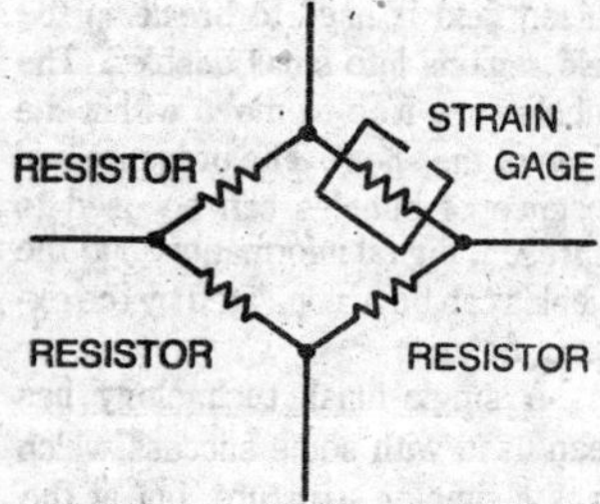

broadband—In data communications, any bandwidth greater than the 4 kHz of voicegrade channels. Loosely, any relatively wide frequency bandwidth.

broadband noise—A noise distribution that is relatively uniform over a wide spectrum of frequencies.

brush—An electrical conductor for reading data from a punched card. The operation of punched-card readers depends upon the movement of the card past a sensing mechanism that has electrical contacts (brushes or photoelectric sensors). The cards are placed in the feed hopper of the reader in the order that they are to be read. They are taken one at a time from the bottom of the stack by the reader and passed to the reading station. The reading devices may be thin flexible springs or brushes which pass through the holes to be read; or light is directed through the holes for sensing, by rows of photoelectric cells. Sometimes the cards are passed through a second reader which is used as a check of the first reader.

BTAM—Abbreviation for *b*asic *t*elecommunications *a*ccess *m*ethod, a technique used in IBM equipment that utilizes macroinstructions for data communications between terminals.

bubble memory—A memory technology that makes use of magnetic bubbles generated from a single-crystal sheet. The bubbles are generated when two magnetic fields are applied perpendicular to the single-crystal sheet. A constant field is used to strengthen the field region and a pulsed field is used to break up the field regions into small bubbles. The bubbles are free to move within the plane of the sheet. The presence and absence of bubbles can be used to represent digital information, and the bubbles can be manipulated by the external fields.

A single-mask technology has been used with some success which gives a simpler structure, but at the cost of higher access times and smaller bit densities than other bubble units. A typical device uses temporary changes in drive field rotation to read, write, and erase data.

A bubble generator is used to pass data through a generator lock to a major loop. Bubbles are also stored in minor loops using input switches. They are transferred back to the major loop with output switches. The unit can also selectively erase information in the data stream using an annihilator loop. The presence of a bubble is read as a one and the absence of a bubble is read as a zero. The bubbles are moved using a magnetic overlay system which forms a closed loop.

A bucket-brigade shift register can be formed which is similar to that used by charge-coupled devices (CCDs); the bubble devices have the advantage of being nonvolatile (retaining memory when power is interrupted). Besides shift registers, bubble technology may be used in the future for switching and logic functions.

In addition to nonvolatility, bubble memories require very small amounts of power; a 10 megabit unit uses about 10W and fits into a space of but four square inches. Applications for bubble memories include an endless-loop recorder which would replace cassettes and floppy disks in data loggers, text editors, point-of-sale terminals, and other applications needing about one megabit of capacity. They will also find use in auxiliary memories which would fill the gap between 1 ns core types and 8 ns disks.

bucket—An expression used to indicate a portion of storage reserved for accumulating data or totals of information. Buckets are labeled 1, 2, 3, etc., and are commonly used during initial system planning.

bucket brigade—A continued shifting of data bits in a given direction.

buffer—A device or unit that serves as an isolator or interface between two dissimilar elements. It is used to match impedances, speeds, or other characteristics while maintaining isolation between matched elements. As a register, a storage buffer would serve as an intermediary storage point between two registers or data handling systems with different access times or data formats.

In a typical communications interface, buffering provides asynchronous communications between Bell 103 or 202 data sets at speeds up to 9600 baud.

buffer storage—Buffer storage indicates:

(1) A synchronizing element between different forms of storage, usually internal and external.
(2) An input device for assembly of information from external or secondary storage for transfer to internal storage.
(3) An output device which copies information from internal storage for entry to external storage.
(4) Any device for temporary storage during data transfer.

buffered computer—A computer system that allows input and output data to be stored temporarily to match transfer speeds of the input and output devices with the speed of the computer. To accommodate a difference in speed changes, a buffer is used to accept the data at one speed, hold the data, and then release it at the required rate.

A card reader might be reading data from cards at about 1000 characters per second, and yet this data may be put into storage at a rate of about 50,000 characters per second. Part of the buffer operates at the lower speed and temporarily stores the data until it has enough data to transmit in a group at the higher speed. In the case of an output buffer, data is transmitted at the slower speed until a new group of input data can be accepted.

Format changing might include:

(1) Rearranging data
(2) Duplication of data
(3) Code generation
(4) Insertion and deletion of data

Some amount of buffering is required for all input and output equipment because of the translation needed in going from one language to another. Buffers are found in a variety of equipment functions, including controllers, synchronizers, electronic amplifiers, transmitters, selectors, adapters, and communicators. They may perform code changes, speed changes, mode changes, format changes, checking, and time-sharing.

bug—1. A usually elusive error in a program, circuit, or machine. 2. A dual-inline-package integrated circuit, so named because of the insect-like appearance of the device.

bug patch—A temporary circumvention of a program element or automatic routine through manual control. The patches are worked out and inserted to fix the errors. After a number of patches are made, they are incorporated into the source program, which is reassembled to complate the documentation of the changes.

building block—A self-contained element that can serve as a stage or subsystem by interconnection with other such elements. This concept of construction provides an approach to system and hardware design which allows expansion of a system using a modular technique.

build-virtual-machine—A modeling process whereby a machine program duplicates an actual defined system configuration. A build-virtual-machine program allows the user to structure programs that will fit the limits of the memory of the actual system.

built-in check—A system, usually implemented in hardware, for verifying the accuracy of information transmitted, manipulated or stored in any part of the computer system. Also called an *automatic check, built-in automatic check,* or *hardware check.*

burst—1. A sequence of signals counted as one unit using a specified criterion. In burst transmission, messages are stored for a time period, then released at a much faster speed for transmission. The received signals are recorded and then slowed down for the user. 2. In color TV reception, the signal that serves as the reference for the 4.58 MHz oscillator; it occurs during video blanking.

bus—A circuit used as a high-traffic path for data or power transmission. A bus often is used as a common connection between a number of locations or switching points and is sometimes called a *trunk* or *trunk line*. Buses are used in microprocessors to speed the data flow, transfer data, and for addressing and control. A single bus can be used in alternate time periods for data, addresses, and control signals. Multibus systems use a dedicated bus for data and another for addressing. Control may or may not be on a dedicated bus. The multibus system allows data and addresses on the same cycle without the serial delays found in a common-bus system.

Some of the features found in data and address buses used to minimize package count and improve performance are:

(1) Multibus systems to eliminate multiplexing and latching.
(2) Three-state output buffers to minimize the use of bus drivers.
(3) Separate output-enable logic to allow bidirectional signal flow.

Most microprocessors are designed for 8-bit bus operation, and programs are more efficient if they use 8 bits or less per message to eliminate the need for multiple-word control.

Typical bus cycles found in microprocessors are:

(1) Data word transfer in, followed by word transfer out.
(2) Data word transfer in, followed by byte transfer out. Data transfer on the bus is sometimes interlocked so that communications can be independent of the length of the bus and response times. Asynchronous operation allows each device to run at maximum speed without the need for clock pulses.

Bus organization is an important part of a system's architecture. Many microcomputers use a single bus for address, data, and control information; others use a memory bus for data transfer between CPU and memory, and another bus for data transfer between the CPU and peripheral devices. A typical data bus may have 60 or more signal lines transmitting information.

The single-bus system acts as a universal interface connecting all parts of the system, while the dual bus treats the CPU as a focal point with separate interfaces to memory and peripheral units.

Buses are usually designed on some form of backplane with a bus motherboard to handle words up to 16 bits long. Bus construction requires control and power lines, variable- and fixed-frequency clocks, and connectors to peripheral devices.

Bus program counters are incorporated as counting registers on chips; one can be used for program location and another for stack counting. The counter contents are sent out on the address bus to allow the memory to fetch the correct instructions; the processor then increments the program counter after each use of the instructions.

Voltage levels and impedances at the bus interface allow rapid transmission and minimize effects due to noise. A number of units can share the bus without excessive loading. In some systems, a bus protocol allows a vectored interrupt. Device polling is not required for interrupts, which reduces processing time in cases where many devices are connected to a common bus. Usually, an interrupt vector is passed to the processor; the vector points to addresses for a new status word and the start of the interrupt service routine.

A priority structure is used to determine which device has control of the bus. Each device on the bus is assigned a priority number so that when two or more devices request use of the bus, the device with the higher priority receives control first.

bus driver—A power device designed to supply signals to all devices on a bus without signal degradation.

bus interface—A circuit or device designed to match a peripheral with a bus.

bypass—A shunt or parallel path around a circuit, device, or unit. A bypass filter, for example, provides a low-attenuation path around the unit to be bypassed, as in the case of a carrier-frequency filter used to bypass a telephone repeater station.

byte—A generic term developed by IBM to indicate a measurable number of consecutive binary digits which are usually operated upon as a unit. Bytes of eight bits representing either one character or two numerals are most often encountered. Words in some systems are divided into high and low bytes and the byte addresses are either odd or even numbers. The high bytes are stored at the odd-numbered locations and the low bytes at the even-numbered ones.

byte multiplexing—The processing of data in sequential chunks by assignment of time slots to individual input/output devices. Bytes, one after another, are then interlaced on the channel going to or from the main memory. Byte multiplexing is used on some 360 and 370 systems.

C

CAD—Acronym for ***computer-aided design***. CAD techniques are used whenever conventional design methods prove excessively time-consuming. Considerable development has gone into computer methods and programs to solve complex network problems. Programs are also available for the design of integrated circuits. Some of these programs in use have included ECAP, NET-1, CIRCUS, PREDICT, NASAP, and SCEPTRE, all of which handle lumped-parameter elements. Depending on the external construction of the device, sometimes frequency-response characteristics can be used to describe a device accurately. The response characteristics are obtained experimentally without regard to the internal structure of the device. This is known as the black-box method, and it offers the following advantages for integrated circuit design:

(1) The model is able to accept experimental or analytical data.
(2) The complete circuit is enclosed in a black box for repetitive analysis of a complete system.
(3) Model parameters can be lumped or distributed.
(4) Solution can be done in sections using small computers.

Some CAD programs are geared towards time-sharing using a larger machine. Here the computer serves many users at the same time at the output and input facilities, while the CPU actually services each user in sequence. The user dials the computer and operates the teletypewriter as if the machine were his alone, while other people are also being similarly served at many distant locations. The circuit designer is in contact with the machine and is able to make changes to save computing time and effort that are not possible with batch processing.

Time-sharing allows a turnaround time of a few minutes and provides the circuit designer with almost instant answers to calculations. This allows rapid interaction with the machine compared to batch processing.

calculator—A processor of data especially suitable for performing arithmetic operations. Data and instructions are usually, but not always, inserted manually. A calculator can be used with a microcomputer and it can be a microcomputer which is used as a calculator. Early digital machines were used primarily for calculations and were assigned as special-purpose calculators.

Present-day calculators are small, highly specialized computers with a memory structure composed of a fixed and variable section. The fixed section is in the form of a ROM and provides the control for changing instructions in a limited fashion.

The simple four-function calculator can be used to do advanced operations such as square roots, squaring, summing of products and quotients, trigonometric calculations and exponents. This is done by altering the order of computations and adding a few extra steps.

The scientific programmable calculator is typically used for complex scientific and engineering problems. These units can be used as portable scratch pads for problem solving and typically have a 10-digit display which operates in scientific notation. Results are computed in degrees or radians and some have 15 or more scientific functions, including trigonometric, inverse trigonometric, hyperbolic, exponential, and logrithmic. Units offer 64 or more steps or programming using eight or more registers. Decimal points systems include floating point and exponential with scientific notation to 10^{99}.

Calculator systems which are operated as batch terminals typically use the following equipment:

(1) A calculator with up to 4000 words of memory
(2) A ROM for stringing variables
(3) Thermal or matrix printer
(4) Data communications interface and modem

Optional equipment for batch terminal use includes:

(1) Tape cassette
(2) Calculator card reader
(3) Tape reader
(4) Line printer or plotter
(5) Memory subsystem

A typical display calculator organization uses:

(1) 700 words of microprogramming
(2) 75 words for storage in registers
(3) 12 inputs and 12 outputs for external connections

The organization allows the user to emulate a ROM program before committing the microprogram to a custom ROM. Signal levels within the system are MOS compatible and all external lines are TTL compatible. The microprogram is written so that the keyboard is scanned in a desired sequence. The position of the keyboard switches provides the signals for the processor to carry out some operation or subroutine as a funciton of microprogram stored in ROM.

Calculators are also used as editing systems in some batch terminals. Both cassettes and mass memory systems are used to add, delete, and insert card data into storage. Many of these systems are used to eliminate the bulkier punched cards or paper tapes as storage media.

Calculators typically operate in a sequential mode with one program step at a time. Following power-on initalization, the input data is strobed through a multiplexer as fast as the system clock will allow. Numbers representing one of the four funcitons are entered in a similar manner, then at the conclusion of the equation, a number representing the equals operation is entered. The output is then provided either to a display, or as latched outputs to external equipment.

calculator terminal—A desktop calculator with microcomputer compatible inputs and outputs, and designed for interactive computations. Terminals designed around desktop calculators can handle such applications as inventory control, processing orders, payroll, and account maintenance with the help of the BASIC language. These applications also use alphanumeric stringing and matrix manipulation and require larger storage capacity than tape cassettes provide. Disk drive units are available for some desktop calculators which will store up to 2 million 8-bit words at fast access speeds.

Other desktop calculators allow time-sharing for many users from their home or office. Remote connections are made through standard telephone channels, and the remote keyboard has all the functions and symbols required for the application. Answers are flashed back to the remote display and many features of powerful minicomputers are available as options. Calculators are also used to communicate calculated data directly to large batch computers for additional processing and storage. The batch computer can then send a final message based on the data for display at the calculator. The batch terminals are usually used in an organization where centralized processing stations are required and large amounts of data are transferred between two or more points. Typical applications for batch terminals include:

(1) Inventory Control
(2) Payroll
(3) Remote job entry
(4) Numerical control tape preparation
(5) Structural design engineering

Use of the calculator terminal brings all of these applications to the remote location. A typical calculator terminal may have the following characteristics:

(1) 2000 bps transmission speed, with ranges from 1200 to 9600 available.
(2) Half-duplex mode with full duplex available
(3) 80-column or 32-column output page width for display

CAM— Acronym for *content-addressable memory.* CAMs are special RAMs in which the addresses of data can be retrieved on command. Programming is usually done by writing into the unit using a separate addressing and control line. CAMs also allow a normal read/write across rows which makes them useful for applications requiring quick data searches, correlation checking, and sorting. Fast CAMs find application in large virtual-memory systems or in applications like airline reservation systems, where searching for items like flight numbers, destinations, and departure times makes up a large part of the processing task.

The higher cost and low bit densities of CAMs have limited applications. Costs are higher compared to conventional RAMs because of the additional space needed for the eual-access system and the additional pins required for the dual control system.

CAN—The cancel character instruction, which is used to indicate data that is in error and should not be accepted.

CANCL—A status word used to indicate that the remote system has deleted information previously transmitted.

capacitor storage—A device that uses the electric field in an insulator held between conductive plates to store digital or analog data.

card—1. An information storage medium of paper stock. Data is typically stored in the form of magnetic-ink characters or punched slots in ordered positions on the card face. Such cards are typically 3¼ inches × 7⅜ inches. A plug-in circuit board containing printed-circuit connections and components. Circuit cards are designed to hold the integrated-

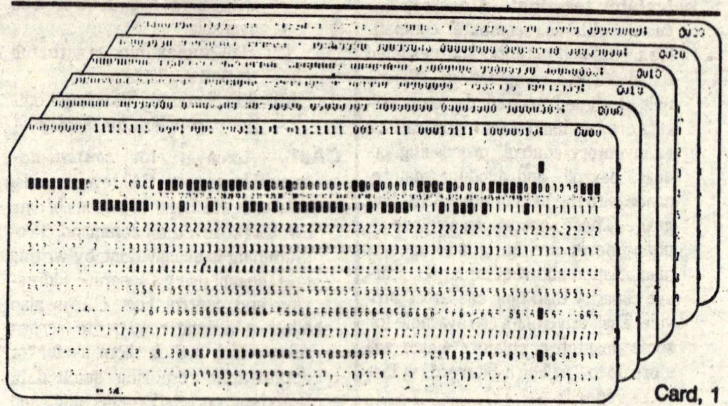

Card, 1

circuit packages and other components that make up the electronics of a functioning microcomputer system.

card cage—The structure that holds the various printed-circuit cards required by the microcomputer. The card cage includes one or more output connectors and may be prewired to hold a minimum number of circuit cards such as the CPU, memory, and output controller. Expansion is allowed by connecting card cages together. The card and card cage system are modular in design, offering:

(1) Simple assembly
(2) Easy access for checkout and troubleshooting
(3) Choice of output connections

card code—The combination of punched holes used in cards to indicate digital information.

card column—The line of punched holes in a card which appears parallel to the short edge of the card.

card field—The columns on the card which are assigned to receive the same type of information for a group of cards.

card deck—A pack of punched cards.

card hopper—That part of a card-processing machine which holds the card deck during processing. The card *hopper* holds the cards to be processed, and a card *stacker* typically holds the cards that have been processed.

card image—A representation of the hole patterns punched in a card. In a card image, each card hole represents a one and each unpunched space represents a zero.

card-programmed—A type of calculating system processing approach that uses punched cards for programming. Card-programmed calculating systems usually involve many different machines and multiple steps in the data flow.

card punch—A device which records data onto cards by punching holes in them whose positions relate to alphabetic and numeric data in accordance with a specific code.

card reader—A device which senses the hole patterns in punched cards and translates the data contained on the cards into the desired form. It is typically used with a controller that provides communications over a bus under direct memory access of the CPU. The CPU issues commands to the controller through the bus, and the controller responds by issuing the

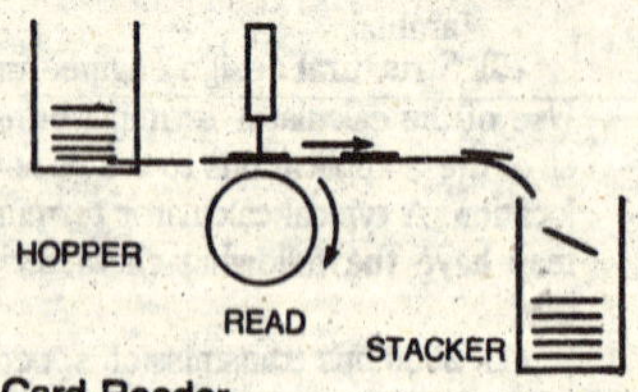

Card Reader

correct timing and control signals to the reader. Data on the cards is then transferred to the system memory until the reader controller issues an interrupt signal to the CPU to signal the end of data transmission. Data can be transferred in one of two formats:

(1) Standard, in which each column is stored right-justified within one word of memory.
(2) Packed, in which eight bits from each column are stored in alternate half-words of memory.

card row—The line of punched holes in a card which appears parallel to the long edge of the card.

card stacker—In a multiple-card processing system, a mechanical device that accepts each card after it has been processed and aligns it so that after the processing operation, all cards may be retrieved as a card deck.

card verifier—1. A special card reader that senses card codes immediately following the punch operation check of their accuracy. The operator of the machine reads the source documents and presses the correct keys on the verifier keyboard. The machine checks each column to verify that the correct holes have been punched and notches the end of the card if all columns are correct. If the verifier cannot match all the holes in a column, a notch is made above that column. 2. An individual who checks card data as an accuracy verification step.

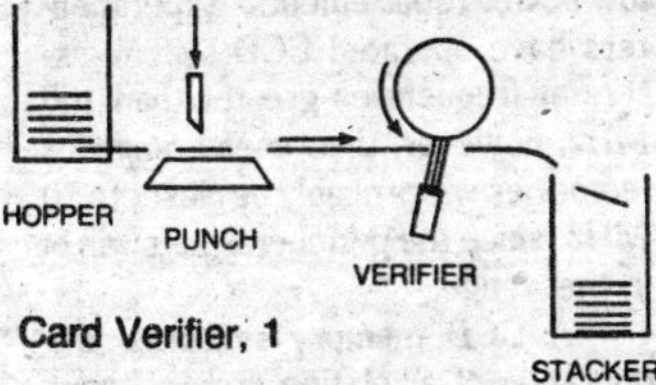

Card Verifier, 1

carriage—The control mechanism for a typewriter or printer, which is usually automatically controlled for such operations as paper feed, spacing, skipping, and ejecting. The term *carriage* was assigned in the typewriter's early days, when the sheet being typed upon was physically carried back and forth in front of a stationary impact printer.

carriage control tape—The tape that controls the line feed for a typewriter or printer.

carriage return—The operation that causes the next character in a series to be printed at the first position on the next line.

carriage return character—The character (abbreviated *CR*) that causes the print position to be moved to the first (usually flush left) space on a new line.

carrier—A radio-frequency signal of a specific wavelength, usually modulated with frequency or amplitude variations that represent intelligence to be conveyed.

carrier transmission—A communications system in which a signal of one frequency (the carrier) may be modulated by signals of other frequencies to convey intelligence over many channels. The signals are demodulated at the receiving end to recover the original information signals.

carry—The operation required when the sum of two digits equals or exceeds the base of the number being used as in adding:

$$\begin{array}{r} 1110 = 14 \\ \underline{+\ 1010 = 10} \\ 11000 = 24 \end{array}$$

Four carry operations are required for addition in binary notation. A carry within a computer results in a forwarding or transfer of the digits to a new digit place. When a carry into a digit place results in an additional carry when the normal adding circuit is bypassed, then the carry is called a high-speed carry, or *standing-on nines* carry. If the normal adding circuit is used, a *cascaded* carry results, which produces a partial sum numeral and a carry numeral; these are added together until no new carries are produced. The *partial* carry results from forming the partial product during multiplication. If the partial carry is propagated to completion, then a complete carry results. The *end-around* carry also occurs in multiplication and other operations, such as the addition of two negative numbers in nines-complement notation. In subtraction operations, a carry results when the difference between the digits is less than zero. This type of negative carry is usually called a borrow.

carry-complete—The signal used by parallel adders to indicate that all carries have been generated and propagated to completion for an addition operation.

carry time—The time required to perform the carry operation. The carry time consists of the time required to transfer a carry digit to a higher position and adding it, or the time required to transfer all the carry digits to higher positions and adding to all the digits in the number.

cascade control—An automatic operations-controlling system in which control units are linked in such a way that each element regulates the input of the next succeeding unit.

cassette—A magnetic-tape housing that contains a tape of a specific length. The cassette includes the supply reel, takeup reel, head pressure pad, and a slot for the capstan drive.

cathode-ray tube—A large vacuum tube with a viewing face like a TV screen, in which an electron beam is focused and controlled to form characters and other images. The beam and pattern are easily varied to produce almost any desired information format. (Usually abbreviated *CRT*.)

A typical application of the CRTs is in drawing display systems, whereby a designer uses a special stylus to draw on a piece of paper placed on a sensing tablet; as the designer draws, the information is sensed and displayed on the CRT screen. Quickly sketched lines are displayed straight, and rough corners appear precise on the display screen. Changes and modifications are easily made and lines are erased with simple stylus movements.

CCD—Abbreviation for *charge-coupled device*, a memory medium that uses carrier movement between potential wells to store digital information. The carriers are stored in the potential wells under electrodes biased in the depletion mode. Pulsing of the electrodes moves the carriers from one electrode to the next. The electrodes are located very close to each other in order to allow the potential wells to couple and move the carriers between them. Two types of structures are used in CCDs:

(1) The surface-channel type, which uses the surface of the substrate for storage and data transfer.

(2) The buried-channel type, which uses both the surface and the bulk of the material for storing and transferring data.

The surface-channel type does not require as much doping, which results in a simpler fabrication. It does offer a higher total charge-carrying capability, but suffers from low transfer efficiency at higher charge transfer rates. (The transfer efficiency is the percentage of the data or charge packet which is actually transferred in a data shift and is typically greater than 99.9%.)

Charge-coupled devices offer high speed, high packing density, and low power requirements. Experimenters have operated CCD shift registers at frequencies greater than 100 MHz; however, their useful range for memories will probably be closer to 10 MHz, since the peripheral units will be in that range.

A CCD memory simulates the operation of a rotating drum without any mechanical movement. A typical 16,384-bit chip is organized for both serial and random-access operation. Four-phase clock signals shift the data between the 64 shift registers of the device. Each shift register can be viewed as representing a single track in a conventional drum unit, with each track divided into 256 sectors, one for each CCD storage cell. The simulated rotation of the drum is controlled by the four-phase clock.

Applications include image sensing, signal processing, and semiconductor memory components. As memories, they may replace disks, drum, and other external storage devices.

cell—The storage memory element for one unit of information, usually one character or one word.

centralized processing—Data processing that is performed at a single central location from data obtained from several locations or managerial levels.

central processing unit—The central processor of a microprocessor. Most microprocessors use a 4-, 8-, 12-, or 16-bit word with 1, 2, or 3 memory cycles required to complete execution of an instruction. The central processing unit (CPU) may contain the arithmetic unit, control registers, main storage, and scratch pad memories.

central processor—That part of a computing machine that controls the interpretation and execution of instructions. The central processor is divided into three main sections:

(1) Arithmetic and control, which performs the calculations, information routing, and control operations for the other sections.
(2) Input and output, which handles all information going into and coming out of the central processor while controlling all peripheral equipment.
(3) Memory, which provides the temporary storage for data and instructions.

The memory cycle time usually determines the overall speed of the central processor.

cer-DIP—Acronym for *ceramic dual-in-line package.* Cer-DIP packages offer higher performance at costs closer to plastic packages than conventional ceramic devices. A military approved package with excellent reliability, this package is finding more and more applications now that some early stability and corrosion problems have been solved.

Cer-DIP

chad—The piece of material removed when a hole is punched in a card or paper tape.

chadless—A type of paper tape in which a chad does not exist. Chadless tape is partially prepunched and each chad is left fastened by about ¼ of the total circumference of the hole. It must be sensed by special readers that use mechanical fingers, as the loose chads interfere with conventional electrical or photoelectric sensors.

chain—A set of items that are serially linked together in specified segments which are processed in tandem, with only one allowed in the mainframe at any given moment. The items may be records or files that are dependent upon one another and each may have access to previously executed segments. Chained files allow open-ended sequential data handling and consist of data blocks with forward and backward pointers.

chain code—A cyclic sequence of words which are related by one bit position from the left or the right. A word must not be repeated before completion of the cycle. An example of a simple chain code is:

000	111
001	110
010	100
101	000
011	

chained list—A list of items in which each item has an identifier to locate the next item in the list.

chaining search—A technique which uses an identifier to locate the next item in a search.

chain printer—A printer mechanism that uses type carried on the links of a revolving chain.

change dump—A dump triggered by those storage locations whose contents have recently changed.

channel—A data pathway for the transmission of signals and data. In a communications system, a channel connects the message *source* with the message *sink*. In a storage unit, a channel may be the track or band that is connected to the read or write circuits. Also called *circuit, line, facility, link* and *path*.

channel capacity—The maximum number of bits or characters that can be handled in a particular channel at any one time. Also, the maximum transmission rate through a channel at a specified error rate. Channel capacity is usually measured in bits per second (for local media) or bauds (for data communications by wire or radio).

channelizing—The subdividing of wideband channels into a number of channels with narrow bandwidths.

character—A letter, numeral, or other symbol that is used to express information. A character is usually part of an ordered set and may be graphic, including English and other spoken languages, and may be any form of numeral, all punctuation marks, and other formatting symbols.

character boundary—As used in character recognition, the largest rectangle having a side parallel to the reference edge of the document.

character check—A verfication that characters have been formed correctly.

character code—An ordered pattern of bits that are assigned in a particular system to represent characters. Baudot and ASCII are character codes.

character fill—The inserting of specific characters, usually all ones or all zeros, to delete unwanted data.

character reader—A device that senses and interprets printed or handwritten symbols and converts the information into machine-language code. Character readers are available for many type styles; they operate optically or magnetically for characters printed with magnetic inks.

character recognition—The process of reading, identifying, and interpreting printed characters and converting them into a machine-language form for computers.

character set—The complete group of representations used as characters. Examples include:

(1) The letters of the alphabet
(2) The binary digits 0 and 1
(3) The complete set of signals used in Morse code

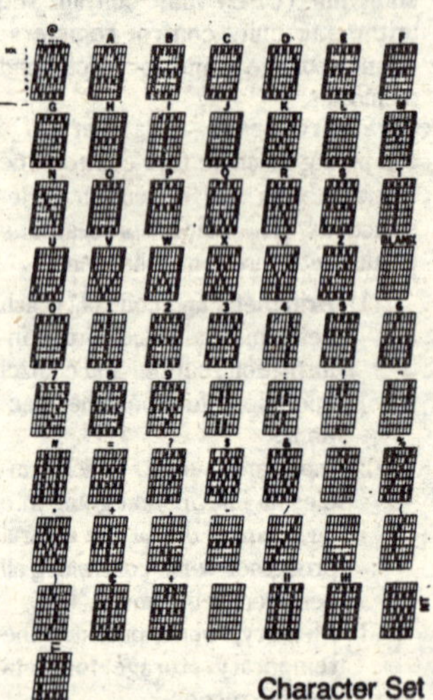

Character Set

character string—A group of connected characters associated by coding, keying, or other programming techniques.

character subset—Selected characters from a character set which have a specified common feature. For example, digits 0–9 are a subset of the ASCII character set.

charge-coupled device—A storage medium that utilizes the transfer of stored charges to achieve high densities for memory applications. (See *CCD*.)

check—Verification of equipment operation and the progress of desired operating conditions along with the correctness of resulting calculations.

check bit—A binary verification digit inserted with other digits as an automatic machine function. A parity check bit, for example, is inserted when the sum of a group of ones is odd, thus keeping the parity always even. When an output contains an odd number of ones, an error is indicated.

check character—A character used to perform a checking operation.

check digit—A digit which is used to perform a check. A check digit is carried as a part of a machine word to report on the other digits of the word. When an error occurs, the check is negative and an alarm is initiated. One or more check digits can be used with either batch processing or real-time computing operations. Data with the check digits can be periodically regenerated and compared with the source data.

check indicator—A device that indicates that a checking operation has uncovered an error. A check indicator may use either visual or audible means to call the operator's attention to the error.

checking routine—A diagnostic program which examines programs or data for the most obvious errors. A typical checking routine will discover errors in misspelling and keypunching and usually does not execute the program to detect programming errors.

checkout—The use of diagnostic tests to verify the correctness of machine and program operation.

checkpoint—A place in a program or routine where a check or a restart can be performed. The checkpoint allows the storage of sufficient information to allow restarting, or it records the information so that the step can be restarted at a later time.

checkpoint and restart—A program verifying technique that allows processing to continue from the last checkpoint rather than from the beginning of the run following an error detection or other interrupt. The checkpoints are determined based upon a desired number of transactions out of the total number required.

check problem—A test to detect errors in programming or machine operation. The check problem results in an error indication when it is not solved correctly.

check register—A register used to store information for checking with the result of a succeeding transfer of data. The check register stores the information until a second transfer of the same information verifies that the information agrees.

check reset—A key that is used to acknowledge an error and reset the program for restart.

checkout routine—A routine to aid programmers during debugging operations. A checkout routine may consist of storage and printout subroutines.

checksum—A summation of bits or digits used for checking purposes. Checksums are usually specified by an arbitrary set of rules fitted to the application. Summation checks provide a redundant checking method in which sums of digits are grouped and checked against previously computed sums for accuracy.

Chinese binary—The binary representation of data on cards which uses the card columns for storing information. Each column in a 12-row card would store 12 consecutive bits. (Also called *column binary*.)

chip—A silicon slab selectively doped with impurities so that passive and active devices, circuit paths, and device interconnections are formed within the solid structure. Thus, a chip is the integrated circuit inside an IC housing.

Microprocessor chips typically utilize large-scale integration (LSI) techniques. Up to 10,000 transistors have been placed on chips of 6 mm square. The chips are usually mounted in dual-inline packages which may have up to 40 pins for mounting on circuit boards.

A microprocessor chip usually includes the arithmetic logic unit (ALU), general purpose registers, and bus controls. The microprocessor chip or chips are combined with memory and input/output chips to form a microcomputer system that will fit on a single circuit board.

circuit—A closed communications path between two or more points. A circuit may have individual high paths and return paths, or the return path may be shared between many circuits. See *channel*. 2. A group of electronic components interconnected to perform specific functions upon application of proper voltages and signals. 3. A closed path of current sources and sinks.

circuit analyzer—Equipment that may consist of one or several test instruments and controlled by a microprocessor which is used to measure one or more quantities or verify performance of a circuit. A typical circuit analyzer is capable of a variety of functional tests on TTL, DTL, MOS, CMOS, and HTL devices using either combinatorial or sequential logic. The equipment may consist of constant-voltage and constant-current supplies, pulse generators, comparators, and a connection matrix. Power supply levels, pulse levels, and comparator limits are all programmable, and the matrix is used to connect the forcing and measuring connections with any lead of the device under test.

circuit breaker—A resettable fuse device for opening a circuit path, usually when overcurrent conditions are exceeded. A circuit breaker may also be used to control and protect circuits from conditions of excessive heat, noise, vibration, voltage, radiation, and other parameters.

circuit capacity—The information capacity and the number of total channels that can be operated in a given circuit at any one time, usually measured in baud or bits per second.

circuit hole—The component mounting hole that appears within or partially within the conductive lines of a printed circuit board; it may or may not be a through-the-board conductive path.

circuit load—The electrical load due to equipment current drain, usually expressed as a percentage of total circuit capability under specific operating conditions for a specific operating time.

circuit noise—Erratic and random electrical impulses generated by electrical switching in a circuit; these impulses, when interpreted by circuits as legitimate signals, cause errors and improper data timing.

circuit reliability—The percentage of time that a circuit meets specified operating conditions. The reliability figure is determined from the testing of enough parts to cause a desired number to fail based on the total population and the circuit application. The number of failures is then subtracted from the total number tested to obtain the circuit reliability.

circulating register—A shift register operated as a closed loop with the data outputs circulated back to the input.

circulating storage—A storage system which operates as a closed loop. Information is stored as a train or pattern of pulses; the pulse train at the output is usually sensed, amplified, and shaped before being inserted at the input.

clear—The placing of storage locations into a desired state, usually a zero or empty condition.

clear area—As used in character recognition, the area that is to be kept free of any markings not related to reading the character.

cleared condition—A destructive read operation which results in placing storage locations into cleared states. The cleared condition is usually permanent and is also called the zero condition.

clock—The usually crystal-controlled timing signal of a precise frequency that is used to time events within a piece of equipment. The clock is the basic method of generating periodic signals for synchronization in electronic equipment, including computers. A clock may be a shift register which changes its contents at specified intervals to mark time, or it may be a data communications clock which controls and limits the number of bits in a data stream.

clock generator—An oscillator, usually crystal controlled, which provides all timing signals within a computer system. A typical clock generator provides the multiphase signals using only one external crystal and internal dividers for signals that are MOS or TTL compatible. ROMs are used with counters for generating clock phases in systems requiring complex clocking.

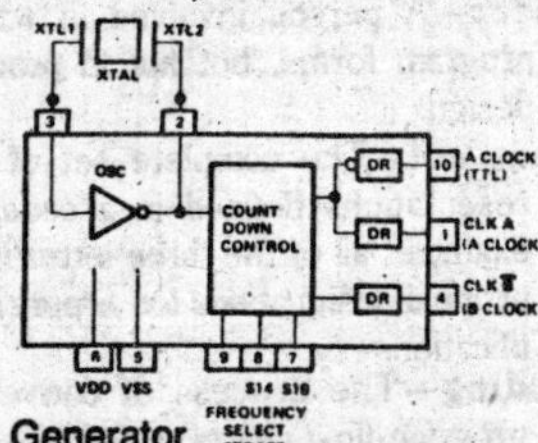

Clock Generator

clock pulse—A signal provided for synchronization of events.

clock rate—1. The number of pulses per unit time that are generated by a clock. The clock rate is typically measured in bits per second or hertz (cycles per second). 2. The rate at which bits or words can be transferred between elements within a system.

clock track—The track upon which a pattern of signals has been cut or traced to provide a reference for the recording of time.

closed loop—A circuit, system, or device in which the output is continuously sampled by the input for comparison and control purposes.

closed-loop program—A program in which there is no exit other than by intervention from outside the program. The closed-loop program is used when a group of indefinitely repeated instructions is required. Closed-loop or feedback control systems are used to control many industrial processes.

closed routine—A routine that is entered by basic linkage from the main routine, instead of inserting a block of instructions through the main program.

closed shop—A computer facility that uses programming specialists for programming rather than the originators of the problems, or one which uses full-time operators rather than user/programmers as operators.

closed subroutine—A subroutine that can be stored in one place and connected to the main routine by one or more linkages. A closed subroutine is usually entered by a jump operation and is forced to return control to the main routine at the end of the operation. The instructions related to the jump and return are known as linkages.

C MOS—An acronym (pronounced "see-moss") for ***complementary metal-oxide semiconductor*** technology employing integrated field-effect transistors in a complementary symmetry arrangement, which simulates "Push/Pull" operation because of the placement of opposing-polarity devices (p-channel and n-channel FETs).

As a logic family, CMOS offers the following advantages:

(1) Low power requirements
(2) Excellent noise immunity
(3) High fanout to other CMOS circuits
(4) High tolerance to power supply variations, allowing low-cost supplies

(5) High temperature range-

coalesce—The combining of two or more files into one.

COBOL—Acronym for *common business-oriented language.* COBOL makes use of English-language statements and was desiged by a committee to serve two purposes:

(1) Provide a specific language for the business data processing industry.

(2) Provide a language to help these users achieve program compatibility.'

The committee was sanctioned by the U.S. Department of Defense and the language was released for publication in 1960.

There are two types of COBOL words—*reserved* and *supplied*. Reserved words such as SELECT, ASSIGN, and READ have a special meaning to the COBOL compiler and must be used according to COBOL rules. Supplied words are those supplied by the user and have meaning exclusive to the program without violating any of the language rules.

A COBOL source program has four basic divisions: identification, environment, data, and procedure. The identification division identifies the program, the program author, and the dates when the program was written and compiled. The environment division is used to describe the specific equipment being used. In the data division are two sections—a file section and a working storage section. The file section is used to describe all information which enters and leaves the CPU storage unit; the working storage section is used to specify the locations needed during processing to hold intermediate results, record descriptions, and items such as reserved words. The procedure division specifies the steps that the computer must use to process the program. The steps of this division make use of the names of records and items which were defined in the data division.

CODASYL—Acronym for *Conference on Data Systems Language*, the assemblage which developed COBOL as a viable language.

code—1. A system of rules and ordered characters used to represent symbols and characters from a different character set. (See, for example, *Baudot code* and *Gray code*.) 2. As a verb, to write or form a routine, as in "code a program."

code conversion—The process for changing the bit grouping for a character in one code to the corresponding grouping in another code. ROMs and other storage elements are useful for code conversion.

coded character set—A set of characters with a code assigned to each character for computer purposes.

code extension character—The control character which indicates that one or more of the succeeding code values is to be interpreted using a different code.

code holes—The holes containing information in perforated tape as opposed to the sprocket holes (used for feeding the tape).

coder—A person involved in writing program forms, but not in program design.

code set—The complete set of representations defined in a code: for example, all of the three-letter international designations for airport identification.

coding—The process of converting program flow charts into the desired language, or the use of codes to represent characters.

coding scheme—The rationale behind a code, the understanding of which could prove helpful in determining character codes in the absence of explanatory data.

COGO—Acronym for *coordinate geometry*, a language used for solving coordinate geometry problems in civil engineering. COGO falls into the general group of a production or process control language along with APT and STRESS.

coincidence—Refers to the property of a circuit or device in which an output is produced only when two or more inputs are received within a specified time period.

collate—To combine items from two or more similar sets to produce another similar set. The collated set may or may not be in the same order as the original set.

collating sequence—The order which is assigned to a set of items, such that any two sets in the order can be collated.

collator—A device used to collate or match sets or punched cards or other collatable data forms. Punched-card collators can combine two sets of cards into a single sequenced deck, or compare two decks of cards without combining them. The collator can also check trays of cards to determine the correct ascending or descending order.

column—A vertical arrangement of characters, bits, or other data on cards, pages, or other matrixed lists.

column binary—The representation of data on cards in which the significance of the punched positions are assigned along the card columns rather than the rows. Also called *Chinese binary*.

column split—A method of sensing or punching card data that allows specified punch positions within single columns to be ignored or treated in a different manner than other punch positions in the same column.

COM— Acronym for *computer output microfilm*. The COM printer transfers the output of the computer in use onto microfilm.

combinatorial logic—Circuits or devices in which the outputs are completely determined by the present state of the inputs. Combinatorial logic includes AND, OR, NAND, NOR, and other circuits that do not rely on previous states to determine the present state.

command—As used in microprocessors and microcomputers, an "instruction" that signals the machine to start, stop, or continue a specific operation. A command is not an instruction in the usual sense, but it is a portion of an instruction word which specifies the operation to be performed. Some examples of commands used in the LSI-11 microcomputer are:

The solidus "/"—used to open a memory location, a general register, or a processor status word.

The carriage return "CR"—used to close an open location.

The "at cost" sign "@"—used to keep a location open using the contents of the location as a pointer.

The GO or "G"—used to start execution of a program at the location immediately before the "G."

command control—Refers to a type of program which handles all user generated console commands sent into the system.

command language—A source language which consists mainly of process operators. Each operator in a command language is capable of executing a particular function or command.

comment—An expression used to identify or explain the steps in a routine. Comments have no effect on the execution of the routine or program and are usually found to the right of instructions on printouts or program lists.

common carrier—A multiple-user communications system licensed and regulated by the Federal Communications Commission to provide services to all users at regulated rates.

common field—A field that can be accessed by independent routines.

common memory—A shared storage medium in which many microcomputers may have access.

common programs—Programs which have common or multiple applications for more than one system. Programs in the following classes can be used for several routines if they are written in a language common to the computers:

(1) Sorting routines
(2) Report generation
(3) Code conversion programs

common software—Common programs.

communication channel—A channel or circuit path reserved for transmitting and receiving. Microcomputers can handle full-duplex communication between a teletypewriter or RS-232 device and the CPU with the interface provided by a UART (universal asynchronous receiver/transmitter). To receive data, the UART converts the asynchronous serial characters from the teletypewriter or RS-232 device into a parallel format for transfer to the CPU bus. During transmission, the parallel characters from the CPU bus are converted into a serial mode for the printer or RS-232 unit. The data transfer is independent, allowing the system to achieve simultaneous two-way data communication.

communication control character—The character which is used to control the transmission of data over communication channels. A communication control character can be used to control printer operation by causing a back space or line skip.

communication link—The means of connecting one location to another for the purpose of transmitting and receiving information. A communications link may be a circuit, channel, or system of equipment which connects the two locations.

communications executive—A program or routine which provides the handling and protocol management for the system of communication links and equipment.

communications satellite corporation—COMSAT. The United States representative in the international INTELSAT organization. COMSAT provides technical and operational services for INTELSAT under a management services contract and coordinates traffic from its operations center in Washington, D.C.

communication statements—These are statements used to link a subprogram to a main program. The communication statements allow the subprograms to be called and returned. A few examples of communication statements are:

PROCEDURE CALL: Used to transfer control from a calling program to the called subprogram. Usually specific procedures are defined and used in this statement.

RETURN: Used to return control to the calling program from the subprogram.

communications terminal—A point in a system or network at which data can be transmitted or received. A large amount of data communications is done over ordinary telephone lines using terminal devices and interfaces. Several leased lines are sometimes linked to improve the bandwidth and allow a heavier flow of traffic than is possible with single voice-grade lines.

communications word—The partial set of characters used as a unit to store or transmit information in a communications system.

commutator pulse—A reference pulse which is used to mark, clock, or control a particular part of a word or a series of words.

compaction—The methods used for reducing space, bandwidth, costs, transmission and storage of data. Compaction techniques tend to eliminate repetition and remove irrelevant operations and steps in coding data.

comparator—A device or method used for checking two or more items for precise degree of similarity, equality, relative magnitude, or order.

comparator check—A check made to compare original data and printed or punched data. The originals and the new data are run through a comparator check to uncover any errors made during processing operations. The checking of cards can be done on a match or nonmatch basis; comparison of alphabetical and numerical data can be done either on selected columns and fields, or on entire cards.

compatibility—The ability to interface without special adapters or other devices. The term relates to the ease of the transfer of data or programs between systems.

compilation time—The time required to compile or translate a program, as opposed to the time when the program is actually being run.

compile—To prepare a machine-language program from a program written in another language using the following techniques:

(1) Using the overall logic structure of the program
(2) Generating more than one machine instruction for each symbolic statement
(3) Performing the function of assembly

compiler—A coding or programming system that inputs source language data and outputs a program either in assembly or machine language. (Source languages used in compilers include FORTRAN, COBOL, APL, ALGOL, PL/1, and others.)

The compiler provides a language that requires fewer statements for algorithm writing and eliminates the requirement for detailed coding to control loops, access data structures, and writes complex formulas and functions. Below is a compiler statement with its equivalent in assembly language for the 8080: Compiler statement is in PL/M (a subset language for PL/1):

```
DECLARE (X, Y, Z) BYTE; IF X
greater   than   Y   THEN

    Z = X - Y + 2;
        ELSE Z = Y - X + 2
```

The equivalent assembly language statement for the 8080 is:

```
          ORG 4000
BEGIN     LLI LOW X
          LHI HIGH X
          LAM;
          LLI LOW Y
          LHI HIGH Y
          LBM;
          SUB;
          ITS LOC2
LOC 1     ADI 2;
          LLI LOW Z
          LHI HIGH Z
          LMA
          JMP FINISH
LOC2      LCI 377
          XRC;
          ADI 1;
          JMP LOC1
FINISH    HLT
LOW X     EQU 70
HIGH X    EQU 10
LOW Y     EQU 71
HIGH X    EQU 10
LOW Z     EQU 72
HIGH Z    EQU 10
          ORG 4070
LOC X     DEF 0;
LOC Y     DEF 0;
LOC Z     DEF 0;
```

The compiler in this case provides instructions that are much easier to read, understand, and write. Programs tend to be easy to read and write, but sometimes at the cost of excessive storage space and slower execution times. A compiler that produces assembly langauge code allows the use of an assembly listing for checking and often helps to eliminate redundant data flow.

compiling routine—A routine used to computer-construct a program.

complement—In any radix system, the difference between any given digit and its base raised to the next higher power. For binary, the complement of 1 is 11. To check the accuracy of a complementing operation, add the number to be complemented with the complement to get the base, or the next higher power of the base. Thus, to verify that 11 is the binary complement of 1, add 1 and 11:

$$\begin{array}{r} \text{carry} \searrow 1\ 1 \\ +11 \\ \hline 100 \end{array}$$

In binary, $100 = 2^2$

The complement C can be obtained by subtracting the given number form the base raised to the power represented by the number of digits in the quantity, or

$$C = B^D - N$$

where B = number base
D = digits in number
N = any number

complement procedure—The method which relates the base and the system used to obtain the complement. See *complement.*

complementary MOS—CMOS. A process that combines both n-channel and p-channel MOS transistors (FETs) on the same chip in a complementary-symmetry configuration.

complementary operator—A logic operator that produces the complement of any given logic operator (the NOT operator).

complementation—An operation which results in the reverse significance in each digit position in a series of digits. If the word is:

0101100

then complementation gives 1010011.

complementing—The use of complements to produce the negative equivalent of a number.

complete carry—A technique used in parallel addition in which all carries are allowed to propagate to completion.

complete operation—A computer operation which includes:

(1) Obtaining all operands from storage
(2) Performing the desired operation
(3) Returning the results to storage
(4) Obtaining the next instruction

component—A functional part of a circuit, module, or system. A component can be a self-contained element or a combination of elements, parts, or assemblies.

composite video—The signal for a CRT consisting of picture signal, blanking, and sync pulses.

compound logic—Logic that furnishes an output that is a function of many inputs.

compound modulation—Modulation of a signal that is already modulated, resulting in double modulation.

compress—To reduce certain parameters of a signal while preserving the basic information content. Compressing usually reduces a parameter such as amplitude or duration of the signal to improve overall transmission efficiency.

compute bound—The limiting of output rate due to delays caused from computing operations.

compute limited—See *compute bound.*

computer—A data processor that performs computations, including arith-

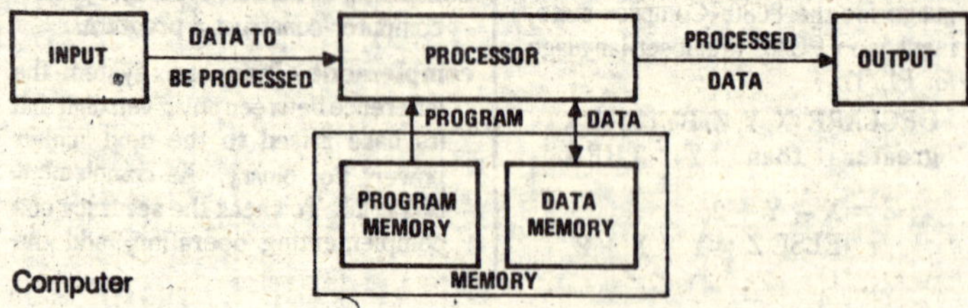

Computer

metic and logic, usually without intervention by a human operator during the processing run.

computer-aided design—The use of a computer for automated design purposes. See *CAD*.

computer-assisted instruction—The use of a computer in a system which is used to assist in the instruction of students. These systems may involve a dialog between the student and the computer which informs the student of errors and offers guidance.

computer code—The machine language or code used within a computer system.

computer instruction—A machine instruction used with a specific computer system.

computer network—A system consisting of two or more interconnected computers. In addition to a host computer, a computer network usually contains the following facilities:

(1) User communications interfaces
(2) Communications networks
(3) Network control hardware and software

computer output microfilm—A system (abbreviated *COM*) designed to replace a line printer as an output device; it is capable of producing high-quality text at 5000 lines per minute or more.

computer program—The series of instructions and statements prepared in order to solve a specific problem or achieve a certain result.

computer run—The processing of a batch of transactions, or the performance of one routine or several routines which are linked to form an operating unit. During a computer run, manual operations are usually not required from the human operator.

computer system—An arrangement which uses several or many computing facilities in a cooperative manner. A computer system generally uses several small computers in dispersed locations for simpler tasks and a larger central computer for the more complex tasks. The central files are stored at the larger computer facility, and the smaller computers call on these files when required. This type of system reduces the load and cost of the central computer and results in overall cost savings.

computer word—The sequence of bits or characters that are treated as a unit and stored in one location. Same as *machine word.*

COMSAT—Acronym for *Comminications Satellite Corporation*, the privately owned United States communications carrier in charge of commercial communications satellite deployment.

COM system—A *computer output microfilm* system serving the purpose of a line printer.

concatenate—To link together in a series. A concatenated data set is one formed by combining the contents of several data sets in a specific sequence.

concentrator—A processor used in communication systems which performs the following services:

(1) Polling of local lines
(2) Formatting of messages
(3) Error correction and flags to operator

concordance—A type of program that uses alphabetic lists of words and phrases with references. Concordance programs sometimes use a free-form assembler to produce the alphabetized listings which are referenced by line numbers.

concurrent—The occurrence of two or more events or activities within the same time period. Concurrent operating allows several programs to share a computer at the same time. Job processing is allowed to continue while the computer performs inquiry or utility operations using time-sharing or multiprogramming.

concurrent processor—A machine capable of operating on more than one program at a time; a *multiprocessor*.

condenser storage—A storage device that uses the capacitance of the medium to store information; capacitor storage.

conditional breakpoint—A point in a program which causes the computer to stop because of a specified condition. The routine is continued from the breakpoint as coded, or another instruction is used to force a jump to another point.

conditional code—Used to define a group of program instructions such as carry, borrow, and overflow. Conditional code instructions are important to program execution and are usually listed in a *condition code register*.

conditional implication—A Boolean algebra operation defined by the following truth table:

OPERAND		RESULT
A	B	C
0	0	1
1	0	0
0	1	1
1	1	1

conditional jump—A jump that occurs only if specified criteria are satisfied. A conditional jump instruction may result in obtaining the correct addresses for the next instruction that produces a transfer of control. The next instruction can be dependent on the specified criteria as to whether or not a jump or skip to another instruction is called for.

conditional stop—A program stop that is dependent upon specified conditions. Conditional stops can sometimes be controlled from the console by the operator.

conditional transfer—A transfer of control which occurs only if specific conditions are met. If these conditions are not met, the program continues in its normal sequence.

condition codes—Codes that are used to contain information about the results of the last CPU operation, such as:

X = 1, if the result was zero
Y = 1, if the result was negative
Z = 1, if an overflow resulted

conditioning—The processing of signals to make them more intelligible or more compatible in a given application. Signal conditioning may include pulse shaping, clipping, digitizing, and linearization.

conductor—That part of a passive circuit path which carries electrical current.

configuration—A group or system of machines that are connected and programmed together.

confidence level—A measure of the degree of confidence of a device's or system's operation, usually expressed as a percentage of the probability of success.

conjunction—The logic operation which uses the AND operator and results in the logical product. The AND function occurs when two or more gates are placed in series and then follow the truth table below:

GATE OR OPERAND	GATE OR OPERAND	AND OUTPUT
A	B	C
0	0	0
0	1	0
1	0	0
1	1	1

The conjunction of the two operands is written as AB or A • B or A × B.

connector—1. A means of converging lines on a flow diagram. A flow-chart connector can be used to represent a break in a flowline, or the divergence of a flowline into several lines. 2. A terminal designed for easy mating with a complementary terminal or adapter, as on a cable.

connect time—The time period when a remote terminal is connected to a time-shared system, usually marked by a *sign-on* and a *sign-off*.

consecutive—The occurrence of two sequential events without the interference of any other event.

consecutive sequence computer—A computer in which all instructions are executed in a defined sequence unless specified to enter a jump operation.

console—The part of a computer system that is used for communication between the computer operator and the CPU. The computer console may contain a start key, stop key, power control, sense switches, and register lights. Other console functions allow manual control, error correction, and status determination for counter and storage circuits. Some consoles allow the programmer to debug the program by slowly stepping the machine through each instruction and observing the status indicators; other consoles include a CRT terminal which may have pictorial capabilities as well as pointing aids such as light pens.

constant—A fixed value or an item of data that does not vary. Constants are those quantities or messages which are available as data for the program and are not subject to change with time. A constant can be one character or a group of characters which represent a value and are used to identify, measure, or compare.

constant area—That part of storage selected to store the invariable quantities required during processing.

constructs—Detailed construction drawings produced using a patented process employing a computer and a plotter. Constructs allow human intervention when required and are commercially available through Control Data Corporation.

contact—The part of a relay, switch, or connector which allows circuits to be closed by physically touching a similar part on a current carrying line. Circuits are opened by breaking the physical connection.

contact sensing—Refers to the techniques used to monitor and convert field switch contacts into digital information for input to a computer. Contact points are usually scanned at programmed intervals.

content addressable memory—A type of RAM in which the addresses of data can be retrieved upon command. CAMs also provide a normal read/write technique, making them useful for:

(1) Quick data searching
(2) Correlation checking
(3) Sorting items

Because of the dual accessing system and larger chips required, CAMs tend to cost more than conventional RAMs.

contingency interrupt—An interrupt which occurs due to one of the following:

(1) Operator requests use of the keyboard
(2) Character typeout
(3) Operator requests program stop
(4) An overflow occurs
(5) An invalid code

continuous simulation—A type of simulation represented by continuous variables scanned at regular intervals. Continuous simulation can be used for either linear or nonlinear differential equations.

control—The act or power of asserting authority in a specific plan of action. The control section of a computer will carry out the instructions in the proper sequence, interpret incoming instructions, and provide the proper output flags.

Instructions which determine jumps are called *control instructions*, and execution of instructions in the correct time sequence is called *flow of control*.

control block—The circuitry which performs the control function of a CPU. In a typical microcomputer the control block will decode instructions and generate all control signals required for operation.

control bus—A data pathway in a computer system that is used to regulate system operations. Control bus signals tend to operate like traffic signals or commands. They may originate in peripheral equipment and be under control of the bus register for access to the bus.

control card—1. A punched card which contains input data for initializing or modifying a program. 2. A punched card used in a sorting program for specifying the sorting parameters.

control character—A character which initiates, modifies, or stops a control operation. A control character is generally not a graphic character, but it may have a graphic representation. A typical control character is used for nonprinting functions such as carriage return or line feed, or to control other operations such as recording, interpreting, transferring, and transmitting.

control circuits—Circuits used to carry out program instructions in the correct sequence. Control circuits also interpret the program instructions and send the control signals through the system.

control console—A console which enables the operator to control and monitor all processing functions from a central location. The control console usually has a typewriter or other keyboard input to allow communication with the processor.

control counter—A device used to record the location of the current instruction word. The control counter is sometimes used to select storage locations.

control cycle—A cycle in the operation of a punch card machine in which feeding is stopped to allow a control change.

control data—Any data item that is used to identify, select, modify, or execute an operation, routine, record, or file.

control field—A location where control information is placed, usually constant and usually as a sequence of similar items.

control function—Any action that affects the recording, processing, transmission and interpretation of data such as starting and stopping, carriage return, font change, or rewinding.

control instruction—An instruction which may (1) move data between the main memory and the control memory, (2) prepare main memory storage areas for processing, or (3) control the instruction sequence and interpretation.

controller—A unit which operates automatically to regulate the performance of a controlled variable or system. Controllers use the data from the input and the output of a device to obtain the maximum and most efficient control of the device or process. Controllers are also used in computer systems for generation of signals to interface the CPU with memory and peripheral equipment. A typical controller chip performs all the control functions required for the flow of data at the interface.

control operaton—Any action affecting the recording, processing, transmission, and interpretation of data; control function.

control panel—The part of a computer console that contains the manual controls. The control panel may be implemented using switches, plugs, pins, or sockets to change instructions manually, or it may be implemented in software. Many microprocessors use a transparent control panel implemented in software with its own memory separate from the main memory. This frees the main memory and allows the control panel to be greated as a unit and plugged in when needed without disturbing the main program.

control program—A sequence of instructions used to guide the CPU through operations. A control program in a microprocessor is usually stored in ROM where it can be accessed, but not erased by the CPU.

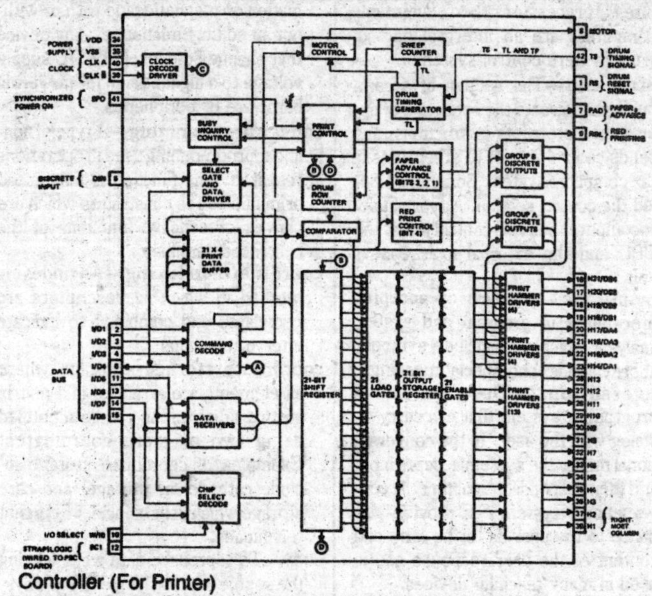

Controller (For Printer)

control read-only memory—CROM. A type of ROM that is designed and microprogrammed to decode control logic. A CROM is a major component of some microprocessors in which all actions of the CPU are controlled from the microprogram stored there. In general, the instructions are basic and have a short execution time, which makes it practical to use a large number of them in the program.

control register—The register which stores the current instruction to control the CPU for the next cycle. Also called *instruction register*.

control routine—Primary routines which control the loading and rerouting of other routines. Control routines are used in automatic coding and are sometimes considered as a part of the machine itself as opposed to another program. Sometimes called monitor routine, supervisory routine, or supervisory program.

control section—The sequence of instructions within a program that can be replaced from outside the program segment which contains it. A typical control section is exchanged with control sections from other segments in many microcomputer systems.

control sequence—The normal order for the selection of instructions for execution. The control sequence can be specified by an address in each instruction, or it may be consecutive except for jumps and transfers.

control statements—Statements are instructions which direct the program flow and convey control information to the CPU. Control statements may cause transfers dependent upon specified conditions, but they do not cause the development of machine-language instructions.

control store—An address register which allows the user to monitor the program point at which program operation is stopped. The control store register aids debugging and is usually monitored through the front panel of a ROM simulator.

control system—A system which controls, analyzes, monitors, or measures a process or other equipment. Computers are an intergral part of many modern control systems.

control unit—The section of a computer that directs the sequence of operations, interrupts instructions, and sends control signals to other units in the computer system. Sometimes called the control section. A typical microcomputer has two control units: the CPU and the external logic control unit.

conventions—Standard or accepted procedures in program and system analysis which may include symbols, abbreviations, and special meanings.

conversational—Descriptive of a program or system that can carry on dialog with the user. In the conversational mode, the system accepts input and then responds in real time. A conversational system can provide guidance to the user as to the form and content of the user response and is used in many teaching devices.

conversational language—A language which uses a character set similar to English to aid communication bewteen the user and the computer. BASIC is an exmaple of a conversational language.

conversion—The act of changing data or information from one form to another without changing the content of the data. Conversion equipment is used in many systems for transposing data from one form to another in order to make it acceptable to the input of another type of processing device.

convert—To change information from one base to another in order, for example, to transfer the data from the output of one unit to the input of another. Numerical data can be converted from binary to decimal, or from cards to tape.

converter—1. A device which changes the representation of data from one form to another and allows the form of data processing to change. For example, a converter may accept data on punched cards and store the information on magnetic tape with or without an editing function. 2. Any device that changes the level of a DC supply voltage to a higher value for powering hardware or peripherals.

convex programming—A type of nonlinear programming used in operations research. The function is maximized or minimized to constraints which are convex or concave functions of the controlled variables.

coordinate indexing—An indexing method in which all descriptors are correlated and combined to indicate interrelationships.

coordinate storage—Storage where all elements are arranged in a matrix so that any location can be identified using two or more coordinates. Examples of coordinate storage include cathode-ray storage, and core storage which uses coincident-current techniques.

copy—To reproduce data while leaving the source data unchanged. The physical form of the data may change as when a deck of cards is copied onto magnetic tape. A *hard* copy refers to any printed form of machine output, such as reports and listings.

cordonnier system—An information retrieval system that uses cards with small holes drilled at the intersections of the column and row designations. Also called *peek-a-boo* and *batten* system.

core—A toroidal memory array using small donut-shaped magnets, the fields of which may be used to represent digital ones and zeros. Magnetic core has been a major type of storage for many computers in the past.

core allocation—The use of core memory as allocated in a system. Since memory is usually limited, core allocation is concerned with the division of memory for:

(1) Programs to be permanently stored
(2) Temporary storage of programs
(3) Data to be permanentl, stored

(4) Temporary storage of data
(5) Working storage

core memory—A memory that uses toroids in matrix arrays for storing binary digits. A core memory is a programmable random-access memory that uses ferromagnetic storage techniques.

core storage—The storage of binary digits using magnetic cores, usually strung through wires in the form of a matrix array.

correction program—A routine designed to be used after a failure, malfunction, or error. The routine is inserted at a point before the error, during a run or rerun of the program.

corrective maintenance—Maintenance designed to eliminate existing faults. Corrective maintenance may occur as a part of emergency maintenance or deferred maintenance, and should not be confused with preventive maintenance, which is designed to prevent failures. Corrective maintenance time may be scheduled or unscheduled.

counter—A device used to measure and represent the number of occurrences of a specific event. Also known as an *accumulator*. Some types of counters can be set to an initial value and then increased or decreased (as an up–down counter). Others may be used as address counters or registers in which address data is loaded to specify the location where the next block of data is to be transferred.

A *B-line counter* is used as an index register which can be set to any number from storage, incremented by a certain number, and then tested against another number in storage. Index registers are used for address modifications and in programs involving repetitive steps.

Counters used as *cycle index counters* measure the number of times a cycle of instructions has been repeated. A cycle index register can be used to determine the number of repetitions required in a loop at any given time.

Program counters are registers used to hold the identification of the next instruction word. The program counter is usually incremented to the address of the next storage location in the program sequence.

coupler—A device which transfers signals and has its input and output isolated electrically. Also known as an isolator, a coupler usually consists of a light-emitting diode (LED) and a light sensor. The input signal activates the LED, which in turn forces current through the output light sensor. When the two devices are separated by an air gap rather than glass or plastic, the coupler can be used to sense motion and encode cards, plates, and slotted disks.

CPE—Abbreviation for *central processing element*. An element of a bit-slice microprocessor that contains all of the major processing circuits necessary to build processors of longer word lengths. CPEs can be cascaded to form a processor of any desired word length. Multiple bus structures allow functions to be executed in a single microcycle instead of several cycles.

CPU—Abbreviation for *central processing unit*. A primary unit of the computer system which controls the interpretation and execution of instructions. A CPU may consist of registers, computational circuits such as the arithmetic and logic unit, control circuits, and input/output ports. The registers may include accumulators, index registers, and perhaps stack registers. All registers are treated as internal memory.

CR—The carriage return character.

CRC—The cyclic redundancy check character.

crippled leapfrog—Refers to a variation of the leapfrog tests to discover computer malfunctions. The crippled leapfrog tests are done from a fixed set of locations rather than the changing locations used in the leapfrog tests.

critical path—A scheduling system which uses milestones to check the progress of the task.

CROM—Abbreviation for *Control Read-Only Memory*, a type of ROM that is designed and microprogrammed to decode control logic. The CROM is a major component of many two-chip microprocessors. One chip contains the CPU and the other a CROM that accesses the correct routine for each instruction, sequences through the routine, and provides the data control signals to the CPU.

cross assembler—A program run on one computer for the purpose of translating instructions for another computer. Many microprocessor programs are assembled by other computer processors. Development time and costs can be reduced by using a larger computer's processing and editing capability. Software is often written in FORTRAN with assemblers available through national time-sharing service companies.

cross compiler—A program that prepares a machine-language program on one computer for another computer. A cross compiler can replace a cross assembler in many high-level language applications to allow extra convenience to the programmer.

cross coupling—The usually unwanted inadvertent transfer of signals and signal components between circuits or channels.

crossfoot—The punching of results of another field in punched cards due to the adding and subtracting of numbers from different fields in the same card.

cross modulation—A form of signal distortion found in multiple-carrier systems; crosstalk. Cross modulation may be caused from the effects of the envelope of one carrier upon the other due to nonlinearity in the common transmitting medium.

crosstalk—The undesirable energy transferred from one circuit to another. The source of the energy is called the disturbing circuit and the circuit receiving the energy is called the disturbed circuit. *Far-end* crosstalk propagates in the same direction as the signals, and *near-end* crosstalk propagates in the opposite direction.

CRT—Abbreviation for *cathode-ray tube*. CRTs are used for both display and storage in computer systems. As a display, the CRT can be operated in the point mode to allow points to be established and displayed on the screen. CRT storage uses the electron beam to sense the presence or absence of spots on the CRT screen.

cryogenics—The study and use of properties of materials at temperatures approaching absolute zero. Cryogenic elements offer high-speed storage from the superconductivity which occurs at near-zero temperatures. Since superconductors have no resistance, they also have the ability to store currents permanently.

cryotron—A device operated at low temperatures to allow changes in small magnetic fields to control large currents; the cryogenic equivalent of an electron tube.

current—The rate of flow of electrical carriers past a given point, usually measured in amperes.

current attenuation—The loss of current in a device or circuit, or along a line, usually expressed as the ratio of output to input current in decibels.

current density—The amount of current passing through a given area of a conductor, usually expressed in amperes per square centimer (A/cm^2).

current instruction register—A register which contains the instruction presently being executed.

cursor—A manually controllable pointer used as a position or location indicator in a display. A cursor is usually employed to indicate a character to be changed or corrected, or a position where data is to be entered via the display keyboard. The cursor may take the form of an underscore, an undertext caret, or an arrow.

cue—The action made by the calling party in a communications mode, which serves as the signal for a subsequent series of events to begin.

curtate—That part of a punched card consisting of adjacent punched rows.

cybernetics—The science of communication and control in living organisms and the corresponding simulation through the use of:

(1) Integration of communication and control technology
(2) Systems engineering development
(3) Hardware and software application development

The field of cybernetics has aided technology forecasting and assessment, systems modeling, policy analysis, pattern recognition, and artificial intelligence development.

cycle—One complete revolution in a repetitive sequence of revolutions; the operations are allowed to vary, but the sequence must retain a regular pattern. A computer cycle refers to a nonarithmetic shift in which digits are taken from one end of a word and moved to the other end, or to repeat a set of operations a required number of times. Cycling may include the supplying of address changes using a cycle counter to measure the number of times the cycle is to be repeated. An *action* cycle is the complete cycle operation performed on a block of data, including origination, manipulation, and storage.

cycled interrupt—A change of control to a specific operation, usually in a predetermined manner such as a specific sequence or operation cycle.

cycle index—An index of the number of times a cycle has been executed or is to be executed. A cycle index register can be set to the number of cycles desired, then each cycle shifts the register down by one until it is empty and the cycle series is complete.

cycle shift—The nonarithmetic shift in which digits are taken from one end of a word and shifted to the other end.

cycle stealing—A method of delaying execution of a program to allow an operation which would normally require a complete cycle for completion. A cycle-stealing data channel will allow the storage of a data word without changing the processor logic. After the word is stored, the program can continue as though never stopped. A cycle steal is different from an interrupt in that it does not change the contents of the instruction register.

cycle time—The interval between calling for and delivery of information from storage, or any regular sequential time interval such as required to complete specific operations or execute instructions.

DECIMAL	CYCLIC BINARY (GRAY)	BINARY
0	0000	0000
1	0001	0001
2	0011	0010
3	0010	0011
4	0110	0100
5	0111	0101
6	0101	0110
7	0100	0111
8	1100	1000
9	1101	1001
10	1111	1010
11	1110	1011
12	1010	1100
13	1011	1101
14	1001	1110
15	1000	1111

cyclic check—A cyclic method of error detection which is used to check the $x + n$ bit where $n = 1, 2, 3....$ The cyclic check is usually preferred over horizontal, vertical, or combinational checks.

cyclic binary code—A binary code, also called *Gray code*, in which sequential numbers differ by only one place and in that one place differ by only one unit place. The cyclic binary code can be used to minimize the error at transition points in a code, since the error can be no greater than one unit space.

cyclic code—Any code that differs by only one bit between numbers. The cyclic binary code or Gray code is useful for positional measurement, since errors between positions will differ by only one significant bit. The cyclic decimal code uses 4-bit binary words to represent decimal numbers. The words from decimal to decimal are separated by a one-digit change.

cyclic memory—A memory that can be accessed only at multiples of the cycle time.

cyclic polynomial—A detection method that uses division by a polynomial to check for errors. A cyclic polynomial check is a good test for single, double, and odd numbers of errors. If, after the division process, a remainder occurs, then an error is present. The division can be done using a shift register which also provides the checksum. A cyclic sum check results if the checksum data from the shift register is fed back through the register again.

cyclic redundancy—An error detection method that uses redundant check bits. A cyclic redundancy generator is used to generate a stream of check bits which are divided by the same polynomial as the data bits; a nonzero remainder indicates that an error has been detected.

cyclic redundancy check character—A character (abbreviated *CRC*) used as a redundant character for error detection in various modified cyclic codes.

cyclic shift—A shift in which data is moved from one end of a word in a register to the other end. If the register holds:

00110011

then a cyclic shift of two bits gives:

11001100

This is also called a *circular shift, end-around shift, logical shift, ring shift,* and *nonarithmetic shift.*

cyclic storage—A storage system which operates as a closed loop; sometimes called *circulating storage*.

cyclic storage access—Descriptive of a storage unit which allows access only during specific, equally spaced intervals. Cyclic access is found in units such as magnetic drums.

cycling—The periodic change allowed on a variable or function by a control system or controller.

D

daisy chain—A bus system used in microprocessors in which units are interconnected and signals are transferred in serial fashion. The F8 microprocessor uses daisy-chain memory chips. Each unit is allowed to accept one interrupt input, and the chips closest to the CPU have priority when requesting service. In a daisy-chain bus system, each unit can modify the signal before passing it on to the next device in the chain; and when a device required service, it blocks the signal. The first units in the chain thus have priority in the bus system.

daisy wheel—A plastic or metal print wheel on certain types of impact printers, so called because of its symmetrical "petals."

damping—The reduction of oscillatory conditions in control devices and systems to improve stability. Damping may be done to electrical and mechanical components and generally falls within three classifications:

(1) *Critically damped*—no overshoot or undershoot occurs (optimum response)
(2) *Underdamped*—overshoot occurs (excessive oscillation)
(3) *Overdamped*—no overshoot or undershoot (response too slow)

Darlington—A monolithic circuit consisting of two direct-coupled transistors connected to function as one. A Darlington circuit provides high current gains, which makes it useful as a driver circuit in computer applications.

data—A graphic or textual representation of facts, concepts, numbers, letters, symbols, or instructions suitable for communication, interpretation, or processing. Data may be source data or raw data, which is then refined to suit the user by processing. Data is the basic element of information that is used to describe objects, ideas, conditions, or situations.

data access arrangement—An interfacing unit required between non-Bell and Bell equipment on a direct-dial network.

data access register—A register used in some microcomputers for RAM stacking address arithmetic. A typical register system uses three registers: a program counter, a stack pointer, and the operand address. Sixteen instructions allow decrement/increment and register transfer within a single clock cycle.

data acquisition and control—The system used to collect or gather data and prepare it for further processing. Data acquisition and control equipment may include transducers, transducer amplifiers, multiplexers, and data converters as well as logging units such as magnetic tape, disks, printers, plotters, and card and paper-tape units. A typical system samples analog voltages, scales them, and converts them to digital format for recording or printout.

data bank—A collection or library of data. An invoice may form a *record* in an application, a set of records forms a *file*, and the collection of files becomes the data bank.

data base—A collection of data, usually larger than a file, that is sufficient for a given purpose in a data processing application.

data bus—A bus used in many microprocessor systems for transferring data to and from the CPU and the storage and peripheral devices. A typical microprocessor uses three buses: a data bus, a timing bus, and a control bus. The data bus is independent of the processor and handles all communications between any pair of devices connected to the bus.

data chain—A combination of two or more data elements in a sequence to provide meaningful information. A data chain called *Date* would consist of these data elements: year, month, and day.

The sequence would range from low to high or high to low for machine processing. Data chaining is used for the gathering and scattering of information within one record from or to more than one region of memory.

data channel—A bidirectional data path or bus between input/output devices and the main memory, which usually allows concurrent operations.

data code—A data code can be a set of numbers, letters, characters, or symbols used to represent a data item such as a record, a file, or a word.

data communication—The transmission and reception of data generally using some form of electrical transmission. Data communication can be aided by using a data communications control unit which scans the central terminal for messages and then transfers them to the processor. Another technique involves using a data station as a remote terminal for communication with a central computer. When not in use for transmission, the data station can be used for data preparation and editing tasks.

data compaction—The methods used to reduce space, bandwidth, generating time, and other factors which add to the cost of data. Compaction methods tend to eliminate needless repetition and other irrelevancies.

data compression—The methods that are used to increase storage space by eliminating gaps, redundancies, and unnecessary data, shortening the length of records, fields, and blocks.

data converter—Devices that convert analog data to a digital format or vice versa. Converters are available in either hybrid or monolithic form.

data conversion line—The channel used to transfer data elements between data banks.

data descriptor—An identifier used to describe a data area by pointing to one or more data locations in storage.

data element—The basic items of data appearing in a set of data. A data element can be used to denote a set of data items. For example, *Monday* is a data item denoted by the data element of *weekday*. Data elements can always be broken down into subcategories of data, usually data items.

data entry—The transferral of information into a computer for processing. Typical data entry equipment includes terminal keyboards, card or tape readers, and teletypewriters. Data entry terminals contain a keyboard, a communications module, status panel, a display, and a power supply.

Many terminals use microprocessors to allow special functions to be programmed by the user. This technique produces cleaner data for the host computer and reduces reruns. Special collection methods can be designed for specific customers in payroll, accounts receivable, and other areas tailored for the application.

data flow chart—A graphical representation of the path of data for a program or problem solution. The flow chart defines the major phases of the process. Also called *data flow diagram*.

data format—The rules and procedures defining the system used to show the data used in records, files, or words. Data formats are usually defined by statements which can instruct the assembly program in the area of constants, spaces, and punctuation.

data hierarchy—The structure of data consisting of sets and subsets of data in an ordered sequence. Each subset of data is of lower rank than each set of data.

data input bus—A single-bus structure used in some microcomputers. The processor, memory, and input/output devices all share this common bus. A switch register is used to transfer address codes and data between units.

data item—An individual member of a set of data, usually classified under a data element. *Tuesday* is a data item of the data element *weekday*.

data link—The communications circuits, lines, and other equipment used in the transmission of information between two or more stations.

data link escape character—A communication control character to form an escape sequence allowing supplementary communication control operations. Only graphic characters along with communication control characters are allowed to construct an escape sequence.

data logging—The recording of data concerning events that occur in a time sequence. Data logging equipment ranges from simple visual readout devices to complex systems using microprocessors. Data logging applications include:

(1) Process monitoring
(2) Environmental monitoring and pollution measurements
(3) Product R&D engineering
(4) Structural testing for strength, stress, strain, and vibration

data medium—The method used to transport or hold data or information. A data medium may be punched cards, punched tapes, magnetic tapes, or other physical methods that can be varied to represent data.

data migration—The movement of data from online or offline as determined by the system or requested by the user.

data name—An identifier for an item of data.

data processing—The execution of systematic operations performed on data using sets of defined rules and procedures. Data processing has evolved as a general term for using computers in business and other applications.

data processor—A device used to perform data processing. A data processor may be a calculator, a microcomputer, a minicomputer, or a large-scale computer. Also called *processor*.

data purification—The reduction of errors in data prior to using the data in the processing system.

data record—A collection of data elements grouped together and considered as an entity.

data reduction—The transformation of raw data into a more useful form using such methods as smoothing, scaling, or ordering.

data set—A set of data elements, or the electronic device used to provide the interface for data transmission to remote stations (as, for example, a modem). The data set is a potential combination, and all elements are not required to be present to complete the set. A *symbolic* data set is a data set used for coding a program; the *actual* data set is determined at a later time during a particular execution of the program.

data sink—A device in a communications system used for accepting signals from a transmission device. A data sink may also check these signals and generate error control signals.

data source—A circuit or device in a communications system used for originating signals for a transmission medium. A data source may also accept error control signals.

data station—A device for supplying remote terminal capability. A data station allows a wide range of input/output devices, including paper tape, punched card, keyboards, page printers, and various readers.

data stream—The serial data that is transmitted through a channel from a single read or write, or other specific operation.

data system—The combination of personnel efforts, procedures, tools, media, and facilities that provide the means for recording, processing, and communicating data. The data system may be fully or partly automated. Also called *information system*.

data terminal—The equipment which provides a complete data sink and/or source. A typical video data terminal combines data entry and display and has its own storage and character generator for selected displays of up to 480 characters on the screen.

data transmission—The sending of data to one or more stations or locations.

data transfer—As used in microcomputers, an instruction which provides the ability to break the normal sequence of control.

Three types of data transfers are used in microcomputers:

(1) Programmed transfers—the easiest and most direct method
(2) Interrupt transfers—peripheral devices initiate the transfer
(3) Direct-memory-access transfers—the fastest method

A data transfer controller can be used to provide the signal sequences to allow data transfers through the bus system, and a data transfer register can simplify the movement of data for transfers. The data transfer register is also called a memory data register (abbreviated *MDR*).

data validation—The checking of data for compliance with requirements. Data validation can be determined with tests such as the *forbidden-code check* to verify reliability and validity.

dB—Abbreviation for the *decibel*, a unit of measure representing a power ratio between two power sources or sinks, in which one decibel represents the ratio multiplied by 10 times its common logarithm. By extension, voltages and currents can be similarly compared (in which case the multiplier must be doubled).

DC—Abbreviation: 1. Direct current. 2. Direct coupled. 3. Digital computer. 4. Direct cycle. 5. Display console. 6. Decimal classification. 7. Data conversion. 8. Design change.

DC coupling—1. Transmission with a modem using a steady stream of pulses. 2. Direct coupling using components other than capacitors so as to avoid loss of direct current.

DC dump—The removal of any constant-sign voltage (and thus power) from a computer system.

DCTL—Abbreviation for *direct-coupled transistor logic*, a logic system that uses only transistors as active circuit elements.

DDA—Abbreviation for *digital differential analyzer*, an early type of computing machine.

dead band—A range of values for which the incoming signal can be altered without also changing the output. Also called *dead space* and *dead zone*.

debug—To detect and remove errors and malfunctions from a program, routine, or machine. Debugging usually involves the running and checkout of programs to detect the errors. One typical method of debugging includes running a similar problem with a known answer through the system for checkout. Debugging aids are available to allow quick development of microcomputer programs. These aids, normally used with a teletypewriter, allow the user to:

(1) Print register contents
(2) Modify memory and register contents
(3) Use breakpoints for start and stop
(4) Search memory

Debug commands are allowed in some systems for tracing errors, and a class of software known as debuggers features debugging programs which can be stopped and examined while slowly stepping the machine through the instructions. Debugging statements are often a part of these programs to permit the user to:

(1) Start and stop the program
(2) Insert and delete control statements
(3) Print value changes as they occur
(4) Transfer control
(5) Cause printout of cross relationships

To facilitate a successful system debugging operation, the user should be able to start, stop, and single-step the system clock. If the system is microprogrammed, there must be a way to set the contents of the control store address register and lock this register so that it cannot be advanced by the system clock or jump instructions. These controls over the register will allow the user to select the starting point for coding, and repeat a single instruction many times in order to completely debug that instruction. Monitoring the control store register is required to allow the user to know where the program is during debugging. This can be done in many microcomputer systems using the ROM simulator and the console control panel.

decentralized processing—Processing of data by individual subdivisions of an organization at different geographical locations.

decibel—A unit (abbreviated *dB*) for expressing the relationship between two power levels, where the number of decibels is 10 times the logarithm of the ratio. Because of the relationship of voltage and current to power, their ratios may be similarly expressed in decibels using 20 log as a multiplier. A doubling or halving of power represents a 3 dB difference. An order-of-magnitude power difference is 10 dB.

decibel meter—An instrument which is calibrated in decibels and used for measuring power levels above a usually arbitrary reference level. Where the reference is 1 mW across 600 Ω, the unit may be abbreviated *dBm*. In audio equipment, 1 dBm equals 1 volume unit (1 VU); 0 VU or 0 dBm is the 1 mW reference.

decimal—The number system which uses 10 as the radix or base.

decimal notation—A fixed radix notation that uses the characters 0–9 and the radix of 10. Using decimal notation, the number 601.2 is expressed as:

$$(6 \times 10^2) \text{ plus } (0 \times 10^1) \text{ plus } (1 \times 10^0) \text{ plus } (2 \times 10^{-1})$$

decision—A determination for future action. A decision in computer systems usually involves a comparison to determine the existence or nonexistence of a specific condition before taking a specific succeeding action. The action may involve a conditional jump or transfer of control. The comparison may take place between words or numerical characters in registers or other temporary storage.

decision box—A rectangle or other symbol used on a flow diagram to mark a choice or branch in a program.

decision circuit—A circuit such as a decision gate that performs a logical operation on binary information.

decision gate—A specific type of decision circuit that uses the states of two or more inputs to make a decision and provide the correct output indication.

decision integrator—A digital integrator used in incremental computers. The decision integrator provides an increment which is maximum positive, maximum negative, or zero, depending upon the input values.

decision instruction—An instruction that causes the selection of a branch of the program, as, for example, a conditional jump instruction.

decision level—The signal amplitude that serves as a reference for determining the output of a comparison circuit. If the input signal is less than the decision level at the time of sampling, the output of the comparison circuit is negative or zero; if the input is greater than the decision level, the output is positive (with a binary 1 indication). Also called the *decision threshold* or *slicing level*.

decision table—A table that contains all aspects of a problem along with the actions that could be taken. Decision tables can be used in place of flow diagrams and are usually arranged in a matrix or tabular format. The upper part of each column can list all conditions to be considered for the problem, and the lower part can list the action to be taken for each set of conditions.

decision threshold—Decision level.

deck—A collection of punched or magnetically imprinted cards.

declarative operation—A coding sequence consisting of a symbolic label, a declarative operational code, and an operand. The declarative operation is used to write labels and codes for data and constants.

decode—The act of applying a set of data rules to restore a previous representation, or to reverse a previous encoding operation.

decoder—A device which determines the meaning of a set of data and usually initiates some action based on the meaning. A decoder may be a matrix of switching elements used to select one or more channels according to the combination of input signals. Many decoder chips can be expanded so that each decoder drives eight or more other decoders for large system applications.

decollate—To separate the parts of a multipart form or document.

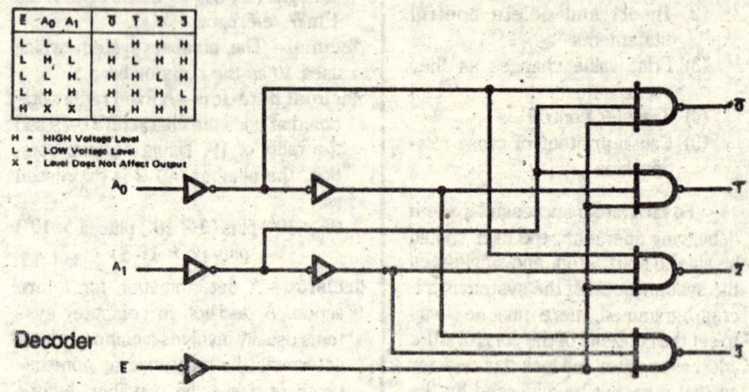

$\overline{E}$	A_0	A_1	$\overline{0}$	$\overline{1}$	$\overline{2}$	$\overline{3}$
L	L	L	L	H	H	H
L	H	L	H	L	H	H
L	L	H	H	H	L	H
L	H	H	H	H	H	L
H	X	X	H	H	H	H

H = HIGH Voltage Level
L = LOW Voltage Level
X = Level Does Not Affect Output

Decoder

decrement—A device or instruction used to reduce, usually be one unit, the contents of a storage location and also the quantity by which the contents are decreased. Usually the decrement is a specific part of the instruction word.

dedicated—Descriptive of machines, programs, or procedures that are designed, tailored, or reserved for specific uses. A dedicated communications line refers to a leased or private line that is used for a particular communications purpose. A dedicated microprocessor is one that is designed and programmed for a specific application, such as instrumentation, traffic control, or arithmetic calculations.

deferred address—Indirect address.

deferred maintenance—Scheduled maintenance intended to correct an existing fault. Deferred maintenance can only be used for faults which do not affect the successful completion of a project or program.

DEL—In ASCII, the delete character.

delay—The amount of time an event is retarded. Delays can be generated by special circuits, devices, elements, units, or lines. A *digit* delay device or circuit is one that retards digits and has the effect of a carry operation in arithmetic. Other elements and units have the ability to accept the data or signal, hold for a period of time *t* and then emit the signal as a function of time minus *t*. Delays *lines* may be electrical, electromagnetic, or acoustical. Some registers use delay lines with feedback to achieve a circulating storage method.

delete character—A character used to obliterate erroneous or undesired data. In punched tape, the delete character will produce perforations at all undesired positions.

delimiter—A flag or character that is used to separate and organize items of data. As a character, a delimiter is used to limit a string of characters, but it can never be a part of the string. A delimiter flag character can be used to mark the end of a series of bits or characters.

delta clock—A clock used for timing subroutine operations. A delta clock can be used to restart a computer using an interrupt after a fault forces the machine into a closed programming loop or causes a halt. The interrupt can be programmed to alert the operator that a fault has occurred.

demand—An input/output coding method in which read/write operations are initiated as the need for them occurs.

demodulate—To recover the information carried by a modulated signal. Demodulation recovers the signal from the modulated wave so that it has the same essential information characteristic as the signal before modulation. Various demodulators are used to receive tone signals and convert them into digital bits for acceptance by computer circuits.

demodulator-modulator—A *modem*, the common device which performs both modulation and demodulation for signals transmitted over communication lines.

derivative action—A type of response found in control systems, the output response of which is the derivative of the input.

descriptor—A word used to define characteristics of a program element such as a record, part of a program, or operation. Also known as *keyword*.

design aids—Special software or hardware elements that are intended to assist in implementation of a data processing system. Design aids for microcomputers range from prototyping cards to software development systems. A prototyping card can reduce circuit design and fabrication time during the early development stage; the card usually contains the microprocessor, system clock, and input/output circuits. (Additional cards may contain RAMs and ROMs along with peripheral controllers.)

design cycle—The complete cycle of development for complex products, which includes breadboarding, prototyping, testing, and production planning. After each phase, the requirements are refined and the specifications modified to reflect everything that has been learned up to that time.

desk check—Analysis of a program for errors in logic or syntax without using any equipment or electrical design aids.

destructive read—A read operation that also erases the data from the source.

deterministic simulation—A type of simulation in which a given input always produces the same output.

development system—A software design aid that enables the user to check and debug programs quickly. A typical development system allows the user to compose and edit programs, run them in real-time in the system environment, diagnose problems, program modificaitons, and document the required changes. The development system console may furnish program control signals such as STOP/STOP ACKNOWLEDGE, INTERRUPT/INTERRUPT ACKNOWLEDGE, and RESET IN/OUT. The user can then half, interrupt, and reset the resident CPU through the console interface. The console also allows the operator to manually write the data into memory, monitor bus contents during subcycles, and step the program to verify data flow.

development time—That part of operating time used for testing and debugging new routines and hardware.

device control character—A control character used for switching various devices in and out of data processing and telecommunications systems.

device selection check—A check to verify that the correct device was selected during a program instruction.

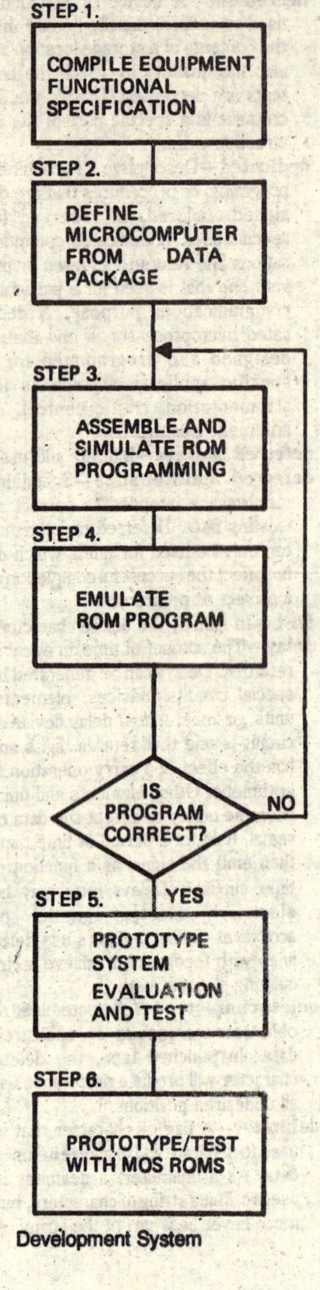

Development System

device status word—A word used to indicate the status of devices such as registers in a computer system. (Abbreviated *DSW*.)

diagnostics—Techniques employed for detection and isolation of malfunctions and errors in programs, systems, and devices. Diagnostics in microcomputers usually involve the use of ROMs. Small systems can store their diagnostics in ROM control. If a compiler is used, diagnostics are available in the following forms:

(1) Precautionary—PRINT WARNING AND CONTINUE

(2) Correctable—CORRECT ERROR, PRINT MESSAGE, AND CONTINUE.

(3) Uncorrectable—PRINT MESSAGE, REJECT STATEMENT, AND CONTINUE

(4) Catastrophic—TERMINATE COMPILATION

Diagnostic routines for programming mistakes are service-oriented; routines for detecting mistakes in data are much more specific. Many of the latter can be implemented from control store to test small portions of the system.

diagnostic test—The running of a program or routine to detect failures or potential failures. Diagnostic tests and routines will usually determine the location errors in programs.

diagnostic trace—A program used to perform diagnostic checks on other programs. The output of the trace program can include the instructions of the program being checked along with the results of those instructions arranged in sequence.

dibit—A group of two bits. As used in some modulation systems, such as the Bell 201 data set, each *dibit* is encoded as one of four unique carrier phase shifts: 00, 01, 10, or 11.

dicap storage—Storage using an array of diodes to control current directed to storage capacitors.

dichotomizing search—A search that divides an ordered set of items into two parts, one of which is rejected; the process is repeated on the saved part in an iterative routine that ultimately results in retrieval of the desired item.

dictionary—A list of code names used in a system or routine along with their intended meaning in that system or routine.

differential analyzer—An analog computer that uses interconnected integrators for solving differential equations.

differential delay—The difference between the maximum and minimum frequency delays occurring across a frequency band.

differential transducer—A transducer that is used to measure two separate parameters and provide a single output which is proportional to the difference between them.

differentiator—A circuit or device with an output function that is proportional to the derivative of the input. A differentiator circuit accepts square waves and produces a spiked or peaked wave of the same rise time and frequency.

diffusion—The process used in the production of semiconductors to introduce impurities into the substrate material. The diffusion process allows the impurities to spread throughout the masked area.

digit—Any symbol that represents a positive integer smaller than the radix of a number system. In the decimal system, a digit is any one of the characters from 0 to 9; in binary, a digit is a 0 or a 1.

digital—Employing discrete integers or voltage levels to represent data and information. A digital format can be used to represent any and all information required for problem solution.

digital-to-analog converter—A device for converting digital signals into continuous analog signals. Digital-to-analog converters usually buffer the input so that the output remains the same until the input changes. Units are available with up to 16 channels that can operate at 10,000 amples per second with a 100 cond conversion time. (Abbreviated *D/A* or *DAC*).

digital—Employing discrete integers ates in a switching mode—for example, a flip-flop.

digital clock—A system clock which operates in a digital mode and produces precisely timed voltage pulses of fixed duration. The output signals have a digital representation and allocate time as set by the system priorities.

digital computer—A computer that processes data using combinations of discrete or discontinuous data representations, and which can perform arithmetic and logic operations on data as well as on its own stored program.

digital control—Descriptive of an automated system which uses a digital computer or other digital elements to perform processing and control tasks for production systems. Also called *direct digital control* (DDC).

digital differential analyzer—1. An incremental computer which uses a digital integrator for computing. 2. A differential analyzer that uses digital representations for all analog quantities. (Abbreviated *DDA*.)

digital logic—Refers to the common types of logic families used for digital integrated circuits and systems, such as:

TTL—transistor-transistor logic
ECL—emitter-coupled logic
HTL—high-threshold logic
IIL—integrated injection logic

digital subset—A collection of data in a specific format. The format is usually set by control information to which the system has access.

digit emitter—A character emitter limited to the 12 rows of a punched card.

digitization—The conversion of analog signals to digital signals. Digitization creates steps at distinct levels of the analog signal.

digitize—To convert an analog signal to a digital representation.

digitizer—The device that converts an analog quantity to a digital format. Also called *quantizer*.

digit place—As used in positional notation, the site where the digit is located in a word. Also called *digit rank* or *symbol rank*.

digit punch—A usually rectangular cutout in any of the rows representing 0 through 9 in a punched card or tape. A punch in the 0 row may also function as a zone punch.

dimension—A FORTRAN statement used to define arrays; used in assembler programming as the maximum number of values that can be assigned to the *set* symbol representing an array.

diminished-radix complement—A complement obtained by subtracting each digit from one less than the radix. For example, the nines' complement in decimal notation and the ones' complement in binary notation. Also called *radix-minus-one* complement.

diode—A usually solid-state electrical valve that permits current flow in one direction and inhibits flow in the other direction.

diode arrays—Multiple diodes usually on a single chip and connected in some kind of matrix.

diode-transistor logic—A logic family (abbreviated *DTL*) that uses diode inputs to transistors which are used as inverting amplifiers.

DIP—Acronym for *dual inline package*, a type of IC package that has double parallel rows of leads for connection to circuit boards. These packages are available in plastic for economy, or ceramic for high humidities and temperatures. Also known as *bugs*.

dipole modulation—The representation of binary digits in a magnetic medium in which part of each cell is magnetically saturated in one of two opposing senses. The rest of the cell is magnetized as background and remains fixed.

direct access—A type of storage in which the access time is effectively independent of the location of the data. The items of data can be addressed or accessed in the same amount of time for each location and program access is independent of any previous accessed location.

direct address—An address that specifies the location of an operand. Direct addressing is a basic addressing method used in many microprocessors. It is designed to reach any point in main storage directly without using other registers. A direct addressed instruction for the 8080 is:

LDA 2131H; load (A with 2132^{12})

This instruction loads the contents of location 2132 (hexadecimal) into the accumulator and is stored in memory as 3A2132.

direct coupling—The coupling of circuits by resistance or inductance so as to allow direct current to pass through the coupling.

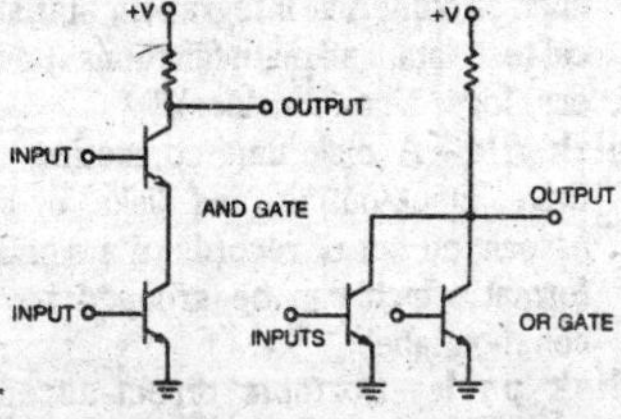

Direct Coupled Transistor Logic (DCTL)

direct-coupled transistor logic—A type of logic (abbreviated *DCTL*) which uses only direct-coupled transistors as active elements.

direct current—Current (abbreviated *DC*) which flows only in one direction at an essentially constant value.

direct digital control—Descriptive of the use of computers and other digital devices for the control of manufacturing processes. A typical direct digital controller might handle up to eight industrial control loops with more flexibility and options than possible with analog controllers.

direct instruction—An instruction which contains the operand for the operation specified by the instruction Also see *direct address*.

directive commands—As used in an assembler, a command that allows the user to generate data words and values for specific conditions in assembly time. Mnemonics are assigned to each instruction operation code in order to describe the hardware function of that instruction.

directive statements—Statements which are used to define the program structure. Directive statements do not generate executable code. Examples of directive statements are ORIGIN STATEMENT, PROCEDURE STATEMENT, PROGRAM STATEMENT, and END STATEMENT.

direct insert subroutine—A subroutine that is inserted into a routine at each place that it is used. Also called an *open* subroutine.

direct memory access—A technique (abbreviated *DMA*) to transfer data directly between memory and peripherals. Sometimes known as the ***data-break technique***, DMA permits transfers to take place without CPU intervention on a cycle-stealing basis. The CPU is only used to set up the transfer, and the transfer rate is limited only by the bandwidth of the memory and peripherals. DMA is the preferred data transfer for high-speed applications. Some DMA channels can transfer up to 500,000 words per second.

A DMA controller is used to handle several input/output channels. The controller generates the priority among the channels along with the interrupts required. The following tasks are required for DMA transfers:

(1) Address selection
(2) Interrupt control
(3) Bus control
(4) Word counting

(5) Input/output data buffering

direct reference address—A type of virtual address that is not modified by indirect addressing. It can be modified by indexing.

disable—A state of the CPU that does not allow certain types of interrupts to occur; also called a *masked* state. As used in communications, a state that does not allow a device to accept incoming calls.

disarmed—A state used to define an interrupt level in a system which cannot accept an interrupt input signal.

disaster dump—A dump that occurs as a result of a nonrecoverable error in the program.

discrete—Individual and separate, as opposed to *integrated*. Discrete *circuits* are electronic circuits manufactured with individual diodes, resistors, capacitors, transistors, and other components. Discrete *data* pertains to variables which can assume one of several distinct states.

discrete programming—A class of procedures used in operations research for locating the maximum and minimum values of a function. All variables must have integer values or similar constraints. If only integer values are used, the programming is called *integer programming*.

discrete simulation—A type of simulation where all major components and events are identified individually and used at irregular intervals. Also called event-oriented simulation.

discrimination—1. The skipping of selected instructions as developed by the programmer. Usually in discrimination, if a conditional jump is not used, the next instructions are allowed to follow in a normal sequence. 2. The process of demodulating an FM signal.

discriminator—In FM radio, a detector circuit used to recover the audio from an RF signal.

disjunction—The logical operation which uses the QR operator and results in the logical sum. In Boolean form, the operation is written as:

$A + B = C$ (A or B equals C)

and follows this truth table:

A	B	C
0	0	0
0	1	1
1	0	1
1	1	1

disk accessing—The process and methods used to transfer data in and out of a disk file. Access is usually accomplished by direct addressing, symbolic addressing, or keyed-record addressing.

disk operating system—A memory system (abbreviated *DOS*) using disks or diskettes that is designed to assemble, edit, and execute programs. A typical system includes an intelligent disk controller, a drive system, and a software system. Programs can sometimes be assembled, edited, and executed in seconds. Using the disk operating system requires the adding of additional memory to the executive.

DOSs allow the efficient use of ROMs for initial loading and storage of frequently used mathematical routines such as numerical integration, statistical test data, and math functions (powers, logs, sine, consines).

disk file—A disk unit consisting of drive, input/output, and disks, or an associated set of records of a similar format which can be grouped by a common label.

disk pack—Portable direct-access storage units which use magnetic disks. Disk packs are mounted on disk storage drives for read and write operations.

disk storage—A memory system that stores data on magnetic disks. The disks are similar in size to a phonograph record and require a disk drive. A typical dual platter drive can provide up to 5 million bytes of storage with an average access time of 30 milliseconds and data transfer times of 2.5 million bits per second. Floppy disks are magnetic disks which are flexible and less expensive to produce and operate. Up to 300,000 words can be stored on a floppy disk using a floppy-disk drive system.

disorderly closedown—Stopping of a system due to an equipment error when it is not possible to shut down in a orderly manner. Special steps are usually taken to prevent the loss or duplication of data.

displacement transducer—A device used to measure linear position or displacement and provide an analogous electrical output.

display—A visual representation of data, which may take the form of numerals (as on a calculator), alphanumeric characters, or graphs. A display unit can provide viewing access into the operation of the microcomputer system.

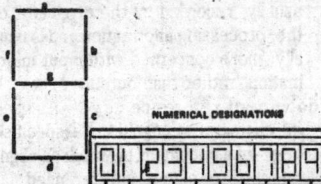

Display

A microcomputer *video-terminal display* unit might use a dot array of 1024 × 1024 dots for character generation. A bright dot can be produced anywhere on the screen, and a series of dots can be used to indicate lines on a graphical display. Data on the CRT display screen can be highlighted by blinking, underlining, use of a different color, increased intensity, or a combination of methods.

Gas discharge displays have a pleasing (orange or green) and large character size, but they are difficult to interface because of the high voltage required for ionization of the gas.

Light-emitting diode displays are compatible with TTL levels, but they have limited sizes and color selection.

Liquid-crystal displays (LCDs) require very little power and are compatible with MOS logic, but they produce no light themselves and are hard to see except under direct-lighting conditions.

Incandescent and *fluorescent displays* can produce high brightness with large character size, but because of costs and power requirements, they are used mostly in specialized applications.

display modes—The various modes used in a display system to denote the points on the screen such as vector, increment, or character point.

display register—A register with corresponding indicators on the display panel; used to display the contents of the register selected by the display switch.

display station—A unit used to indicate alphanumeric information in a communications or computer system.

display switch—Switches used to select the register that is to be shown on the display panel.

display tube—An indicating type of vacuum tube (such as a CRT) that is used to display data in a form recognizable to humans.

dissector—A mechanical or electrical transducer that detects in sequential order the light intensity of an illuminated space. The dissector is used in optical character recognition. Also known as an *image dissector*.

distortion—Any variation in a reproduced waveform that was not present on the original waveform.

distributed environment—See *distributed system*.

distributed-intelligence microcomputer system—A multiprocessing method (abbreviated *DIMS*) in which the tasks assigned to the distributed system remain fixed. In a multiprocessing environment, the tasks are allocated by software algorithms. With the DIMS, each processor may be assigned a fixed combination of the following tasks:

(1) Input/output controller activity

(2) Data concentration
(3) Information processing
(4) Remote communication

Distributed intelligence is used in some modular instruments, POS terminals, networks of remote sensors, and scientific computers.

distributed processing—Systems that use intelligent input/output controllers and direct-memory-access control to free the CPU of the details of block transfers. Distributed processing makes use of complex LSI chips similar to those used in microcomputers. These chips allow low-cost intelligent controllers for keyboards, displays, printers, card readers, modems, and floppy disks.

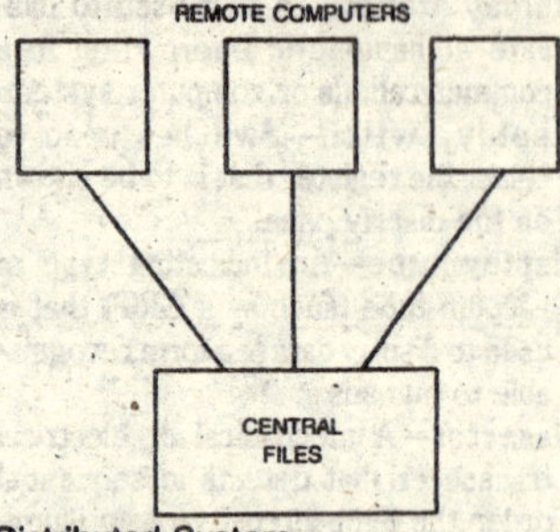

Distributed System

distributed system—An arrangement of computers in an organization in which a number of computers at separate locations work in a cooperative manner. The system may use one large computer and several smaller machines, with the central files located with the larger machine and the smaller computers calling on the files when required. Distributed systems can provide fast response to local events, maximum availability for single failure modes, and simplified system programming with good user access.

DMA—Abbreviation for *direct-memory access*, a method used to obtain direct access to the main memory without involving the CPU. The CPU is essentially disabled during DMA data-transfer operations. The approach usually taken bypasses the registers for direct access to the memory bus. DMA channels allow faster transfer speeds than otherwise possible, sometimes improving instruction times by as much as an order of magnitude.

DMA controllers are used to provide the interface between system buses and the user's peripheral. The controller provides the logic for the required tasks for DMA transfer: address selection, interrupt control, bus control, word counting, and input/output buffering.

document—1. Any representation of data that can be interrupted by humans or machines, as well as the process of creating the same representation. 2. A paper voucher, form, report, or other record containing stored information; the information is usually recorded by the originator of the processing information and is usually more concerned with input information rather than output.

document reference edge—As used in character recognition, a specified edge of a document to which all alignment of characters is referenced.

documentation—1. The presentation, organization, and communication of information. Documentation involves the creating, collecting, organizing, and disseminating of the information contained in documents. 2. A collection of documents or records on a particular subject.

document reader—A device used to sense and interpret the codes contained in punched cards or printed materials. A typical card reader operates at speeds of up to 300 cards per minute.

domain tip—A type of memory device that uses thin films to create magnetic domains for storing digital data. Thin aluminum layers are deposited on a glass substrate, and channels are etched into the aluminum and filled with a thin magnetic film which is used to form the domain regions. Costs are below core memory; applications include backup memories for microprocessors in areas like point-of-sale terminals, numerical control, and data logging.

DOS—Abbreviation for *disk operating system*.

double-precision—Descriptive of the use of two computer words to represent data. Sometimes called double-length processing. Double-precision arithmetic uses two words to represent numbers in order to obtain greater accuracy than is possible with a single word. If the normal word length is eight bits, then in double-precision arithmetic 16 bits are handled by breaking each number into two parts. Each part is handled separately, but in a manner that allows carries between them. Double-precision processing allows the system to operate as if its registers were twice as large, but operating at a slower speed.

double-pulse recording—A type of recording in which each memory cell uses two regions magnetized in opposite polarities with neutral regions on each end. Zeros and ones are represented by the sequence of opposite polarities in the cell.

double rail—A type of self-timed asynchronous logic circuitry which uses twin lines and three states: high, low, and undecided.

downtime—The time interval when a system is malfunctioning or not operating correctly and is thus not being used. Downtime is opposed to available time, idle time, and standby time in which the system is functional.

driver—1. A small program used to execute other programs. 2. A circuit or device used to power or control other circuits or channels.

drop-dead halt—A type of halt from which there is no recovery. A drop-dead halt may be programmed in deliberately, or it may be the result of an error in the program.

drop-in—The reading or recording of a spurious signal with an amplitude greater than nominal by a specified percentage.

dropout—A temporary loss of transmission or the failure to read a bit from a magnetic storage system. In transmission, a dropout is usually due to noise or a malfunction. Dropout in a magnetic storage system is mainly caused by an output too low to be detected.

dry run—A checking of the program flow chart, coding, and all program documentation before putting the program on a computer.

DTL—Abbreviation for *diode-transistor logic*, a logic family using diodes as inputs and transistors as inverting amplifiers.

D-type flip-flop—A type of bistable multivibrator that is triggered on the leading or positive edge of the clock pulse. D-type flip-flops are typically used for buffer and shift registers, and ripple counters.

dual-inline package—A popular type of IC package (abbreviated *DIP*) that uses twin-rows of leads. This configuration allows standardization, low-cost manufacturing, and a degree of second-source replaceability.

dual operation—The negation of the result of the original operation. The dual operation is found by replacing all zeros with ones and all ones with zeros in the truth table of the original operation. The dual operation for a logical OR is the NOR operation.

dual system—A system configuration in which two computers are used for processing and the results compared for accuracy. Identical inputs and routines are used. The dual system is employed for applications requiring a high degree of reliability.

dummy—Related to appearance or characteristic without functional capability of suggested function. A dummy may be an artificial character, statement, address, or instruction usually inserted to complete format conditions, such as fixed word length. A dummy *argument* or definition is a prototype card field in a macro definition that is variable and is to be replaced with a parameter later.

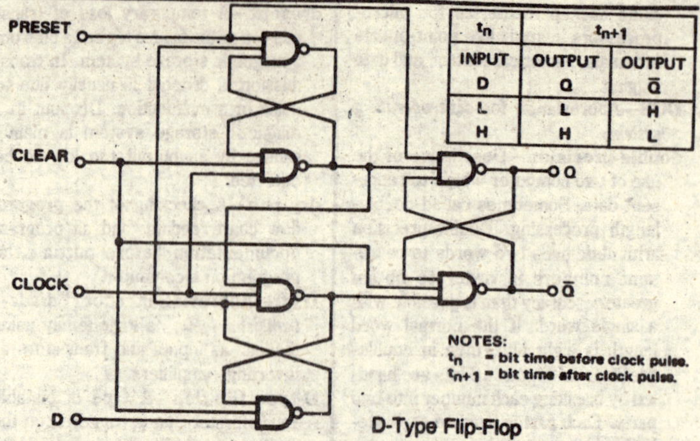

t_n	t_{n+1}	
INPUT D	OUTPUT Q	OUTPUT $\bar{Q}$
L	L	H
H	H	L

D-Type Flip-Flop

Dummy *instructions* are used to complete block lengths without affecting program operation.

dummy load—1. The act of transfer to storage of a program without execution in order to determine if all specifications and requirements have been met. 2. A resistor that simulates electrically a sink for an electric current.

dump—A transfer in operation or contents of a computer system. A power or *DC dump* results in the removal of power from the computer. Power dumps can result in the loss of operations and data unless specific measures are taken to prevent losses. *Binary* and *change* dumps cause a printout or output into binary form, or a printout or output only, for locations that have changed since the last dump. A dumping program usually has a restart provision to allow the program to start again at the last dump point if an interrupt such as that caused by a machine malfunction should occur.

Dump commands such as the following are used to transfer the contents of memory between two specific locations to a specified output format:

D x, y; (dump memory between locations x and y)

dump check—A check to verify data being transferred during dumping. One method adds all of the digits during dumping and checks the sum when retransferring.

dump point—The point in a program where it is desirable to have a transfer operation. Dump points are usually designed to protect against machine failure.

duodecimal—Relating to the number system with a radix of twelve.

duplex—Containing two sets of operational elements that may or may not operate simultaneously. In communications, a duplex system is one in which data may be received and transmitted over the same lines simultaneously.

duplicate—1. To copy such that the result is in the same form and indistinguishable in content from the original, such as, to make another punched card with the same pattern as the original. 2. A copy of an original document or program.

duplication check—A check which requires that the results of two independent operations be identical. A duplication check may be performed at the same time on different equipment, or at different times on the same equipment.

dwell—A programmed time delay of variable duration. A dwell is not sequential or cyclic, nor is it an interlock.

dyad—An operator indicated by writing the symbols of two vectors with no symbol or other sign between them.

dyadic operator—A Boolean operator with two operands. Dyadic operators include AND, OR, NAND, NOR, and exclusive-OR. A *dyad*.

dynamic check—A test of any function or process that is conducted by subjecting the device, process, or function to the rigors of its anticipated operational environment.

dynamic dump—A dump that is performed during program execution.

dynamic debugging—The debugging of routines at full system speed. The routines are first checked using the single-step mode; only when they are completely debugged at low speed should dynamic debugging be undertaken.

dynamic memory—See *dynamic storage* and *dynamic RAM*.

dynamic programming—Programming which allows a number of decisions for each stage of a multistage problem. Dynamic programming seeks to optimize the probelm solution by the integration of the cumulative effects of each stage on the overall goal.

dynamic RAM—A RAM in which data is stored capacitively and which must be refreshed, or it will be lost. Dynamic RAMs offer high bit densities, low cost, input/output compatibility with TTL levels, and speed compatibility with many microprocessors.

dynamic relocation—A program which can be moved to a different location in a partially executed state without affecting its ability to complete the processing.

dynamic storage—A type of memory, usually semiconductor, in which the stored data gradually leaks away and is lost, unless it is refreshed periodically by special circuitry.

dynamic subroutine—A subroutine that has a skeletal form with regard to certain parameters which are selected later as the processing proceeds. These parameters may include the number of repetitions, decimal point position, or item size. The computer can be used to derive these parameters during program execution.

E

EAE—Abbreviation for *extended arithmetic element.*

EAM—Abbreviation for *electrical accounting machine.*

EAROM—Acronym for *electrically alterable ROM*, a specialized random-access read/write memory that may be programmed by writing into the array and used as a ROM. Read cycle time is 10–20 microseconds and writing takes about one millisecond. The contents can be erased in one operation. EAROM costs tend to be high due to low production yield and the long test times required to check the data patterns. EAROM testing may take up to 30 minutes per unit while testing of conventional RAMs can be done in a 30 seconds.

EBCDIC—Abbreviation for *extended binary-coded-decimal interchange code*, a code which uses a set of eight bit-coded characters. EBCDIC is used for representation and transmission in data processing systems, communications, and associated devices. Some examples of the EBCDIC code follow:

EBCDIC SYMBOL	CODE
1	1111 0001
2	1111 0010
3	1111 0011
4	1111 0100
5	1111 0101
A	1100 0001
B	1100 0010
C	1100 0011
D	1100 0100
!	0101 1010
$	0101 1011
*	0101 1100
)	0101 1101

EBR—Abbreviation for *electron beam recording.*

ECAP—Acronym for *electronic circuit analysis program*, a language for modeling and analyzing electrical networks. ECAP allows the synthesizing of device models using function generators or tables of functions in conjunction with passive components.

Eccles-Jordan trigger—A once-common tube-type bistable multivibrator in which the output of one section is directly coupled into the input of the other section. The circuit is capable of storing one bit of information.

echo—The return of a sufficient portion of a transmitted signal due to reflection. An echo is usually received as interference, but in an echo check, the received echo data is compared with the original for accuracy.

ECL—Abbreviation for *emitter-coupled logic*, a logic family that uses signal coupling directly into the emitters of transistors. ECL is very fast, requires only a 1 volt of signal swing in 3–4 nanoseconds, and inherently generates little noise. Power requirements tend to be higher than other logic families. Microprocessors have been implemented with ECL using the bit-slice approach.

edit—To modify the form or format of data, such as inserting or deleting characters or decimal points.

editor—An interactive system or a program which allows users to prepare programs or text and to make changes using simple commands. Some time-sharing services offer such editor systems. Using the time-sharing programs, users can prepare assembly-language programs and correct them quickly. They can also add and store documentation as well as combine and retrieve programs. Editors allow the programs to be output into tape or printout with ease. Editing terminals allow the following functions:

(1) Character replacement
(2) Insertion and movement of characters, words, and blocks
(3) Batch balancing
(4) Check-digit verification

Text is punched using the teletypewriter or keypunch.

An editor allows the microcomputer designer to prepare the original assembly language programs and correct them using simple commands. Commands may be typed in at any time during the edit process in place of a source statement. Some types of editors are portable, with built-in displays and data entry keys.

EDP—Abbreviation for *electronic data processing*.

effective address—An address that is derived by indexing or indirect addressing techniques that is actually used to identify the current operand.

effective instruction—A method used to modify a presumptive instruction using a stored program computer. The method uses modifier or index words which are added to the original instruction to produce the effective instruction.

effector—A device used to produce a desired response from a change in its input upon another device where the end result is required.

EFTS—Abbreviation for *electronic funds transfer system*, a computerized means of transferring financial information from one location to another.

EIA—Abbreviation for *Electronic Industries Association*, an organization of electronic manufacturers that maintains certain standards in various product areas. The EIA has interface standards that cover signal characteristics, voltages, currents, and time periods; connections to modem units; and the physical dimensions of hardware. The EIA also has standards for character codes and coding.

electrical impulse—Any momentary transient voltage, whether inadvertent or intentionally produced.

electrically alterable ROM—A specialized random-access memory (abbreviated *EAROM*) which is programmed by writing into the array and used as a ROM. EAROM applications include machine controllers and replacements for semiconductor memories in minicomputers.

electrically erasable ROM—A ROM that can be erased in one second or less. A typical EEROM is organized as

512 words of two bits each and it can be erased and reprogrammed as many as one million times.

electrical schematic—A diagram that represents all circuit elements using symbols and interconnecting lines.

electric circuit—A continuous closed path consisting of wires and elements for the flow of current.

electric delay line—A delay line that uses lumped or distributed capacitive and inductive elements.

electric transducer—A device which converts nonelectric energy into electric energy, such as the microphone, solar cell, or strain gauge.

electrochromeric display—A type of display that uses materials that change from transparent to opaque under the control of an electric field. A field can be used to turn the ECD on, and it will hold that state until a field of opposite polarity switches it back to its original state.

electronic—Descriptive of any circuit or network employing solid-state or vacuum-tube active devices.

electronic beam recording—The use of an electron beam to store and read information on a target. Targets are usually silicon dioxide, and the data is stored as electrostatic charges or magnetic bubbles on materials like vitrium iron garnet.

electronic control—The general use of electronic devices for industrial and consumer control applications.

electronic data processing—Data processing performed largely by electronic devices. EDP includes the functions of entering, classifying, computing, and recording information and devices such as internally stored program computers, and automatic data processors. Disk units, but not disk packs, are considered as electronic data processing equipment.

electronic digital computer—A machine which uses electronic circuitry to perform arithmetic and logic operations by means of an internally or externally stored program of machine instructions.

electronic funds transfer system—A type of national banking system that uses electronics for the transfer of funds, as well as clearing and settling of accounts.

Electronic Industries Association—A trade association (abbreviated *EIA*) for electronics manufacturers which sets industry technical standards, disseminates market data, and maintains contact with government agencies affecting the electronics industry.

electronic multiplier—An all-electronic device for forming the product of two variables.

electronic pen—A stylus that is used with a CRT display for input to the system computer. Also called a light pen, the stylus signals the computer with electronic pulses which the computer interprets.

electronics—The branch of science and engineering that deals with the phenomena associated with the flow of electrons in devices and the utilization of these devices.

electronic switch—A usually solid-state device that provides an automatic on/off switching action and functions primarily as an electronic circuit element.

electrostatic storage—A type of memory based on capacitor principles, in which a dielectric sandwiched between a pair of electrodes holds electrostatic charges representing information.

else—An operation such as disjunction, OR, or inclusive-OR that is programmed to take place when conditions are not explicit. The *else* conditions are handled as "don't care" or left blank. In a program, *else* conditions usually cause a halt which must be covered to allow recovery for continued processing.

EM—The ASCII *end-of-medium* character.

embossment—As used in character recognition, the distance from the distorted surface of a document to a specified part of a printed character.

emitter-coupled logic—A logic family (abbreviated *ECL*) that uses semiconductors that switch without being driven into full saturation. ECL circuits are faster than TTL, but more expensive because of the extra diffusion steps in device processing.

emulate—A procedure used to imitate one system with another such that the imitating system accepts the same programs and achieves the same end results as the imitated system. Emulation, which involves the software techniques used to imitate the original system, can minimize the impact of conversion from one system to another during program development.

Emulation of a number of devices can sometimes be done using a single general-purpose unit. The general-purpose device, adapted to several different configurations through microprogramming, becomes a host serving the more specialized devices. One in-circuit emulator system uses two processors—one to execute commands and control peripherals, and the other to interface directly with the user's prototype system. Emulation allows custom instructions through microprogramming, which permits software designed for larger machines to run on microprocessors. The user is also allowed to run programs and integrate hardware and software very early in the development cycle.

emulsion laser storage—A storage system that uses a controlled laser beam to expose small sections of a photosensitive area.

enable—To permit, either automatically or under manual control, the operation of a specific function.

encode—To apply a code to represent data or information. Encoding may be done for convenience, or to hide the meaning of information from others. Also called *encipher*.

encoder—Any device or circuit that provides an enabling code to permit an otherwise unusable system or device to be used in an environment where the code is required. In a selec-

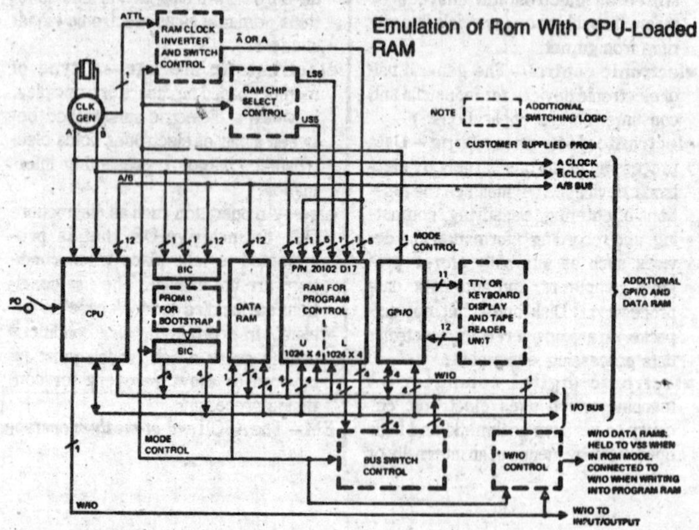

Emulation of Rom With CPU-Loaded RAM

tive calling communications system, an encoder may be a simple tone oscillator of a specific frequency.

end-around carry—A carry from the most significant digit position to the least significant digit position.

end instrument—The final device in a communications loop. End instruments include all generating and loop-terminating units at receiving and transmitting stations.

end-of-data marker—A character or code word that indicates that the end of all data held in a storage unit has been reached.

end-of-file—The termination or completion of a quantity of data, usually indicated by end-of-file marks (abbreviated *EOF*).

end-of-medium character—The ASCII EM character. A control character used to indicate the physical end of a data medium. The character usually gives ample warning to allow the user to make changes in the system operation. In the 7-digit ASCII, the EM is represented by a binary 25: 1001 1001 (the first character given is an even-parity indicator).

end-of-message—A character or group of characters which indicates the termination of a message or record (abbreviated *EOM*).

end-of-run—A type of routine used for housekeeping just before a run is completed. An end-of-run routine may be used for rewinding tapes or printing out totals.

end-of-tape arrangement—A programmed routine employed during the processing of the final tape in a multireel program. See also *end-of-run*.

end-of-tape marker—A character or special device to alert an operator that the end of the recording area is approaching. The marker may be a photoreflecting strip, a transparent section of tape, a unique bit pattern, or any other flagging arrangement.

end-of-text character—A control character used to denote the end of a text. In ASCII, this is the ETX character symbolized by a binary 3.

end-of-transmission-block character—The ASCII ETB character which indicates the end of a block of data being transmitted. The ASCII value of ETB is binary 23, or 0001 0111.

end-of-transmission character—A control character used to indicate the conclusion of transmission. In ASCII, this is the EOT character symbolized by a binary 4.

engineering data—Data contained in an original source document prepared under a design activity. Engineering data may include: configuration description, performance specifications, reliability and maintainability goals, and operational practices and procedures.

engineering improvement time—Machine time that is set aside for installing and testing modifications to the computer system. Engineering improvement time is a part of the total machine time necessary for servicing. Engineering time includes preventive servicing, repair time, and testing following repairs. Time spent to improve reliability without improving the facilities is called *supplementary maintenance time*.

enlarger printer—A unit which projects an enlarged image from microfilm, and develops and fixes the image on a hard-copy medium.

enquiry character—A control character used to request a response from a remote station. The ENQ character is usually for station identification or status data.

entry block—A block of main memory storage assigned for receipt of each entry into the system and associated with that entry for the life of the system.

entry conditions—The initial conditions required to be satisfied for the execution of a given routine.

entry instruction—The first instruction to be executed in a subroutine. The entry instruction may have several entry points at different locations of the subroutine.

entry point—A place where control can be transferred, other segments of the program can reference, and where the program can be activated by the operator or the system.

envelope—The configuration of a modulation waveform in which the carrier may be seen as a different and more complex configuration.

envelope delay—The propagation time between two fixed points of the envelope of a modulated wave. When the delay is variable over the frequency range of transmission, a distortion known as envelope delay distortion results.

EOF—Abbreviation for *end-of-file*.

EOM—Abbreviation for *end-of-message*.

EOT—Abbreviation for *end-of-transmission*.

epitaxial growth—The process of manufacturing semiconductor material by depositing a vapor on a seed crystal. The deposited layer can then continue to "grow" a larger single-crystal structure.

EPROM—Acronym for *erasable programmable read-only memory*, a ROM in which the data pattern written in may be erased to allow a new pattern to be used. Some types use a transparent lid to expose the chip to ultraviolet light for erasure. The chip is supplied in the erased condition with all bits in the zero state. EPROMs allow fast turnaround times during the microcomputer development stage.

equalization—Circuit and techniques employed to compensate for the detrimental effects of methods used to reduce frequency and phase distortion in transmission lines. Equalization may involve the use of compensating networks to reduce delays due to frequency and phase shifts.

equation solver—An analog device used to solve systems of equations.

equation statements—Statements which are used in high-level languages which appear as mathematical equations, but which might not have any mathematical validity.

An equation statement as used in FORTRAN, BASIC, or PL/1 is an instruction to replace the variable to the left of the equals sign with the value of the expression to the right. Thus:

G = D/2 + G ;(replace G with D/2 plus G)

may not be valid algebraically, but it is a valid equation statement.

equivalence—The logic operator that states: if P is a statement, Q is a statement, R is a statement, then the equivalence of P, Q, and R is true if P, Q, and R are all true or all false.

equivalence element—Any logic element that performs the following equivalence operation:

INPUTS A	INPUTS B	OUTPUT C
0	0	0
1	1	1
0	1	0
1	0	0

equivalent binary digits—The number of digits required to express in binary notation a number expressed in another number system.

erasable programmable ROM—A programmable ROM that allows fast turnaround time for prototype work. Some types use a package with a quartz lid to allow ultraviolet light to erase the bit pattern, then a new pattern is written into the device.

erase—To clear or obliterate information in a storage medium. Erasing results in the replacement of all digits with zeros in magnetic storage, or the replacing of all digits in paper tape with holes, also called rubout or letter-out. Erasing in some EPROMs is done with a specified level of ultraviolet light.

error—Any discrepency between the observed or measured quantity, and the true or specified value. An error may be an incorrect step, process, or result in a data processing system; it may be attributable to a machine malfunction or a human mistake. Errors can tend to average out to produce a balanced error which may have no system effects.

Boundary errors can occur in a system when the processing arrives at a limit condition. This may occur in systems that have not been completely tested for overflow.

error ambiguity—A gross error which occurs in the reading of certain digital codes as the parameters represented by the codes change. Error ambiguity is common in analog-to-digital conversion because of imprecise digit positions. It is usually transient in nature if the parameter continues to change. Antiambiguity circuits can be used to minimize this condition.

error burst—A grouping of errors in a short period of time compared to error activity before and after the occurrence. In some transmission systems, a burst may be defined by a specific criterion such as three consecutive correct bits or words after any errors to terminate the error burst.

error condition—The state that results from an attempt to execute programs or instructions that are invalid, or that operate on invalid data.

error control—The various methods which are used to detect and correct errors. Errors can be corrected by operating on the detected errors, or by retransmission from the source. An error control character can be used to indicate if the data with it is to be disregarded or corrected. This character is also called an *accuracy control character.*

error correcting codes—A code in which expressions must conform to specific rules of construction. The code may define equivalent expressions that are not acceptable so as to allow the correction of errors. Some codes may use retransmission for correction.

Error detecting codes may use similar methods for detecting without correcting errors. The code may be arranged so that single errors produce forbidden or impossible code combinations. Errors may be deleted or printed out for user correction.

Some compilers will continue through a program using error diagnostics; the errors are then listed along with the final printout.

error dump—The dumping of a program into a medium so that the cause of an error interrupt can be analyzed.

error message—An indication that an error has been detected.

error ratio—The ratio of the number of units of data in error to the total number of data units.

error signal—The feedback signal used in a closed-loop control system for correcting the output.

ESC—The escape character. A control character which signals a change in meaning for characters following it, or forms an escape sequence for the development of additional operations. In ASCII, ESC is symbolized by the binary 27 (00011011).

ETB—The end-of-transmission-block character.

ETX—The end-of-text character.

evaluation system—A group of parts from a specific microcomputer family which are mounted on a circuit board to allow the user to become familiar with the parts in a typical configuration. The user can run simple programs and connect the module to peripheral devices for operational tests. The evaluation module is usually interfaced with peripherals using a peripheral adapter for connection to keyboards, printers, displays, or other devices. A typical evaluation module may contain a CPU, RAMs, a clock generator, power-on initialization circuitry, and various input/output ports.

evoke module—A module containing hard-wired circuits used for dedicated automatic control systems. Evoke modules are used where changes to the program are not expected. Up to

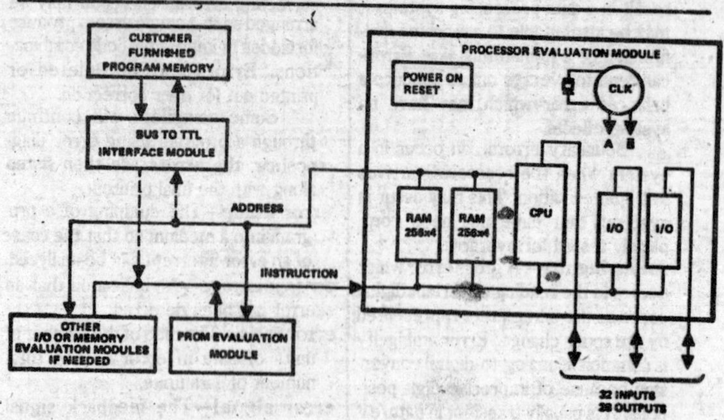

Evaluation System

100 instructions are feasible and the system can be very fast, since fetching and decoding are not required. A low-cost system can be built using evoke module control, but if program changes are ever required, expensive rewiring must be done.

exalted carrier—A method used for receiving amplitude- or phase-modulated signals. The carrier is first separated from the sidebands, filtered, amplified, and then combined again with the sidebands for demodulation.

exception—A logic operation that states: if P and Q are statements, then the statement P EXCEPT Q is valid only if P is true and Q is false.

exception reporting—A reporting of only the exceptions, such as: values over limits, changes, or deletions.

exclusion—A logic operator having the property: if P and Q are statements, then P EXCLUSION Q is true if P is true and Q is false; and P EXCLUSION Q is false if P is false or P and Q are both true.

Exclusion can be represented by P AND NOT Q, or P NAND Q.

exclusive-NOR—A logic operation which has a true output if the input statements are the same, and a false output if they are different. The exclusive-NOR function is:

INPUTS		OUTPUT
A	B	C
0	0	1
1	0	0
0	1	0
1	1	1

exclusive-OR—A logic operation which has a true output only if the input statements are different or odd. The exclusive-OR operation can be shown as:

INPUTS		OUTPUT
A	B	C
0	0	0
1	0	1
0	1	1
1	1	1

EXEC—An abbreviation for *executive statement*, or *executive system*.

execute phase—The part of the computer operation cycle when a command is performed.

execute statement—A job control command which designates the load module to be executed along with the specific job steps.

execution cycle—That part of the machine cycle when the execution of instructions is taking place. Divide

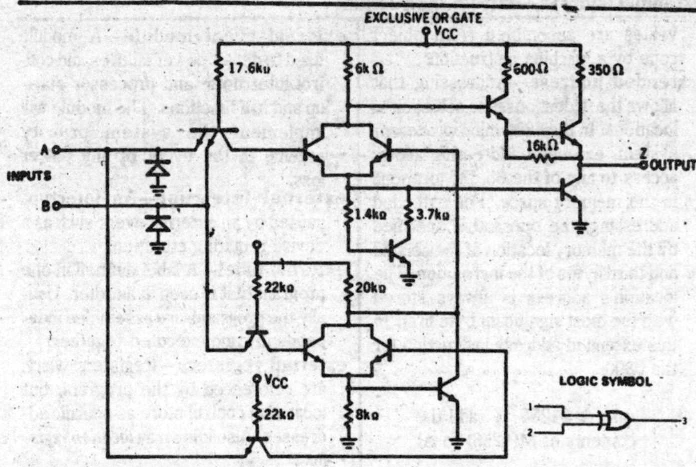

Exclusive-Or

and multiply operations may require a number of execution cycles to complete an operation. The execution cycle is usually the same as the clock period, which can vary from a few hundred nanoseconds to a few milliseconds.

execution time—The time required to complete an instruction, procedure, or cycle. The execution time is the portion of an instruction cycle when the actual operation is taking place, such as decoding and executing an instruction. It is usually expressed in terms of clock cycles.

executive—A program, routine, or system that has supervisory control over others. Executive instructions are designed and used to control the execution of other routines and programs. The executive command language should be open-ended to allow easy expansion for additional features and functions. Statements need not be restricted to card formats and may be of variable length.

An executive program usually consists of controlling loaders, an editor, an assembler, a FORTRAN compiler, a debug monitor, input/output devices, and a library of routines. After the executive program is loaded into memory, all operations are executed using teletypewriter commands to the executive, editor, and debug programs. The executive program coordinates and controls the running of all other programs and essentially converts a collection of software into an operating system.

Parts of the executive program are resident in the memory at all times. The main tasks of the program include job scheduling, storage allocation, and output control.

executive routine—An automated computer procedure used to control the loading, relocation, scheduling, and execution of other routines. The routine usually maintains control of the computer at all times and returns control from all functional operations back to the excutive routine upon completion.

exit—A method used to interrupt or leave a repeated cycle of operations in a program.

explicit address—An address reference that is specified as two absolute values, one of which supplies the displacement value. The explicit address values are assembled from object code by a machine instruction.

extended address—Addressing that allows the widest possible selection of locations. In the 6800 microprocessor system, extended addressing allows access to any of the 65,536 locations in the memory space. For extended addressing, the operand is specified by the memory location of the second and third bytes of the instruction. The location's address is always stored with the most significant byte first. In this extended address instruction for the 6800:

Add A $1256 ; (add the contents of M(1256) to A)

the $ indicates that 1256 is a hexadecimal number to the assembler.

extended addressing—An addressing mode designed to reach almost anywhere in the memory system.

extended arithmetic element—A central processor element (abbreviated *EAE*) that is implemented with hardware to multiply, divide, and normalize functions.

extension register—A register which provides expansion for the accumulator register or the quotient register.

external clocking—A type of clocking used in synchronous communication in which the bit timing signal is supplied from a modem.

external delays—Lost system time due to causes beyond the control of operators and service crews.

external device code—An address code for an external device which specifies the operation to be performed. The code is used in systems with common bus lines for a number of external devices. The external device code addresses a particular device and only that device will respond to the instruction that is part of the code.

external event module—A module used to detect power failures and control interrupts, and processor start-up and half functions. The module will implement the system priority scheme in the event of any power loss.

external interrupt—An interrupt caused by an external event such as a device requiring attention.

external label—A label defined in one program that is used in another. Usually the programs are assembled independently and executed together.

external registers—Registers which are referenced by the program, but located in control store as specific addresses. Also known as *location registers*.

external storage—Storage that is separate from the computer unit. External storage includes magnetic tapes, punched cards, or paper tape. Also called *offline storage*.

external symbol—A symbol that is used in several program modules, or in a program module dictionary.

extracode—Machine instructions that are used to provide increased capability for machine software. For example, an extracode may provide floating-point arithmetic for a machine that does not already have floating-point capability. Extracodes are stored within the system, or in ROMs.

extract—1. To remove from a set of items all items that meet a particular criterion. 2. A procedure used to replace the contents of certain columns of data with the contents of other columns.

extract instruction—An instruction that requests the formation of a new expression from selected parts of another expression. A typical extract instruction might remove the first, second, fifth, and sixth bits from an 8-bit word and combine them to form a new word.

F

FACE—Acronym for ***field-alterable control element***, a chip used in some systems to allow the user to write microprograms. The FACE chip allows field microprogramming for low-volume applications. A typical system uses a writable control store, a logic unit, and a display-and-debug unit. The FACE chip is similar to a control ROM (CROM) and uses external memory for microprogram storage.

facsimile—A television-like system (abbreviated *FAX*) for the transmision of images of documents. The image is scanned and the information converted into signal waves for transmission to remote locations. The information is usually duplicated on hard copy for final use and documentation. Facsimile transmission involves scanning of the image with a revolving drum and use of photoelectric sensors to create the electrical signals.

failsafe—Descriptive of a system, circuit, network, or component with built-in protective measures which preclude system failure. Failsafe systems usually allow some degradation of performance that does not prevent proper system operation.

fail-soft—A method of system implementation which prevents the loss of data and facilities due to an outage in some part of the system. Degraded performance usually results from a failure, but the system may continue to run.

failure logging—A procedure used in some systems to record the system state following the detection of an error. A section of the monitor using machine-check interrupts logs the data which is stored for diagnosing errors at a later time.

failure prediction—The methods and techniques used to determine when failures are most likely to occur in specific parts and equipment. Failure prediction attempts to allow a schedule for the replacement of parts and equipment before failure occurs. These methods are used to determine the *mean time to failure* (MTTF) and *mean time between failures* (MTBF) for a part based on test data which is used to calculate the average time that the part will operate under normal conditions before failure occurs.

fallback—A condition where substitute hardware is employed for malfunctioning systems. Fallback is used to increase capacity for malfunctioning systems, or take over completely in the case of total system failure.

fallthrough—A software "step" that results in machine cycling to the operation represented by the next lower block on a flowchart.

false add—To form a partial sum without carries.

FAMOS—Acronym for *floating-gate avalanche-injection metal-oxide semiconductor*. A type of erasable PROM which uses ultraviolet light for erasing and an avalanche transport mode. The FAMOS device uses silicon-gate field-effect transistors with no connection to the silicon gate. Memory operation then depends on charge transport by avalanche injection from a source or drain.

fan-in—The number of inputs connected to a specific logic device or function.

fanout—The number of output circuits that are connected to a specific logic device or function. A device must be capable of driving the amount of devices specified in the fanout specification.

fault—Any physical condition that causes an element of a system to fail or malfunction. A fault may be a broken wire, an intermittent device, or a failed element.

fault-location—A type of program used for identification or information regarding equipment faults. The fault-location program is designed to identify the location and type of fault and is usually an important part of the diagnostic routine.

FAX—Abbreviation for *facsimile*, a system used to convert images to electrical signals for transmission to remote points.

FDM—Abbreviation for *frequency-division multiplexing*, a type of multiplexing in which a communications channel is divided into a group of independent lower-frequency channels. Each channel is assigned a slot for its unique pair of transmission end frequencies, and channels are easily cascadable (allowing low costs in many applications). FDM is used on voice-grade lines where it provides asynchronous transmission speeds of up to 150 bits per second.

FE—Abbreviation for *format effector.*

feasibility study—A preliminary system analysis to allow decision-making. A feasibility study may be directed at the suitability, capability, or compatibility of a new system or modifications to present systems and equipment.

feedback—Refers to the return of a part of the output to the input. As used in a closed-loop control system, feedback provides the information about the condition under control. Feedback is used in analog amplifiers using various feedback elements. Negative feedback is used in most amplifiers and control systems to stabilize the output and reduce distortion generated within the stage. Positive feedback in an amplifier increases gain, but causes instability and accentuates distortion. Positive feedback is not always undesirable, however, as an oscillator depends on positive feedback for its operation.

feedforward—A type of control action in which conditions that can disturb the control variable are minimized or converted into corrective actions.

feed holes—The holes that are punched in a tape to allow it to be driven by a sprocket. The distance between the centers of the feed holes is called the feed *pitch*.

ferrite—A high-permeability iron compound used for the construction of magnetic cores. Ferrite compounds contain iron and other metallic oxides combined with ceramic materials to form toroidal cores with high magnetic flux properties. The cores are pulsed by electric currents in wires wound about it and assume one or the other states of magnetic flux to allow storage, switching, or gating. Ferrite-core memories are arranged in columns and rows to provide the function of state retention.

ferroelectric—Descriptive of a phenomenon in certain materials which exhibit spontaneous electric polarization along with dielectric hysteresis.

ferromagnetic—Descriptive of the ability of certain materials to be highly magnetized and exhibit hysteresis. Ferromagnetic materials such as iron, nickel, and cobalt alloys have marked hysteresis properties and are used for storage in computers.

ferrous oxide—One medium used to contain encoded information on magnetic tape.

FET—Acronym for *field-effect transistor,* a type of transistor which operates in a manner of field conduction and whose characteristics are similar to those of a vacuum tube. The field is set up in a channel of semiconductor material which is made more or less conductive, depending on the applied gate signal. Since FETs are controlled by voltages rather than currents, power requirements can be low and impedances quite high.

fetch—1. To locate and load a program from storage, as in bringing a program phase into main storage for execution from the memory library. 2. That portion of a computer cycle from which the location of the next instruction is obtained. A fetch can also be used to retrieve phases of a program and load them into main storage, or transfer control to a system loader. A typical fetch routine includes:

(1) Obtaining the requested phase of the program
(2) Loading into main storage
(3) Transferring control to the phase entry point

fetch instruction—The instruction or procedure used to locate and return instructions that have been entered in the instruction register.

fetch phase—That part of the computer cycle in which the instruction is brought from memory into the program register. The fetch phase may be used to form the address, access the machine instruction from memory, and store it in the instruction register.

FF—The form-feed character.

Fibonacci search—A dichotomizing search in which the set or remaining subset is divided, using successively smaller numbers in the Fibonacci series. The Fibonacci series contains integers in which each integer is equal to the sum of the two preceding integers and is found from:

$$x_i = x_{i-1} + x_{i-2}$$

Where:

$$x_0 = 0 \qquad x_1 = 1$$

Thus:

$$x_i = 0, 1, 1, 2, 3,$$
$$5, 8, 13, 21\ldots\text{(Fibonacci numbers)}$$

If the number of items in a set is not equal to a Fibonacci number, then the number of items in the set is assumed to equal the next higher Fibonacci number.

field—A group of data such as characters which can be treated as a single unit, or a specified area which is used for a particular category of data. A field might be a group of particular card columns or a set of bit locations assigned for specific items of information. Code fields can be assigned by source statements of the assembler or assembly program. Typical code fields include label, operand, comment, and operator. Fields are also used for data storage procedures: 8-bit words can be divided into two 4-bit fields, or eight 1-bit fields.

field-effect transistor—A type of transistor (abbreviated *FET*) that uses conduction due to a field in a channel between depletion layers. The resistance of the channel may be altered by appropriately altering the applied gate voltage.

field-protected—A display field in which the user is not allowed to enter, modify, or erase data from the keyboard.

BIT	REGISTER A	REGISTER B
1-3	ESTABLISHES 1 OF 8 BASIC I/O MODES	ESTABLISHES 1 OF 8 BASIC I/O MODES
4	NOT USED	NOT USED
5	CA1 INTERRUPT CONTROL	CB1 INTERRUPT CONTROL
6	CA2 INTERRUPT CONTROL	CB2 INTERRUPT CONTROL
7	DMA END-OF-BLOCK INTERRUPT CONTROL	NOT USED
8	DMA ENABLE	NOT USED

Fields for Registers

FIFO—Acronym for ***first-in-first-out***, a priority basis used in many computer registers and storage elements. A FIFO system is useful for system applications where it is desirable to read out data in the same order that it was written. Excessive read time in a FIFO system may cause delays in communication rates. FIFO read and write operations should be completely independent of each other and system timing. In a FIFO system, the data to be written in memory is stored in the next available location, and the read operation advances the outputs to the next memory word. Once the read is advanced, the previous word cannot ordinarily be used again. The main advantage of a FIFO system is the absence of external addressing; since control is automatic, the system requires only data inputs, read outputs, and clock lines.

FIFO queue—A first-in-first-out "waiting line" in which the most recent arrival is placed at the end of the line and the item waiting the longest receives service first. Also called a ***pushup list***.

FIFO storage—A storage system that uses the FIFO technique. One method of FIFO implementation uses shift register circuits to insure the proper first-in-first-out order. When data is entered, it is shifted to the last register stage. The next data entry is shifted to the next-to-last register stage; this is repeated until the register is full. A status register is used to identify full locations so that data is shifted only to the last empty stage. FIFO is also used in stack registers and in stack storage systems where it is desirable to read data in written order.

figurative constant—A preassigned fixed character string using a preassigned fixed data name in a particular programming language.

file—A collection of related records or data sets which are used as a unit. A line on an invoice may be an item, a complete invoice may form a record, and a complete set of records may form a file. A *permanent* data file is one maintained with new data, while a *working* file is a temporary collection of data sets which is destroyed once the data is utilized or transferred to another form.

file gap—The area of a data medium which is used to indicate the end of a file or the start of another. A file gap may also be used as a flag to indicate the beginning or end of a particular group of data.

file maintenance—Any activity required to keep a file up to date by changing, adding, or deleting data.

file manager—An online executive program that is used to create, delete, and retrieve programs by name from storage. A file manager can be used with disks, tapes, or cassettes in systems with as few as 4000 words.

file protection—Any device or technique used to prevent accidental erasure of data from a file.

file separator—An information separator used to identify the boundary between adjacent files.

FILO—Acronym for *first-in-last-out*, a pop-up register in which the most recent entry is retrieved first. Also called *stack*.

filter—A device or program that "sifts" signals, data, or other materials according to specified criteria, with the purpose of separating usable portions from the unusable. An *electrical* filter may contain inductors, capacitors, and resistors that allow it to select desired frequencies in communication channels, or provide a path to ground for noise signals.

firmware—That part of software that cannot be easily changed once it is implemented. Firmware might consist of those microprograms that are contained in ROM, and may be an extension to the basic instruction package for creating microprograms for a user-oriented instruction set. If the extension is done in read-only memory instead of software, it is called firmware. The ROM is used to convert these extended instructions to basic instructions for the computer.

Firmware tends to have a hardware compatibility while offering software-type implementation techniques. Firmware is generally used only for the movement of data between hardware elements and tends to be defined by the hardware. Additional formats and data modes usually require additional hardware, if implemented with firmware.

first-in-first-out—A priority basis (abbreviated *FIFO*) in which the item waiting the longest is serviced first. The FIFO system is used in many stack registers where the register outputs must be read in the same order that data was entered. It is also used for compiling and code conversions.

first-in-last-out—See *FILO*.

first-level address—See *direct address*.

fixed area—That part of main storage occupied by the resident section of the control program.

fixed-cycle—Refers to a type of computer operation cycle where a specific amount of time is used for each operation. Fixed-cycle operation involves clocking so that all events occur as a function of measured time.

fixed data—Data that is not likely to change or affect the results, date, operator, designator, or dump format. Also known as *housekeeping data*.

fixed length—Refers to records, words, or other elements that always contain the same number of characters, bits, or fields. A fixed length may be a restriction due to equipment or a requirement to simplify and speed processing operations.

fixed-point—1. A type of arithmetic in which the computer does not consider the location of the radix point. In a desk calculator using fixed-point arithmetic, the operator must keep track of the decimal point. In a computer, the location of the decimal point is the programmer's responsibility. 2. A type of arithmetic in which the operands and the results of all operations must be scaled to have a magnitude between certain fixed values. The LSI-11 allows fixed-point arithmetic with an extended arithmetic option. The following instructions are used for the manipulation of fixed-point numbers:

MUL; (multiply)

DIV; (divide)

ASH; (shift arithmetically)

ASCH; (arithmetic shift combined)

Operand formats are allowed for 16-bit single words or 32-bit double words.

fixed-program—A type of computer which uses instructions that are wired in or stored permanently. In a fixed-program computer, the instructions are not changed except by rewiring or changing the storage locations.

fixed storage—Storage in which contents are not changed by computer instructions, as in photographic disks or magnetic cores with a lockout feature. Also known as *read-only storage, permanent storage,* and *nonerasable storage*.

flag—An indicator used to signal the occurrence of a specific condition. A flag may be a specific bit that indicates a point of demarcation such as a carry, overflow, or interrupt. Also known as a *mark, sentinel,* or *tag*.

flip-flop—A circuit that is capable of assuming either one of two stable states; a *bistable multivibrator*. The flip-flop will assume a given state depending upon the previous history of the inputs. The circuit is capable of storing one bit of information. For a flip-flop with two inputs, the state of the outputs will correspond to the past and present conditions of the two inputs. Flip-flops can be coupled to other circuits with capacitors, or the circuits within the flip-flop can be coupled with capacitors, permitting operation only for alternating currents. Flip-flop circuits have a variety of configurations, including D, J–K, R–S, T and R–S–T.

D flip-flops perform a delay function since the output will be the input which appeared one pulse earlier. If a 1 appeared at the input, the output after the next clock pulse will also be a 1.

J–K flip-flops have a J input and a K input following the clock pulse; a 1 on the J input and a 0 on the K input will set the output to 1. A 0 on J and a 1 on K will reset the output to 0. Where a 1 appears on both inputs, a change of state results, regardless of any previous states; a 0 on both inputs inhibits any change of state.

R–S flip-flops operate like two NAND gates which have been cross-connected. The circuit has a reset (R) input and a set (S) input. A 1 on the S input and a 0 on the R input will clear or reset the output to 0. A 1 on the R input and a 0 on the S input will set the output to 1. If 1's are on both inputs, the output will remain the same; a 0 on both inputs is not considered.

T flip-flops have only one input. A pulse on the input causes the output to change states. T flip-flops are used for ripple counters.

R–S–T flip-flops have three inputs labeled R, S, and T (reset, set, and trigger). The circuit operates like an R–S flip-flop except that the T input is used to change the state of output.

Flip-flops can be strung together so that the state of one can be transferred to another. Then a number stored in one string can be transferred to another, allowing numbers to be transferred in computer systems. Flip-flops are used to form storage registers, counters, and controls as used for interrupt level signals. Level-enable flip-flops control the interrupt level from a waiting state to an active state.

floating address—An address that can be easily converted to a machine address by indexing, assembly, or some other means.

floating-point arithmetic—A type of arithmetic in which the computer keeps track of the decimal point. Floating-point arithmetic uses the floating-point notation to eliminate carrying a great amount of digits which may occur in many calculations. Seven or eight digits are retained along a two-digit characteristic:

NUMBER	SCIENTIFIC NOTATION	FLOATING POINT NOTATION
0.0024	0.24×10^{-2}	.24E – 2

Some floating-point subroutines for conversion include:

(1) Floating-point to ASCII
(2) ASCII to floating-point

(3) Floating-point to integer
(4) Integer to floating-point

Floating-point instructions for the LSI-11 microcomputer are:

FADD; (floating add)
FSUB; (floating subtract)
FMUL; (floating multiply)
FDIV; (floating divide)

floating symbolic address—A label used to identify a word or other item in a routine independent of the location of the information within the routine.

floppy disks—A magnetic storage medium that uses flexible disks that resemble phonograph records. Floppy disk systems provide random access storage for 300,000 or more bytes and are used to replace paper tapes or cassettes in many applications. Some systems use reusable diskette cartridges with up to four disk drives.

flow chart—A graphical representation of the definition or solution of a problem, in which symbols are used to represent functions, operations, and flow. Also called a flow diagram. A flow chart might contain all of the logical steps in a routine or program in order to allow the designer to conceptualize and visualize each step. It defines the major phases of the processing, as well as the path to problem solution.

The flow chart can contain logical operations by using symbolic notation to describe the arithmetic operations in terms of inputs and outputs. Functional flow charts define all operations sequentially, but do not contain enough detail to allow program coding. Detailed charts are derived from the functional flow chart and the command codes along with the way each command code acts in the system. The detailed charts include every operation in step-by-step form that must be performed during coding. The programmer is only required to know the microprocessor programming language.

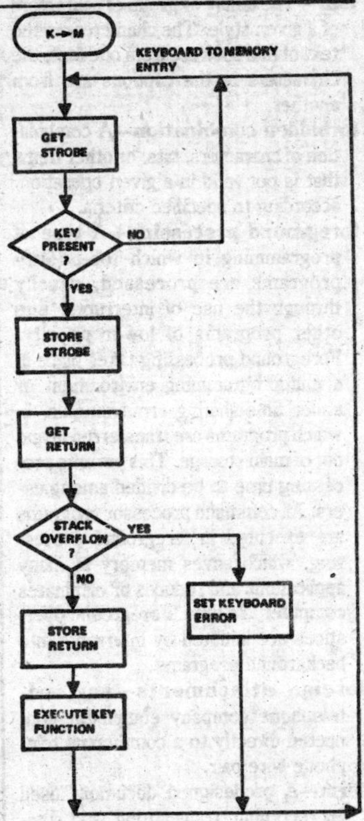

Flow Chart for a Keyboard-To-Memory Routine

flow process diagram—A graphic representation of work in process. The major steps of work in process are defined by illustrative symbols which may represent documents, equipment, or operations.

flow line—The line providing the connecting path between flow-chart symbols. Flow lines are used to indicate the sequential processes of the operation they represent.

flying-spot scanner—A device used in optical character recognition which uses a moving spot of light to scan each character's space. The difference in light levels as the light moves over dark lines and white spaces denotes the character printed.

font—The family or group of characters of a given style. The characters in the text of this book are from one font; the characters in the captions are from another.

forbidden combination—A combination of characters, bits, or other items that is not valid in a given operation, according to specified criteria.

foreground processing—A type of programming in which top-priority programs are processed, usually through the use of interrupts, into other programs of lower priority. Foreground processing takes place in a multiprogramming environment or under time-sharing arrangements, in which programs are transferred in and out of main storage. This permits processing time to be divided among users. All command processor programs are executed in foreground processing, which saves memory in many applications and reduces or eliminates computer idle time. Foreground operations are initiated by interrupts into background programs.

foreign attachments—Any non-telephone company equipment connected directly to a commercial telephone wire pair.

form—A predesigned document used for recording, transmitting, and summarizing data. Forms may be printed or reproduced in other manners, and they usually contain spaces for the insertion of information.

form-feed—The format effector that controls the movement of the printing position to the next form or page. In ASCII this is the FF character represented by the binary 12 (0000 1100).

format—A predetermined arrangement of data, words, letters, characters, files, etc.

format designator—The letters and symbols used in instruction words to specify and establish a given format.

format effector—A control character (abbreviated *FE*) used for control of the layout and position of information in printing and display devices.

FORTRAN—Acronym for *formula translator*, one of the most widely used languages for scientific and business problems. FORTRAN requires a compiler for each particular model of computer. It is well suited for problem solving with mathematical and English-language conventions. Statements, used as sentences in the language:

(1) Define the arithmetic steps for the processor

(2) Provide the control required during program execution

(3) Define the required input and output operations

(4) Define such additional areas as dimensions of variables.

Arithmetic statements appear as equalities; the right side can involve parentheses, operation symbols, constants, variables, and functions. These are combined using a set of rules similar to ordinary algebra. The following operation symbols are used in arithmetic statements:

+; (addition)

−; (subtraction)

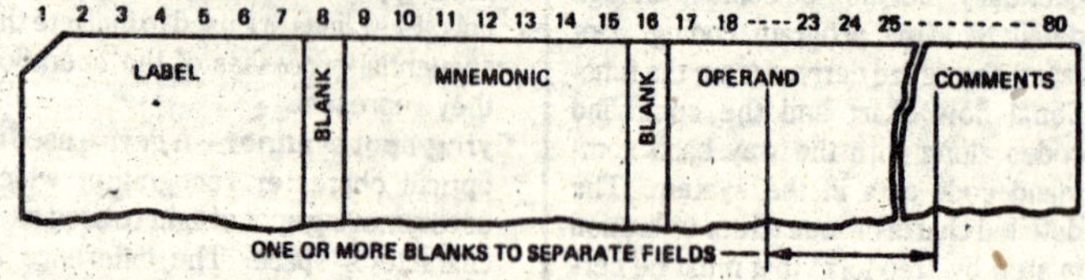

Format for Punched Card

*; (multiplication)

/; (division)

**; (exponentiation)

An example of an arithmetic expression as it would appear on a FORTRAN coding sheet is:

A**B*C + D**E/F – G + H

Which is interpreted as:

$A^BC + D^E/F - G + H$

Besides the ability to indicate constants, variables, and operations, it is also possible to use functions such as:

ABSF (X); (absolute value of *x*)
SQRTF (X); (square root of *x*)
SINF (X); (sin *x*)
COSF (X); (cos *x*)
ATANF (X); (arctan *x*)

Input/output statements such as the following bring data into the processor and output the results:

READ 1,A,B,C; (read the next card and the numbers stored in locations A,B and C)

PRINT 2, ROOT; (print the number identified as the variable ROOT in storage)

PUNCH 4, SUM A; (punch the value of SUM A on a card)

Control statements are used to state the flow of the program. Any statement that is referred to by another is given an identifying number which allows branching from one part of the program to another. Some examples of control statements are:

GO TO 3; (the next statement to be executed is number 3)

GO TO (3, 18, 20) K; (the next statement to be executed depends on the previous value of *k*; if *k* = 1, the next statement is number 3)

IF (A*B) 3, 18, 20; (allows one of three alternate instructions if the value of *a* times *b* is less then, equal to, or greater than zero)

FORTRAN IV is an upgraded version that provides (1) more power for interfacing with more complex configurations, (2) greater flexibility, (3) improved accuracy, and (4) a more powerful instruction set. The FORTRAN IV compiler permits intermixing between assembly language and FORTRAN statements to produce an object listing for diagnostics. Programs are compiled in the ***operating system*** (OS), or as task modules under real-time executive control. Some extended features of FORTRAN IV are:

N-dimensional arrays
Mixed-mode expressions
Unformatted inputs and outputs
Alphanumeric stringing
Conditional compiling
Tracing and debug facility
Inline assembly language capability

Many microprocessors use FORTRAN IV assembly and simulators which allow the use of large general-purpose computers for developing microcomputer programs.

Fourier analysis—A method used to determine the harmonic components of a waveform, based on the theory that any waveform can be constructed using the appropriate number of selected harmonics from a sinusoid of a given frequency.

four-address—An instruction format which contains four address parts.

four-plus-one address—An instruction which contains four operand addresses and one control address.

four-wire—A two-way communications circuit which uses two discrete paths for transmission. Data is transmitted in one direction only on one path, and in the other direction on the other path. The circuit may or may not use four wires, but the *effect* of a 4-wire system is achieved in that no crosstalk or intercoupling exists between the two circuit paths.

fox message—A standard message used to test communication systems, since it contains all of the alphamerics and many of the function characters. The standard fox message is:

THE QUICK BROWN FOX JUMPS OVER THE LAZY DOG 1234567890 (station name) SENDING.

FPLA—Abbreviation for *field-programmable logic array*, an array which uses fusible links for programming the logic configuration. High current is passed through the links to achieve the desired logic design. FPLAs offer 50-nanosecond speeds along with editing capability and good flexibility. In typical FPLAs, product terms can be added or deleted from any output function, input variables can be deleted from any output function or product term, and programmed active-high outputs can be reprogrammed to active-low. A typical device may provide eight output functions and 48 product terms; all outputs can be programmed active-high true or active-low true, which allows complements to be implemented using fewer product terms. FPLAs are used with a small auxiliary memory to repair core memory systems as an alternate to restringing methods.

frame—An area which is one recording position long and extending across the width of magnetic or paper tape. A single frame may have several bits or punch positions through the use of different recording positions across the width of tape.

freeze mode—An operational mode whereby the computer is stopped with all values held as they were when the interrupt occurs.

frequency—The number of occurrences of a periodic phenomenon within a specified period of time, usually one second. The clock frequency refers to the master frequency of the periodic pulses used to schedule the operation of a computer.

frequency modulation—A method of modulating a radio-frequency carrier of fixed amplitude, in which the instantaneous frequency deviates from the center frequency at a rate that corresponds with the signal. The amount of deviation is proportional to the *amplitude* of the modulating signal, but the frequency of the deviation is proportional to the *frequency* of the applied signal.

front-end processing—A processing system in which smaller processors such as microprocessors are used to interface the communication terminals to a larger host information processor.

FSK—Abbreviation for *frequency-shift keying*, a form of signal transmission in which the 1 and the 0 are represented by two distinct frequencies (tones).

full adder—A circuit or device that performs complete addition with carry operations. Many adders can be cascaded to increase word-length capability.

full-duplex—In communication systems and devices, refers to simultaneous two-way independent transmission in which transmission and reception occur mutually and on a noninterference basis.

full-read pulse—As used in coincident current selection, the result of partial drive pulses which are applied at the same time.

full shift—The capability of having more than just a single-place shift in-

TRUTH TABLE

C_n	B	A	$\overline{C_{n+1}}$	$\overline{\Sigma}$	Σ
L	L	L	H	H	L
L	L	H	H	L	H
L	H	L	H	L	H
L	H	H	L	H	L
H	L	L	H	L	H
H	L	H	L	H	L
H	H	L	L	H	L
H	H	H	L	L	H

NOTES:
1. $A = \overline{A^* \cdot A_C}$, $B = \overline{B^* \cdot B_C}$ where $A^* = \overline{A_1 \cdot A_2}$, $B^* = \overline{B_1 \cdot B_2}$

Full Adder

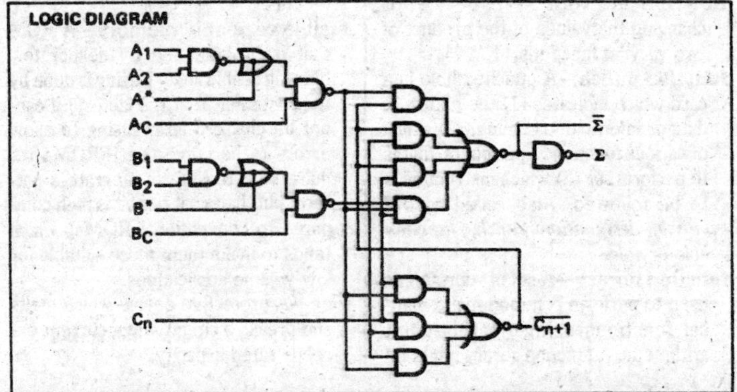

struction. Full-shift includes single or multiple-place, left or right, or logical or circular shift instructions.

full-write pulse—The result of partial-write pulses which are applied at the same time in coincident-current selection.

function—The purpose of an entity or its action, such as a machine action for carriage return or line feed.

functional diagram—A diagram that represents the functional relationships of a circuit, device, or system in a logical sequence.

functional interleaving — The technique of having input/output operations and computing operations proceed independently of one another, but sharing the memory.

functional partitioning—A method of microprocessor partitioning directed towards user microprogramming. Microprogram storage is separate from the CPU and also from macroprogram storage. It is usually implemented in ROM, PROM, or RAM. Microinstruction address generation and internal register storage (along with all arithmetic processing) are also separated to allow a very flexible configuration.

function digit—A coded instruction used for setting a branch order for linking subroutines into the main program.

function element—The smallest building block in a computer system that can be represented by logical operators using symbolic logic. Typical function elements include AND, NAND, OR, and NOR gates.

function generator—A circuit or device capable of generating sine, square, and triangular waveforms. Some analog function generators provide arbitrary output waveforms which can be changed at the discretion of the operator; others may follow a curve drawn on a surface to generate the waveform function automatically.

function key—A specific button on a keyboard that initiates a desired functional operation. A function key might cause a carriage return, query the system, or have it perform a specific operation. Specialized function keys are used in airline consoles, badge readers, and stock quotation systems.

function multiplier—A device for changing the values of the product of two varying functions.

function punch—A punched hole in a card which indicates (1) the nature of data or information coming, (2) which of various functions a peripheral unit is to perform, or (3) which instruction is to be followed. Also called *control punch, designation punch, function hole* or *hole*.

function library—A set of subroutines used to perform common mathematical functions using floating-point arithmetic. A function library might include square roots, exponentiation, logarithms, and trigonometric functions.

function table—1. The arrangement of two or more sets of data such that an entry in one set selects one or more entries in the remaining sets, providing a tabulation of the values of a function for a set of values of the variable. 2. A hardware device which decodes multiple inputs into a single output, or encodes a single input into multiple outputs.

fusible read-only memory—A ROM that is programmed by deliberately blowing fusible links. Fusing is done by the customer or at the factory; it cannot be changed after fusing to allow errors to be corrected. FROMs require little tooling to generate a pattern, but their cost per bit is high compared to conventional ROMs, which tends to make them more suitable for low-volume applications.

fuse—A protective device which melts and breaks a circuit when current exceeds rated capacity.

G

gain—The ratio of signal-level increase between the output and the input of a circuit or device.

gamma ferric oxide—An oxide used to coat magnetic tapes for recording.

gang punch—The punching of identical information into a group of cards simultaneously.

gap—A space or interval which appears between items of data. A magnetic gap refers to the air space in the magnetic circuit. A head gap refers to the separation between the pole pieces of a magnetic recording head. A data gap may appear as an interval of space or time to indicate the end of a word, record, or file on tape, or it may be the complete absence of information for a length of time or space on the recording medium.

gap digit—A special character used to mark the beginning and end of gaps in some variable-word-length machines.

gapless—Descriptive of a magnetic tape on which raw data is recorded in a continuous manner. The data is recorded onto the tape without word gaps, but it may still contain signs and marks in the gapless form.

gapped—Refers to a magnetic tape on which blocked data is recorded. Gapped tape contains all of the flag bits required; the format can be read directly into a computer.

garbage—A term facetiously used for unwanted and meaningless information in a computer system.

gas discharge—A type of display that uses the glow produced by ionized neon gas to illuminate segments of alphanumeric display characters. Gas-discharge displays can be viewed in bright sunlight and have lifetimes in excess of 200,000 hours. Their main disadvantage is the high voltage required to operate them and the interfacing circuitry required for computer applications.

gate—A circuit or device having one output and one or more inputs with the output state completely determined by the previous and present states of the inputs. A gate can also be a trigger used to allow the passage of other signals through a circuit. Logical gates can take many forms, some of which are shown in the following table:

Logical Gates

GATE TYPE	OPERATION
Conditional Implication	A OR NOT B; (output is false only if A is false and B is true)
EXCEPT	A EXCEPT B; (output is true only if A is true and B is false)
Exclusion	A AND NOT B; (output is true only if A is true and B is false)
IF-THEN	A OR NOT B
IF-THEN-NOT	A OR NOT B
Implication	A OR NOT B
Inclusion	A OR NOT B
Inclusive-OR	OR
Majority	Implements the majority logic operator
Negation	Reverses the signal or state into its alternate or opposite
NOT IF-THEN	A AND NOT B
AND	Output true if all inputs are true
OR	Output true if one or more inputs are true
OR-NOT	A OR NOT B
NAND	Negative AND
NOR	Negative OR
Coincidence	Any gate that depends on the input history
Sheffer stroke	NAND

Gates can be implemented in software, individual hardware devices, or large gate arrays using integrated circuits.

gating—The selection of a part of a waveform due to its time interval or amplitude, or the operation of a gating circuit when a signal is allowed to pass during a specific interval.

gating circuit—Any circuit that operates in a selective manner, allowing conduction only under specified conditions.

gating pulse—A pulse that permits the operation of a gating circuit.

Gaussian—Refers to a distribution which is encountered when a large number of samples is collected. The Gaussian distribution is characterized by equal probabilities of values at equal positive and negative deviations from the mean. Also called *normal distribution*.

Gaussian noise occurs when unwanted signals are distributed in a Gaussian or normal manner. Some amplifiers are designed to furnish a response which can be differentiated with respect to time to match a Gaussian distribution curve.

G-code—A command used in manufacturing process control which changes the mode of operation, as for example from positioning to contouring.

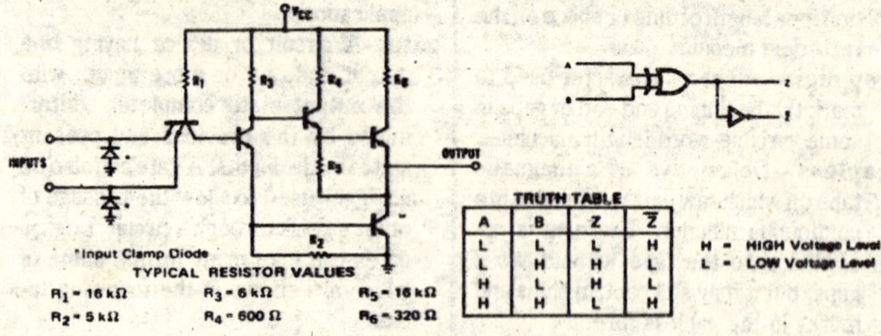

A	B	Z	$\overline{Z}$
L	L	L	H
L	H	H	L
H	L	H	L
H	H	L	H

TTL NAND Exclusive-OR Gate

generalized routine—A routine used to solve a general class of problem. The generalized routine is used to solve specific problems by inserting the appropriate values into the program.

general-purpose computer—A stored-program computer designed to solve a wide variety of problems and to be adapted to a large class of applications.

general-purpose register file—A file (abbreviated *GPR*) usually made up of 2 to 16 registers for holding temporary memory data and addresses. GPRs are also used for calculating memory addresses and combining and moving memory data.

general register—A register used for arithmetic operations and to compute and modify addresses. General registers perform such operations as addition, subtraction, multiplication, and division and are used in place of special registers such as accumulators in many microcomputer systems.

A typical central processor in a microcomputer might contain eight 16-bit general registers which can serve as accumulators, index registers, autoincrement registers, autodecrement registers, or stack pointers. Arithmetic operations are performed from one general register to another, one memory location to another, or between memory locations and registers. A general register unit may also serve as a scratchpad memory for the microprogram and provide a skeletal interrupt system to allow microprogram emulation.

generate—To create or produce; especially, to formulate a program by selecting subsets from a set of skeletal coding under the control of specific parameters. Also, to produce assembly-language statements from model statements of macro definitions when called for by a macroinstruction.

generated address—The number or symbol which is generated by instructions and becomes part of the address.

generating routine—A compiling routine that performs a generating function.

generator—A program or compiling routine that allows the computer to write other programs automatically.

germanium—A semiconductor material with properties similar to silicon. Germanium is used primarily for the manufacture of special-purpose diodes and transistors where sensitivity is a criterion, as in communications detectors and passive front ends.

get—To locate, fetch, and transfer an item from storage, as the activity required to develop or make a record from an input file available, or to obtain or extract a coded value from a field. The GET command might be used to obtain a numerical value from a series of decimal digits.

gibberish—A term used for totals or accumulations of records or data. The totals have no meaning or particular sense on their own, but are useful for control purposes. An example would be the cumulative account number for a customer's accounts-receivable total.

giga—A prefix denoting a quantity of 10^9, and used for any unit in the International System of Units.

GIGO—Acronym for *garbage-in, garbage-out*, a term used to describe the reason for meaningless computer output data: improper input.

glitch—A short-term voltage transient that usually occurs too fast for detection, but which causes improper machine operation because it is interpreted as a legitimate signal.

global—That part of an assembler program which contains the body of any macro definition called from a source module and the open-code portion of the source module.

global variable—Any variable with a name that is accessible by the main program and all its subroutines.

global variable symbol—A variable symbol used in assembler programming to communicate values between macro definitions and open-code sections.

go to—A multilanguage statement that directs the computer to leave the current sequence of instructions and begin operating at another point in the program. A typical FORTRAN go-to instruction might be:

GO TO 5; (the next statement to be executed is number 5)

In some languages such as BASIC, the space between the words is omitted, so the statement takes the form GOTO.

grandfather cycle—A term used to indicate the time for magnetic records to be retained before rewriting to allow records to be reconstructed in the event of losses or errors.

graphic—1. Any assembly of symbols or characters that is used to denote any concept, configuration, or idea nontextually. 2. Any symbol produced by printing, drawing, handwriting, etc.

graphic character—A character represented using a graphic rather than a control character.

graphic display—A nontextual display which reproduces data on a video screen, panel, or page.

graphic panel—The master control panel used in automated control systems which displays all the relationships and functions of the control equipment using colored block diagrams.

graphic plotter—A plotting machine used as a computer output device. Graphic plotters can provide high-quality graphics in several different colors for displaying complex patterns.

graphic terminal—1. A communications terminal which displays data on a screen or moving paper. 2. A video terminal.

Gray code—A cyclic binary code in which sequential numbers are represented by expressions that differ only in one place and in that place only by one unit. The Gray code is very useful in positional systems, since the maximum error between positions is never greater than the least significant bit. See code table under *cyclic binary code*.

Gray cyclic code—See *Gray code*.

grid—As used in optical character recognition, any two mutually orthogonal sets of parallel lines used for specifying or measuring character images.

ground—The point considered to be at zero potential voltage and to which all other potentials in the system are referred.

ground absorption—The energy loss in radio frequency waves due to absorption.

grouped record—The combining of two or more records into single sections of information. Grouped records tend to decrease the time required for tape acceleration and deceleration and conserve tape space. Also known as *blocked record*.

group mark—A mark which identifies the beginning or end of a set of data, such as words or blocks.

group separator—An information separator used to identify the boundary between groups of items (abbreviated *GS*).

guard band—1. The frequency band left vacant between two communications channels to prevent overlapping and mutual interference. 2. The unused area which isolates components on a printed-circuit board.

guard bit—A bit used to indicate the status of words or groups of words of memory. A guard bit can be used to indicate to hardware units or programs if the contents of a memory location can be changed by a program, or if a core or disk memory word is to be filed or protected.

guard digit—The hexadecimal zero attached to each operand fraction in a single-word floating-point addition or subtraction operation.

guard signal—A signal which allows values to be read only when all values are not in a changing state. The guard signal is usually an extra output generated when all operations are completed.

gulp—A term for a small group of bytes processed as a unit.

gun—The group of electrodes constituting the electron beam emitter in a CRT.

H-

half-add—An instruction that performs bit-by-bit half-adder operations. Half-add can be done using an exclusive-OR operation without carries.

half-adder—A circuit that has two input and two output channels which operate according to the following table.

INPUTS		OUTPUTS	
A	B	C	S
0	0	0	0
0	1	0	1
1	0	0	1
1	1	1	0

Where S = sum without carry
C = carry

Two half-adders can be combined to perform binary addition.

half-duplex—A communications arrangement which permits alternate one-way transmission between two given points at any one time.

half-duplex channel—A two-way channel used to transmit *or* receive at any one time.

half-duplex circuit—A communications system, or portion of a system, with single loops to terminals for two-way nonsimultaneous operation.

half-duplex operation—A communications mode in which transmission and reception take place, but not at the same time. Operating modes may be defined by the following:

S/O; (send only)
R/O; (receive only)
S/R; (send or receive)

half-shift register—A term used for a type of flip-flop used in shift registers; it requires two half-shift registers to make one stage of a shift register.

halftime emitter—A device that produces pulses halfway between two other pulses. Halftime emitters are used in some punched-card equipment.

half-word—A continuous sequence of bits or characters which make half a computer word and are capable of being addressed as a unit.

halt—A condition occurring after the sequence of operations in a program stops. A halt may be due to a halt instruction, an unexpected halt, or an interrupt. The program would normally continue after the halt unless a *drop-dead halt* occurs. In this case there is no recovery. A drop-dead halt may be programmed to shut down the system, or it may be due to an error in programming such as division by zero, or transfer to a nonexistent instruction. A drop-dead halt is sometimes called a *dead halt*.

halt indicator—An indicator on the console or panel which is true whenever the processor is in the halt mode.

halt switch—A switch on the console or panel which causes the processor to stop executing instructions.

Hamming code—A general term for a data code that is capable of being corrected automatically. The Hamming code contains four information bits and three check bits.

Hamming distance—The number of digit positions in which two corresponding digits of two binary words having the same length are different. Also called the *signal distance*.

handshaking—A term which implies an initial exchange between two units or items in a system connection. Handshaking usually requires a matching at an interface, as when signals are exchanged between data set devices when a connection is made. A typical handshaking procedure takes place when a connection between a modem and an ACIA channel is established:

(1) Local modem is enabled from the ACIA *request to send* signal.

(2) Remote modem answers the call and sends back its carrier frequency.

(3) Local modem detects this carrier and enables its *clear to send* output, which is detected by the computer.

handshaking protocol—A sequence in a program that greets and assists the programmer in the use of procedures or programs of the system. Handshaking in input/output control allows interfacing between peripherals with different response times. Control flags and jumps can be used to reduce decoding and software.

hands-on—A descriptive term for actual operating experience of hardware and equipment as opposed to educational or tutorial knowledge of that equipment.

hangup—A condition in which the central processor performs an illegal operation, keeps repeating the same routine, or stops execution. A hangup may be caused by the inability to escape from a loop, the improper coding of an instruction, or the use of an improper or nonexistent code.

hangup prevention—The design of a program such that no sequence of instructions can cause a halt or a nonterminating condition. Hangup prevention may include nonterminating indirect addressing and an infinitely nested execution of instructions.

hard copy—A printed record of a machine output, such as printed reports and program listings.

hard limiting—A circuit which restricts the excursion of a variable with a very small variation of the limited output.

hardware—The physical components of a computer system, including all electronic and electromechanical devices and connections.

hardware assembler—An assembler that usually consists of PROMs which are mounted on simulation boards. A hardware assembler allows the prototype unit to assemble its own programs.

hardware check—A check performed by built-in equipment. Also called a built-in check or an automatic check.

hardware interrupt—Any interrupt that schedules input/output equipment. A hardware interrupt allows input/output operations to be performed simultaneously with processing.

hardware priority interrupt—An interrupt that resolves priority when several events occur at the same time. Hardware priority interrupts can provide automatic vectoring and fast response to events. The routines are usually easy to write and take less memory space compared to polling methods.

hard-wire logic—Any system of logic elements that uses formed or wired connections. Hard-wire logic includes hand-wired diode-matrix boards and any logic board that cannot be reprogrammed with little difficulty.

harmonic—A sinusoidal wave whose frequency is an integral multiple of the fundamental waveform. The *second harmonic* is twice the frequency of the fundamental, although logically it is the first actual harmonic (multiple) of that signal.

hartley—1. A unit of information content, equivalent to 3.32 bits. The hartley is defined as the equal of one decadal position, or the designation of one of ten possible and equally likely states or values. 2. (usually capitalized) A type of oscillator characterized by a feedback element consisting of a split inductance.

hartley principle—The principle that the gross information content is the number of bits or hartleys required to transmit a message in a noiseless system with a specified accuracy, without regard to redundancy.

hash—Electrical noise which causes interference or unwanted and meaningless information to be carried in memory.

hash total—A sum formed for error-checking purposes by adding fields or other items that normally are not related, such as the total of invoice serial numbers.

head—A device used to read, write, or erase data in a storage medium. A head can be the small electromagnet for reading, writing, and erasing data on magnetic drums or tapes, or any of the marking devices used for punching, reading, and printing paper tape.

header—The initial part of a message which contains information such as routing, addressee, destination, and time of origin.

header card—A card that contains supplemental information related to the data in cards to follow.

header label—A block of data at the start of a magnetic tape which contains information to identify the file. A header label may include:

(1) The date when recorded
(2) File name and number
(3) Reel number
(4) Retention time

head gap—The space between the pole pieces of a magnetic recording head.

heading—1. The sequence of characters preceded by the *start of heading* character, which is used as address and routing information. 2. Azimuth bearing of an aircraft or target.

heatsink—A device used to dissipate heat away from a component or chassis.

HELP—Name of a program and system of files that provides assistance to the programmer in the use of software and hardware.

henry—The unit of inductance in the International System of Units (SI) and equal to the inductance present when a current change of one ampere per second produces one volt of potential in a closed circuit.

hertz—The SI unit of frequency, and equal to one cycle per second.

hertzian wave—The electromagnetic radiation which carries a radio signal through space.

heterodyne—To *beat* or combine two sinusoidal waves with a nonlinear device (such as a mixer) to produce sum and difference frequencies.

heterodyne interference—Interference resulting from the simultaneous reception of two signals whose wavelengths are separated by a frequency difference in the audio range.

heuristic—Refers to exploratory methods of problem solving in which solutions are found by evaluating the progress towards a final result.

heuristic routine—A routine which uses a trial-and-error method using a learning technique rather than a direct algorithm approach.

hexadecimal—Pertaining to the use of character sets with 16 possibilities, or number systems with a base or radix of 16.

hexadecimal notation—A notation system that uses 16 integers represented by the numerals 0–9 and the letters A–F, as shown in the following table:

hierarchy—A structure that consists of ranked sets and subsets. A hierarchical file system can eliminate the requirement for a separate data base definition language.

high—Refers to the higher voltage or the most positive level in a two-level logic system. Usually, true states are represented by a *high* (relative to the alternate state) voltage, a binary 1, and a closed switch; false states are denoted by a logic *low*, a binary 0, and an open switch.

high frequency—Any frequency falling between 3 MHz and 30 MHz.

high-level compiler—A compiler for high-level languages.

high-level language—A computer language that uses English-like statements for instructions. In high-level languages, each instruction or statement corresponds to several machine-code instructions. Tests using microprocessors show that such languages require 10% less time for programming and debugging than assembly languages.

high-level modulation—A level of modulation produced in the output circuit of an AM transmitter system that permits 100% modulation.

high-order digit—A digit that occupies a significant or highly valued position in a notational system.

high-noise-immunity logic—A type of logic (abbreviated *HNIL* or *HiNIL*) that offers protection from noise generated in nearby sources. HiNIL offers a DC noise immunity almost ten times greater than TTL and will block transients large enough to cause TTL malfunctions.

high-pass—Descriptive of a circuit or device (such as a filter) that permits the passage of all electrical signals above a certain critical frequency and shunts all other signals to ground.

BINARY	OCTAL	DECIMAL	HEXADECIMAL
0000	0	0	0
0001	1	1	1
0010	2	2	2
0011	3	3	3
0100	4	4	4
0101	5	5	5
0110	6	6	6
0111	7	7	7
1000	10	8	8
1001	11	9	9
1010	12	10	A
1011	13	11	B
1100	14	12	C
1101	15	13	D
1110	16	14	E
1111	17	15	F

Hexadecimal and Equivalent Numbers

high-speed logic—A logic family such as ECL which offers relatively high switching speeds.

high-speed printer—A typing machine which operates in excess of 300 lines per minute with 100 characters per line.

high-speed read/punch diagnostic—A test for peripherals and controllers which uses a test tape for reading and punching operations.

HiNIL—Acronym for ***high-noise-immunity logic***, a logic family designed especially for applications where transients are likely to occur and create a noisy environment. HiNIL can be used directly with CMOS to protect the CMOS circuits from static electricity and transients during turn-on. HiNIL is also compatible with many analog circuits.

hit—A momentary electrical disturbance in a circuit or system.

HNIL—See *HiNIL.*

hold—A condition which suspends operation of a system or circuit for a specified time (as, for example, to allow the user to study the parameters).

hold button—A button used in analog computer consoles which allows the operation to be temporarily stopped for observation by the operator. All integrating capacitors are disconnected during a hold to maintain the correct charges.

hold instruction—An instruction which causes data called from storage to be retained after it is called out.

hole—1. The blank left in a card after punching. 2. A mobile void in a transistor that is quickly filled by an electron and which gives the illusion of movement in a direction opposite that of electron flow.

hole current—Current caused from the movement of electrons into holes, creating new holes in semiconductors.

hole pattern—The punched configuration in a card column that represents a single character or a character set.

Hollerith code—A punched-card code which uses 12 rows per column and usually 80 columns per card. It is a 12-level code which represents the alphabet plus digits 0-9, using zone bits and data bits. The Hollerith code lends itself readily to error-detection methods.

hologram—A type of imaging that uses lasers instead of lenses.

homeostasis—A steady-state condition in a system where the input and output are precisely balanced.

hopper—The portion of a card processing machine which holds the cards to be processed for the card feed mechanism.

horizontal tabulation character—A format effector (the HT character) that causes the printing or display position to be moved to the next series of positions along the display or printing line. In ASCII, this character is represented by a binary 9 (0000 1000).

host—The primary or controlling computer in a multiple computer installation. Host computers are also used to prepare programs for use by other computers and to compile, edit, link, and test programs used in other systems.

hot—A terminal or conductor that is connected, alive, or energized, but which is not at ground potential.

housekeeping—Any operation in a routine that does not contribute to the solution of the problem, but which is required for machine operation (such as setting up constants and variables).

housekeeping operation—Machine operations that must be performed before actual processing begins. Housekeeping operations include:

(1) Establishing controlling marks
(2) Reading the first record
(3) Setting up auxiliary storage units
(4) Initializing parameters

housekeeping routine—Initial instructions which are executed only once, such as clearing storage locations or initializing instruction addresses.

HT—The ASCII horizontal tabulation (HT) character, designated by a binary 9 (000 1001).

human engineering—The science and art of designing machines for use by human operators. Human engineering is concerned with the limits and habits of the human operator.

human factors—Machine design considerations that are based on the inherent limitations and psychological or physiological needs of human operators.

hunting—1. A condition in which a system appears to seek a state of equilibrium continuously. 2. Repeated oscillation to limits above and below a desired value.

hybrid circuit—A circuit fabricated by interconnecting circuits of different classes, such as tubes and transistors, transistor discretes and ICs, or thin-film and thick-film ICs.

hybrid computer—A computer that uses both analog and digital representations. Hybrid computers are used in many simulation applications in which a close relationship with the physical world is required.

hybrid integrated circuit—An integrated circuit that uses a combination of technologies or components which are interconnected on a common substrate or package.

hybrid interface—An interface for connecting analog and digital devices together.

hybrid system—A system in which digital and analog computing elements are used, or a system where a small computer is used for immediate quick-response processing and a larger remote location machine is used for off-site processing of large blocks of data.

hypertape—A high-speed tape unit that uses cartridges to house the supply and takeup reels to permit automatic loading.

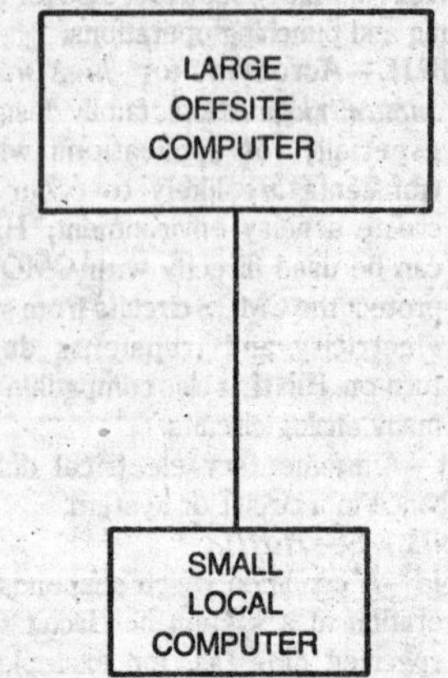

Hybrid System

hysteresis—1. A lagging in the response of a signal or property which may depend upon the past history of the signal or device being observed. 2. The difference between the turn-on threshold of a device or circuit, and the turn-off threshold of that same device after turn-on.

hysteresis error—The difference in readings obtained in a system with and without hysteresis present.

hysteresis loop—The loop or closed curve which results when parameters are plotted for devices exhibiting hysteresis.

I—Symbol for *current*.

IC—Abbreviation for *integrated circuit*, an electronic self-contained assembly fabricated on a single chip of semiconductor material.

An IC usually starts out as a schematic diagram, then a layout drawing is prepared which is 20–100 times larger than the final product. Mixtures of paste-like inks are used for conductors, and for each type of ink used a separate mask is produced by reducing the layout drawings. When the inking is completed, the chips are placed in a furnace, where the temperature is controlled and diffusion is used to achieve the proper resistivity of the semiconductor. Laser trimming can also be used for producing resistors with fine tolerances. Etching is used for trimming and removing unwanted paths on the chip.

icand register—A register which contains the multiplicand during a multiplication operation (from the last two syllables of *multiplicand*).

idealized system—A conceptual system which is often used as a standard to measure the performance of other systems.

idealized value—An expected or desired value of a parameter. The idealized value may be assumed to exist even though it may be impossible to determine.

identifier—Any symbol which is used to tag, name, or indicate data.

identifier word—A full-length word used in search, or search-and-read operations. The identifier word may be stored in a special register and then compared with each word in the suspected sequence.

identity element—A logical element that provides a true output when all inputs are the same. The term is usually used for circuits with only two inputs, while identity gates and units may have more than two inputs. Also called *equivalence element*.

identity gate—A gate which produces an output when all of the inputs are the same.

INPUTS	OUTPUT
0 0 0	1
1 0 0	0

(continued overleaf)

INPUTS	OUTPUT
1 1 0	0
1 1 1	1
0 1 0	0
1 0 1	0
0 1 1	0

Also called an *identity unit*.

idle time—That portion of available time when the hardware is not being utilized. Idle time may be the time when cards, tapes, and control panels are being prepared for the next run, or it may be the time between runs when no work is scheduled.

ier register—A register which holds the multiplier during a multiplication operation (from the last two syllables of *multiplier*).

IF—Abbreviation of *intermediate frequency*, the signal in a superheterodyne receiver which appears at the output of the first detector.

IF-THEN—A logical *inclusion* or *implication* operator which states: if P and Q are statements, IF P-THEN Q is false if P is true and Q is false; IF P-THEN Q is true if P is false and Q is true or P and Q are both true.

IF-THEN gate—A gate which performs the IF-THEN operation. An IF-THEN gate may be implemented in hardware or software.

ignore—1. A typewriter character used to indicate that no action should be taken. 2. An instruction to inhibit execution.

illegal character—A character or character code that is not valid according to specified criteria. Illegal characters can be detected to indicate machine malfunctions.

illegal code—A symbol that is not a true member of a defined code or language.

illegal operation—An operation that cannot be performed, or an operation that is performed with invalid results.

image—A one-to-one representation of the hole patterns of a punched card. Also called a *card image*.

image dissector—As used in optical character recognition, any transducer that detects the light intensity in different areas of a sample space. Also called an *image sensor*.

image sensor—A type of light intensity transducer that can detect differences in light within a sample space. One type of image sensor uses silicon chips in a continuous array.

immediate access store—A store operation with an access time that is very small compared to other operating times.

immediate address—An instruction in which the address contains the value of the operand. Sometimes called a *zero-level address*. In the 8080 microprocessor, the operand is provided by the second byte of the instruction as shown in the following example:

```
SBI  4  ; (A = A – 4)
```

which subtracts the constant 4 from the accumulator.

immediate addressing—A forn of addressing in which the operand contains the value to be operated on. Immediate addressing requires address reference, since the operands and instructions are in the same location. Almost all microprocessors use immediate addressing for jump and call instructions.

immediate instruction—An instruction which contains the operand itself rather than an address. The use of immediate instructions allows only half as much memory to be required since instruction and operand are contained in the same word. Immediate instructions include addition, subtraction, load, and compare in some microprocessors.

impedance—The ratio of voltage to current in alternating-current circuits. Impedance contains a resistance term and a reactance term and is expressed in ohms.

impedance compensator—A network used in a transmission path to obtain a desired characteristic over a specific frequency range.

imperative statement—A statement defining an action in a symbolic program which is converted into machine language. Imperative statements consist of verbs and operands and usually express a complete unit of procedure.

implication—A logical IF-THEN operation which states: if P and Q are statements, *P inclusion* Q is false if P is true and Q is false. *P inclusion* Q is true if P is false and Q is true, or P and Q are both true.

implication gate—A device or circuit that performs the implication operation. Also called *IF-THEN* or *inclusion gate*.

implicit address—An address reference used in assembler programming which is specified as one absolute expression. An implicit address is converted into explicit form before it can be assembled into object code.

implicit differentiation—A procedure used in analog computers in which functions are derived implicitly. For example, if the output is the square of the input, then the input is the square root of the output; if the output is the integral of the input, then the input is the derivative of the output.

imprinter—A device for marking characters onto a form. Imprinters include typewriters, printers, presses, pressure plates, and stamping machines.

imprinting—The act performed by an imprinter; the output function of an imprinter.

impurity—A material added to semiconductor crystals to produce excess holes or electrons. Excess holes are produced by acceptor impurities and excess electrons are produced by donor impurities.

impurity level—The energy level in a material due to the addition of impurity atoms.

in-circuit emulator—A unit for emulating the user's prototype and production microcomputer in its actual operating environment. An in-circuit emulator allows early system control by using the emulator in place of the processor. The user is able to interrogate, revise, and debug the system in a real-time enviornment.

in-circuit test—The testing of individual integrated circuits by checking their outputs. With an in-circuit test, logic inputs can be programmed while the outputs are measured to isolate pins stuck at zero or one, along with solder splashes and open connections.

in-circuit tester—An automated test unit for performing in-circuit tests on mounted components. Some in-circuit testers can prescribe repairs and test simple components such as resistors in less than six milliseconds each.

inclusion—See *IF-THEN*.

inclusion gate—A circuit or device that performs the inclusion operation.

inconnector—A connector used in flow-charting to indicate the continuation of a broken flow line.

increment—To move ahead by one step at a time; it refers to a software operation used with stacks and stack pointers. The stack pointer is used to hold the addresses of information stored in the stack register. The pointer is incremented after each byte is removed from the stack and decremented (moved back one step) as each byte is added to the stack.

incremental—An arrangement of outputs used in rotating sensors. The outputs are arranged such that the phase shift is 90 degrees apart, which allows the direction of rotation to be determined.

incremental compaction—A data compaction method which uses only the initial value and changes in storage for transmission. Incremental compaction allows a saving in time and space since only changes at specific intervals are processed.

incremental computer—A computer which mainly uses an incremental representation of data or a special-purpose computer designed to process changes in variables as well as the absolute values of the variables.

incremental data—Data which represents the change from the value of the data which just preceded it; each data word or value is referenced to the prior position.

incremental integrator—A digital integrator which has an output that is maximum positive, zero, or maximum negative when the input is maximum positive, zero, or maximum negative.

incremental representation—A representation of a variable in which the changes in the variable are represented rather than the variable itself.

independent program loader—A program which allows the *operation system* user to load nonsystem programs from *operating system* file devices.

index—1. Symbol or number used to identify a specific quantity in an array of similar items. 2. An ordered reference list of the contents of a file with keys for identification of the contents and the action required to prepare such a list. 3. In numerical control, movement of a machine part to a predetermined location.

indexed address—An address which is modified by the contents of an index register or similar technique. As used in the 6800 microprocessor system, the operand will be in a memory location with an address formed by adding the second byte of the instruction to the value contained in X, such as:

ADD A 3, X ; (add X + 3 to accumulator A)

This instruction adds the contents of the memory location referenced by the contents of X + 3 to accumulator A. This instruction becomes the same as direct addressing if X contains zero. Sometimes called a *variable address*.

indexed addressing—A form of addressing in which the address contained in the second byte of the instruction is added to the index register.

indexed files—A file structure consisting of a series of pointers to data blocks throughout the disk. Indexed files are used for applications with a large amount of random-access data. They have the open-end characteristic of chained files with a much faster access time.

indexing—A technique of addressing modification that usually requires an index register for implementation.

index register—A register used to hold the addresses of information subject to modification prior to or during the execution of an instruction. The index register contents are available for loading into the stack when required. Modification may be either by addition or subtraction, yielding a new effective address.

index value—A desired preset value of a controlled quantity used as a target value for an automatic control system.

index word register—A register which stores a word used to modify addresses under the direction of the control section of the computer.

indicator—A device which registers conditions resulting from computations.

indicator chart—A chart or table used by the programmer to record items concerning the indicators in the program. The indicator chart can be a useful part of the program documentation, since indicators are often used to vary the sequence of operations within the program.

indirect address—An address that specifies a location that contains either a direct address or another indirect address. Also called ***multilevel address*** or *deferred address*.

indirect addressing—A system of addressing a location that contains the address of data instead of the data itself. Indirect addressing is any level of addressing other than the first level of direct addressing. It forms a system of computer cross referencing.

inductance—The property of a metallic conductor or circuit element containing metal which opposes changes in the current flowing through the circuit.

inductive coupling—Coupling between circuits and conductors due to mutual inductance and a source of potential interference.

industrial control—The control of machines, processes, and systems involved in manufacturing operations.

industrial control modules—Electronic control modules designed primarily for industrial control applications. Examples include analog multiplexers, transducer amplifiers, analog-to-digital converters, sample-and-hold devices, and digital-to-analog converters.

industrial control communications—Communications equipment designed for industrial control applications.

industrial data processing—Data processing used for industrial applications.

industrial microcomputers—A microcomputer family designed specifically for industrial applications. Industrial microcomputers usually require a full range of memories and interface equipment for the specific applications. The microcomputer can monitor the process and transmit control signals when desired by the programmer. Typical applications include pollution control, utility control, machine tool control, and material control systems. Interface equipment should be rugged and simple (such as pushbutton controls with fixed displays), although more complex applications use keyboards, alphanumeric displays, printers, floppy disks, and tape cassettes.

inequivalence—A Boolean *exclusive-OR* operator which produces a true output if only one of the two input variables it connects is true.

INPUTS		OUTPUT
A	B	C
0	0	0
1	0	1
0	1	1
1	1	0

inequivalence gate—A device or circuit which performs the inequivalence operation.

information—The aggregation of data which produces a whole idea, condition, or situation. Information may be a set of symbols which indicates alternatives for a situation. Information is usually derived from data.

information bits—Any bits that are generated by the data source and not used for error control. Information theory provides that all information can be represented by some collection of bits, regardless of the complexity of the information.

information content—The gross information content is the number of bits needed to transmit a message over a noiseless system with a specified accuracy, regardless of redundancy. *Net information content* is the minimum number required for essential information only.

information feedback system—An information transmission system used in telecommunications which utilizes an echo check to verify the accuracy of the transmission.

information heading—That portion of a message which contains control information such as the identification of originating station, the identification of a sending device or system, message priority, and message routing information.

information processing—The execution of a systematic sequence of operations performed on data or information. In a typical microprocessor system, the processor accepts data, interprets it, and outputs the results.

Information processing activities include routing operations, arithmetic, and diagnostic operations. In small systems, these operations will be performed by one processor or a single arithmetic processor and another processor for routing and diagnostics. Larger systems will use a separate processor for system diagnostics.

information retrieval—The methods and procedures required for recovering specific information from stored data. Information retrieval may involve the cataloging of data so that all or part may be called out at any time.

information separator—The IS character, used to identify the boundary of information in a message.

information system—The network of all communication methods within an organization.

information theory—A branch of science involved in the likelihood of accurate communications and transmission of information. Information theory uses mathematical analysis to determine the efficiency of communications techniques.

inherited error—An error which is carried forward from a previous step in processing. An inherited error produces an initial error or offset for the next processing step.

inhibit—A computer operation that prevents another operation from taking place. An inhibit might be used on a bus system to disable a channel to allow another control of the bus.

inhibit gate—A circuit used as a switch and usually placed in parallel with the circuit it is controlling.

inhibiting input—A computer gate input which can prevent outputs which might otherwise occur.

inhibiting signal—A signal which prevents an operation from taking place.

inhibit pulse—A pulse used to prevent an operation from taking place.

initial condition mode—A mode in analog computers where all integrators are inoperative and the required initial conditions are applied to the system.

initialize—To set the preliminary steps for a routine that are not to be repeated, such as setting counters and addresses to zero.

initializing—The preliminary steps of arranging instructions and data in memory that are not to be repeated.

initial program load—The procedure required to cause an operating system to begin execution. Also referred to as initial program loading, or initial program loader (abbreviated *IPL*). Load and loading usually refer to the procedure, while loader may refer to a routine which makes it possible to load and execute another program.

inline—A method of processing in which all individual transactions are completely processed without the records being grouped or arranged.

inline assembly—A mechanical assembly operation in which a line of assembly heads inserts electrical components into circuit boards.

inline package—See ***dual-inline package***.

inline procedures—A set of statements used in COBOL for the controlling of program operations.

inline processing—A system that processes transactions in the sequence in which they arrive, without any sorting or arranging.

inline subroutine—A subroutine inserted directly into the operational sequence of processing. Inline subroutines are recopied at each point they are required in a routine.

input—A device or set of devices used to bring data into another device. An input may be a channel for impressing or inserting a state or condition on another device, or a device or process involved in an input operation. Many times input is used as an all-encompassing term for input data, input signal, or input terminal when such usage is clear within a given context.

input area—Internal storage area into which data from external storage is transferred.

input block—A section of internal storage reserved for data from external storage concerning processing and storage operations.

input buffer register—A register that receives data from input devices such as tapes and disks and then transfers it to internal storage.

input channel—A channel for impressing a state or condition on a device or circuit. Also called an *input*.

input data—Data entered into a computer system for processing.

input device—A device used for conveying data into another device, such as the units designed to bring information into a computer: card readers, transducers, and keyboards.

input editing—Operations done on input data to convert the format for more convenient processing and storage. Input editing may also check the data for proper format, completeness, and accuracy. Many times, the input data has been formatted for the convenience of humans and must be reformatted for efficient machine usage.

input equipment—Equipment used for transferring data and instructions into a data processing system. Input equipment includes all peripherals used to gather or collect data.

input impedance—An impedance which is measured at the input terminals of a device, usually under no-load or other specified conditions.

input module—A packaged functional device or unit used for conveying data into another device.

input converter—An analog-to-digital converter packaged for process control applications.

input/output—Pertaining to either input or output or both. Abbreviated *I/O*.

input/output channel—A circuit path which allows independent communication between the processor and external devices. Input/output channels may transfer data between memory and external interfaces in blocks of any size without disturbing working registers in the processor. Multiple channels are allowed to operate concurrently with hardware priority control of each channel. Transfers are in full words, with automatic packing and unpacking allowed in some systems.

input/output control program—The control of input and output operations by the supervisory program.

input/output control system—A group of macroinstruction routines (abbreviated *IOCS*) for handling the transfer of data between main storage and external devices. The routines can be divided into two parts: physical and logical.

input/output devices—Hardware capable of entering data into a machine and accepting data from the machine for processing into a form suitable for humans or other processing units. Also called *input/output equipment*.

input/output device controller—A control unit with the necessary logic circuitry to interconnect one or more peripheral devices with the input/output interface. Many controllers can operate multiple devices as long as they are the same type.

input/output executive—A modular programming technique for peripheral input/output device management and support. The executive program can free the user from time-dependent service routines and provide a well-defined protocol system.

input/output processor—A secondary processor (abbreviated *IOP*) used to transfer operations to and from the main memory.

input/output request words—Control words that are used for input/output requests that are stored in the message reference block until the I/O operation is completed.

input/output table—A plotting machine which generates a function representing the input of a device plotted against the output.

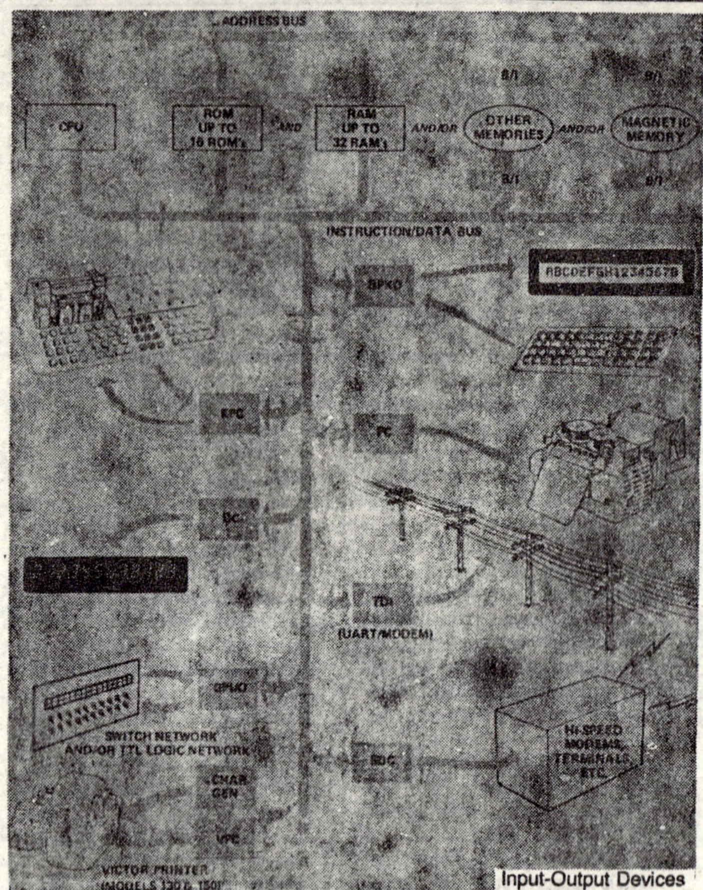

Input-Output Devices

input/output unit—A device such as a modem or terminal designed for manual, mechanical, electronic, video, or audio entry to and output from the computer.

input program—A routine to direct or control the reading of programs and data into the computer system. Input programs may be internally stored or wired and may use a bootstrap operation for housekeeping and control operations.

input reference—A value used to compare the deviation or error of a measured variable. The input reference is a selected value and is also known as the set point or desired value.

input register—A register which accepts data from outside the computer at one speed and supplies the information to the computer calculating unit at a different, usually much higher, speed.

input storage—Containment of input data for processing. Successive groups of data can be compared for the correct format and are held until signaled for by the program.

input stream—The sequence of job control statements submitted to an operating system on an input unit. Also called *input job stream* or *job input stream*.

input translator—A section of a program that converts a programmer's instructions into operators and operands for the computer. A translator can also check the input for errors of syntax.

input unit—Hardware used to supply the computer with coded information for processing.

input work queue—A waiting line of job control statements from which jobs and job steps are selected for processing.

inquiry—The interrogation of the contents of storage from a local or remote point by keyboard, keypad, or other device.

inquiry processing—A type of processing in which inquiries and records from a number of terminals are used to interrogate and update one or more master files maintained by the central system. Also called inquiry and transaction processing.

inquiry station—A remote terminal from which interrogation into computing or data processing equipment is made. Information is placed into the computer through a keyboard and is simultaneously displayed on a screen. A reply to the inquiry is then displayed on the screen until the operator desires to erase the display using an erase button on the console. Also called *inquiry terminal*.

inserted subroutine—A subroutine that must be relocated and injected into the main routine at each place it is used.

instability—A measure of the fluctuations or irregularities in the performance of a variable, circuit, device, or system.

installation time—Time required for installing, connecting, and testing either hardware or software (or both) until acceptance is complete.

instruction—A statement containing information which can be coded and used as a unit in a digital computer to command it to perform one or more operations. An instruction usually contains one or more addresses and may specify arithmetic operations such as addition or multiplication, or control operations for data manipulation. Instructions can be grouped as follows:

(1) Data transfers between registers and memory
(2) Branching operations
(3) Input/output control
(4) Loading and storing accumulators
(5) Restoring registers and accumulators
(6) Jumps and stack-pointer operations
(7) Binary and decimal arithmetic
(8) Set and reset interrupts
(9) Increment and decrement registers and memory

instruction address—The address which must be used to fetch an instruction.

instruction address register—The register (abbreviated *IAR*) which holds the address of the instruction to be executed next in the program sequence without regard to branching or interrupts. Also called *program counter*.

instruction area—That part of storage selected to store the group of instructions to be executed. The instruction area normally is used to hold the microcomputer program.

instruction characters—Characters used as code elements to initiate, modify, and stop control operations. An example would be the CR (carriage return) character.

instruction code—All of the symbols and definitions used to systemize the instructions for a given computer or executive routine.

instruction control unit—Those parts of a computer (abbreviated *ICU*) that allow the retrieval of instructions in the proper sequence with the interpretation of each instruction and the application of the proper commands to the ALU and other parts in accordance with that interpretation. A typical ICU contains a read-only memory in which the microinstructions are stored along with the address control logic for microprogram branching.

instruction counter—A counter used to indicate the location of the next instruction to be interpreted.

instruction deck—A deck of punched cards which contain data defining the operations to be performed by the computer system.

instruction diagnostic—A device using hardware and software that completely tests all CPU instructions in all modes, including interrupts.

instruction execution logic—The logic that allows each instruction to be retrieved or fetched from memory, decoded, and executed. The instruction execution logic may involve program counters, address registers, instruction registers, and the general-purpose register, along with many transfers between these units and memory.

instruction modification—An alteration in the operational code of a command or instruction such that if the routine is repeated, the computer will perform a different operation.

instruction register—A 4- to 16-bit register (abbreviated *IR*) used to hold the instruction currently being processed after it is brought to the control section from memory. The instruction register can be used to specify the initial step in a microprogram, and as an internal register to store temporary data for microprogram control.

instruction repertoire—The set of operations represented in a given operational code.

instruction set—The total structured group of characters and definitions to be transferred to the computer as operations are executed. Usually the instructions are listed in alphabetical order and include binary and decimal arithmetic along with logic, shift, store, rotate, load, branch, interrupt, and stack operations. Instruction sets can be encoded in binary, octal, or hexadecimal, with the names of operations in mnemonic form using combinations of letters and numbers.

instruction word—The grouping of letters or digits into a single unit which defines operations to be performed by the computer. The instruction word may be a complete computer word, or part of the computer word which is executed as an instruction.

instrumentation—Devices for measuring, recording, and controlling physical processes and quantitative phenomena.

integral action limiter—A program or device that limits the output value of a signal due to integral action at a predetermined value.

integral boundary—A location in main storage at which a fixed-length field must be positioned. The integral boundary may be a half-word or double word, and its address is a multiple of the length of the field.

integral control action—A control action in which the rate of change of output is proportional to the input.

integrated circuit—An interconnected array of components fabricated from a single crystal of semiconductor material by etching, doping, and diffusion, and which is capable of performing at least one and sometimes many complete circuit functions.

integrated component—A single structure with a number of elements which cannot be separated without destroying the function or functions of the device.

integrated data processing—A data processing approach (abbreviated *IDP*) in which all stages of processing are carried out using a coherent systems approach, such as, a business system where data for orders and buying are combined to accomplish the functions of scheduling, invoicing, and accounting.

integrated emulator—An emulator program whose execution is controlled by an operating system in a multiprogramming environment.

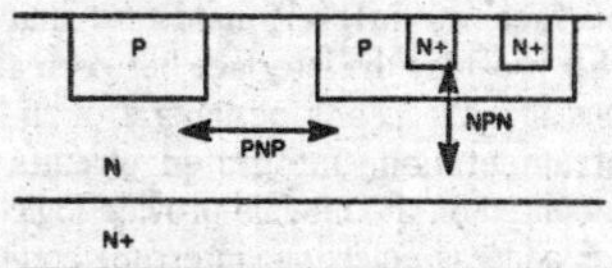

Integrated Injection Logic

integrated injection logic—An integrated circuit logic (abbreviated *IIL* or I^2L) that consists of interconnected bipolar transistors of both polarities. A cross section of an I^2L chip consists of an npn transistor operated in a vertical mode, while a lateral pnp transistor is used as a current source and a load for the preceding stage. Isolation is automatically accomplished between the collectors, allowing high packing densities. Besides high packing density, it offers a good speed-power product along with versatility and low cost.

integrated monolithic circuit—A one-chip circuit that uses geometric etching and conductive ink deposition techniques to achieve circuit functions on a single semiconductor chip. Also called an *integrated circuit*.

integrated amplifier—1. An analog-computer amplifier that has an output voltage proportional to the area under a time-curve plot of a variable between a reference time and any arbitrary point in time. 2. A high-fidelity stereo amplifier that includes an integral preamplifier with all necessary controls.

integrator—A unit or device that performs the mathematical function of integration, usually with reference to time. Integrators include circuits which integrate signals over a period of time and any system with an output proportional to the input.

intelligent cable—An interfacing system which allows input and output operations along with word and byte transfers to occur in any mix on all channels concurrently. An intelligent cable provides a low-cost parallel interface while freeing the designer from costly development time involved in interfacing the peripherals. Some features of intelligent cables include:

(1) TTL compatibility with low-power Schottky circuits
(2) Handshaking and strobing capability
(3) Multiple device control
(4) Microprogrammed interface control
(5) Standard ribbon cabling

intelligent disk storage—A disk system that does its own data base management; only commands from the host computer and data field information need to be passed to the system controller. All indexing, searching, and deblocking are done on the disk system controller.

intelligent keyboard system—A keyboard system that performs all alphanumeric and numeric operations for keying, editing, calculating, storing, compressing, and printing.

intelligent terminals—A terminal capable of data processing using storage and a stored program which is available to the user. Typical configurations include 4096 bytes of user memory with a minidisk system or magnetic tape cassettes. Expansion allows up to 16,384 bytes with additional cassette stations and panel displays. Intelligent terminals allow more of the communications function to be done outside of the host computer, thus increasing the potential for terminal applications.

interacting simulator—A simulator that precisely duplicates the timing of the microcomputer to allow the user total interactive control to execute and alter the program.

interblock gap—The area on a data medium used to indicate the end of a block or record. Also called *block gap*.

interconnection line—A transmission line connecting two systems or networks which allows energy to be transferred in either direction. Also called *tie line*. A large interconnection is called *giant tie* or *regional interconnection*.

interface—1. A common or shared boundary between instruments, devices, or systems, which is functionally compatible with connected units. An interface enables devices to exchange information among devices and implies a connection to complete the interchange. 2. The specification required for the interconnection between two systems. For example, the EIA interface is a standard set of signal characteristics including voltages, currents, and time durations for communication terminals.

interface bus—A bus that provides the interface connections and timing to interconnect different types of instruments, and either programmable calculators or computers to form complete instrumentation systems.

interface cards—Circuit boards or cards that permit the connection of various instruments and peripherals to the CPU.

interface module—A hardware unit that provides the interface between a bus and the user's peripheral or instrumentation. Integrated circuits mounted on the module provide logic for address selection, interrupt control, and byte input/output transfer. Interface modules for industrial microcomputer systems may include modules for digital communication, power switches, analog-to-digital and digital-to-analog conversion, timekeeping clocks and pulsers.

interface standard—A format that allows matching the characteristics of two or more units, systems, or programs so that they can be easily joined together.

interference—Electrical or magnetic disturbances that cause unwanted responses or effects (usually voltage spikes or *transients*).

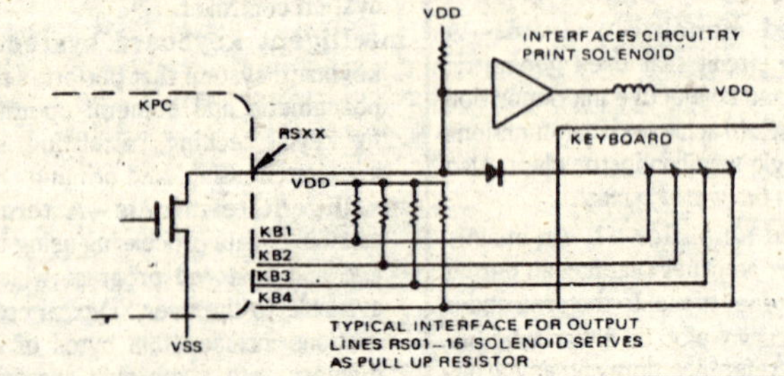

TYPICAL INTERFACE FOR OUTPUT LINES RS01–16 SOLENOID SERVES AS PULL UP RESISTOR

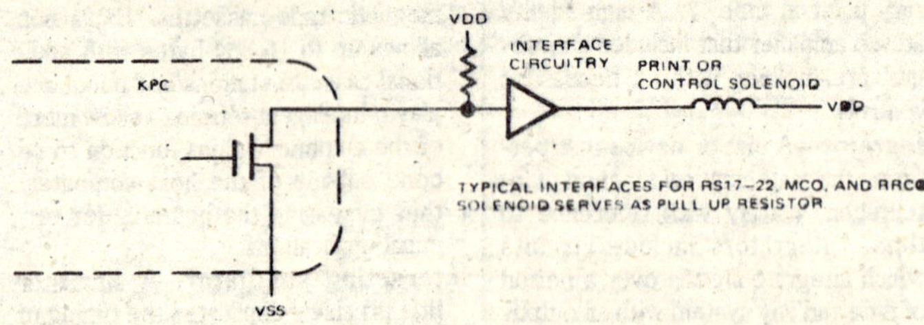

TYPICAL INTERFACES FOR RS17–22, MCO, AND RRCO. SOLENOID SERVES AS PULL UP RESISTOR

Interfaces

interlace—1. To assign successive storage location numbers to physically separated storage locations on a magnetic drum to reduce access time. 2. To superimpose two TV raster scans so that the lines formed by one scan appear as alternating lines of the other.

interleave—To arrange parts of one sequence or group with parts from another such that each sequence or group retains its identity.

interleaving—1. The inserting of segments of one program into another program to allow the two to be executed essentially in a simultaneous mode. 2. A process of splitting memory into two sections with two paths to the central processor to speed processing. Interleaving allows a second word to be read during the half-cycle when the previously read word is being written back into the memory.

intermediate cycle—An unconditional branch instruction that may address itself.

intermittent control—A control system in which the control variable is monitored periodically with an intermittent correcting signal supplied to the controller.

intermittent error—A sporadic error which may not be detected when diagnostic programs or routines are run.

internal arithmetic—Computations performed by the arithmetic and logic unit.

internal interrupt—A control signal which diverts the attention of the computer to consider an extraordinary event or circumstance. An internal interrupt causes the control of the program to be transferred to a subordinate, which then corresponds to the stimulus. Internal interrupts are used primarily to synchronize the program with the termination of input/output transfers, and to signal the occurrence of errors.

internally stored program—The set of instructions stored in internal memory as contrasted with those stored on cards, disks, or tape.

internal memory—Addressable storage directly controlled by the CPU of the microcomputer. Internal memory is the total memory or storage accessible to the CPU and forms an integral part of the microcomputer. Also called *internal storage*.

internal storage—See *internal memory*.

interpolation—The process of finding a value between two known values, and the procedure for determining values of a function between known and observed values.

interpret—To translate or decode, as in converting nonmachine language into machine language, or to print the graphic characters represented by the holes in a punched card.

interpret program—A program that translates and executes each source language statement before operating on the next statement.

interpreter—1. A machine that will accept a punched card with no printing on it, read the information from the punched holes, and print a translation using characters in specified rows and columns. 2. An executive routine which translates a stored program expressed in a machine-like pseudo code into machine code and performs the indicated operations using subroutines as they are translated.

The interpreter is used like a closed subroutine which operates successively on the sequence of pseudo instructions and operands. It is usually entered as a closed subroutine and left with a pseudo-code exit instruction. Since the interpreter operates on the instructions one by one and executes each statement before starting on the next, it tends to be slower than other methods of translation.

interpretive code—Interpretive routine.

interpretive routine—A routine that decodes and immediately executes instructions written as pseudo codes. The essential characteristics of an interpretive routine is that a particular pseudo-code operation must be decoded each time that it is executed. This is contrasted with a compiler, which decodes the pseudo codes into a machine language routine for execution at a later time.

interpretive translation program—A program designed to translate each instruction of a source language into computer instructions and allow each one to be executed before translating the next instruction. If the program allows programs written for one type of computer to be run on a different type, it is often called a *simulator program.*

interrecord gap—An interval of space or time left between recording portions of data or records. Interrecord gaps are used to prevent errors from overwriting, and tape start-stop operations.

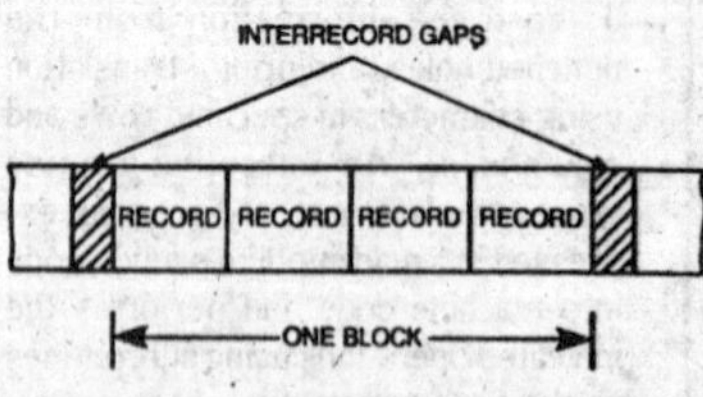

interrupt—To temporarily disrupt the normal operation of a routine by a special signal from the computer. Usually the normal operation can be resumed from that point at a later time. As the peripheral units interface with the CPU, interrupts occur on a frequent basis. Multiple interrupt requests will require the processor to delay, or prevent further interrupts, or break into a procedure to modify operations.

With the use of interrupts, throughput increases because the processor is allowed to perform calculations concurrent with input/output operations. The major characteristics of interrupts include:

(1) *Latency*, the time to recognize the interrupt and branch to the service routine.

(2) *Response*, the time to identify the interrupted device and begin execution of the device service code.

(3) *Software overhead*, the time required to get to the service routine and return to the main program.

An example of interrupt usefulness occurs in printer buffering. Serial printers tend to be slow and to print a line of characters without interrupts; a microprocessor transfers a character to the printer and then waits until that character is printed until it transfers the next character. Character transfer

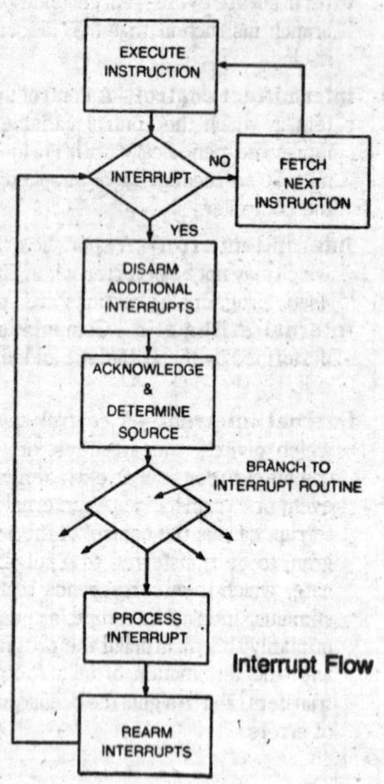

Interrupt Flow

takes only a few microseconds, while character printing may take up to 100 milliseconds per character; the microprocessor spends most of the time waiting for printing completion. A program interrupt can eliminate this waiting time, so that when the printer is busy, the microprocessor can be involved in other tasks and return only when required to transfer a character.

interrupt count pulse—An interrupt level that is triggered from pulses provided by the clock. Each pulse causes an instruction in the count-pulse location to be executed.

interrupt device—The external device requesting an interrupt, such as a communications unit or timing signal.

interrupt enable and disable—Instructions used to set and reset an interrupt control flip-flop.

interrupt input lines—Signal channels that are used for inputs that set the interrupt flags of the control registers.

interrupt mask bit—A specific bit used to prevent the CPU from responding to further interrupt requests until cleared by execution of programmed instructions. It can also be manipulated by specific mask bit instructions.

interrupt mask word—A word used to enable or disable interrupts in a system. Each bit of the word is interrogated to enable or inhibit a specific device interrupt.

TYPICAL INTERRUPT MASK WORD

BIT POSITION	DEVICE
0	DISK UNIT 1
1	DISK UNIT 2
2	DISK UNIT 3
3	MEMORY PROTECT VIOLATION
4	REAL-TIME CLOCK
5	TELETYPE
6	PAPER TAPE READER
7	COMPUTER CONSOLE
8	TEMPERATURE RECORDER

interrupt freeze mode—A condition in analog computers where all computing action is stopped and all values are held as they were when the interrupt occurred.

interrupt module—A device which acts as a monitor for a group of field contacts and notifies the computer when an external priority request is generated.

interrupt response time—The elapsed time between an interrupt and the start of the interrupt-handling subroutine. The difference between the total time elapsed and the actual execution time is the overhead time.

interrupt signal feedback—A signal indicating that the interrupt signal has advanced to the waiting or active state. The signal is not present once the interrupt level is reset to the disarmed or armed state.

interrupt vector—1. An interrupt channel reserved for the highest priority external function; in many cases this is a real-time interrupt from the 60 Hz line source. 2. A polling scheme in which the highest priority device or devices are hard-wired to achieve fixed-priority encoding. The encoded value is then used as a system address to transfer control to the interrupt response routine.

interval polling timer—A control program which keeps track of the time of day in order to interrupt the system periodically as required.

interstage punching—A form of card punching in which either the odd or even columns are not used.

interword gap—The time or space allowed between words on a tape, disk, or drum. The interword gap allows the medium to be switched and is used for the control of individual words.

inversion—1. Any procedure which is used to reverse the order of items of data. 2. The process of reversing the polarity of any DC voltage or signal.

invert—1. To place in contrary order, as to exchange the numerator with the denominator in a fraction. 2. To reverse the polarity of any voltage or signal, whether DC or pulsed.

inverter—1. A circuit or device that takes in a positive signal and outputs a negative one, or takes in a negative signal and outputs a positive signal. 2. A device that changes direct current to alternating current, with or without a voltage level change.

inverting amplifier—An amplifier with an output voltage that is equal in magnitude to the input, but opposite in sign.

involuntary interrupt—An interrupt which is not caused by the object program, but affects the running of the object program. An example is the termination of a peripheral transfer which causes the operating system to stop the object program while the interrupt is serviced.

I/O—Abbreviation for *input/output*.

ion—Any atom or molecule that has a resultant electric charge due to loss or gain of valence electrons.

ion implantation—A method of introducing impurities into semiconductors that uses high energy ion impingement on the silicon surface. Ion implantation allows shallow emitter junctions with a high degree of control. Ion implantation is used in CMOS circuits, shift registers, semiconductor memories, solar cells, and even resistors.

IOCS—Abbreviation for *input/output control system*.

IOP—Abrreviation for *input/output processor*, a device which performs bidirectional data transfer between the main memory and peripheral units. A typical IOP can handle up to 32 peripherals, but only one device operates at a given time.

I/O test program—Refers to a special PROM containing a program which plugs into and checks input/output circuit boards.

IPL—Abbreviation for *initial program loader*, a program that reads the supervisor into main storage and then transfers program control to the supervisor.

ipot—Acronym for *inductive potentiometer*, a variable resistor which uses a metallic resistive element such as nickel-chromium wire rather than deposited carbon.

irreversible process—A device or mechanism which does not return to its original state after a disturbance is removed.

isolated digital output module—A unit that provides an output interface along with electrical isolation between the microcomputer and a process control or peripheral device. Isolation is typically 1500V, and outputs of up to 50V can be provided.

isotropic—Used to describe a medium with physical properties that do not vary with direction.

isotropic dielectric—A dielectric insulator material with electrical properties that are independent of the direction of the applied field.

I^2L—Abbreviation for *integrated injection logic*, a logic family that uses only npn and pnp transistors. I^2L offers high performance and low costs along with ease of interfacing with other circuits.

item—A unit of information relating to a single object, as a set of one or more fields, or a collection of data characters which are treated as a unit. For example, a record may contain a number of items such as fields, and a file may contain a number of items such as records.

item advance—A technique used for the grouping of records by operating successively on different records in storage.

item design—A specification which contains the fields that make up an item, the order in which the fields are to be recorded, and the number of characters to be allocated to each field.

item size—The magnitude of an item expressed in words, characters, or blocks.

iterate—To repeat a loop or a series of steps in a program or routine.

iterative—Descriptive of a procedure or process that repeatedly executes an operation or series of operations until some condition is satisfied.

iterative process—A process for calculating a desired result by repeating a cycle of operations, which comes progressively closer to the result. For example, the square root of a number may be approximated by an iterative process using addition, subtraction, and division.

iterative impedance—The impedance of a four-terminal network when a large number of identical networks are cascaded.

J

jack—A connecting device into which the wires of a circuit or device are attached.

jack panel—An assembly of a number of jacks mounted on a board or panel.

jam—A pileup of cards in a card processing machine.

JCL—Abbreviation for *job control language*, a programming language specifically used to code job control statements.

jitter—A distortion caused by shifts in the time or phase position of pulses which can cause difficulty in synchronization and detection.

J-K flip-flop—A flip-flop with two inputs, J and K, with the following features:

(1) A clock pulse will not cause a transition if either input is enabled.

(2) If both inputs are enabled, the output will change states.

(3) No indeterminate conditions are allowed.

job—A group of tasks prescribed as a unit of work for the computer. A job consists of one or more steps and may include programs, linkages, files, and instructions for the operating system.

job control program—A program that is called into storage to prepare each job or step to be run. It may assign input/output devices and set switches for program use.

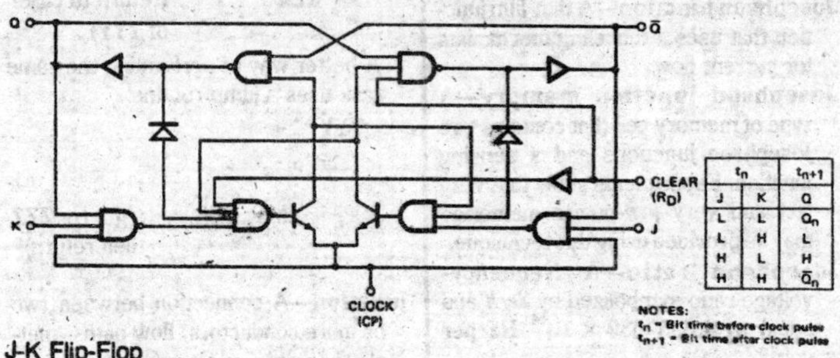

Q
$\bar{Q}$
CLEAR
(R_D)
K
J
CLOCK
(CP)
t_n		t_{n+1}
J	K	Q
L	L	Q_n
L	H	L
H	L	H
H	H	$\bar{Q}_n$
NOTES:
t_n = Bit time before clock pulse
t_{n+1} = Bit time after clock pulse

J-K Flip-Flop

job control language—A language (abbreviated *JCL*) used to code job control statements.

job control statement—A statement used in identifying a job or describing its requirements to the operating system.

job input stream—The input, usually consisting of tape or punched cards, that is first sent to the operating system. The job input stream may contain the beginning of job indicators, directions, and programs.

job-oriented terminal—A type of terminal designed to receive source data associated with the job to be performed and capable of transmission with the operating system of which it is a part.

job processing control—That portion of a program that starts job operations, assigns input/output operations, and controls the transfer from one job to another.

job stream—The set of computer jobs in an input queue waiting for initiation and processing.

job step—The execution of that portion of a program identified by a job control statement. Most jobs will have several job steps.

join—To form the logical sum or union.

joint denial—A logical operation that has a true output only if all inputs are false.

joint denial gate—A circuit or device that provides a true output only if all inputs are false.

Josephson junction—A thin-film junction that uses a tunneling mechanism for current flow.

Josephson junction memory—A type of memory cell that contains two Josephson junctions and a sensing junction. Experiments show that very fast and very low-power memories may be provided using this technique.

Josephson ratio—A frequency-voltage ratio symbolized by $2e/h$ and equal to $4.835\ 939 \times 10^{14}$ Hz per volt.

joule—The unit of energy (symbol, J) which describes the work performed when the point of application of one newton is displaced a distance of one meter in the direction of force.

joule effect—The production of heat due to current flow in a conductor.

joule magnetostriction—The effect which causes the length of an iron core to increase when subjected to a longitudinal magnetic field.

JOVIAL—A computer language used for command and control applications that is a version of the *international algebraic language*, an early version of ALGOL. JOVIAL contains facilities for numerical computations along with some data processing.

jump—A departure from the normal sequence of executing instructions. Jumps usually differ from branches in that they do not use the relative addressing mode. Also called *transfer*.

jump instruction—An instruction designed to control the transfer of operations from one point to another in a program.

jump routine—A routine designed to have the computer depart from the regular sequence of instructions and shift to another routine or program. For example, the following sequence in the 8080 microprocessor calls the ZZZ routine:

```
YYY .
    .
    .
      CALL ZZZ   ; (call routine for ZZZ)
      RET        ; (return to caller
                    of YYY)
```

A better way of performing the same task uses a jump routine.

```
YYY .
    .
    .
        JMP ZZZ     ;(go to ZZZ
                     then return)
```

junction—A connection between two or more conductors, flow paths, metals, or semiconductors.

junction box—An enclosure used for connecting different runs of cable in a raceway or conduit.

junction circuit—A circuit connecting two exchanges together which are closer than those found in trunk lines or circuits.

junction diode—A two-terminal device with a single-crystal structure that permits current flow in only one direction. Also called a *junction rectifier*.

junction rectifier—Junction diode.

junction transistor—1. Bipolar transistor. 2. Field-effect transistor without an insulated gate.

junction summing—A technique used in computing amplifiers and control systems where various signals are connected to a common point at the input of the amplifier or control unit.

junk—A term used for unintelligible signals, especially those received from a communications channel. Also called *garbage* and *hash*.

justify—1. To adjust the printing positions of characters on a page such that the rightmost edge of each line is flush with all other lines. 2. To shift the contents of a register such that the least significant bit is at a desired position.

K

K—1. Symbol for ***kelvin***. 2. Symbol (on drawings) to indicate presence of an electromechanical relay. 3. Symbol for ***cathode***. 4. Nonstandard but often used symbol for ***kilohm***. 5. In lowercase form, the SI prefix for ***kilo-***, the prefix meaning thousand. 6. In lowercase form, symbol for ***constant***. 7. In lowercase form, symbol for ***coupling coefficient***. 8. In microcomputer usage, symbol for 1024 (which is the first power of 2 above 1000).

Karnaugh map—A chart or table which shows the combination of logical functions and tends to eliminate duplicate logical expressions by listing all of the similar functions. The Karnaugh map is drawn as a rectangular diagram of variables with overlapping subrectangles such that the intersection of the subrectangles represents a unique combination of variables, and such an intersection is shown for all logical combinations.

kayser—The obsolete unit for wave number, which is the reciprocal for wavelength. The SI unit for wave number is ***reciprocal meter***.

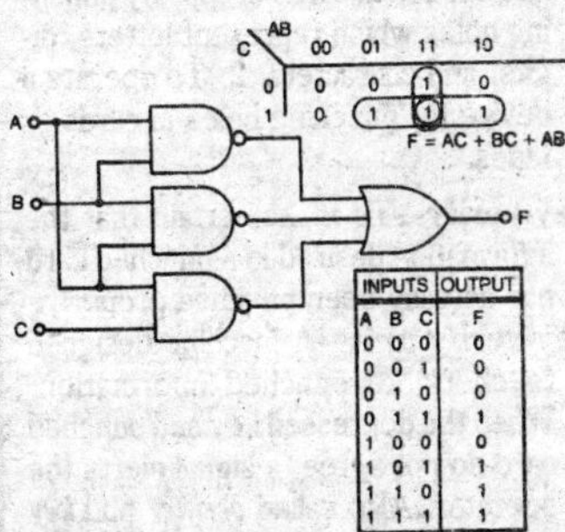

INPUTS			OUTPUT
A	B	C	F
0	0	0	0
0	0	1	0
0	1	0	0
0	1	1	1
1	0	0	0
1	0	1	1
1	1	0	1
1	1	1	1

Karnaugh Map With Logic and Truth Table

Kelvin effect—A property of high-frequency currents in which most of the current flow concentrates near the surface. Also called ***skin effect***.

key—A group of characters used to identify an item or record. 2. A marked lever or switch used for entering a character or command into the system.

keyboard—A unit containing keys for entering data or information into a system. Keyboards may be ***alphanumeric*** (as used for word processing, text processing, and data processing) or ***numeric*** as used for Touch-Tone telephones, accounting machines, and calculators.

keyboard control keys—Switches used in terminals to control and move the cursor on CRT displays, to change the terminal application, or to change the communications mode.

keyboard encoder—A circuit or device that identifies each key function and produces a word corresponding to that function. Some encoders allow the use of custom encoding with the use of PROMs, and error detection for simultaneous key depressions.

keyboard function key—A key which sends out a unique string of characters that represent a code (to the computer), a set of data, or commands to activate peripherals.

keypunch—1. A device used to record information in cards or tape by punching holes which represent letters, digits, and characters. 2. To operate a device for punching holes in cards or tapes.

key-verify—To make certain that the information desired in a punched card has actually been punched properly.

key-verify unit—A machine designed to check keypunched information. When the depressed key and punched card do not agree, a signal alerts the operator. Also called ***verifier*** and ***key verifier***.

keyword—A significant word in the title, abstract, or text that can be used alone or with other significant words to describe a document. A keyword or set or keywords may describe a document's contents, label the document, or assist in identifying or retrieving the document.

keyword-in-context—An index of programs (abbreviated *KWIC*) which lists the programs in alphabetical order with entries for each keyword in the title. The index is prepared by highlighting each keyword of the title in the context of the words on either side of it, and aligning the keywords of all titles alphabetically.

kilo—Prefix indicating multiplication by a factor of 10^3; thousand.

Kipp relay—An alternative term for an electromechanical one-shot or monostable multivibrator, a circuit that has a stable and an unstable state and which goes through a complete cycle in response to a single triggering action.

kit—A set of parts and software assembled by the user for a specific application or specification. Microcomputer kits allow the user a cost-effective system without special hardware design. Kits are available as complete standalone systems for writing, debugging, and executing programs on the microprocessor. They include not only the processor and memory, but also a low-cost set of peripherals. A typical system has an alphanumeric display, an ASCII keyboard, and cassette tape units. Software may include a monitor, editor, and assembler package. A universal system bus may be included to allow the connection of memory and peripherals with several microprocessors.

KSR—Abbreviation for ***keyboard send/receive***, a teletypewriter transmitter and receiver unit that has transmission capability from keyboard only.

KWIC—Abbreviation for ***keyword-in-context***, a title index based upon the use of keywords for programs. The keywords are listed in alphabetical order for identification.

L

label—1. A set of symbols that identify or describe an item, record, message, or file. 2. A code name that classifies a name, term, phrase, or document.

laced card—A card with extra multiple punching in a column to signify the end of a card run. The term is derived from the lacework appearance of the card.

lacing—The extra punching used in a card to indicate the end of a run.

lag—The relative difference between two events, states, or mechanisms.

language—A system for representing and communicating information or data between people or different types of machines. A language consists of a carefully defined set of characters and rules for combining the characters into larger units such as words or expressions. There are also rules for word arrangement and usage to achieve specific meanings. Most computer languages have the following features:

(1) Data objects or structures with descriptions that correspond to nouns and adjectives in natural languages.

(2) Operations and commands which act upon the data objects, corresponding to verbs and adverbs in a natural language.

(3) Control structures to specify the sequence of operations which correspond to phrasing and forming paragraphs in natural languages.

language interpreter—A processor, assembler, or other routine that accepts statements in one language and produces equivalent statements in another language.

language translator—A program or routine that converts statements in one language to equivalent statements in another language. The languages may be computer or machine languages, or natural languages such as English.

large-scale integration—Fabrication of integrated circuits with more than 1000 equivalent transistors on a single semiconductor chip.

laser—Once an acronym for *light amplification by stimulated emission of radiation*, the term has become legitimized as a word describing an amplifier and generator of a narrow and coherent beam of energy in the visible light spectrum.

latch—An arrangment or circuit used to hold data in a ready position until required, usually controlled by another condition or circuit. Also called *lock*.

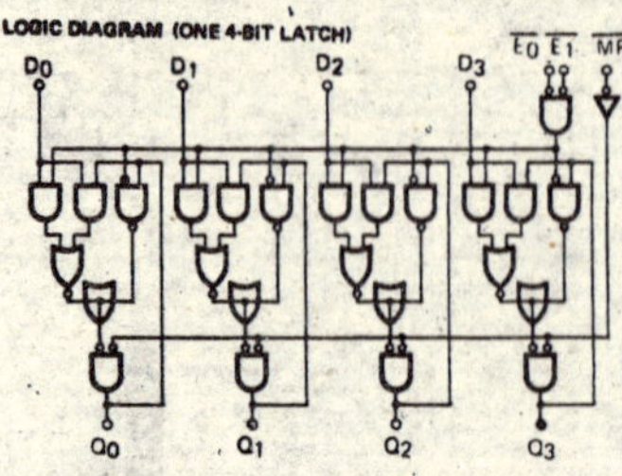

TRUTH TABLE

$\overline{MR}$	$\overline{E_0}$	$\overline{E_1}$	D	Q_n	OPERATION
H	L	L	L	L	Data Entry
H	L	L	H	H	Data Entry
H	L	H	X	Q_{n-1}	Hold
H	H	L	X	Q_{n-1}	Hold
H	H	H	X	Q_{n-1}	Hold
L	X	X	X	L	Reset

X = Don't Care
L = LOW Voltage Level
H = HIGH Voltage Level
Q_{n-1} = Previous Output State
Q_n = Present Output State

Latch

latching—A technique in which data is held in a circuit until other circuits are ready to change this circuit.

latency—Refers to the time required by a computer to deliver information from its memory. In a serial storage system, the latency time becomes the access time minus the word time. In a rotational system, it becomes the time required for the desired location to appear at the heads.

latency time—The time lag between a command for data and the delivery from memory.

lattice filter—A wave filter composed of four branches connected together to form a mesh which functions as a section of the filter. The filter may have a single section, or it may be composed of several sections.

lattice network—A circuit with four branches connected together to form a mesh with the two nonadjacent junctions serving as inputs and the other two serving as outputs. Also called *bridge network*.

lattice spacing—Refers to the length of an edge in a unit cell of a crystal.

layout—The overall plan, structure, or design of a circuit, system, or device. The layout may include the arrangement of data, sequence, size, schematic diagrams, flow diagrams, and outlines of operation or procedure.

LCD—Abbreviation for *liquid-crystal display*, a display technique that uses segments of a liquid crystal solution in a sandwich of glass plates. The light-reflecting properties of the solution are controlled by an electric field.

leader—1. A record which precedes a group of detailed records, giving information about the group which is not in the detailed records. 2. An unused or blank length of tape or film at the beginning of a reel.

leakage—Refers to undesired losses due to stray conductive paths in components and circuit boards.

leakage current—Current flow due to undesirable conductive paths across or through insulating surfaces or barriers.

leapfrog test—A checking routine that copies itself using storage. A typical leapfrog routine might:

(1) Perform a series of operations on one group of storage locations.
(2) Transfer to another group of storage locations.
(3) Check the correctness of the transfer.
(4) Repeat the series of operations for the new locations.
(5) Continue transferring and repeating until all storage locations are occupied.

left-justify—1. To adjust the printing positions of characters on a page such that the left margin is aligned flush. 2. To shift the contents of a register so that the most significant bit is at a specified position.

level—1. The absolute magnitude of a quantity. 2. The degree of subordination in a hierarchy, as in the different levels of recorded information on paper tape.

library—A collection of routines and subroutines available to a computer. A typical microcomputer library might consist of:

(1) A loading and debugging program
(2) Text editor
(3) Resident assembler
(4) Cross assembler
(5) Floating point arithmetic program.
(6) PROM programming package
(7) Tape conversion program
(8) Multiply/divide package

LIFO—Acronym for *last-in-first-out*, a queue technique in which the last line in is the first to be operated on. LIFO is used in pushdown stack operations. Also called *FILO*.

light-emitting diode—A diode with a light-producing characteristic used as a low-cost, low-power indicator on panels and in displays. Light-emitting diodes are available in several colors and operate at current levels of 5–10 mA.

light pen—A photosensitive device that can cause the computer to change or modify the display on a CRT screen. As the display information is selected by the operator, the light pen signals the computer using a pulse. The computer then instructs other points or lines to be plotted on the screen following the pen movements.

limited integrator—An integrator which ceases to integrate when the output exceeds a specified limit.

limiter—1. A transducer in which the output does not vary above a critical threshold value. 2. A circuit that restricts amplitude to a specified level. 3. In an FM receiver, a circuit that eliminates variations in amplitude to prevent AM components from being processed.

linear—A function that varies in direct proportion to the input.

linear amplifier—A class A or AB amplifier that develops an output in direct proportion to the input signal.

linear displacement transducer—A transducer that produces an output that is a direct function of position along a single axis.

linear interpolation—A mode of machine-tool control which uses the data contained in a block to produce constant velocities for two or more axes simultaneously.

linearity—A relationship between two quantities when a change in one is directly proportional to a change in the other.

linear network—A circuit with electrical elements that remain constant in magnitude with varying currents.

linear optimization—The set of procedures used to find maximum and minimum values of a linear function subject to specific constraints or conditions.

linear program—An algorithmic program used to select one solution from a set of possible solutions to a given problem based on desired maximum or minimum requirements.

line circuit—A physical circuit path, as a transmission or communication line.

line code—A single instruction contained on one line in a program. A line code may contain one or more addresses, or one or more operations. Also called *program line*. A line code for addition in the 6800 system is:

ADD A 1, Y ; (add Y + 1 to accumulator)

line control block—An area of main storage (abbreviated *LCB*) used to hold control data for operations on communication lines.

line discipline—The procedures and rules used to adjust the operating values of transmission systems for the desired control. Line discipline includes considerations in polling and queuing priority.

Controllers are available to make the printer transparent to the host computer.

link—1. A transmit and receive system for connecting two terminal locations. 2. A connecting path between two units of switching apparatus, or that part of a subprogram that connects it with the main program. 3. A 1-bit register used as an extension of the accumulator in some systems. As a link register, the link is used in arithmetic operations and can be cleared, set, and complemented as part of the accumulator.

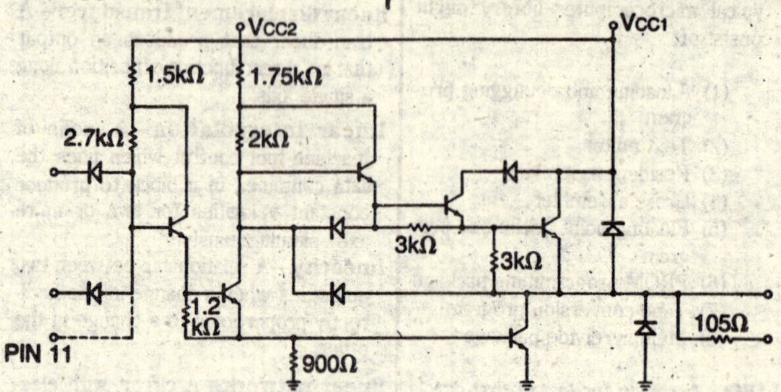

Line Driver

line driver—An amplifier used to transmit analog or digital signals over a transmission line or circuit.

line feed character—The LF character, a format effector that causes the print or display position to be moved to the next line. In ASCII, the LF character generates a binary 10 (0000 1010), which is decoded to cause line feed at the receiving terminal printer.

line printer—A machine that prints an entire line of characters at one time. The characters are typically contained on a series of continuously rotating disks. The machine stops the disks at the right characters and stamps a single line in a fraction of a second. High-speed line printers may operate at a rate of 1000 lines per minute or more.

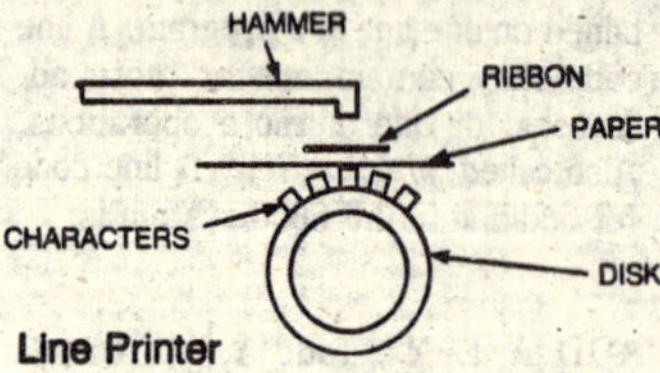

Line Printer

linkage—A technique for providing connections for entry and exit of a closed subroutine from the main routine.

link bit—Refers to the single bit contained in the link register. The link bit can be used as an indicator for overflow from the accumulator or other diagnostic operations. (See also *link*, 3.)

link editor—A software system used to load and connect the object program output from a BASIC or FORTRAN compiler, or an assembler into a main program.

link indicator—An indicator used to display the contents of the link register.

liquid crystal—A type of display technology that uses segments of a liquid crystal solution between glass plates. An electric field at the plates causes the solution to change its light-reflecting properties selectively. Energizing the proper segments produces the desired display output.

LISP—Acronym for *list processing*, an interpretive language designed for the handling of symbolic lists and recursive data. LISP can also be used for manipulation of mathematical and logical operations.

list—An ordered set of items. A pushdown list is a set of items where the last item entered is the first item of the list, and the position of the other items is pushed back by one. A pushup list has items entered at the end of the list, and the other items maintain the same relative position in the list.

listing—A printed list that is a by-product of a program or operation. For example, an assembly listing would contain in logical instruction sequence the details of a routine with the coded and symbolic notation along with the actual notation established by the assembly routine.

list processing—A method of processing data in the form of lists. Chained lists are used to allow the order of items to be changed without altering their physical contents.

list-processing language—A language such as LISP designed for symbol manipulation. List-processing languages are used mainly as research tools and have proved valuable in the design of compilers and problem-solving simulation. Other uses of list processing languages include:

(1) Mathematical proofs
(2) Information retrieval
(3) Pattern recognition
(4) Algebraic programming

list-processing structure—A technique where list structures or sets of data items are used to organize the memory in computers. The memory is organized into several lists having symbolic names, headers, or starting records and a number of entries. The header contains the first data entry address, and each data entry contains one or more data items and the address of the next entry in the list.

list structure—A set of data items with each element containing the address of the successor item or element. It is relatively easy to insert or delete data items in a list structure, and such lists tend to reach the capacity of fixed storage systems.

literal—A symbol which represents the value expressed rather than a reference to data. A literal in a source program is data and not a reference to data. The literal 8 represents the value eight.

literal operand—An operand that specifies precisely the value of a constant rather than an address where the constant is stored. Literal operands allow coding to be more concise than operands using data name references.

load—The process of filling a storage unit in a computer. Loading includes the reading of the beginning of a program into virtual storage and the modifications necessary to the program for transfer of control for execution. Loading also includes the transfer of storage between memory units. A typical load operation transfers the contents of a memory byte and stores it in the accumulator. The memory is read bit by bit, and as each bit is read, the next sequential accumulator bit will be set or reset to reproduce the status of the memory bit just read.

load-and-go—A machine operation and compiling technique which uses pseudo language for conversion directly into machine language. The program is then run without the need of an output machine language.

loader—A program that operates as an input device to transfer data from offline memory to online memory. A loader usually performs the following functions:

(1) Load a string of bytes into memory.

(2) Check each byte for correct transmission.
(3) Check each word to insure that it is a valid instruction.
(4) Check the number of bytes read.
(5) Convert relocatable addresses to absolute addresses.
(6) Satisfy all external references and labels.

loader routine—A routine generated to perform program-loading operations. A loader routine usually includes printout of memory content upon request. Also called loading routine, since once it is in storage, it is able to bring other information into storage.

loading routine—*Loader routine.*

location—A storage position which can store one word and which is usually identified by an address.

location counter—Refers to the control section of a computer and the register contained in it where the address of the current instruction is held. Also called *instruction address counter* and *program counter.*

locking—1. Use of code extension characters to change the interpretation of a specified number of following characters. 2. Control of an oscillating circuit using a correction signal. 3. Latching.

log—The process of recording, or collecting messages pertinent to a machine run. These include:

(1) Run identification
(2) Input/output identification
(3) Identification of stops and action taken
(4) A history of manual switch settings or key-ins

logarithmic amplifier—An amplifier with an output that is a logarithmic function of the input signal, such as in decibel meters and some types of recorders. Also called *log amp.*

logger—A device which records physical processes and events, usually chronologically. Loggers or data loggers are used in control systems to scan and record pressure, temperature, humidity, and other parameters.

logic—1. The systematic scheme which defines the interaction of signals in data processing systems. Logic includes the application of truth tables and the relationships between switching circuits involving arithmetic computation. 2. The science dealing with the formal principles of reasoning and thought.

logic analysis—The determination of the specific steps required to produce the desired output or intelligence from given input data.

logic analyzer—A device used to test and troubleshoot equipment containing digital logic. Logic analyzers can be used to trace logic states and timing; to examine the activity on each line of a data bus by displaying that line on a CRT screen or using a string of light-emitting diodes; to design microprocessor-based products for examining the flow of command and data words on multiline buses. Logic analyzers perform the first steps in locating the problem; from there conventional instruments such as signal generators and oscilloscopes can be used.

logic card—A circuit board which contains components and wiring which perform one or more logic operations or functions.

logic circuit—A set of elements connected or programmed to perform logic operations or represent logic functions such as AND, OR, and NAND.

logic coincidence element—An operation defined by the equivalence operator. A logic coincidence element produces a true output when the two input signals are the same and a false output when they are different.

logic comparator—A testing device that compares an in-circuit integrated circuit with a tested device. Any differences in the outputs are detected and displayed, usually by light-emitting diodes. A fault can be traced to a specific IC using a logic comparator.

logic design—The specification of the operation of a system in terms of symbolic logic without primary regard to the hardware required to implement the system.

logic diagram—A graphic representation of the logical elements and their interconnections without regard to construction details.

logic element—The smallest part of a computer system that represents a function or operation of symbolic logic. Typical logic elements are flip-flops and gates.

logic file—A data set that is composed of one or more logical open records. A logic file may operate through the use of a file-definition macroinstruction.

logic flow chart—A detailed solution of the work order or arrangement in terms of the logic for a specific machine or process. Symbolic notation is used to represent the information and describe the inputs, outputs, arithmetic and logical operations. Types of operations can be shown using block symbols.

logic gates—A circuit or single component capable of performing a logic operation. A gate may have several inputs but only one output.

logic high—The voltage state furthest from zero in a two-state logic system, usually signifying a true, yes, on, or closed state. Also called *high level*.

logic instruction—An instruction that executes an operation defined in symbolic logic.

logic level—The voltage levels that represent binary conditions in a logic circuit.

logic low—The voltage state nearest zero in a two-state logic system, usually signifying a false, no, off, or open state. Also called *low level*.

logic operation—An operation in which logical quantities expressed in ones and zeros are used to make comparisons, decisions, and extractions.

logic operator—Any of the Boolean operators such as AND, OR, NOR, and NAND.

logic probe—A logic testing tool which provides a direct readout of logic levels by connecting to or placing over in-circuit ICs. The logic probe uses one or more lamps to indicate if a logic signal path is at logic one or logic zero or toggling between these levels. Some units use the relative brightness to indicate duty cycle, some rely upon blinking effects for frequency indication, and others are designed to be used in conjunction with a high-quality oscilloscope.

logic product—The result obtained from the logical multiply operation or the AND operation.

logic pulser—A testing tool which drives a logic path to a desired state for a short time to check for faults and short circuits.

logic shift—A shift in which all bits are treated the same with no special consideration given to the sign bit as in an arithmetic shift. A logic shift affects all positions.

logic swing—The voltage difference between the two logic levels representing a zero and a one in a gate or circuit.

logic symbol—A graphic character used to represent a logic operator.

logical add—A Boolean operation performed on two bits at a time such that the result is one if either or both are one, and the result is zero if both bits are zero. Logical add is the same as the OR operator.

LOGICAL ADD

INPUTS		OUTPUT
A	B	C
0	0	0
1	0	1
0	1	1
1	1	1

logical connectives—Operators or words such as AND, OR, OR ELSE,

IF-THEN, and EXCEPT, which make new statements from given statements.

logical decision—The choice between two alternatives based upon certain criteria pertinent to the application.

logical difference—A relation in set theory which includes all members of one set which are not members of another. For example, if set A includes 1, 3, 5, 7, 9, 11, and set B includes 2, 3, 5, 6, 7, 8, then the logical difference is 1, 2, 6, 8, 9, and 11.

logical multiply—The AND operator.

LOGICAL MULTIPLY

INPUTS		OUTPUT
A	B	C
0	0	0
1	0	0
0	1	0
1	1	1

logical relation—A term used in assembler programming in which two expressions are separated by a relational operator such as EQ, GE, LE, LT or NE.

logical sum—Logical add.

long instruction format—An instruction which occupies more than one standard position or length, such as a two-word instruction. The second word may be used for address modification or as an operand.

longitudinal magnetization—A magnetization used in magnetic recording which is in a direction parallel to the line of travel.

look-ahead—1. A logic characteristic resulting in machine-sensing that all carries required for addition are generated. 2. The ability of a CPU to mask an interrupt until the following instruction is completed.

look-ahead carry—See *look-ahead,* 1.

look-ahead-carry generator—An adding circuit that anticipates carries to provide high-speed operations.

lookup—A procedure for obtaining the value of a function from a table of function values. If the values of the function are equally spaced, the locations of associated functions can be generated by a linear relationship. If the arguments are not equally spaced, the addresses can be separated using constants and a comparison operation.

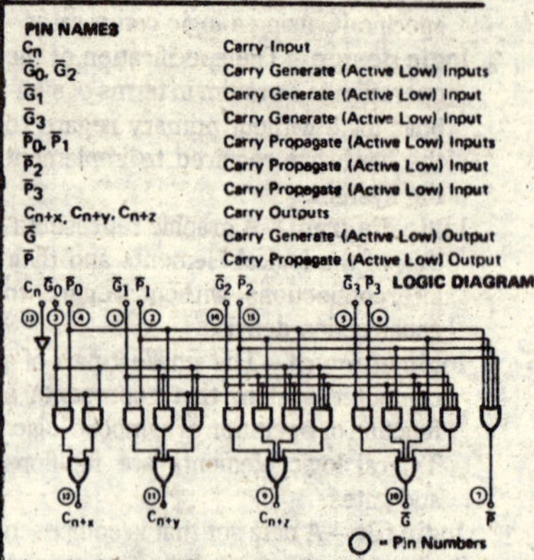

Look-Ahead-Carry Generator

lookup table—A collection of data in a form suitable for ready reference, frequently stored in sequenced machine locations or in the form of rows and columns. The intersection of rows and columns can serve to locate specific items of data or information.

loop—1. A communications circuit between two private subscribers or a subscriber and the local switching center. 2. A direction-finding antenna. 3. A closed-circuit path within an electronic circuit or collection of circuits (such as a ground loop). 4. A self-contained series of instructions in which the final instruction can modify itself, causing the process to be repeated until a terminal condition is reached. Productive instructions in the loop are used to manipulate operands while housekeeping or bookkeeping instructions modify the productive instructions and keep track of the number of operations and repetitions. A loop may be terminated under any number of conditions. Loops are also used as return paths in control systems and other functions or operations requiring a feedback path.

loopback test—A test or check in which signals are looped from a test center through a loopback switch or data set, and then back to the test center for measurement.

loop checking—A method for checking the accuracy of transmission of data in which the received data is returned to the sending unit for comparison with the original data.

loop code—Coding that uses a program loop for repetition of a sequence of instructions. Loop coding generally results in storage savings, but it also requires more execution time compared to straight line coding.

loop counter—A counter used in assembly programming to prevent excessive looping during conditional processing.

loop error—The error due to departure of the loop output signal from its desired value.

loop feedback—The signal that is fed back to the input to produce the loop-actuating signal in a feedback control system.

loop gain—The ratio of output to input amplitude in a control loop.

looping—A repeating or recursive property of many programs and instructions used in microcomputers. Looping is often performed at delayed speeds, and many looped instructions are stored in ROM and then jumped to when required. Looping can also occur when the CPU is in a wait condition or as a result of errors and malfunctions.

loop initialization—The instructions prior to a loop which set addresses and data to their initial values.

loop jump—A jump instruction which causes a jump to itself.

loop program—A series of instructions which are repeated until a terminal condition is reached.

loop test—A series of instructions used to determine when a loop function has been completed.

loop transfer function—The mathematical function representing the relationship between the output of a feedback loop control system and its input.

loss—The decrease in power of a signal as it is transmitted from one point to another, usually expressed in decibels.

lower sideband—In an AM signal, that band of frequencies adjacent to and immediately below the carrier and spaced from the carrier by an amount equal to the frequency of the modulating wave. Since the sidebands (upper and lower) contain the intelligence, the carrier and one of the two sidebands may be discarded before transmission, so that only one of the two sidebands (upper or lower) is sent.

low frequency—Electromagnetic radiation between 30 and 300 kHz.

low level—1. The most negative voltage in binary logic systems. If the true level is most positive, as it is in positive logic or positive true logic, then the low level is the false or zero level. 2. Characterized by a comparatively small value, as in *low-level signals*. 3. Relatively crude or primitive when compared with other members of the same genre or class.

low-level language—A "primitive" language which resembles a machine code or has a one-to-one relationship with a machine code, by contrast to a *high-level language*, which uses English-like statements.

low-order—Refers to the weight or significance assigned to the digits of a number. For example, in the number 2,345,768, the low-order digit is 8.

low-pass filter—A device or circuit which permits the passage of relatively low-frequency signals and attenuates high-frequency signals.

low-performance equipment—Equipment which has insufficient performance characteristics to allow its use in trunk or link circuits. This equipment may be used in subscriber line circuits whenever it meets line circuit requirements.

low-power Schottky—A variation of the Schottky TTL logic family. Low-power Schottky circuits allow smaller, less costly power supplies, improved packing density, and less noise generation, along with simplified MOS-to-TTL interfaces.

low-speed storage—Descriptive of storage devices that have long access times compared with the time required for arithmetic operations of the CPU, and low access times compared to other peripheral units.

LSI—Abbreviation for *large-scale integration*, a name applied to integrated circuits with 1000 or more functional units or gates on a single chip.

lug—A device provided on the end of a conductor for inserting screws at terminal strips.

lumped—Circuit elements that are concentrated in discrete units rather than distributed over a transmission line or circuit path.

lumped parameter—A circuit parameter which may be considered to be localized for the purpose of analysis.

Lukaseiwicz notation—A notation used in forming mathematical expressions in which the operator precedes its operands. For example, the term *A plus B multiplied by C* is written as $+ABC$. Also called prefix notation, parentheses-free notation, and Polish notation.

lux—Obsolete unit of illumination equal to one lumen per square meter.

M

machine—1. A general term for a device such as a microprocessor or microcomputer that can store and process numeric and alphabetic information. Machine is used to refer to both analog and digital computers along with related data processing equipment. 2. An automatic radio receiving and transmitting station.

machine address—Absolute address.

machine-check indicator—A device which is switched on when programmed conditions are detected by the machine-checking circuits. The system is then programmed to run a diagnostic routine to find the cause of the interruption.

machine code—An operation code that a machine is designed to recognize directly and without translation.

machine-code instruction—The symbols that state a basic computer operation that is to be performed. The machine-code instruction is the combination of bits specifying the machine-language operator, which becomes a part of the instruction that designates the operation of logic.

machine cycle—The shortest complete action or process that is repeated in order; also, the time required for this action or process. Also called *microcycle*.

machine equation—The equation that an analog computer is programmed to solve.

machine instruction—Any instruction that a machine can recognize and execute; machine-code instruction.

machine language—A language that can be used directly by a microprocessor; a binary language. All other languages must be translated or compiled into binary code before entering the processor. Users generally write the program in coded instructions that are more meaningful to them. Then assembly programs are used to translate the symbolic instructions into binary machine code. Also called *object code*.

machine learning—The ability of a device to improve its performance based on its own prior experience.

machine length—Refers to the working word length used by a device.

machine-oriented language—A language designed for interpretation and use by a specific machine or class of machine. The language may include instructions which define and direct machine operations along with any information to be acted upon by the machine during specific operations.

machine-readable—The capability of being sensed or read by a specific device. Cards, drums, disks, and tapes are all machine-readable media.

machine unit—The voltage used in an analog computer to represent one unit of the simulated variable.

machine variable—Refers to the signal in an analog computer used to reproduce the variations of the simulated function.

machine word—A word with the standard number of bits that a computer normally handles in a register or during a transfer. Typical machine words in microcomputer systems are 4, 8, and 16 bits long.

macro—1. A large mainframe computer facility able to handle very large volumes of data. 2. A single instruction as written in source code which may require a number of successive operational machine steps to execute, each step involving a machine instruction in *microcode*; a macroinstruction. 3. A group of often used instructions treated as a unit entity.

macroassembler—A language processor that accepts words, statements, and phrases to produce machine instructions. A macroassembler allows segments of a large program to be created and tested separately. The full macro capability of a resident macroassembler eliminates the need to rewrite similar sections of code repeatedly and simplifies program documentation.

macro call—A call for a subroutine jump to a macro command.

macro code—1. That coding system which permits a macroinstruction to call upon specified groups of instructions for execution as if it were a discrete machine operation. 2. Any instruction that results in a call for a jump to a routine that is not machine-peculiar, and which usually consists of a body of inseparable instructions. 3. Collectively, the procedures used to provide code segments which are used frequently throughout a program.

macro command—A command or statement used to bring a string or strings of frequently used instructions into operation.

macro definition—The specification of a macro operation, including the name of the operations and the fields, fixed and variable.

macro facility—That feature of an assembler which allows it to produce a sequence of statements from a macro definition.

macro generating program—A program designed to construct a group of instructions in object code from a macroinstruction in the basic source language.

macro generator—Macro generating program.

macroinstruction—An instruction in a source language that is equivalent to a specified sequence of machine instructions and requiring several microcycles to execute. A macroinstruction is a powerful command which results from combining several operations into a single instruction. A macroinstruction may also generate a debugging routine to be used with a particular program.

A macroinstruction set may be register- or stack-oriented, and may be original or a copy from another machine. Lower cost and higher performance usually result when an original macroinstruction set is developed. If more than eight bits of operation code are used in a macroinstruction, the interpretation becomes complex and additional logic

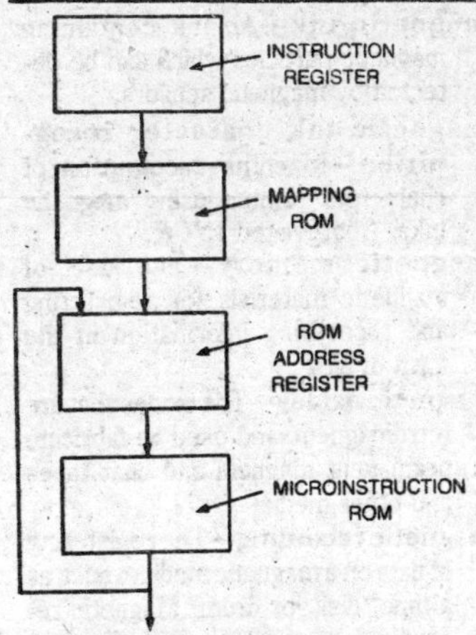

Macroinstruction Decoding System

may have to be added to the hardware design.

macroprogramming—The procedure and methods used for writing machine statements in terms of macroinstructions.

magnadur—A ceramic material made from sintered oxides of iron and barium, used for permanent magnets and as an electrical insulator.

magnetic—Descriptive of phenomena and devices depending essentially on magnetism.

magnetic bias—A steady magnetic field added to the signal field in magnetic recording. A magnetic bias can improve the linearity of response during recording.

magnetic bubble memory—A technology that uses a single-crystal sheet with perpendicular magnetic fields to produce magnetic "bubbles." A pulsed field is used to break up and control the bubbles as groups of data bits. Densities of 10 million bits per square inch have been realized, and densities to one billion bits per square inch have been projected for this technology.

magnetic character reader—A device that reads magnetically inscribed square inch have been projected for this technology. data from cards and paper documents into a computer. The reader may be used for both online and offline operations.

magnetic circuit—A closed path for magnetic flux.

magnetic coating—The magnetic layer consisting of oxide particles held in a binder applied to magnetic recording materials such as tapes, disks, and drums.

magnetic code—The specific manner in which data bits are represented on magnetic recording materials. A phase-encoding format records a one as a flux transition at the midpoint of the data cell towards the level representing erased tape. A zero is recorded as a flux reversal in the opposite direction.

magnetic core—A memory device in which information is represented by the magnetic polarity of a wire-sensed permeable ring. Small rings called cores are used to represent bits 0 and 1. The cores are made of ferrites and variations of the ring form includes tapes, rods, and thin-film configurations. The cores are usually arranged in the form of a matrix.

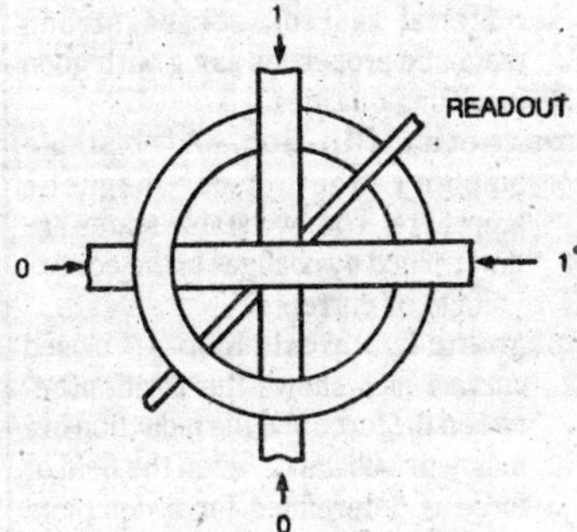

Magnetic Core

magnetic core storage—A storage system that uses a core of magnetic material coupled by wires or other conductors. The cores are magnetized to represent binary ones or zeros.

magnetic cycle—The sequence of changes in magnetization of an object corresponding to one cycle of alternating current.

magnetic delay line—A delay medium that uses magnetic material to slow the propagation of magnetic or sound waves.

magnetic disk—A storage device or medium which uses a coated disk for storing information. The data is stored in the form of magnetic spots representing binary data and is arranged in circular tracks around the disks. The tracks are accessed by movable read and write heads which are positioned to the desired disk, and then to the desired track. The information is obtained sequentially as the disk rotates.

magnetic drum—A storage device which uses a rotating cylindrical drum surfaced with a magnetic coating. The data is stored as magnetized spots on closed tracks that circle the drum. A read-write head is used for each track, and the proper head is selected by switching. Data is read or written sequentially as the drum turns.

magnetic ferrite—A ceramic-type material that possesses strong magnetic properties along with good insulating qualities.

magnetic flip-flop—A bistable amplifier that uses magnetic amplifiers. The two stable states are determined by changes in the control voltage or current.

magnetic hysteresis loop—A closed curve which shows the relation between the force and the induction in a magnetic substance when the field or force is determined for a complete cycle.

magnetic instability—The property of magnetic material on tape that causes variations to occur from temperature, aging, and mechanical strain. Magnetic instability is a function of particle size and magnetization.

magnetic ink—An ink containing magnetic particles which can be detected by magnetic sensors.

magnetic ink character recognition—Machine recognition of characters printed using magnetic inks. Abbreviated *MICR*.

magnetic memory—The use of magnetic materials for registering and recovering information in the form of bits.

magnetic oxides—The oxides that are ferromagnetic and used to fabricate permanent magnets and coat tapes and other media.

magnetic recording—The registering of data on a magnetic medium such as a tape, disk, or drum. Magnetic recording parameters include tape speed, transfer rate, and packing density. Tape speed refers to the speed or velocity at which the tape moves past the recording head and is usually expressed in inches or centimeters per second. Transfer rate is a measure of how fast data can be handled by the recording system and is expressed in bits or bytes per second, or in baud. Packing density refers to the number of bits per unit length stored on the tape.

magnetic saturation—The limiting value of magnetic induction in a medium when magnetization is complete.

magnetic shift register—A shift register in which the pattern of a row of magnetic cores is moved one step along the row by each new pulse.

magnetic storage—A storage system that uses the magnetic properties of materials such as magnetic cores, tapes, and disks to store data.

magnetic strip—A line of magnetic ink on the back of a ledger card which contains coded information. The magnetic strip may or may not be printed on the face of the card.

magnetic tape—A flexible oxide-coated tape on which data can be stored by selective polarization of portions of the surface. One side is usually coated with a uniform layer of dispersed magnetic material. The tape can be used for audio, video, or binary data recording.

magnetic tape diagnostic—A routine used to check tape controller and tape transport operations.

magnetic tape reader—A unit which transforms the pattern of magnetic spots on a tape into pulse signals for a computer.

magnetic thin film—A layer of magnetic material used for logic and storage elements. Thin films are usually less than one micrometer (micron) in thickness.

magnetic wire—A wire composed of or coated with a magnetic material and used for recording.

magnetohydrodynamics—The study of the motion of electrical conducting fluids in the presence of a magnetic field.

magnetostriction—A phenomenon where certain materials increase in length in the direction of a magnetic field and return to their original length when the field is removed.

magnetostriction transducer—A device that uses the property of magnetostriction to convert electrical energy to mechanical energy, or vice versa.

magnetostrictive delay line—A delay device which uses the magnetostrictive effect to convert electrical signals to sonic waves or sonic waves to electrical signals. Also called *magnetostrictive acoustic delay line.*

mailbox—A set of locations in a common RAM storage area which is reserved for data addressed to specific peripherals and other microprocessors located in the immediate area. The mailbox arrangement helps the coordinator microprocessor and the supplementary microprocessors transfer data among themselves with minimal hardware.

mainframe—1. The heart of a computer system, which includes the CPU and ALU. 2. A large computer, as opposed to a mini or a micro.

main storage—The general-purpose storage area of a computer. Main storage is usually accessed directly by the operating registers and may be the fastest storage device in the computer, since it is used to execute all instructions.

maintenance—Activity used to eliminate faults and keep hardware and programs in satisfactory working condition. Maintenance may include tests, measurements, replacements, adjustments, and repairs.

maintenance control panel—A panel of indicators and switches used to display a sequence of routines for repair checks.

maintenance time—Time used for hardware repair, including corrective and preventive operations.

major control data—The various high-priority items of data used to select, execute, or modify another data value, routine, record, file, or operation.

major cycle—The time interval between successive appearances of a given storage element. Usually it is the time of one rotation of a recirculating storage element, and it is composed of a number of minor cycles.

majority—The logic operator having the property of unanimity: if P, Q, R are statements, then the majority of P,Q,R is true if more than half the statements are true, and false if more than half the statements are false.

majority carrier—Refers to the predominant type of current carrier in a semiconductor region. For npn transistors, the majority carrier is the *electron;* for pnp it is the *hole.*

majority decision gate—A device or circuit used to implement the majority logic operator.

majority gate—Majority decision gate.

major state—A basic control state in a computer, such as fetch, defer, or execute. Major control states are used to determine and execute instructions. During any one instruction, a state lasts for one cycle.

major state logic generator—The logic circuits of the CPU which are used to establish the major state for each computer cycle. The major state logic generator determines the machine state as a function of the current instruction, the current state, and the conditions of the peripheral units.

makeup time—1. The part of available time that is used for reruns due to malfunctions and mistakes from a previous operating time. 2. The unproductive time required to prepare a system to perform a specific task.

malfunction—A failure in the operation of a computer system.

malfunction routine—A routine used to locate a malfunction in a computer or as an aid in locating mistakes in the program. Also called *diagnostic routine*.

management information system—An organized assemblage of management activities performed with the aid of automatic data processing. One example is a data processing system which provides management with the information required to manage or supervise a particular organization or function. Another example is a communications data processing system where data is recorded and processed for operational purposes. The problems are isolated for different levels of decision-making, and information is fed back to upper management to reflect the progress made in achieving objectives.

manipulated variable—The quantity or condition that is altered by the computer to initiate a change in a regulated process.

manual input—The entry of data by hand.

manual input generator—A device which accepts manual input data and holds the contents for sensing by the computer or controller.

manual storage—A type of storage in the form of manually set switches, usually arranged in an array or matrix.

map—A graphic portrayal of the correspondence between the elements of one set and the elements of another set, such as the listing which relates data names to core addresses.

marginal check—A preventive maintenance technique that uses the variation of operating conditions such as voltages and frequency to detect and locate incipient defective components.

marginal test—A built-in check system that uses resistor networks and variable voltages. All working registers are usually displayed on the console panel.

mark—1. A sign or symbol used to signify or indicate an event in time or space. Examples include end of message marks, file marks, drum marks, and end-of-tape marks. Also called a *marker* or *flag*. 2. The radioteletype signal that causes a character to print.

marker—1. An intentionally displayed pip on a scope to show a specific frequency 2. Mark, 1.

Markov chain—A probabilistic model in which the probability of an event is dependent only on the event that preceded it.

mark reader—A device used to detect pencil marks on documents.

mark sensing—The electrical detection of manually recorded conductive traces on a nonconductive surface such as paper.

mark-to-space ratio—In radioteletype, the ratio of the duration of positive and negative cycles of a square waveform; the positive cycle is a

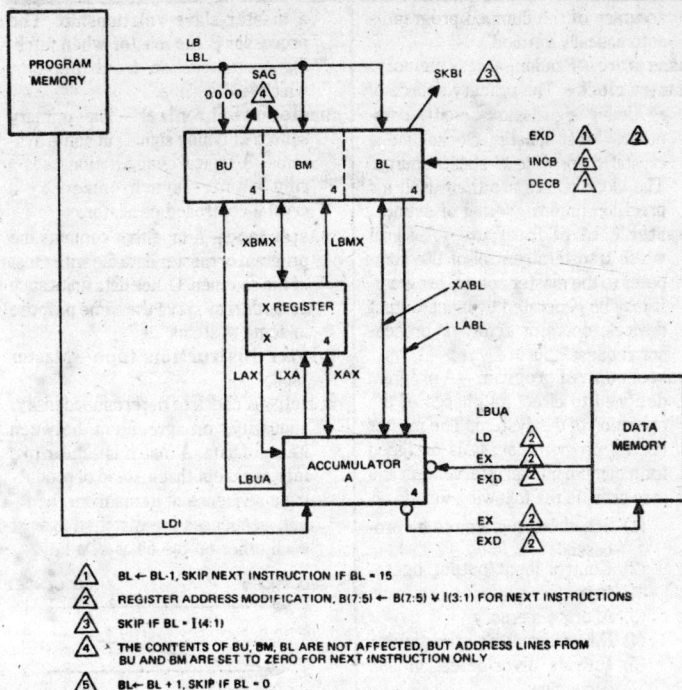

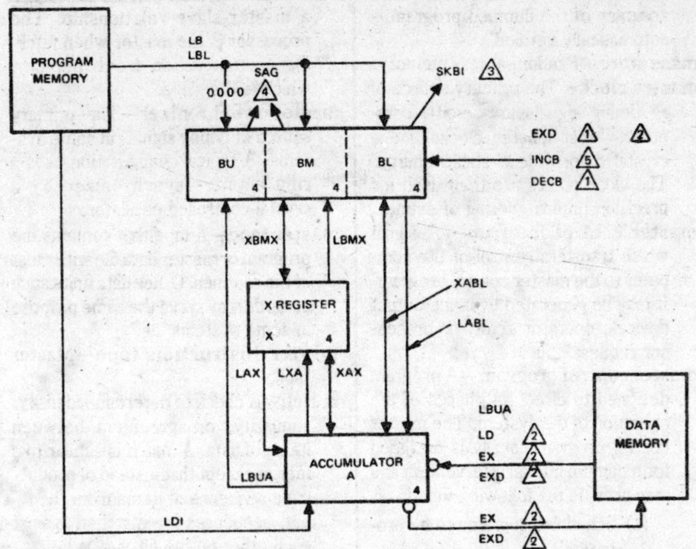

1 BL ← BL-1, SKIP NEXT INSTRUCTION IF BL = 15

2 REGISTER ADDRESS MODIFICATION, B(7:5) ← B(7:5) ∨ I(3:1) FOR NEXT INSTRUCTIONS

3 SKIP IF BL = I(4:1)

4 THE CONTENTS OF BU, BM, BL ARE NOT AFFECTED, BUT ADDRESS LINES FROM BU AND BM ARE SET TO ZERO FOR NEXT INSTRUCTION ONLY

5 BL← BL + 1, SKIP IF BL = 0

Map of Address Modification Instruction

mark or a one, and the negative cycle is a space or a zero.

M-ary—A term used to refer to devices and operations with more than two states or conditions.

mask—1. A machine word that specifies by selective inhibition the parts of another machine word that is to be operated on. 2. A thin sheet with open and closed portions used in device photoprocessing.

mask bit—A specific bit used with a pattern of bits to extract selected bits from a string.

masking—The process of extracting certain bits or sensing certain binary conditions while ignoring others by inhibition. One technique of masking uses zeros in bit positions of no interest and ones in positions to be sensed.

mask programmable read-only memory—A type of PROM which is programmed during the final steps of manufacture. The surface of the wafer is coated with a layer of aluminum that is selectively etched to give the desired interconnecting pattern. The devices are fabricated up to this step of manufacture and then held in storage until a customer's data pattern is defined. Then the chips are mask-programmed and delivered to the user.

mass-storage device—A device with a large storage capacity such as a magnetic disk or drum.

mass-storage dump—A program used to transfer a specified area of memory to a mass-storage device. If an autoloadable format is used, the accuracy of the dumped program is automatically verified.

mass store—Random-access memory.

master clock—The primary source of all timing signals in a digital computer. Most master clocks use a crystal to provide a stable source. The clock pulses are then used for precision time-triggering of events.

master control interrupt—A signal which transfers control of the computer to the master control program. It may be generated by input/output devices, operator error, or processor request.

master control program—A program designed to direct all phases of the operation of the system. The master control program usually is designed for minimum human intervention and may provide the following functions:

(1) Schedule programs to be processed
(2) Control input/output operations
(3) Allocate memory
(4) Direct compiling operations
(5) Provide error-detection and correction
(6) Provide printed instructions
(7) Adjust operation according to system environment

master control routine—1. A part of a program used to control linking of other routines and subroutines, or calling selected program segments into memory. 2. A routine used to control the operation of hardware.

master scheduler—A control program that allows the operator to initiate special actions designed to override the normal functions of the system.

master–slave—A term for a configuration in which one device or function, the master, always has control over another device or function, the slave. In a computer system, the master computer schedules and transmits tasks to the slave, which performs the computations as directed. Bus control can also be under a master-slave relationship. The processor is the master when fetching an instruction from memory, which is the slave.

master synchronizer—The primary source of timing signals in some systems. A typical configuration uses a ring counter synchronized by a crystal-controlled oscillator.

master tape—A tape that contains the program or master data file with most of the routines. Other data units such as cards may serve the same purpose in some systems.

master instruction tape—Master tape.

match—A check to determine identity, similarity, or agreement between items of data. A match is similar to a merge except that instead of producing a sequence of items from the input, sequences are matched against each other on the basis of a key.

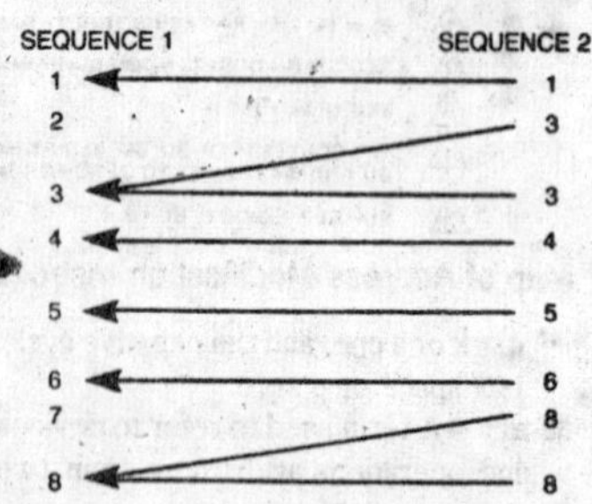

Match Schematic for Two Items

matching—A technique used to verify coding. Individual codes can be compared by machine against master codes to determine any that are invalid.

material implication—A Boolean operation defined by the following truth table:

OPERANDS A	B	RESULT C
0	0	1
1	0	0
0	1	1
1	1	1

mathematical check—A check that uses mathematical relationships. Also called *arithmetic check*.

mathematical control mode—The control mode or control action used in a control system, such as proportional, integral, or derivative.

mathematical model—The mathematical representation of a process, device, or system.

mathematical programming—A procedure used in operations research for locating the maximum or minimum values of a function subject to specified conditions.

matrix—An array of quantities or elements in a prescribed form. A matrix is usually capable of being subject to a mathematical operation using an operator or another matrix. A matrix of circuit elements can be capable of performing functions such as code conversion. The matrix elements may be diodes, transistors, magnetic cores, or other binary devices.

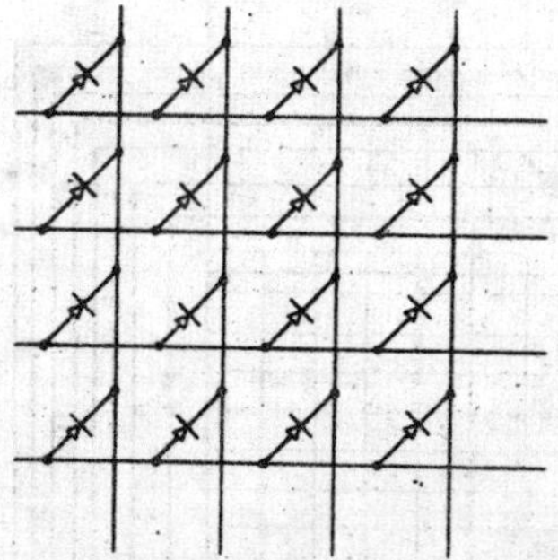

Matrix of Diodes

matrix printer—A device that uses an array of dots to form characters. Dot-matrix character formation is also used in some display devices. Sometimes called *dot matrix printer*.

matrix switch—An array of circuit elements used to perform a specific function as interconnected. Functions include word translation, encoding, and number-system transformation. Elements include switches, transistors, diodes, and relays.

matrix storage—A storage system with elements arranged such that access to any location requires the use of two or more coordinates. Examples are magnetic-core storage and CRT storage.

matrix table—A set of quantities arranged in a rectangular array according to specific mathematical rules and conventions.

maximum frequency operation—The maximum repetition or clock rate at which the electronic circuits will perform reliably under continuous worst-case conditions.

maxwell—In the centimeter-gram-second system, the unit of magnetic flux. One maxwell is equal to 10^{-8} webers.

m-derived filter—An electric filter element derived from the constant-*k* element by transformation.

mean repair time—The average repair time per failure. The mean repair time, if taken over a given performance period, can be used to assess reliability of the equipment.

mean-time-between failure—The average time between failures (abbreviated *MTBF*) taken as a function of the operating time. The MTBF represents the expected failure-free operating time for the equipment. Also called ***mean time to failure (MTTF)***.

measurand—A measured physical variable such as pressure, temperature, flow, or distance.

measurement error—Anticipated deviations in a measurement due to:

(1) Sampling variability
(2) Sample preparation variations
(3) Stability variations or lack of precision

measurement reproducibility—The degree of agreement between repeated measurements under the same operating conditions over a given period of time.

mechanical dictionary—A language translating machine used to provide a word-for-word substitution from one language to another. The mechanical dictionary is used in automatic searching systems for encoding.

mechanical differential—A device used in analog computers to provide a mechanical rotation equal to the difference of two input rotations.

median—The average of a series of values, or that value for which there are an equal number of items with lesser magnitudes and greater magnitudes.

medium—1. The physical substance upon which data is recorded, such as magnetic tape, disk, or card. 2. Any carrier of any commodity, especially data.

medium frequency—Radio frequencies from 300 kHz to 3 MHz, sometimes called ***hectometric waves***.

medium-scale integration—Integrated circuits with more than 100 but less than 1000 circuits or gates on a single chip. Abbreviated *MSI*.

meet—A Boolean operator that gives a true output only when both variables connected by the operator are true.

mega—Prefix denoting one million, abbreviated *M*.

megabit—A unit equal to one million bits.

megahertz—A unit of frequency equal to one million cycles per second.

memory—A basic component of a computer which stores information for future use. Memory and storage are interchangeable terms.

A memory is used to accept and hold binary numbers until required. To be effective, a computer must be able to store the data that will be operated on as well as the program which directs what operations are to be performed. Memory units are designed to store large amounts of information and must allow rapid ac-

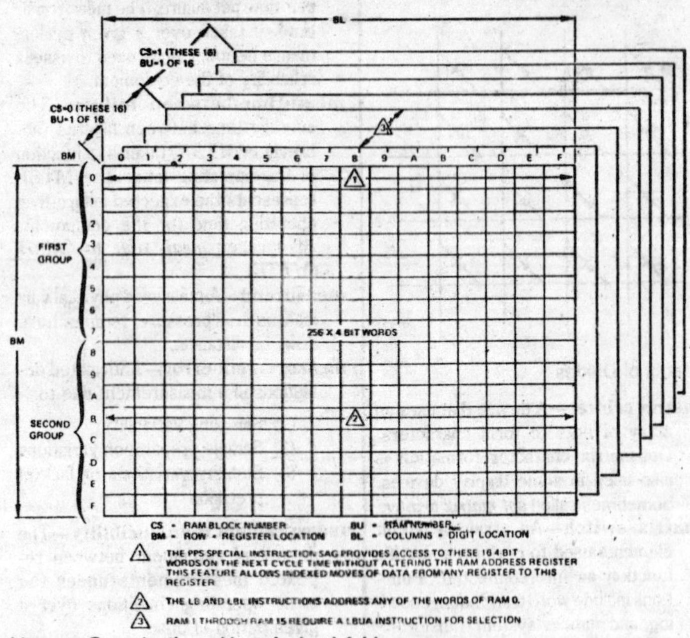

Memory Organization—Hexadecimal Addresses

cess to any desired part of that information in time of need. These two requirements tend to increase the cost of the memory. Various types of memory in use include core, disk, drum, tape, and semiconductor. Typical access times are:

SEMICONDUCTOR	
TTL RAM	60 ns
MOS RAM	300 ns
CORE	500 ns
FIXED HEAD DISK OR DRUM	8 ns
MOVING HEAD DISK	50 ns
FLOPPY DISK	100 ns
CASSETTE AND REEL TAPES	10 s

memory address counter—A register used to point to the next location in memory for an instruction-fetch operation. The memory address counter may be a regular working register or a specially designed unit.

memory address driver—A device or circuit used to supply signal requirements over transfer lines in memory systems.

memory address register—A register (abbreviated *MAR*) used to hold the address of a data word to be read from or written into memory. The memory address register can also be used as an internal register for microprogram control during data transfers to and from the memory and peripherals.

memory and device control unit—A unit which provides the external signals to communicate with peripheral devices, switch registers, and other memories.

memory buffer register—A register used to store words as they come from memory (read operation) or prior to entering memory (write operation).

memory bus—The circuit path for communication between the CPU and memory. A memory bus may actually consist of three buses which are time-shared over a single bus:

(1) Memory address bus
(2) Memory-to-CPU data bus
(3) CPU-to-memory data bus

memory cache—A memory system that uses a limited but very fast semiconductor memory along with a slower but larger capacity memory. The overall effect of a larger and faster memory is achieved at reduced cost. Look-ahead procedures are used to locate and deposit the right information into the fast memory when it is needed.

memory cycle—The operation and the time required for reading from and writing into memory.

memory data register—A register (abbreviated *MDR*) that holds the last data word read from or written into the memory location addressed by the contents of the memory address register.

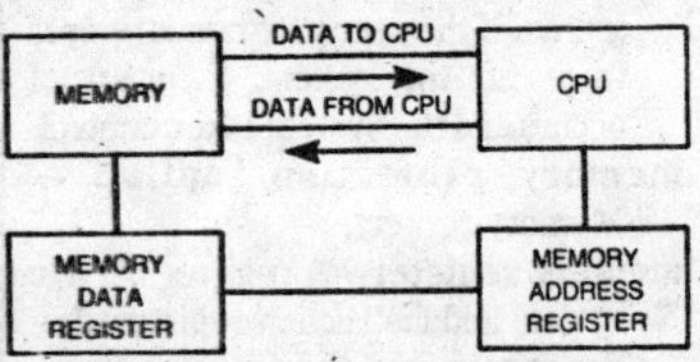

Memory Data and Address Registers

memory diagnostic—A routine used to check all memory locations for proper operation with a set of worst-case pattern tests.

memory dump—An operation that causes a microcomputer to produce a listing of the contents of a storage device. A *dynamic* memory dump is concerned with only certain sections of memory under program control as a main routine is executed. A *differential* memory dump is concerned with only those words and bits that have been changed during execution of a routine.

memory fill—The placing of patterns of bits in memory registers not in use in order to stop the computer if the program seeks instructions from these registers.

memory latency time—The time required for the memory control hardware to move the memory medium to a position where it can be read.

memory map—A listing of all variable names, array names, and constants used by the program with relative address assignments. The memory map also includes all subroutines called and the last location when called.

memory module—Refers to a semiconductor memory unit. One typical module contains 4096 words of 16 bits each. Modules may be stacked to obtain up to 65,536 words.

memory protect—A CPU option that protects the system from accidental modifications. The memory is set up into two segments, separating the operating system from user programs. If the user program attempts to modify the system, an interrupt occurs and the system takes control.

memory protection option — Memory protect.

memory register—A register used in all data and instruction registers between memory, the arithmetic unit, and the control register. The memory register may be involved in all transfers of data and instructions in either direction between memory and the ALU. The contents may be added to or subtracted from and are usually available until cleared. Also called *distributor, high-speed bus, arithmetic register, auxiliary register*, and *exchange register*.

memory scan—An option which provides a rapid search of any part of memory for any word. With a memory-scan option, any block of locations may be searched using a single instruction.

memory timing generator—Circuits used in multiple-memory systems to determine where addresses should be written, which words should be sent to the CPU, and in what order they should be sent.

mercury delay line—A delay circuit or system in which mercury is used as the medium of sound transmission.

mercury storage—A storage system that uses the acoustic properties of mercury to store data.

merge—To combine items into one sequenced file from two or more similarly sequenced files without changing the order of the items.

mesa—A type of transistor in which one electrode is made smaller than the other to control bulk resistance. The base and emitter are raised above the collector.

mesh—A set of branches forming a closed path in a network.

message—A transported item of information or a group of words which is transported as a unit.

message blocking—The linking of several messages into a single transmission or record. Message blocking results in lower transmission overhead by reducing the delays due to changing the transmission direction of the communications link.

message control program—The top-priority program which controls the sending and receiving of messages to and from remote terminals.

message exchange—A device placed between a communication line and a computer to free the computer for other functions.

message routing—The function of selecting the path or the alternate path by which the message will proceed to the next point in reaching its destination.

message switching—The operation in which a message is received at a central location and stored on a direct-access device until the proper outgoing circuit is available for transmission to its destination.

metal-oxide semiconductor—A semiconductor (abbreviated *MOS*) device in which a conducting channel is induced in the region between two electrodes by applying a field created by a voltage. MOS devices are self-isolating and can be fabricated in a smaller area than bipolar devices. They are less expensive to make in LSI configurations, but switching speeds are slower than bipolar units. MOS devices employ field-effect transistors in one of three functional configurations: NMOS, PMOS, and CMOS (for negative, positive, and complementary).

metal-oxide-semiconductor memory—A memory using MOS technology.

MICR—Abbreviation for *magnetic-ink character recognition*.

MICR code—A magnetic-ink character-recognition code developed for the American Bankers Association. It uses a set of 10 numeric symbols along with 4 special symbols; the characters are visually readable through the use of magnetic sensing heads in various types of sensing equipment.

micro—1. Prefix for one-millionth (10^{-6}). 2. A microcomputer, microprocessor, or the system built using either.

microcircuit—A circuit fabricated from integrated elements in such a way as to make the elements inseparable and the circuit miniaturized.

microcode—The microprocessor operational instructions that cause the device to respond to user-programmed instructions. A single user-programmed instruction may involve many microcode instructions, and each microcode instruction occurs during a microcycle. Some microcodes are user-programmable, and this allows tailoring a microprocessor to fit a particular language, making it competitive with larger machines that do not allow modifications of their basic structure.

microcommand—A command issued in microcode used to specify elementary machine operations or microcycles which are to be performed within a basic machine cycle.

microcomputer—A complete small computing system consisting of hardware and software. The hardware includes the microprocessing unit, memory, auxiliary circuits, power supply, and control panel. The main processing blocks are typically fabricated with LSI circuit packages.

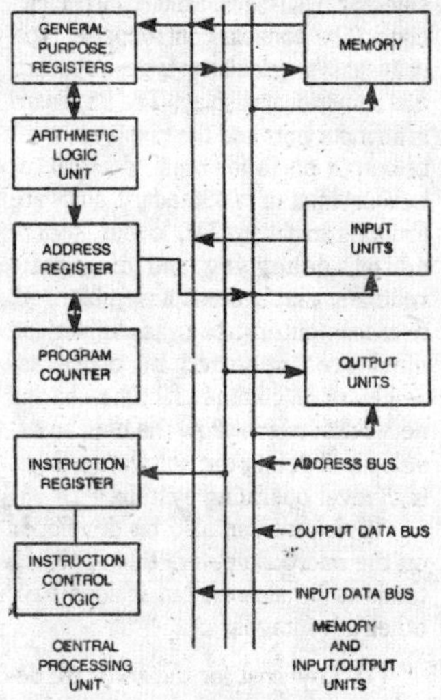

Microcomputer Structure

Dramatic decreases in the costs of microcomputer hardware, achieved through a high level of circuit integration, have opened up new aplications for computers. These include consumer and control applications where low-cost programmable logic is required. Microcomputers have been applied to games, controllers, terminals, and instruments with considerable success. A number of features of microcomputers have led to this success.

(1) Product costs are greatly reduced
(2) Products get to market faster

(3) Product capability is greater, allowing a higher product price
(4) Development time and costs are lower
(5) Reliability is increased, reducing service costs

A typical microcomputer has the CPU on a single chip or circuit board; the system also contains ROM storage for programs and data along with clock circuits, input and output units, selector registers, and control circuits. The console control panel typically has a calculator-type keyboard and a multidigit display. The keyboard is an input port and the display is a set of output ports for octal, decimal, or hexadecimal data. Standard software includes an assembler, loader, source editor, debugging and diagnostic routines, and a cross assembler. All microcomputers use an assembler and most are supported by cross assemblers on commercial time-sharing networks which allow the user to develop and debug the software using a high-level operating system.

Software can also be developed on the microcomputer; this approach tends to be slower, but it does have other advantages:

(1) Low cost for the software development tools
(2) Online program execution
(3) Debugging of the actual hardware

Despite their many advantages, microcomputers do have some disadvantages. They cannot be used for high-speed applications such as data acquisition, communications, and CRT refreshing as easily as minicomputers and larger machines. Microcomputer speeds are increasing and microcomputers are beginning to find applications in these areas. Because of the high level of integration, testing is difficult and sometimes places a burden on the user in trying to develop effective diagnostics during product development.

microcomputer development system—A prototyping system of hardware and software which allows the user to design, debug, and modify programs. These systems can compose programs; emulate the CPU, memory, and input/output units; and automate all debugging operations. Errors in the programs can be detected before masks are made, and implementation of high-level languages is allowed. Many systems operate in parallel with the standard instruction set. A typical development system includes:

(1) Console or panel for control and monitoring functions
(2) Processor card or board
(3) Random-access-memory card
(4) Programmable read-only-memory card
(5) Input/output ports
(6) Teletypewriter interface
(7) PROM programmer
(8) Self-contained enclosure with power supplies

Software includes a debug program, editor, assembler, and PROM programmer. Standard documentation consists of instruction books and programming manuals.

microcomputer execution cycle—The microcyles required for a microcomputer to execute an instruction. A typical execution cycle is:

(1) Fetch instruction from memory
(2) Store in instruction register
(3) Decode instruction
(4) Execute operation defined by instruction

microcomputer instrument—A scientific instrument that used microcomputers to control the collection, conversion, and recording of data. Examples include spectrometers and interferometers.

microcomputer interfacing kit—A set of hardware designed to permit customer interfacing of peripherals. A typical kit has a prewired card frame that will accommodate from 6 to 18 modules. The user selects the proper modules and wires in the mating system connector.

microcomputer kit—A set of hardware or software or both that allows the user to configure a microcomputer system to a particular product application. A kit can be a collection of logic modules which are assembled by the user to a prewired system unit. Kits are available which allow the processor to communicate with a variety of peripherals. Provisions are included which enable interrupts at a hard-wired priority level and conversion of analog monitoring voltages.

Many kits are complete enough so that they can be wired for the user's configuration and used immediately. They include all the components needed as well as full documentation. Many have enough input/output and memory capacity to implement an instrument controller, a point-of-sale terminal, a communications interface, an industrial robot, or a sophisticated game. Kits contain the microprocessor, RAM, EROM, input/output ports, and support circuitry including a master clock, interrupts, DMA control, control panel circuits, and display. Some kits have interfaces for a teletypewriter and cassette tape unit.

Software usually includes a monitor, an editor, and an assembler program. The programs can be run directly on the CPU and loaded on cassette tape in less than 60 seconds. System capabilities include:

(1) Program load and dump on cassette tape
(2) Debug commands
(3) Display and store memory
(4) Display, set, and clear breakpoints
(5) Display and set contents of all registers
(6) Manual interrupt for program start and restart
(7) Execute programs from memory
(8) Memory protect

microcomputer kit assembler—A software package used to generate object programs from a source program written in symbolic assembly language. Some assemblers process the source program in two passes. In the first pass, the assembler reads the source tape and generates a symbol table for storage in the memory. During the second pass, the symbolic instructions from the symbol table are converted into binary data. This system allows a number of options during the second pass, such as:

(1) Generate a listing on the CRT display
(2) Generate a listing for the printer
(3) List only lines with errors
(4) Generate an object tape

microcomputer POS—A *point-of-sale* system in which the cash register is a special-purpose computer terminal. The POS system can monitor and record transactions directly in the store's data files, perform credit checks, and handle other marketing functions.

micromputer prototyping system—A hardware and software kit which allows the user to develop a prototype system to his own specifications. The system includes a chassis, control panel, power supplies, and one or more RAMs in addition to the processor cards. Using a teletypewriter unit, the system provides everything needed for evaluation of the processor cards.

microcomputer support devices—Equipment used to complement such peripherals as paper-tape readers and punch machines, card readers, printers, floppy disk drives, cassette drives, PROM programmers, and terminals.

microcomputer terminal—A terminal that uses a microcomputer for intelligence. Microcomputer terminals usually have formatting and error-correction capability and can act as stand-alone data collection centers.

microcomputer timing modules—Circuits used to clock the microcomputer. The real-time clock module, the resettable clock module, the pulse accumulator, and the time-of-day module are considered as *special* timing modules.

microcontroller—A device or instrument that controls a process with a high degree of resolution; it typically consists of a microprocessor, memory, and appropriate interfaces. A microcontroller is distinguished from a data-processing microcomputer by its shorter word length and inability to accommodate some types of arithmetic operations.

microcycle—One of the operational steps required for a microprocessor to execute an instruction. Typically, one microcycle might be used to fetch the instruction, one or two more might be used for data access, and several more may be required for execution.

microdiagnostic—A test routine used to exercise the microprocessor and detect faults. Microdiagnostics are usually controlled by the microprocessor control store, which may be a RAM to allow writing capability. On most systems, microdiagnostics can detect a problem in a few seconds.

microelectronics—The technology of fabricating functional circuits using subassemblies comprised of integrated-circuit packages.

microfilm—A film in the form of a strip which is used to hold a photographic record of printed or graphic material which may be enlarged for viewing or reproduction.

microfiche—A sheet of film, usually 4 by 6 inches, used to store printed or graphic material which has been reduced 12 to 38 times by photographic methods.

microfunction decoder—An MSI arithmetic logic functions especially useful in microcomputer systems. Microfunction decoders perform lookahead operations for carry and shift functions, usually in a single microcycle.

microinstruction—The microcode required for a microcycle. Microinstructions are stored within a microprogram; they specify the sequential operations of individual computing elements.

microinstruction decoder—The logic used to interpret the microinstructions and provide signals to control data transfers, arithmetic operations, and sequences.

microinstruction sequence—The series of microinstructions that the microprogram control unit selects from the microprogram to execute a single macroinstruction or command.

microkit—A microcomputer system kit that usually consists of a CPU, keyboard, CRT display, and cassette tape units.

micrologic cards—Circuit boards which provide a logic family for use in wired or programmable logic systems. Typical micrologic cards include flip-flops, arithmetic functions, counters, converters, timing circuits, analog and digital converters, line and lamp drivers, motor controls, signal shapers, and input/output isolation circuits.

microminiaturization—The production and use of circuits and components with very small dimensions, especially with regard to the scaling down of already-miniature circuits. An example of microminiaturization is the development of LSI chips that perform the functions once performed by circuit cards containing several MSI chips.

micromodule—A small electronic device capable of performing one or more circuit functions, and possessing the feature of replaceability as a (usually) plug-in element.

micron—A unit of length equal to one millionth of a meter. The term has recently been supplanted in the International System of Units (SI) by ***micrometer***.

microprocessing unit—The main part of the hardware (abbreviated *MPU*) for a microcomputer. The MPU consists of the microprocessor, the main memory, input/output ports, and the clock circuit. It does not contain power supplies, enclosure, or control panel, and it is usually on a single circuit board. The level of complexity of the microcomputer is a direct function of the MPU.

microprocessor—The LSI equivalent of a computer's central processing unit, designed to work as a sequential computational or control unit by executing a defined set of instructions contained in memory. In a microcomputer with a fixed instruction set, the microprocessor may consist of an arithmetic logic unit and a control logic unit. For a microcomputer with a microprogrammed logic set, it may contain an additional control memory unit. The microprocessor determines what devices should have access to data and makes these decisions based upon timing requirements. It also correlates the activities of the memory and input/output units.

All microprocessors use large-scale integrated circuit technology; some feature a single-chip construction while others use several chips. The division or partitioning of functions is based on considerations of word length, flexibility, and performance.

Programmability can be obtained on one or two levels. The microinstruction level provides a very detailed level of control. The microinstructions can be combined to obtain a macroinstruction set which is then used to write control programs.

Control programs can sometimes be written in microcode to provide increased execution speed and more detailed control at the expense of more difficult programming. Microprocessors that are not microprogrammable use fixed, general-purpose instruction sets which are usually adequate for most applications.

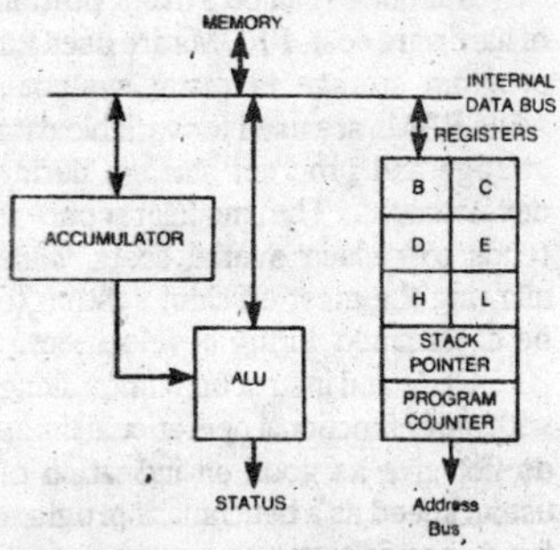

8080 Microprocessor Structure

Key features of individual microprocessors include word length, architecture, speed, and programming flexibility. Word length depends upon the requirements for resolution, accuracy, and the width of parallel inputs and outputs.

Microprocessors are structured for fixed word lengths, or for modular expansion using the bit-slice approach. In some microprocessors, the word lengths used for addresses are greater than those used for instructions. Longer word lengths for either instructions or addresses provide higher system throughput and more powerful memory addressing; shorter word lengths can require less hardware and smaller memories.

Architecture can include general-purpose registers, stacking, interrupts, interface structure, and some integral memory. General-purpose registers may be used for addressing, indexing, and status. They can simplify programming and reduce memory by eliminating memory buffering. Stacking permits subroutine nesting and temporary storage of data when programs are placed in ROM. Stacks consist of RAM memory locations maintained by software or stack register hardware.

The interface structure should be simple to use and not too costly for the application. Separate buses for addressing, data and memory are usually the best solution.

Memories can be a major portion of hardware cost. PROMs are used for program storage in many systems, while RAMs are used for variable data storage and program storage during development. The modular concept tends to reduce overall costs while allowing the most efficient system to be determined during development.

Cycle and instruction times along with other functional operational times do not give as good an indication of useful speed as a benchmark program for a specific task.

Programming flexibility can be determined from the nature of the instruction set. Multiple addressing modes conserve memory, simplify programming, and increase processing speed. Indexing and pointer addressing can be used to access tables stored in ROM or PROM. Custom instructions using microprogramming can improve overall performance by optimizing the microprocessor structure. Other features that aid programming include bit and byte manipulation, microprogram emulation, multiply and divide instructions, and double-precision arithmetic capability.

A typical microprocessor has an ALU and a number of registers to provide temporary storage. The accumulator is usually the one essential general-purpose register. It can serve as both a source and a destination register for operations involving another register, the ALU, or memory. Other general-purpose registers are used to store intermediate data and operands.

The program counter is a dedicated register used to count and track the program instructions by maintaining the address of the next instruction in memory. Each time that the microprocessor fetches an instruction, it increments the program counter so that it always indicates the following instruction. The fetched instruction, in the form of an operation code, is sent to the instruction register to be decoded.

microprocessor analyzer—An instrument used for designing, troubleshooting and testing both hardware and software in systems that use microprocessors. The analyzer is used with an oscilloscope and can display data related to a selected instruction cycle. Some types interface to the system using a connector that clips directly onto the microprocessor.

microprocessor assembler simulator—A program that accepts microprocessor assembly langauge, edits the text, and then allows the user to debug the software on a simulation of the microprocessor. A microprocessor assembler simulator provides about 60% to 80% assurance that the final software product will work.

microprocessor cache memory—A storage area which is used in addition to the main memory. A typical cache memory contains a cluster of bipolar devices in four blocks of four words each. When addressing memory, the CPU checks the cache and the main memory. If the cache is full, data is transferred to the main memory. A cache system can save CPU time when checking for errors.

microprocessor card—A circuit board which contains a microprocessor or microprocessing elements. A 144-pin edge connector is used for interfacing to other units.

microprocessor chip—The single piece of doped silicon upon which the microprocessor CPU is fabricated.

microprocessor chip set—A group of LSI semiconductors which can be connected to form a microcomputer.

microprocessor code assembler—Assembler programs for microcodes. The code assembler can also test the microprogram and is generally written in FORTRAN IV for running on a large computer system.

microprocessor compiler—A program which translates the source program into machine language. Compiler programs can be run on medium to large computers, and are available from time-sharing service firms.

microprocessor components—The hardware parts of a particular microprocessor configuration such as ALU, control logic, and register array.

microprocessor controller—A usually dedicated controller built around a microprocessor; a microcontroller.

microprocessor debugging program—A program that resides in microprocessor memory and used during system development to assist in debugging operations. A typical debugging program has the following capabilities:

(1) Load paper tape
(2) Punch contents of memory
(3) Inspect memory
(4) Move and set program breakpoints
(5) Start program typeout
(6) Modify memory

microprocessor educator system—A microprocessor-based communications terminal used for program development. A typical system contains:

(1) 53-key input keyboard
(2) A 64-character, 31-line CRT display
(3) 110 bps teletypewriter
(4) Composite video output for remote display

microprocessor instruction set—The group of instructions that are a part of the basic software for a given microprocessor. A typical instruction set may have 50 to 100 different instructions, including binary and decimal arithmetic, shift, rotate, load, store, interrupt, and stack.

microprocessor instrument—A scientific instrument that contains a microprocessor for calculations and error corrections due to drift and other variations.

microprocessor intelligence—The control program used to guide the microprocessor through the various operations it must perform.

microprocessor language assembler—A software package used to assemble source code on a minicomputer and convert it into binary output for loading into the microprocessor.

microprocessor language editor—A software set provided in the form of a binary tape which is then loaded into memory using a special program. Language editors are used primarily for creating and modifying source program tapes. Once in memory, the program text can be changed, deleted, and reformatted.

microprocessor maintenance console—A diagnostic tool which interfaces with some types of microprocessors. The maintenance console can display and simulate the contents of any memory location and register in the microprocessor system. It can also display outputs and simulate inputs.

microprocessor modem—A modulator-demodulator device under dedicated microprocessor control.

microprocessor ROM programmer—A program which is used to load, verify, and modify programs in a PROM device. Data is usually entered by means of paper tapes produced from a teletypewriter keyboard.

microprocessor slice—Refers to the building-block approach of a 2- or 4-bit microprocessor that can be ganged to build 8-, 16-, 24-, or 32-bit systems. A longer word length provides higher thoughput and easier programming, while shorter word lengths require less hardware and smaller memories.

microprocessor system analyzer—An instrument used to design, troubleshoot, and test both programs and hardware in microprocessor systems. A system analyzer can test programs and hardware either together or individually and can be connected or disconnected in a short time using clip-type connectors.

microprocessor terminal—A terminal that uses microprocessor circuits for intelligence capabilities; a smart terminal.

microprocessor training aid—A hardware unit designed to help the user master the software of 4- and 8-bit microprocessors. The training aid contains memory circuits for program and data storage, with a front panel for display and control of addressing and CPU status. It gives the student training in the use of the instruction set and provides software solutions to hardware problems.

microprogram—A program of instructions that do not reference the main memory. The microprogram is constructed from the basic subcommands, and it is sometimes a sequence of pseudo commands which are translated into machine commands by hardware. A microprogram tends to obtain maximum utilization of the subcommands by directly controlling the operation of each functional element in the microprocessor by using microcode. The microprogram can be used to implement a higher-language program by storing the microinstructions in ROM.

microprogram control section—Refers to the area of a microprogrammed computer that determines control action for the microprograms. The control section is similar to a processor within a processor; actions are usually determined by a microprogram stored in ROM, the control store. Instructions usually are very basic, and control is at a detailed level with a very short execution time.

microprogram control unit—A functional unit (abbreviated *MCU*) used in bipolar microprocessors to maintain and generate microprogram addresses. It is also used to control carry and shift operations and, with an interrupt control unit, to set the interrupt structure. The MCU uses the next address field rather than a program counter. The microprogram addresses are arranged in a two-dimensional array or matrix. Each microinstruction is selected by its row and column address.

microprogram display—A special board used on some systems for display and debug operations. It can be used to trap, latch, and display the control signals from the microprogram for an interface into the machine operations.

microprogram indexing—A technique used to locate data within a memory and count the number of times an operation is performed in a microprogram. Indexing can be used to point to a data item in a list of words, or count the number of times an inner loop in an instruction is used.

microprogrammable instruction—An instruction which does not reference main memory and may have several shift, skip, or transfer commands to be performed.

microprogrammable processor—A processor in which the instruction set is not firmly fixed. The instruction set is defined in memory, which is fetched to control the data paths of the machine. Since the contents and interpretation are defined in memory, the meaning and effect of the instruction can be changed by changing the contents of the memory.

microprogrammed processor—A processor or computer whose instruction set is not fixed, but can be tailored to specific needs by the programming of ROMs or other memory units; a microprogrammable processor.

microprogrammed sequencer—A device that generates, increments, and stores addresses. It can branch anywhere in memory, perform a subroutine, and then return.

microprogramming—The techniques of modifying an instruction set by building higher-level instructions from basic elemental operations. The higher-level instructions can then be directly programmed. For example, if a machine has basic instructions for addition, subtraction, and multiplication, an instruction for division could be defined by microprogramming. Microprogramming adds flexibility to the microcomputer. Compared to conventional programming, the distinctive feature is the storage associated with the control unit. In microprogramming, a user instruction determines an address in control memory which provides the starting point for executing the microprogrammed steps.

The development of inexpensive semiconductor memory has resulted in a wider use of microprogramming techniques. Microprogramming enhances flexibility by allowing the machine to optimize its control memory for specific applications. This ability to adjust can greatly simplify programming. Microprogramming is generally slow, since each user instruction requires that a sequence of programmed steps be executed. Control storage ROM must be fast enough to allow the use of a separate clock that is five to ten times faster than that used for main memory.

In *monophase* microprogramming, each microinstruction requires a clock pulse period for execution, while in *polyphase* microprogramming, the microinstruction requires more than a single clock period. Monophase operation involves shorter instructions and a shorter instruction set. Polyphase operation needs fewer instructions and is faster, but more complex to implement.

Microprogramming can aid system testing. Checking all data paths is difficult at the machine-language level, but microdiagnostics can check each path to isolate faults by checking functions rather than combinations of functions, as with conventional diagnostics.

Microprogramming is not, however, without its disadvantages:

(1) Expensive compared to writing programs
(2) Tends to be application- and machine-peculiar
(3) Relatively slow
(4) High debugging costs

Microprogramming techniques have been implemented in terminals, calculators, peripheral controllers, processors, and instruments with success.

microprogramming parameterization—A technique of microprogramming which uses stored parameters to characterize the state of the program. These parameters can be stored as program status words which are then tested to determine what actions should be initiated.

microsecond—A time period equal to 10^{-6} second (one millionth of one second).

microwave—Electromagnetic wavelengths shorter than 300 cm (frequencies above 1 GHz).

MIIS—Abbreviation for *metal-insulation-insulation-semiconductor*, a semiconductor "sandwich" which uses stored charges between two layers of insulation for nonvolatile memory. MIIS is used with the silicon-on-sapphire process to produce a memory that is independent of the external power supply.

miniaturization—The reduction in size of components and circuits to increase packing density and reduce power dissipation and signal propagation delays.

minicartridge—A magnetic tape holder that is smaller than a cassette. A typical minicartridge holds 140 feet of tape, 54% less than a cassette. The drive unit records on a single track at 800 bpi with storage for 115 kilobytes. The minicartridge is expected to outlast the life of a cassette by a factor of six or seven.

minicomputer—A small general-purpose-computer with a central processor, memory, and interface components which has more computing power than a micro, but less than a full-scale mainframe computer. Minicomputers are characterized by word lengths of 12, 16, or more bits; high-level language programming; extensive data processing capability; and a capacity that permits time-sharing.

minicomputer terminal—1. A terminal that contains a minicomputer for computation and processing, as well as interface control; a smart terminal. 2. A user-interactive input/output device that interfaces with a minicomputer system.

minicomputer communication processor—1. A processor unit containing a minicomputer that is connected between a central computing facility and a communications network to perform communications control functions for a full-scale mainframe central computer. 2. A communication processing unit that interfaces with a minicomputer system.

minimal latency coding—A method of programming in which the access time for a word depends upon its location; the location is chosen to reduce or minimize the access time. Also called *minimimum delay coding* or *optimum coding*.

minimum access code—A coding system is which the effects of delays for the transfer of data or instructions between storage and other sections is minimized.

minimum access programming—Programming aimed at minimizing the waiting time required to obtain information from storage; minimum latency programming.

minimum access routine—A routine coded such that the *actual* access time is less than the *expected* random access time.

minimum latency code—Minimum access code.

minimum latency programming—Minimum access programming.

minimum latency routine—Minimum access routine.

minor cycle—The time interval between the appearance of corresponding parts of successive operations used to provide serial access in a storage device. A major cycle usually contains several minor cycles.

minority carriers—Nondominant charge carriers in a semiconductor device.

minuend—The quantity from which another quantity is subtracted, or is to be subtracted.

minus zone—The bit positions in a code or coding which represent the albegraic minus sign.

mistake—A human action that produces an unintended result such as faulty arithmetic, an incorrect formula, or incorrect instructions. Mistakes are sometimes called gross errors to distinguish them from rounding and truncation errors. In the strict sense of the word, humans make mistakes and do not malfunction, while computers malfunction and do not make mistakes.

mixed-base notation—A positional representation in which the ratios of significances for all pairs of adjacent digits are not the same. For example, let three digits represent hours, tens of hours, and minutes. The significances, taking one minute as a unit, are:

60, 10, 1

The radixes of the second and third digits are 6 and 10. The ratio of the significances must be an integer.

mixed-radix notation—Mixed-base notation.

mnemonic—1. A word-like symbol used in assembly languages to code a computer to execute an instruction whose description resembles the word symbol. In BASIC, for example, the term MOV A, B is a mnemonic for "move the contents of register B into arithmetic register A." 2. Descriptive of any technique involving memorization of simple words and elements to recall complex words, rules, names, etc.

mnemonic address code—An address code that uses an easy-to-remember abbreviation related to the destination, such as LAX for Los Angeles International Airport.

mnemonic operation code—Refers to an operation code in which the names of operations are abbreviated and expressed in mnemonic terms to aid programmers. Examples include:

ADD for addition
CLR for clear
SQR for square root
MPY for multiply

Source statements are usually written using mnemonic code for translation by an assembler into machine code, which consists of only ones and zeros.

mobile systems—Computer, radio, and other complex systems which are to be installed on ships, planes, or motor vehicles.

mobility—Refers to the characteristics of the movement of charge carriers in vacuum or in materials.

mode—Any of the various methods of operation in a system, or the most frequent value in a series of values. Examples of modes in a system include:

(1) access mode
(2) interpretive mode
(3) binary mode
(4) alphameric mode
(5) byte mode
(6) conversation mode

model—A characterization, usually involving mathematical terms, of a process, device, concept, or system. A model may be a schematic representation of a system or process. It usually allows some manipulation of variables to enable a study of the system or process under various conditions or modifications.

modem—An electronic device that performs the modulation and demodulation functions required for communications. A modem (formed from a blending of modulator and demodulator) can be used to connect computers and terminals over telephone circuits. On the transmission end, the modulator converts the signals to the correct codes for transmission over the communications line. At the receiving end, the demodulator reconverts the signals for communication to the computer using the computer interface unit. Also called *data set*.

modem chip—An LSI chip that can be used to build a stand-alone modem unit. A modem chip can be used to develop full-duplex, half-duplex, simplex, automatic answer, automatic disconnect, answer only, or answer/originate configurations. All that is required for a complete unit that can perform all supervisory functions, including handshaking routines, is an input filter, output buffer, and threshold amplifier.

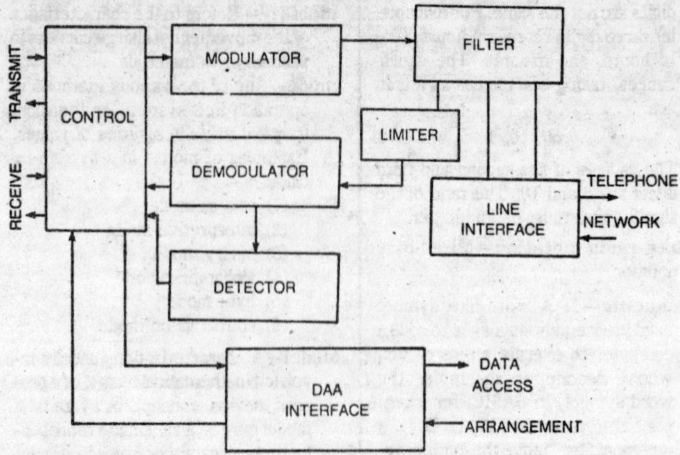

Modem

modification loop—A group of instructions which form a closed path to alter or change instruction addresses or data.

modifier—A quantity used to alter the normal interpretation and execution of an instruction, such as an index tag or indirect address tag.

modify—To alter a portion of an instruction or subroutine such that its interpretation and execution will be different from its usual interpretation and execution. The modification may permanently change the instruction or affect only the current execution. A typical modification is the changing of effective address through the use of index registers.

modular—Possessing a building-block capability, whereby standard replaceable components can be grouped to form a variety of configurations of subassemblies, assemblies, or systems.

modular converter—A data conversion unit that can be interconnected to form data acquisition systems and subsystems. These modular converters are available in epoxy-encapsulated form for analog-to-digital and digital-to-analog conversion along with sample-and-hold circuits and multiplexers.

modulate—To vary the amplitude, frequency, or phase of a carrier wave (such as light or a radio signal) proportionally with intelligence (such as speech), for transmission and ultimate demodulation.

modulated carrier—A wave whose magnitude, frequency, phase, or other characteristic has been varied according to the intelligence to be conveyed.

modulating signal—The signal which causes a corresponding variation in the characteristics of the carrier wave.

modulation—The variation of any wave or parameter in direct correspondence with an intelligence-bearing signal.

modulation code—The code used to cause variations in a signal in accordance with a predetermined scheme.

modulator–demodulator—A device that converts data signals to a form suitable for transmission and decodes transmitted signals to a form suitable for processing; a *modem*. Also called *data set*.

module—A software or hardware device that is of standardized design for easy replaceability or system expandability.

module boards—Interchangeable circuit boards that may contain a complete or partial functional circuit for building up a microcomputer system.

module extender boards—The connecting boards which, when inserted between a modular circuit board and its receptacle, permit access to the circuit without breaking the existing electrical connections. Module extender boards are used during system testing and maintenance operations.

modulo check—A checking operation which anticipates a remainder when the processed number is divided by a number carried through with data during the process.

modulo *n*—A ring of integers derived from the set of all integers:

> Let n be an integer greater than one, and A and B two other integers; if n is a factor of $A - B$, then A is congruent to B modulo n.

modulo *n* check—A check that makes use of a check number that is equal to the remainder of the desired number when divided by n. For example, if $n = 4$, the check number will be 0, 1, 2, or 3 and the remainder of A must equal the check number B when divided by 4.

mole electronics—The technique of growing solid-state crystals to form transistors, diodes, and resistors in one mass for microminiaturization. Also called *molecular electronics*.

monadic Boolean operator—A Boolean operator with only one operand, such as the NOT operator.

monadic operation—An operation on one operand, such as negation. Sometimes called *unary operation*.

monitor—1. To supervise and verify the correct operation of a program during its execution. 2. Software, hardware, or a human that observes, supervises, controls, or verifies the operation of a system or process. 3. A unit in a computer which prepares machine instructions from a source code. It may use built-in compilers for one or more program languages. The machine instructions are sequenced into the processing unit once compiling is complete.

monitor program—A computer software routine used to check for error conditions which may occur when the program is being executed. These error conditions may consist of numerical overflow, infinite loops, or attempts to access protected areas of memory. The monitor will attempt to provide error recovery along with diagnostics.

monitor system—The hardware and software used to control computer system functions. The monitor system can simulate the processor, maintain continuity between jobs, observe and report on the status of input/output devices, and provide automatic accounting of jobs.

A time-sharing monitor system usually remains permanently in memory to provide overall coordination and control of the total operating system. It allows several user programs to be loaded simultaneously into memory and prevents one user's program from interfering with another's during execution and control of all input/output devices.

Monte Carlo generator—A random-number generator or program for obtaining a random number.

Monte Carlo method—1. A trial-and-error method of obtaining a solution to a problem by repeated calculations. 2. Any technique for generating a number that is truly random.

monolithic—Fabricated on a single silicon chip.

monolithic storage—A computer memory made up of monolithic integrated circuits.

monostable circuit—1. A circuit that has one stable state. A monostable circuit repeats one complete cycle of operation for each trigger pulse. 2. A one-shot multivibrator.

monostable multivibrator—A one-shot device that provides a single output pulse for each input trigger pulse.

Morse code—A system used in signaling and telegraphy which uses combinations of dots and dashes to represent characters.

mosaic—A photoelectric pattern composed of a large number of photoemissive granules on an insulating support.

MOS—Abbreviation for *metal-oxide semiconductor*, a basic technology for fabricating integrated active devices employing field-effect transistors in any of a variety of different configurations. MOS devices tend to have a high capacitance, which makes them slower than their bipolar counterparts; but MOS devices achieve a higher functional density with fewer process steps, so fabrication costs are lower.

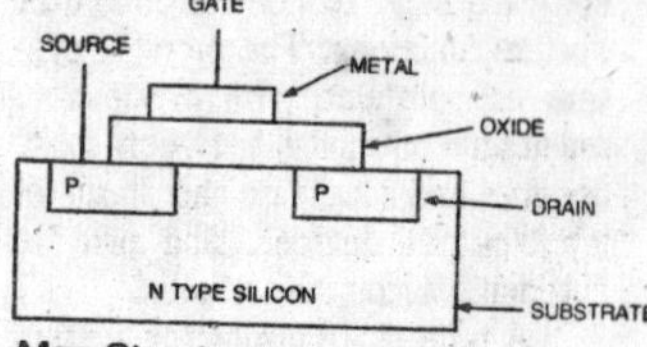

Mos Structure

MOS character generator—An LSI device that uses MOS circuitry to generate the voltage patterns required to form numbers, letters, and symbols for visual displays.

MOS DMOS—A double-diffused MOS device. The second diffusion process results in a product capable of handling higher voltages and currents with very little parasitic capacitance and low noise.

MOSFET—Acronym for *metal-oxide-semiconductor field-effect transistor*, a field-effect transistor made from a sandwich of metal and oxide layers.

MOS memory—A computer storage medium that uses MOS LSI devices rather than devices such as drums or disks.

MOS ROM—Acronym for *metal-oxide-semiconductor read-only memory*, a storage medium that uses MOS transistor cells to store binary ones and zeros.

MOS transistor—*Metal-oxide-semiconductor transistor*, a field-effect transistor that uses a sandwich of metal and oxide layers. Also called *MOSFET*.

most significant bit—The leftmost bit (abbreviated *MSB*) in a word. The MSB contributes the most weight to the numerical value of the word in most codes.

MPS—Abbreviation for *microprocessor system*.

MPU—Abbreviation for *microprocessor unit*.

MSI—Abbreviation for *medium-scale integration*, that level of active-device integration that yields more than 100 but less than 1000 active devices on a single substrate.

MSI Interconnections

MTBF—Abbreviation for *mean time between failures*, the predictable average time between anticipated malfunctions of an equipment item or system.

MTL—Abbreviation for *merged transistor logic*, a type of logic that uses multicollector transistors. Also called *integrated-injection logic* (I^2L).

MTTF—Abbreviation for *mean time to failure*.

multiaccess—Descriptive of a system which permits several users to interact with a single central computer using a number of online terminals. Access points are connected to the central processor by data transmission lines from remote terminals which may use teletypewriters, CRT displays, or satellite processors. Most multiaccess systems operate in a conversational mode with a fast response time.

multiaddress—An instruction format that contains more than one address part.

multiaspect—Descriptive of searches or systems which allow more than one facet of information to be used to identify and select operations.

multichannel—A system which divides the frequency spectrum of a signal into a number of bands which are separately transmitted and then recombined.

multichip IC—An integrated circuit that uses two or more semiconductor chips in a single package.

multilayer board—A printed circuit board that has two or more layers of circuit tracks (abbreviated *MLB*). Multilayer boards increase logic speed and packing density, and cut electrical crosstalk.

multilevel address—Indirect address.

multiple address code—An instruction code in which an instruction word may specify more than one address to be used during the operation. Examples include the *two-address* code and the *four-address* code. In a typical instruction of a *four-address* code, the addresses specify:

(1) The location of the two operands
(2) The location where results are stored
(3) The location of the next instruction

multiple-aperture core—A magnetic core with two or more holes for wires. Multiple-aperture cores can be used for nondestructive reading.

multiple system—A computer system which contains two or more central processing units with input/output devices and other hardware units that are related and interconnected for simultaneous operation.

multiple device—Two or more semiconductor chips in a single package, connected together to function as a single unit.

multiple modulation—A modulation technique that uses a succession of modulation processes where the wave from one stage becomes the modulating wave for the next stage. For example, PPM-AM is a system where pulse-position modulation is used to amplitude-modulate a carrier.

multiple-precision—The use of two or more words to represent a quantity or numeral, resulting in increased accuracy for computation.

multiple programming—Programming which allows two or more logic or arithmetic operations to be executed simultaneously.

multiplex—The concurrent transmission of two or more messages or information streams over the same channel.

multiplex data terminal—A device that transfers data from units operating at low transfer rates to units operating at high transfer rates in such a way that the high-speed devices are not required to wait for the low-speed units.

multiplexed operation—Refers to simultaneous operations which share the use of a common unit in such a

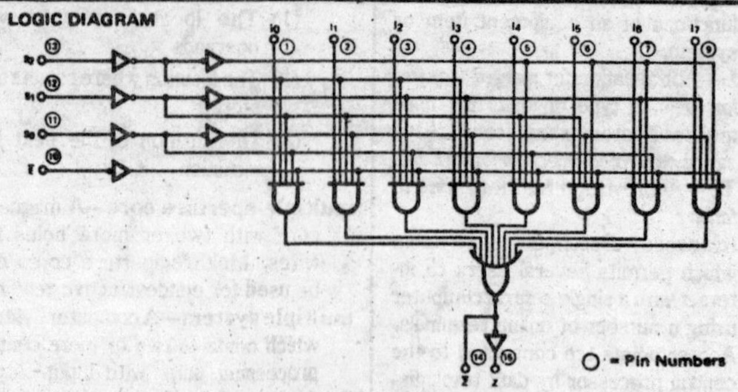

TRUTH TABLE

$\bar{E}$	S_2	S_1	S_0	I_0	I_1	I_2	I_3	I_4	I_5	I_6	I_7	$\bar{Z}$	Z
H	X	X	X	X	X	X	X	X	X	X	X	H	L
L	L	L	L	L	X	X	X	X	X	X	X	H	L
L	L	L	L	H	X	X	X	X	X	X	X	L	H
L	L	L	H	X	L	X	X	X	X	X	X	H	L
L	L	L	H	X	H	X	X	X	X	X	X	L	H
L	L	H	L	X	X	L	X	X	X	X	X	H	L
L	L	H	L	X	X	H	X	X	X	X	X	L	H
L	L	H	H	X	X	X	L	X	X	X	X	H	L
L	L	H	H	X	X	X	H	X	X	X	X	L	H
L	H	L	L	X	X	X	X	L	X	X	X	H	L
L	H	L	L	X	X	X	X	H	X	X	X	L	H
L	H	L	H	X	X	X	X	X	L	X	X	H	L
L	H	L	H	X	X	X	X	X	H	X	X	L	H
L	H	H	L	X	X	X	X	X	X	L	X	H	L
L	H	H	L	X	X	X	X	X	X	H	X	L	H
L	H	H	H	X	X	X	X	X	X	X	L	H	L
L	H	H	H	X	X	X	X	X	X	X	H	L	H

H = HIGH voltage level
L = LOW voltage level
X = Level does not affect output.

Multiplexer

way that they are considered independent operations.

multiplexer—A device which samples a number of channels and produces data that is the composite of all sampled channels, for transmission over a single channel. On reception, demultiplexing recreates all original channels.

multiplexer channel—A channel designed to operate with a number of devices simultaneously. A multiplexer channel allows several devices to transfer records at the same time by interleaving items of data. The multiplexer channel acts as a communications coordinator in many complex system configurations.

multiplexer polling—A method of polling or voting which allows each remote multiplexer to query the terminals conntected to it. Multiplexer polling is usually more efficient than polling from a central computer, since it involves fewer control messages.

multiplexing—The process of transmitting more than one signal at a time over a single channel, usually by sequentially sampling all signals and coding them into a single data stream. Frequency-division multiplexing (abbreviated *FDM*) allows a number of devices to share a link by dividing its frequency spectrum into a number of subchannels. Time-division multiplexing (abbreviated *TDM*) assigns a time slot into which each device may place information.

multiplication shift—A shift which results in multiplication of the number by a positive or negative integral power of the radix.

multiplication time—The time required to perform a multiply operation. In most binary operations, it is equal to the total of all addition times and shift times.

multiplier—A device that generates a product from two numbers. A digital multiplier generates the product from two digital numbers by additions of the multiplicand in accordance with the value of the digits in the multiplier. It then shifts the multiplicand and adds it to the product if the multiplier digit is a one, or shifts without adding if the digit is a zero. This is done for each successive digit of the multiplier.

mutiplier-quotient register—A register in which the multiplier for multiplication is placed, and the quotient for division is developed.

multiply—The logic operation which makes use of the logical product and is given by:

MULTIPLIER	MULTIPLICAND	LOGICAL PRODUCT
0	0	0
1	0	0
0	1	0
1	1	1

Same as the AND operation.

mutiply-divide instruction—An instruction or set of instructions which allow multiply and divide operations directly. Multiply and divide instructions are standard or optional on some microcomputers.

mutiply-divide package—A collection of subroutines that perform single- and double-precision multiplication and division for signed and unsigned binary numbers. The multiply-divide package is usually supplied in the form of a source program tape with an assembly listing for the specific microcomputer.

multiport register—A register that is capable of reading two locations and writing one location simultaneously. A typical 8-bit multiport register uses two sets of eight latches for address selection.

multiprocessing—Use of more than one independent processor and the processing of several programs or program segments concurrently. Each processor is only active on one program at any one time, while operations such as input/output transfers are performed in parallel on the programs. The processor can address adjacent storage modules in an odd or even fashion to reduce storage access conflicts in a multiprocessing system. Modules 0, 2, 4, and 6 would be referenced for even addresses,

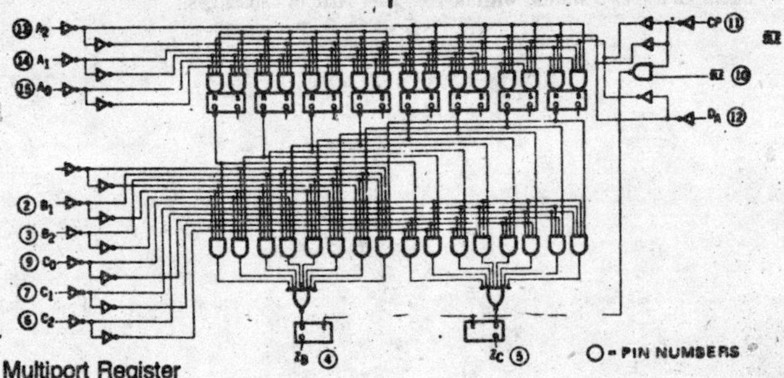

Multiport Register

while modules 1, 3, 5, and 7 are referenced for odd addresses.

Multiprocessing microcomputer systems can be used to provide increased computing power, but hardware and software costs can outweigh the advantages compared to larger computers.

multiprogramming—Refers to the concurrent execution of two or more programs. Multiprogramming generally uses overlapping or interleaving techniques to allow more than one program to time-share machine components.

multiprogramming executive—A software block that provides the operating system for concurrent execution of more than one program. A typical multiprogramming executive includes a priority scheduler along with memory allocation and deallocation.

multitasking—The procedures in which several separate but interrelated tasks operate within a single program identity. Multitasking differs from multiprogramming in that common routines and disk files may be used. Multitasking may or may not involve multiprocessing.

multithread—A section of a program that can have more than one logical path through it executed simultaneously.

multivibrator—An electronic switching circuit with two distinct states. When the device alternates rapidly between the two states, with no external crystal for frequency control, it is said to be *free-running*. When it is crystal-controlled, it is usually called an *oscillator*. When one of the two states is stable, it is called a *one-shot*. When both states are stable, it is called a *flip-flop*. In the free-running or crystal-controlled state, the multivibrator is said to be *astable*. As a one-shot, it is said to be *monostable*. As a flip-flop, it is considered *bistable*.

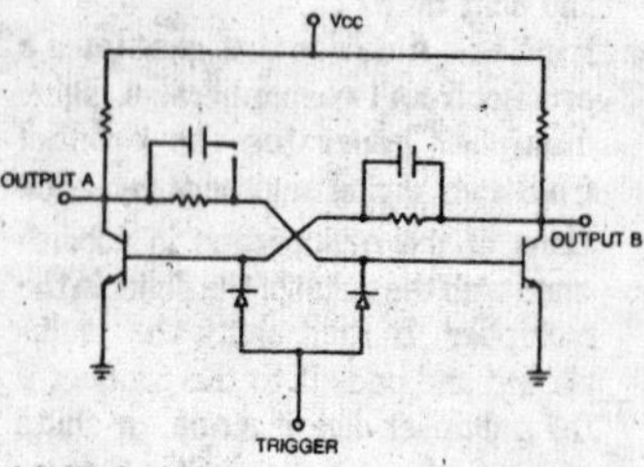

Multivibrator

multiwire process—A customized pattern of insulated wires laid on an adhesive-coated surface to form a circuit board.

mutual inductance—The generation of an electromotive force in one conductor by a variation of current in another conductor which is linked to the first conductor by magnetic flux.

MUX—Abbreviation for *multiplex, multiplexing,* or *multiplexer*.

Mylar—Tradename for a type of polyester film widely used as a base for magnetic tape and for the dielectric of capacitors.

N

NAK—The negative acknowledge character. A signal sent by the receiver as a negative response to the sender to indicate that the previous block was unacceptable and the receiver is now ready to accept a retransmission.

NAND—The logical operator having the property: if P and Q are statements, then the NAND output of P and Q is true if either P or Q is false; and it is false if both P and Q are true. (Also called *inverted AND* and *negated AND*.)

NAND flip-flop—A flip-flop such as the R-S type which can be constructed from NAND gates.

NAND gate—A device or circuit that performs the NAND operation.

nanocircuit—An integrated microelectronic circuit in which each component is fabricated on a separate chip or substrate for maximum high-speed performance.

nanoprocessor—A processor that operates with a cycle time in the nanosecond range.

nanosecond—An amount of time equal to 10^{-9} second. Abbreviated ***ns***.

nanosecond circuit—A circuit that processes pulses or waveforms with rise and fall times measured in billionths of a second or less.

narrowband—Descriptive of a communications channel whose bandwidth is restricted to some specified value less than originally allocated for such channels.

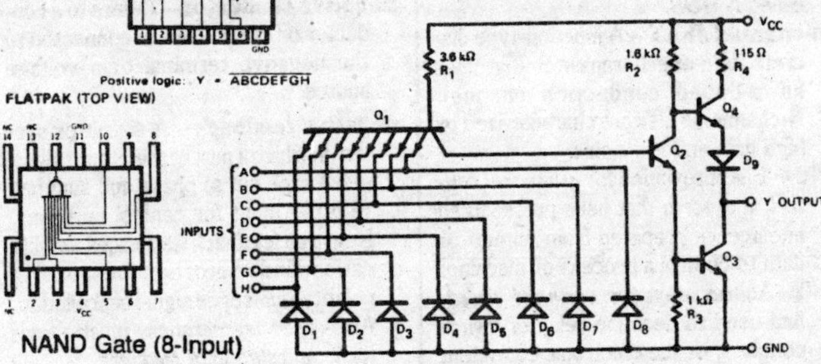

NAND Gate (8-Input)

natural frequency—The frequency of free oscillation; thus, the frequency of resonance of any device or circuit.

natural function generator—An analog hardware unit or a software program used to solve differential equations using methods based upon physical laws.

n-channel—A semiconductor material using n-type dopants and used for the conduction channel in MOS field-effect devices. N-channel MOS devices have several advantages over p-channel types. The majority carriers are electrons rather than holes, as in p-channel devices; thus, the mobility is increased, thereby allowing a theoretical improvement in speed. Threshold voltages are lower than with p-channel devices, which allows circuits to operate at lower supply voltages. The lower voltages result in fewer parasitic effects and permit tighter packing densities.

Compared to bipolar devices, n-channel MOS offers lower power consumption for the same speed, but bipolar offers higher speed if power is not a consideration.

n-channel modem—A modem that uses n-channel MOS circuits. N-channel modems operate from a single power supply and are fully TTL-compatible.

n-channel MOS—MOS devices that use an n-channel region for field-effect conduction. Such devices tend to be faster and use less semiconductor real estate than p-channel units. Also called *NMOS*.

n-channel JFET—A junction-type discrete field-effect transistor that uses an n-doped conduction channel. N-channel JFETs are characterized by high gain and low noise.

NC—1. Abbreviation for *numerical control*, a system that uses prerecorded intelligence prepared from numerical data to control a process or machine. 2. Abbreviation for *normally closed*, and used to describe relay or switch contacts, or the electronic equivalent of such contacts. 3. Abbreviation for *no connection*, usually written adjacent to a depicted contact or conductor on a schematic to show that the absence of another conductor is not an inadvertent omission.

negate—To perform the logical operation of reversing a signal, condition, or state to its alternate or opposite state.

negation element—A device, circuit, or gate with the capability of reversing a two-state signal, condition, or event into its alternate or opposite state.

negation gate—Negation element.

negative—1. Less than zero, the opposite of positive. 2. Having a surplus of electrons (negative charges). 3. The minus terminal of a battery or power supply. 4. The *NOT* function. A negative OR gate is the same as a NOT OR or NOR gate; a negative AND is a NOT AND or NAND.

negative-acknowledge character—A communication control character (abbreviated *NAK*) transmitted by a receiver as a negative response to a sender. The negative acknowledge is sometimes used as an accuracy control character.

negative bias—A potential, negative with respect to ground, applied as a constant voltage to an electronic circuit element for the purpose of keeping the circuit element in a ready-to-operate state. A negative bias on an amplifier input electrode, for example, establishes the operating point of that stage.

negative conductor—Refers to a conductor or cable which is connected to the negative terminal of a voltage source.

negative feedback—A circuit or system in which a part of the output signal is fed back out of phase and summed with the input for control purposes. Negative feedback decreases amplification and distortion because of polarity-difference signal cancellation. Also called *degeneration, inverse feedback,* and *stabilized feedback*.

negative impedance—A condition occurring in electronic devices where an increasing voltage at some point begins to produce a proportionate decrease in current.

negative resistance—See *negative impedance*.

nesistor—A type of transistor that operates as a result of a bipolar field effect.

nest—1. To store subroutines or other data within subroutines or data of a different hierarchy such that the different levels can be accessed or executed recursively. 2. To store subroutine addresses or general register data in such a fashion that the most recent stored data must be accessed first, and all subsequent data accessed in that same order (the reverse order of storage).

nesting—1. Stacking of index addresses and other register data so that they can be accessed sequentially, in reverse order of storage. 2. A program technique of enclosing subroutines within program subroutines; the blocks of data or subroutines in the inner "ring" or loop are not necessarily part of the outer ring or loop.

nesting level—Refers to the relative hierarchical level at which a term or subexpression appears in an expression in assembler programming, or the level at which a macro definition containing an inner macro instruction is processed by an assembler.

net loss—The sum of gains and losses between two terminals of a device, circuit, or system.

network—1. An interconnected combination of elements used to provide a communications path between two or more points. 2. An assemblage of components usually containing many similar elements and devoted to a common function. 3. Any system of multiple interrelated circuits or elements.

network analysis—The process of calculating the transfer characteristic and other properties of a usually passive circuit from its configuration, elements, voltages, etc.

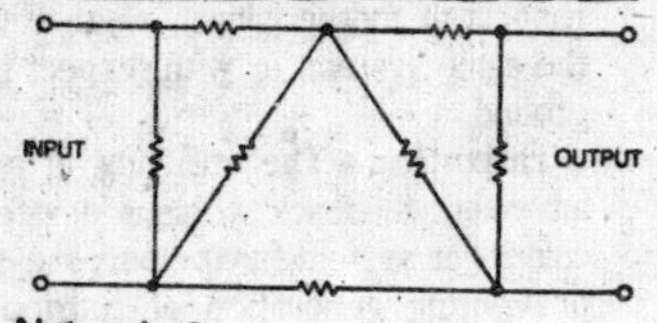

Network, 2

network analyzer—1. A group of circuit elements which can be interconnected to form a model of a network or system. Electrical measurements can then be used to determine desired quantities in the simulated system. Also called a *network calculator*. 2. An electronic test-equipment item designed to make qualitative tests on specific circuit networks.

network buffer—A storage device used to compensate for a difference in the rate of flow of data received and transmitted in a computer communications system. The buffer has memory and control circuits for storing incoming messages and holding outgoing messages which must be delayed because of busy lines.

network calculator—A combination of electrical elements used to simulate the operation of a system such as a power generating plant.

network relay—A relay used for the protection and control of alternating current networks.

network service—A multiuser computer service. Typical network services include highly systematized programs and data bases.

network synthesis—The process of formulating a network with specific requirements.

network transfer function—The ratio of output to input in a network, usually expressed in incremental units over a specific time period.

neuron simulation—Refers to the study of neuron cells and networks using electronic devices and systems.

neutral—A conductor, device, or contact with no net charge or voltage with respect to another similar element in the same system, or with respect to ground.

neutralization—The nullifying of inadvertent feedback within a device, circuit, or system for the purpose of preventing generation of spurious signals and unwanted radiation.

neutral zone—1. An area in space or time in which no control action takes place. 2. A period between words used for switching or other operations. Also called *dead band.*

new input queue—Refers to a group of new messages in system awaiting processing. The main scheduling routine will scan them along with the other queues for processing at the right time.

new line character—A format effector that causes the printing or display position to be moved to the first position of the next printing or display line. Abbreviated *NL.*

nines' complement—The radix-minus-one complement in decimal notation.

ninety-column card—A punched card with 90 vertical columns representing 90 characters.

Nixie tube—Tradename for a gas discharge tube used as a visual alphanumeric display unit.

NMOS—Abbreviation for ***n-channel metal-oxide semiconductor***, a semiconductor technology that uses MOS devices with n-channel regions for conduction.

NMOS driver—A circuit used to interface NMOS memories with emitter-coupled logic. A typical NMOS driver has a propagation time of 10 ns and a transition time of 20 ns with a 400 pF load.

NMOS RAM—A random-access memory that uses NMOS technology for high speed and low power. NMOS RAMs compete with bipolar units for many high-speed cache applications. A typical NMOS RAM has the following features:

(1) Access time of less than 100 ns
(2) Maximum power dissipation of less than 600 mW
(3) Fully static operation
(4) Single 5V supply
(5) Standard 16-pin package

n-n junction—A junction produced between two n-type regions in a semiconductor having different electrical properties.

no-address instruction—An instruction specifying an operation that the computer can perform without referring to its storage or memory unit.

node—A terminal common to two or more branches in a network or system. Also called ***junction point, branch point, nodal point***, and ***vertex***.

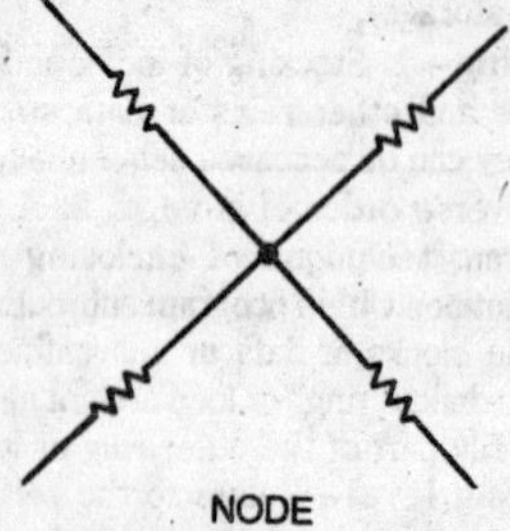

NODE

noise—Any unwanted disturbance in a system, such as random variations in voltage or current, or bits or words which are extra and must be removed before the data is used. *Steady-state* noise may consist of Gaussian noise, thermal noise, white noise, and random noise. *Impulse* noise is characterized by peaks of large amplitude and pulses of short duration. This type of noise can block out data signals and cause errors, especially in high-speed systems where more bits are affected in a given time period.

noise immunity—Refers to the insensitivity of a circuit or device to spurious signals or noise. CMOS logic offers a noise margin of 1.5V compared to a noise margin of 0.4V for TTL circuits.

noise level—Refers to the strength of extraneous signals in a circuit or system.

noise margin—The difference in potential between a signal and either the noise existing when the signal is removed or the threshold level of the device being rated.

noise ratio—The ratio of the noise level to the signal level, usually expressed in decibels.

noisy digit—A digit (usually zero) that is produced during the normalizing of a floating-point number and inserted during a left shift operation into the fixed-point part.

noisy mode—The mode during the normalization of a floating-point number in which digits are inserted with a left shift operation into low-order positions.

nominal bandwidth—The band of frequencies, including guard bands, assigned to a channel.

nominal impedance—The impedance of a circuit or device under normal conditions, usually specified for a specific frequency. For example, a loudspeaker with a nominal impedance of 8 Ω is considered to have an 8Ω impedance when the speaker's input signal is a 1000 Hz sine wave.

nonarithmetic shift—A shift in which the digits dropped off at one end are returned at the other in an end-around carry operation. If a register holds 23456789, a nonarithmetic shift of two bits produces 45678923. Also called *end-around*, *ring shift*, or *cyclic shift*.

nonconductor—An insulator through which no current can flow.

nondestructive read—A read operation that does not result in erasure of the data in the source (abbreviated *NDR*).

nondestructive readout—1. A reading process that does not result in destruction of the data in the source. 2. A storage medium that cannot be erased and reused.

nonequivalence element—A two-input logic element that furnishes a *true* output only when its two input signals are different.

nonequivalence operation—A logical operation applied to two operands which produces a 1 for those bits that are different and a 0 for those bits that are the same.

OPERANDS	RESULT
110110	101100
011010	

nonlinear distortion—Distortion that is caused by a deviation from a linear relationship between the input and output of a system or device.

nonlinearity—A relationship between the output and input which cannot be represented by direct proportioning.

nonlinear network—A network of circuit elements that cannot be specified with linear variables such as differential equations or functions.

nonlinear programming—A procedure used in operations research for locating the maximum and minimum of a function subject to nonlinear constraints.

nonlinear system—Refers to a control system model which cannot be represented by linear equations.

nonoperable instruction—An instruction whose only effect is to increment the instruction index counter. Usually written as CONTINUE.

nonpolarized return-to-zero recording—A recording method in which the reference condition is the absence of magnetization. Ones are represented by a specified condition of magnetization, and zeros are represented by the absence of magnetization.

nonreturn-to-change recording—A recording method in which ones are represented by a specified condition of magnetization and zeros are represented by another condition.

nonreturn-to-reference recording—A recording method in which ones are represented by a change in the condition of magnetization and zeros are represented by the absence of change. Also called *nonreturn-to-zero recording.*

nonreturn-to-zero—A method of writing information on a magnetic surface in which the current through the write head does not return to zero after the write pulse. Abbreviated *NRZ*.

nonreturn-to-zero recording—Nonreturn-to-reference recording.

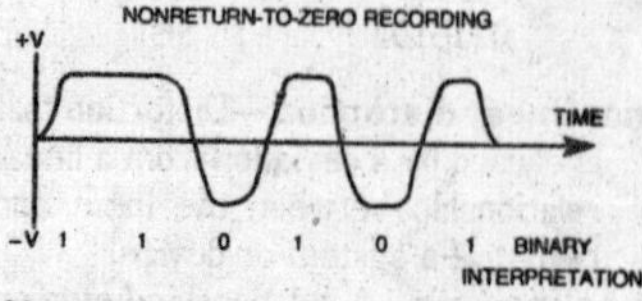

Nonreturn-to-Zero Recording

nonswitched line—A service or connection between a remote terminal and a computer that does not have to be established by dialing.

nonvolatile—Descriptive of a memory or storage medium that retains data in the absence of power so that the data is available upon restoration of power. A magnetic memory is nonvolatile; most semiconductor read/write memories are volatile. PROMs and EAROMs remain intact after they are programmed if power is removed and then reapplied.

nonvolatile memory—A memory, such as magnetic tape or disk, which retains information if power is removed.

nonvolatile storage—Storage media that retain information in the absence of power and which allow the information to be available when power is restored.

NO .OP—A no-operation instruction which causes the computer to do nothing except proceed to the next instruction in sequence. Also, NOP.

no-operation—The computer instruction which causes the computer to do nothing except proceed to the next instruction. Abbreviated *NO OP*, NOP.

NOP—The no-operation instruction, NO OP.

NOR—A logical operation that has a true output only if all inputs are zero. The negative-OR operation.

NOR circuit—A circuit or gate that has a true output only if all inputs are false.

NOR gate—A circuit that performs the NOR operation.

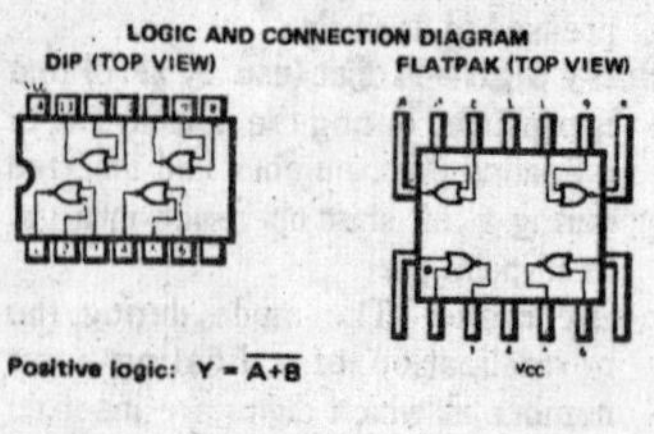

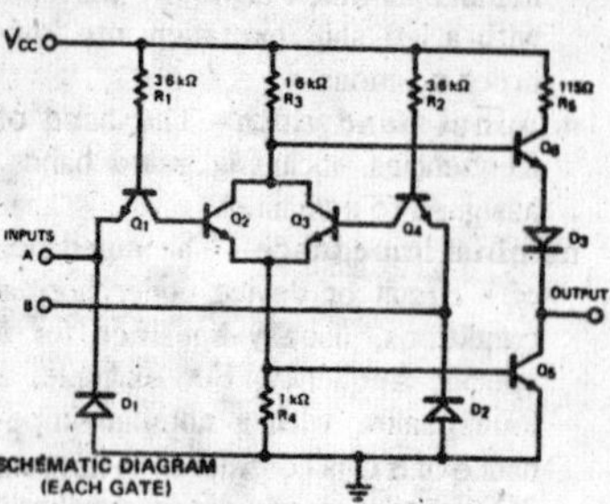

NOR Gate (Quad 2-Input)

normal direction flow—A flow in a direction from left to right or top to bottom in a flow chart.

normalization—The multiplication of a variable by a numerical coefficient to make it assume a desired value. Also called *scaling*.

normalization routine—A floating-point arithmetic operation related to the normalization of numerals in which digits other than zero are developed in the lower order or less-significant positions during a left shift.

normalized form—A form used in a floating-point number which is adjusted so that its mantissa lies in a specified range. Also called *standard form*.

normally closed—The designation applied to the contacts of a switch, relay, or solid-state switching device such that the circuit is completed when no input power is applied. Abbreviated *NC*.

normally open—The designation applied to the contacts of a switch, relay, or solid-state switching device such that the circuit is not completed until power is applied. Abbreviated *NO*.

normal stage punching—A card punching system in which only the even-numbered rows are punched.

normal state—Refers to the condition of operation in a computer where the instructions are concerned with conventional aspects of computation such as adding, subtracting, and data transfer.

Norton's theorem—A theorem that states that any linear network of impedances and sources, if viewed from any two points in the network, can be replaced by an equivalent impedance in shunt with an equivalent current source.

NOT—A logic operator having the property: if P is a statement, then the NOT of P is true if P is false; and it is false if P is true. The NOT operator in represented by an overline.

NOT AND—The NAND operation.

NOT AND gate—An AND gating circuit combined with an inverter; a NAND gate.

notation—The act, process, or method used to represent technical facts or quantities. In computer practice, the term typically describes the number radix, as follows:

NOTATION	RADIX
BINARY	2
TERNARY	3
QUATERNARY	4
QUINARY	5
DECIMAL	10
DUODECIMAL	12
HEXADECIMAL	16
DUOTRICENARY	32
BIQUINARY	2,5

notational system—Any of the various number systems used to indicate radix values, such as binary, decimal, or hexadecimal. See *notation*.

NOT circuit—A circuit or gate in which the output is opposite in polarity to the input.

NOT gate—A circuit which has a true output when the input is false, and a false output when the input is true.

NOT if-then gate—A gate that performs the *A AND NOT B* and *B AND NOT A* operations.

NOT operation—A Boolean operation which specifies that the output will always be the inverse of the input. A circuit or device that performs the NOT operation is called an *inverter*.

NOT OR—The *negated OR* operation; or *NOR*.

npin transistor—A transistor which has an intrinsic (undoped) layer between the base and collector to extend the high-frequency range.

npip transistor—A transistor which has an intrinsic layer between two p regions.

np junction—The region in a semiconductor where the n-doped and p-doped areas meet. It is characterized by a high resistance in one direction and a low resistance in the other.

n-plus-one address instruction—A multiple address instruction in which one address serves to specify the location of the next instruction in the normal sequence of execution.

npn—A transistor with a p-region base and an n-region emitter and collector. Such transistors are characterized by electrons as majority carriers (rather than holes).

NRZ—Abbreviation for *nonreturn to zero*, a recording technique in which write-pulse voltages do not return to zero following application.

n-type—A semiconductor region which is doped to provide excess electrons.

null—A balanced condition which results in zero output from a circuit, device, or system.

null character—A control character that serves to accomplish media fill or time fill functions. For example, in ASCII the null character is a string of zeros. Null characters can be inserted or removed without affecting the meaning of a sequence, but control of equipment or the format may be affected. Abbreviated *NUL*.

null cycle—The time required to cycle through a program without introducing data. The null cycle represents the lower boundary for program processing time.

null indicator—A device which indicates when a parameter is zero.

null matrix—A matrix of values in which every element is zero. Also called *zero matrix*.

null set—A set which contains no numbers. Also called the *empty set*.

null suppression—The bypassing of all null characters in a data string to reduce the amount of characters transmitted. Also called *data compaction*.

number—A mathematical entity that indicates quantity or amount of units; a numeral.

number system—Notation system.

numeral—A discrete representation of a number using a single-digit symbol. For example, the number 12 is composed of two numerals.

numeral system—A system for representing numbers by agreed sets of symbols according to agreed rules.

numeration—The representation of numbers by agreed sets of symbols according to agreed rules.

numeration system—Numeral system.

numeric—1. Pertaining to numerals or representation by means of numerals. 2. A set of numerals with an established meaning within a given context. For example, 10-4 is a communications numeric for "okay."

numerical—Pertaining to numerals or representations using numerals.

numerical analysis—The study of methods for obtaining useful quantitative solutions to problems that have been expressed mathematically. Numerical analysis also includes the study of errors and the bounds of errors in obtaining these solutions.

numerical control—The automatic control of a machine or process using numerical data that is introduced using punched tapes or other input methods. Most numerical-control devices have limited logical capability, and they rely on the input medium for detailed guidance.

A computer is generally used to prepare the control media. Direct numerical control uses a system of numerically controlled machines which are connected to a common memory. Direct numerical control systems may have provisions for collection and display of data along with limited editing and operator instruction capabilities.

Other types of numerical control systems may use methods with interchangeable connections for modifying the control sequence.

numerical control system—A system for controlling industrial machine operations automatically by insertion of numerical data at some point.

numerical control tape—A punched-paper or magnetic tape that is used to feed instructions to a numerical control machine.

numeric code—A code that consists only of number symbols and associated special characters.

numerical data—Data in which information is expressed by a set of numbers which can assume only discrete values or configurations.

numerically controlled machine—A machine which is under the control of numerical data. See *numerical control*.

numeric coding—A system of abbreviation in which all information is reduced to numerical quantities, in contrast to alphabetic coding.

numeric constant—A term which is treated as an octal or decimal number, depending upon the conversion mode in effect at the time.

numeric word—A word composed of characters from a numeric code. For example, in the Dewey decimal classification system, 621.39 is a numeric word used to identify a specific class of literature.

Nyquist rate—Refers to the maximum rate at which code elements can be resolved in a communication channel of limited bandwidth.

O

object code—The output from a compiler or assembler which is itself executable machine code or is suitable for processing to produce executable machine code. A line of object code might be a 16-bit string of ones and zeros whose combination is the machine-language equivalent of an instruction.

object deck—A stack of punched cards forming a computer program in machine language. The object deck is usually prepared from an equivalent source deck by a compiler.

object language—The language which is the output of an automatic coding routine. Object language and machine language may be the same; however, if the coding routine is done in a series of steps, the object language of one step may serve as the source language for the next step.

object program—A source program that has been translated into machine language, or the final or target program which is the end result of processing. Typically, translator modules are used to translate the user-generated code into executable machine code; other operating modules add the utility routines to generate the executable object program.

OCR—Abbreviation for *optical character recognition*, the recognition by machines of printed or written characters using optical sensing devices.

octal—A number system whose radix is 8, composed of the digits 0 through 7.

octal debug technique—A debugging and loading program used in octal systems. It is usually supplied on two preprogrammed PROMs with a supplementary tape and includes the following features:

(1) Memory list/modify
(2) Register list/modify
(3) Tape load/punch
(4) Memory dump

octal digits—The symbols 0 through 7 when the radix is 8.

odd-even check—Parity check.

odd-even interleaving—The splitting of memory into several sections and independent paths with the odd and even addresses in alternate sections. Odd-even interleaving allows additional segmenting over normal memory interleaving.

odd-parity check—A check in which the sum of all binary digits in a word is odd. An additional character position permits insertion of a 1 when the total is even, and insertion of a 0 when the total is odd.

OEM—Abbreviation for *original-equipment manufacturer*.

off emergency—A console or control panel switch which can be used to disconnect all power in the event of an emergency situation.

offline—1. Equipment which is not under direct control of the CPU. 2. Terminal equipment not connected to a transmission line.

offline operation—An operation which is independent of the system's operating time base. Offline operation usually refers to the operation of peripheral units independent of the CPU.

off-punch—A punched hole in a card or tape that did not compare favorably with the proper position for that hole.

off-the-shelf—Refers to production items which are available from current stock, or software that can be used as purchased.

ohm—The unit of electrical resistance.

ohmmeter—A portable battery-operated instrument for measuring electrical resistance and determining electrical continuity.

one-address—A system of instructions such that each complete instruction explicitly describes one operation and one storage location.

one-address instruction—An instruction that consists of an operation and exactly one address. The instruction code of a single-address computer may include both zero and multiaddress instructions as special cases.

one-cell switching—Refers to an array of magnetic cells and the selective switching of one cell in the array by the application of selected drive pulses.

one-digit adder—A binary adding circuit which adds one digit at a time.

one-for-one—A term used with assembly routines where one source-language instruction is converted into one machine-language instruction.

one-level storage—A concept which treats all online storage as having one level of appearance to the user. One-level storage makes all online storage appear as main storage.

one-plus-one address—An instruction that contains one operand address and one control address.

ones' complement—The radix-minus-one complement in binary notation.

one-shot—1. A monostable multivibrator. 2. Any circuit or device having only one stable state.

one-shot multivibrator—A multivibrator that has one stable state.

one-step operation—A method of operating a computer manually in which a single instruction or part of an instruction is performed in response to a single manual control operation. One-step operation is generally used for debugging procedures.

one-to-zero ratio—The ratio of a one output level to a zero output level.

online—1. Equipment, devices, and systems in direct interactive communication with the CPU. 2. Descriptive of terminal equipment connected to a transmission line.

online data processing—Data processing in which all changes to records and accounts are made at the time that each transaction or event occurs. Online processing generally requires random-access storage.

online debugging—The debugging of a program while sharing its execution with an online process program. Online debugging must be accomplished in such a way that any attempt by the program being debugged to interfere with the process program will be detected and inhibited.

online diagnostics—The running of diagnostics while the system is online, but off peak to save time and to take corrective action without shutdown of the system.

online equipment—Equipment under the direct control of the CPU.

online mode—A mode of operation in which all devices are responsive to the CPU.

online storage—Storage devices which are under direct control of the computing system.

online system—1. A system where the input data enters the computer directly from the point of origin and the output data is transmitted directly to where it is used. 2. A system which has no need for human intervention between the source of data and the processing by the CPU.

op codes—Operation codes which are decoded to serve as instructions in microcomputer systems. The op code usually contains source statements which are used to generate machine instructions after assembly.

open-loop—A control system in which there is no self-correcting action and no feedback path; also a family of control units, which may include computers which are linked together manually by operator action.

open-loop control—A type of control in which no feedback is employed.

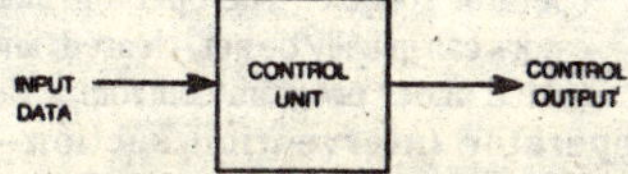

Open-Loop Control

open-loop control system—A control system without feedback where the output is directly controlled by the system input.

open routine—A routine that can be directly inserted into a larger routine with a linkage or calling sequence.

open running—Refers to a teletypewriter which is connected to an open line. The teletypewriter appears to be running, as the type hammer continually hits the type box, but does not move across the page.

open shop—The operation of a computer facility in which most of the problem programming is performed by the problem originator rather than by a group of programming specialists.

open subroutine—A subroutine which is directly inserted into the linear operational sequence where it is used. It does not require a jump and must be recopied at each point where it is needed in the routine.

operand—1. The fundamental quantity on which a mathematical operation is performed. A statement usually consists of an operator and an operand; in an add instruction, the operator will indicate "add," and the operand will indicate what is to be added. A result, parameter, or the address portion of an instruction.

operand call syllable—A specific syllable which calls for an operand to be brought from the stack either directly from the program reference table or indirectly using a descriptor.

operating code—A specific code containing source statements that generate machine code after assembly. Also called *op code*.

operating console—A unit which contains all controls and indicators necessary for the operation of the processor. A typical microcomputer operating console may include the following functions:

(1) Run indicator and switch
(2) Halt indicator and switch
(3) Reset switch
(4) Link indicator
(5) Interrupt indicator
(6) Accumulator, program counter, and memory display

operating system—A basic group of programs under the control of a data processing program or an integrated collection of service routines for supervising the sequencing and processing operations.

Operating systems may provide scheduling, debugging, input/output control, accounting, compilation, storage assignment, data management, and other services. A typical disk operating system features extended file management, program chaining, page loading, and mixing programs of different languages. Up to 100 million bytes of storage can be accessed with some systems.

A floppy disk operating system can eliminate the need for paper tape or cards during microcomputer development. The source programs are written and edited at the system keyboard and stored on the floppy disk for assembly.

Supervisor and executive operating systems include a supervisory program, system programs, and system routines. The executive brings together the system software components to make an operating system.

operation—A defined action, usually specified by a single instruction or pseudo instruction. An operation may be arithmetic, logical, or transferral; and it may be executed under the direction of a subroutine.

operational amplifier—A usually integrated amplifier with high gain and wide bandwidth which can be used to perform mathematical operations. Also called *op amp*.

operational character—A character used as a code element to initiate, modify, or stop a control operation. A typical operational character is the *carriage return*.

operational relay—A relay that is controlled by an operational amplifier or a relay amplifier.

operation code—A code that represents specific actions. Also called *instruction code*.

operation cycle—The portion of a machine cycle when the actual execution of the instruction takes place. Operations such as multiply or divide may require a large number of these cycles for completion. Also called an *execution cycle*.

operation decoder—A device that selects one or more channels of operation according to the operator part of the machine instruction.

operations analysis—The use of analytic methods to provide criteria for decisions in systems involving repeatable operations. The usual objective is to provide management with a logical basis for making predictions and decisions. The following techniques may be used:

(1) Linear programming
(2) Probability theory
(3) Information theory
(4) Game theory
(5) Monte Carlo methods
(6) Queuing theory

operations research—Operations analysis (abbreviated *OR*).

operator—1. The mathematical symbol which represents the process to be performed on an associated operand. 2. The portion of an instruction which indicates the action to be performed on the operands.

operator console—A hardware unit which allows the operator to communicate with the computer. The operator console is used to enter data or information, to request and display stored data, and to actuate the various command routines.

operator indicator—Any display light used to show conditions on the operator console. The operator indicators can usually be set, cleared, and tested under program control.

operator intervention section—That portion of the control equipment in which operators can intervene in normal programming operations.

op register—A register used to hold the operation code of computer instructions.

optical character recognition—The machine identification of graphic characters using photosensitive devices. Optical character recognition (abbreviated *OCR*) includes characters of all fonts or types.

optical coupler—A photon-coupled amplifier used to isolate electrical outputs from inputs. Optical couplers can operate at speeds of up to 10 MHz with isolation voltages as high as 5 kV. Also called *optocoupler* and *optoisolator*.

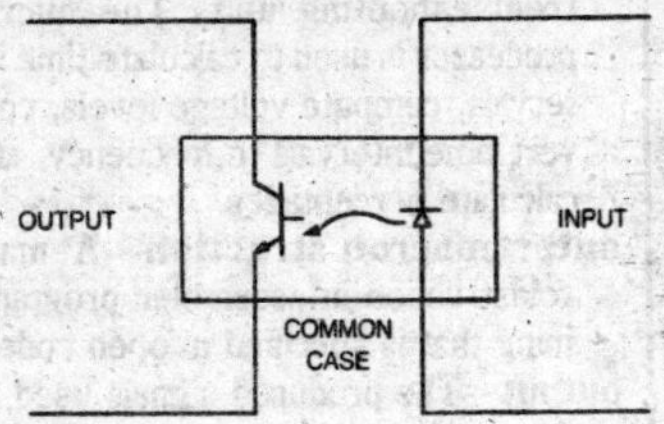

Optical Coupler

optical image chip—An integrated circuit that converts optical images into electrical signals. Optical image chips are used in some TV monitors and in small inexpensive TV cameras.

optical isolator—Optical coupler.

optical mark reader—A device that can read forms with pencil marks, punches, and printed marks.

optical scanner—A device that scans patterns of incident light and generates signals which are functions of the data represented. The data may be printed or written using a bar code or other representation.

optical sensor—A device or transducer capable of detecting light and producing an electrical output.

optimize—To rearrange instructions or data in storage such that a minimum number of jumps or transfers are required in the running of the program.

optimum code—A computer code which is particularly efficient in regard to a specific aspect, such as:

(1) Minimum time of execution
(2) Most efficient use of storage space
(3) Minimum coding time

optimum programming—Programming in order to maximize efficiency with respect to some criterion.

option board—A circuit board family which allows customers to implement certain basic system options. Typical option boards include real-time clocks, serial interfaces, and input/output circuits.

optocoupler—Optical coupler.

optoisolator—Any device using a light-sensing element and light source to avoid direct contact in a circuit.

OR—A logic operator having the following property for logical quantities P and Q:

P	Q	P OR Q
0	0	0
0	1	1
1	0	1
1	1	1

The OR operator is represented in electrical and FORTRAN terminology by a "plus" symbol.

OR circuit—A circuit or device that implements the logical OR operator. An output occurs whenever there are one or more inputs present.

order—1. The weight or significance assigned to a digit position in a number. 2. To sequence or arrange in a series according to specified conditions.

orderly closedown—The stopping of a system in such a way that allows an orderly restart with no destruction of data. An orderly closedown or shutdown provides that all records are updated that should be updated, and no records are erroneously updated when the restart begins.

ordinary symbol—A symbol used in assembler programming to represent an assembly time value when used in the name or operand field of an instruction in assembly language. Ordinary symbols are also used to represent operation codes for assembly language instructions.

OR ELSE—A logical operator which states that if P and Q are statements, then P OR ELSE Q is either true or false. Also called *EITHER/OR*.

OR gate—OR circuit.

origin—The absolute storage address in relative coding to which addresses in a region are referenced.

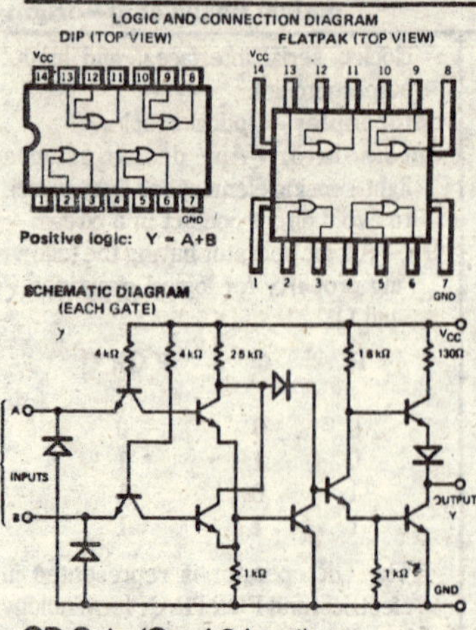

OR Gate (Quad 2-Input)

origination—Refers to the creating of a record in machine sensible form, directly or as a byproduct of a human readable document.

OR operation—The logical operation defined for two integers as follows: if A OR B = 1, then the result is 1; otherwise the result is 0. The OR operation is represented by a plus sign, A OR B = A + B.

OR operator—The logical operator which produces an OR function.

OR unit—OR gate.

OS—Abbreviation for *operating system*, the basic software used for scheduling, debugging, and other operations in a computer system.

oscillation—The cyclic alternation of conditions (as voltages, currents, etc.) in a circuit or system.

oscillator—A low-current source of an alternating voltage at any frequency. Oscillators may be electrical, electronic, or mechanical. Most microcomputer systems use an oscillator with a piezoelectric crystal to provide a stable reference frequency for clocking.

oscilloscope—A test instrument that uses a cathode-ray tube to display graphic representations of pulses and waveforms. Digital testing requires oscilloscopes with wide bandwidths and short rise times. Several manufacturers have combined oscilloscopes with microprocessors and display units to produce a high-performance troubleshooting unit. The microprocessor is used to calculate time intervals, compute voltage levels, convert time intervals to frequency, and calculate percentages.

outer macroinstruction—A macroinstruction in assembler programming that is specified in open code.

output—The produced signals used to drive peripheral terminals.

output area—A segment of internal storage reserved for output data. Also called the *output block* or *output working storage*.

output block—Output area.

output bus driver—An amplifier used to drive the impedance loads used for the output lines in a system.

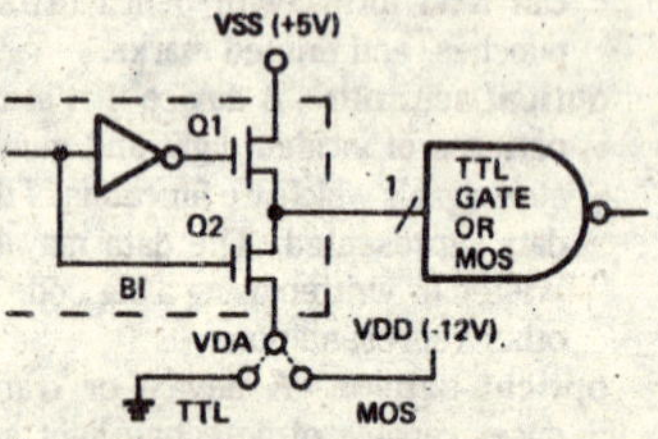

Output Bus Driver

output channel—A path for conveying data from a device or logic element.

output data—Data delivered from a device or program, generally after processing.

output device—A unit used for conveying data out of another area, block, or unit.

output formatter—A special program used to produce punched card or tape versions of assembled microprocessor programs in formats compatible with available storage media. Output formatters are available for the following media:

(1) Mask-programmable ROMs
(2) Laser-encodable ROMs

(3) Assemblers
(4) ROM emulators

output impedance—The idealized load impedance of a device producing signals for use in another system or another part of the same system.

output module—Refers to a machine or part of a machine that translates electrical impulses representing data into permanent results such as printed forms, punched cards, or magnetic recordings.

output module valve—A section of the computer which converts output data into analog control signals.

output record—The current record stored in the output area prior to being output, or a specific record written to an output device.

output register—The register used to hold data until it can be output to an external device.

output steering—Refers to the sharing of one UART serial output among two separate serial output devices under program control.

output stream—The messages and other output data issued by a system or program on the output device or devices activated by the operator. Also called *job output stream* or *output job stream*.

output table—A device that plots curves, graphs, charts, and other graphic output.

outside loop—A program loop that executes the control parameters being held constant while the current loop is being carried through possible values. Outside loops are considered nested loops when loops within it are entirely contained.

overdamping—Damping in excess of critical damping in a control system. Overdamping produces a slow nonoscillatory return to equilibrium following a disturbance.

overflow—1. The condition which occurs when the result of an arithmetic operation exceeds the capacity of the storage space allotted for it. 2. The digit or digits which occur from overflow conditions. Overflow develops when attempts are made to write longer fields into a location of specific length; for example, a 10-digit product will overflow an 8-digit accumulator.

overflow check indicator—A device which indicates an overflow condition.

overflow indicator—A device which changes state when an overflow occurs in the register it is monitoring. The overflow indicator can be interrogated and restored to its original state.

overflow operation—An operation which exceeds the capacity of the storage device, leading to the generation of an overflow condition.

overflow position—The extra position in a register used to hold an overflow digit.

overhead—The distribution of operating time of the executive routine for checking, monitoring, and scheduling all jobs or tasks related to the total cost of the complete system, usually expressed in percentages or ratios.

overlay—A technique for bringing routines into high-speed storage from some other form of storage during processing, such that several routines will occupy the same storage locations at different times. Overlay is used when the total storage requirements for instructions exceed the available main storage. New information which is required is laid over information no longer needed. Usually the sets of information are not related, except that they are needed in the same program at different times. The same data for successive cases is not an overlay.

overlay module—A software load module that has been divided into overlay segments and provided with the information to implement the desired loading of the segments when requested.

overlay program—A program in which certain control sections can use the same storage locations at different times during execution.

overlay region—An area of main storage where segments can be loaded independently of paths in other regions. Only one path within a region can be in main storage at any one time.

overlay supervisor—A routine that controls the proper sequencing and positioning of segments in limited storage during execution.

overlay tree—A graphic representation showing the segments of an overlay program and their relationships.

overload—A condition in a computing element which results in a substantial error in computation because of the saturation of one or more parts of the computing element.

overload module test—A hardware test designed to detect substandard units by using operating conditions or parameters outside the normal.

overload recovery time—The time required for the output to return to its proper value after an overload condition is removed.

overmodulation—Amplitude modulation which exceeds 100%. Overmodulation can produce the loss of signal transmission for a fraction of the modulation cycle, along with considerable distortion.

overpunch—To add holes in a card column that already contains one or more holes.

overshoot—1. The extent to which a control device or system carries the controlled variable or output past a final or desired value. 2. The amount by which an output pulse exceeds its stabilized value momentarily.

overwrite—The act of placing information in a location and destroying all previous information contained there.

Ovshinsky effect—The switching action found in some types of glass semiconductor materials. The impedance of the device changes with an applied electric field and is independent of the polarity.

oxide—A chemical coating used in semiconductor devices, magnetic tapes, and other electronic products.

oxide buildup—The accumulation of magnetic tape residue on the surface of magnetic heads from repeated use. Oxide buildup causes a loss in output and accelerates tape and head wear.

oxide isolation—The separation of elements on semiconductor chips using oxidized regions. Oxide isolation results in high packing density along with higher speeds. Without oxide isolation, the electrical isolation is achieved with reversed-biased junctions that occupy more space and have higher capacitance.

P

P—1. Symbol for ***power***. 2. Symbol for ***poise***. 3. Symbol for ***permeance*** (webers per ampere). 4. Symbol for prefix *peta* (10^{15}). 5. Abbreviation for *positive*. 6. In lowercase, symbol for *pico* (10^{-12}).

pack—To compress data by taking advantage of known characteristics of the data in such a way that the original data can be recovered. Packing involves the use of bit or byte locations that would otherwise go unused and may be used to combine several fields of information into one machine word.

package—The container used to house an active semiconductor device. Packages are available in plastic and ceramic housings with up to 40 pins. In general, microprocessors with fewer pins are easier to physically install, while those with larger numbers of pins are easier to interface with the rest of the equipment required for the microcomputer system.

packaged—Descriptive of equipment which is complete and ready for use, such as modules which are sealed or encapsulated; thus, *off-the-shelf*.

packaging—The process of containing, connecting, protecting, and sealing components and their associated circuitry into standardized enclosures (such as dual-inline devices and transistor housings).

packaging density—The relative number of units of information or devices in a dimensional unit area or volume of a system. Also called *packing density*.

packet transmission—The segmentation of messages and the subsequent transmission and reassembly at the destination. The separate routing of packets can be completely invisible to the host computers and terminals. The packets are typically stored in core memory, and flow control procedures insure that the core storage does not become overloaded while still maintaining loadings close to maximum. Packets can be checked for errors during transmission and retransmitted until they are correctly received. All messages can also be acknowledged from destination to source to insure against their loss.

packing density—The relative number of useful storage units or components per unit of dimension, such as the number of bits per inch on a magnetic tape, or the number of equivalent FETs on an LSI chip.

packing factor—The number of words, bits, or characters that can be written or stored in a given length or volume of a device or medium.

pad—1. A device used to match or control impedances in a transmission line or between an rf generator and receiver terminals. 2. To add capacitance in parallel with existing capacitors to alter the frequency of a tuned circuit. 3. To add dummy characters for the purpose of maintaining bit or timing integrity.

pad character—A character inserted to fill a blank time slot in synchronous transmission, or to fulfill the character count requirement for transmission of fixed block lengths.

padding—1. A technique used to fill out a block of information with dummy records, words, or characters. 2. See *pad*, 2.

page—1. A segment of a computer program which has a virtual address and can be located in main storage or in auxiliary storage. A page can be moved into main memory by the operating system whenever the instructions of that subdivision need to be performed. A program can be divided into pages in order to minimize the total amount of main memory allocated to the program at any one time. Pages are normally stored on a fast-access store. Pages are typically a set of 4096 consecutive bytes, with the first byte located at a storage address that is a multiple of 4096.

page addressing—A procedure of addressing in which memory is divided into segments to make full use of addressing capability. See *page*.

pager—A tiny pocketable receiver designed to receive personalized messages from a central dispatcher in a communication network.

paging—1. The procedure used to locate and transmit pages between main storage and auxiliary storage, or to exchange them with pages of the same program or other programs. Paging can be used to assist in the allocation of a limited amount of main storage among several concurrent programs. 2. The process of calling a nontransmitter-equipped member of a communications network.

paired cable—A cable with two insulated conductors, or with several sets of two conductors each.

PAM—Abbreviation for *pulse-amplitude modulation*, a form of pulse modulation in which the amplitude of the pulses is varied.

panel—The part of a computer console that provides an operator interface. A panel may be an interconnection unit with removable wires, or plugs which allow specific functions to be changed by the operator. Other panels may pictorially show the relationship of system equipment using graphic indicators. Many panels contain all the switches and indicators required for the operation of the CPU and allow bit-by-bit manual entry into registers for program setup and debugging operations.

paper tape—The long, narrow paper strips used to record and store information in the form of punched holes, partially punched holes, chemical impregnation, or magnetic-ink imprinting.

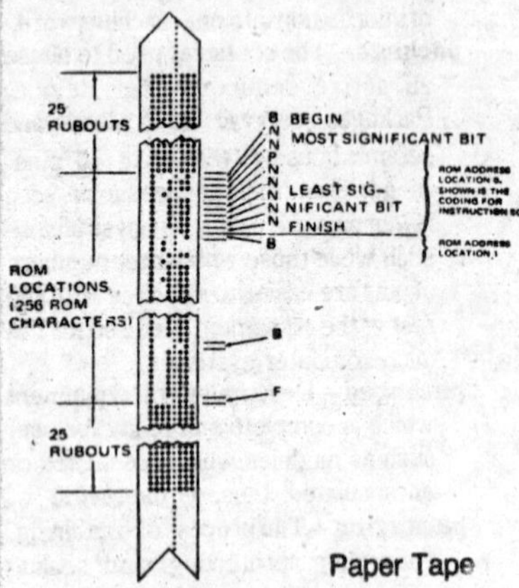

Paper Tape

paper tape automatic development system—A software system consisting of loaders and utility programs for paper tape users. The system includes an executive which causes the utilities to be loaded at the highest memory address to leave maximum room for the user's program. A typical system includes programs for debug, binary load, binary dump, verify, and object loader.

paper tape reader—A device that senses the positions of holes in perforated tape and translates them into electrical signals. High-speed paper tape readers operate at 200 characters per second and are compatible standard software and hardware interfaces.

parabolic interpolation—A procedure used in the numerical control of a machine tool to control the centerline of a cutter path. The method uses parabolic segments defined by three programmed points.

parallel—Arranged in blocks for simultaneous transmission, storage, or logical operation of items (as opposed to *serial*).

parallel adder—An adding circuit which processes all of the corresponding pairs of two numbers simultaneously.

parallel addition—An addition method in which all the corresponding pairs of digits of two numbers being added are simultaneously processed.

parallel by character—The handling of all characters of a machine word simultaneously in separate lines, channels, or storage units.

parallel circuit—A circuit in which all elements are connected to two common points with the same applied voltage across all elements.

parallel connection—The connection of two or more parts of a circuit to the same pair of terminals. Also called *shunt connection*.

parallel input/output card—A circuit board which has the necessary handshake flags for conventional parallel interfacing and contains all the required addressing circuitry.

parallel operation—The performance of several actions simultaneously using similar or identical devices for each action. Parallel operation can include the processing of all the digits of a word or byte by simultaneously transmitting each digit on a separate channel or bus. Parallel operation can save time over serial operation, but usually requires more equipment.

parallel-plate package—A method of packaging circuits which uses a stacking arrangement to increase packing density.

parallel processing—The processing of more than one program at a time using more than one active processor, in contrast to multiprocessing, where only one processor is active on one program at a time.

parallel processing system—A microcomputer system (abbreviated *PPS*) that uses a compatible set of LSI chips to achieve the capability of a parallel minicomputer. The system uses a single-chip CPU which receives an instruction word to perform all operations. The large number of instruction words available allows the system to approach the capability of a minicomputer. The large number of available chips in the set allows the implementation of a broad class of data processing products.

parallel processing system evaluation board—A circuit designed for system development which usually contains a CPU, RAM, input/output ports, and a clock circuit.

parallel search—A memory scanning and sensing operation in which the locations are identified by their contents rather than their addresses. A parallel-search memory allows fast interrogation for retrieving specific data elements.

parallel-series circuit—A circuit in which several series strings of components are paralleled, or in which several paralleled sets of components

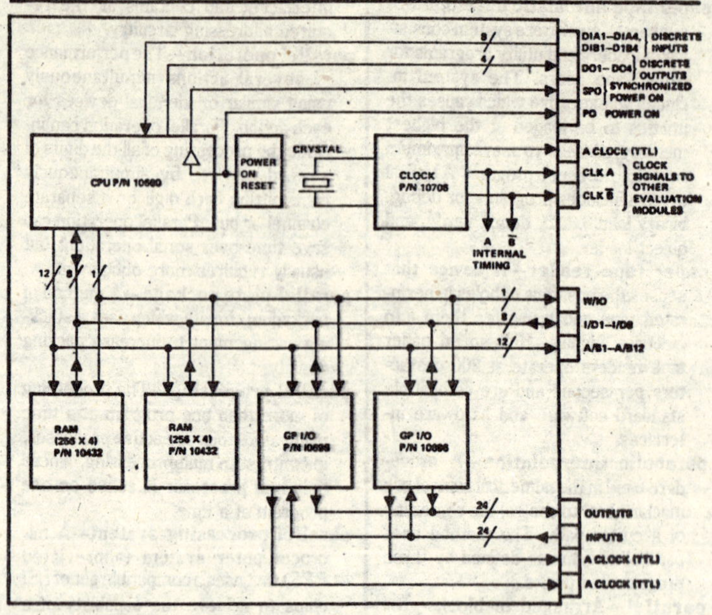

Parallel Processing System

are series-strung. Also called *series-parallel.*

parallel storage—Storage in which all characters, words, or bits are equally available. When words are in parallel, the storage is referred to as *parallel by word*. The use of parallel characters or bits implies a storage which is *parallel by character* or *parallel by bit.*

parallel transfer—Data transfer in which the characters of an element of information are transferred simultaneously over a set of paths whose number equals the number of bits transferred at one time.

parallel transmission—The simultaneous data transmission of a number of signal elements over separate lines or communication channels.

parameter—A variable which is usually given a constant value for a specific program or run. In a subroutine, a parameter may have different values when the subroutine is used in different main routines or in different parts of one main routine, but it usually remains unchanged throughout any one such use.

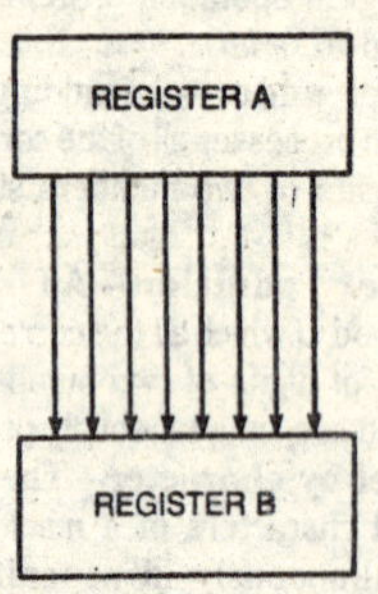

Parallel Transfer

A macro parameter refers to the symbolic or literal elements in the operand part of a macro statement. The macro parameter is usually substituted into specific instructions in the incomplete routine to develop a complete open subroutine.

parametric potentiometer—A potentiometer used in analog computers to represent parameters such as coefficients or scale factors.

parametric subroutine—A subroutine which involves parameters. The computer is expected to adjust and generate the subroutine according to the parametric values chosen.

parametron—A device which uses two stable states of oscillation to store binary digits

parasitic—An undesirable radiation parameter in an electronic circuit, such as oscillation, which disappears when circuit operation ceases.

parasitic stopper—A device or component which attenuates or eliminates a parasitic condition.

parity—The anticipated state (odd or even) of a set of binary digits. Parity is achieved by use of a self-checking code employing binary digits in which the total number of ones in each expression is deliberately kept odd or even by the addition of an extra digit whenever necessary. In ASCII, the leftmost digit is used as a parity bit. (See ASCII and associated table.)

parity bit—In an even-parity system, a bit added to a group of bits whose total of ones would otherwise be odd; in an odd-parity system, an added bit to make an even number of ones total an odd number. The parity bit is error insurance; if odd parity is specified, an error condition will be flagged each time that an even number of bits is counted with a parity bit present. In some systems, the transmission is specified as always odd or even so the parity bit does not change; in others the parity bit is added to make the sum of the bits odd or even when required.

In the ASCII table referred to previously, note that the leftmost bit is a parity bit added to character groups whose complement of ones is odd.

parity check—A check used to determine if the total number of ones or zeros in a word or byte is odd or even. This sum is checked against a previously computed parity digit. Also called *odd-even check.*

parity error—A condition that occurs when a computed parity check does not agree with the parity bit; that is, when a parity bit exists in a digit group of an even-parity system, a parity error occurs when the total of bits (including the parity bit) is odd.

parity generator-checker—A hardware unit used to generate and check parity conditions on data words. Available units can be used for either *odd* or *even* parity applications, and cascading allows expansion to any word length.

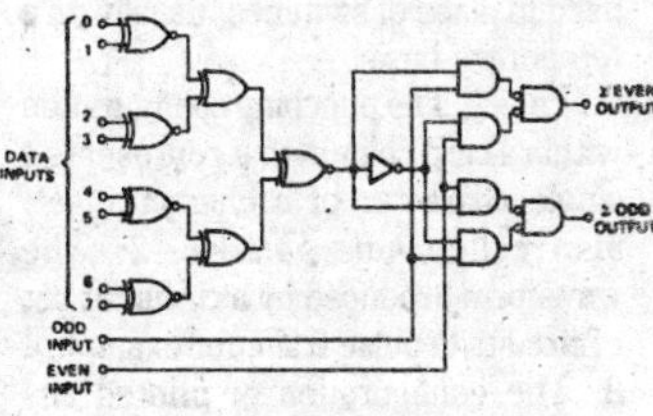

TRUTH TABLE

INPUTS			OUTPUTS	
Σ OF 1's AT 0 THRU 7	EVEN	ODD	Σ EVEN	Σ ODD
EVEN	H	L	H	L
ODD	H	L	L	H
EVEN	L	H	L	H
ODD	L	H	H	L
X	H	H	L	L
X	L	L	H	H

X = irrelevant

Parity Generator-Checker (8 Bits)

parity interrupt—An interrupt that occurs because of a parity error.

parsing—In language theory, the procedures for dividing components into structural forms.

part—A discrete component in an electronic circuit or system.

part failure rate—The anticipated or recorded number of occasions in a specified time period when a component will malfunction.

partial carry—A technique used in parallel addition in which some or all of the carries are stored temporarily, rather than being allowed to propagate.

part operation—The part of an instruction that specifies the kind of arithmetic or logic operation to be performed, but not the address of the operands.

pass—A complete cycle of reading, processing, and writing. Also called *machine run*.

patch—1. To insert corrected coding. 2. A section of coding inserted into a routine to correct a mistake or alter the routine. A patch does not have to be inserted into the routine sequence being corrected; it can be placed somewhere else with an exit to the patch and a return to the routine provided. 3. A temporary repair to a malfunctioning system. 4. A wired connection or set of wired connections used in place of switches, usually on a temporary basis.

pattern—1. The punching configuration within a card column that represents a single character of a character set; also called *hole pattern*. 2. The waveform produced by a circuit or set of circuits (a pulse train, for example). 3. The configuration of printed circuitry on a board or chip.

pattern recognition—The identification of shapes, forms, or configurations by automated methods.

pattern-sensitive fault—A fault that occurs in response to some particular pattern of data.

PC—1. Abbreviation for *program counter*, the index address register. 2. Abbreviation (usually lower case) of *printed circuit*.

pc board—Abbreviation for *printed-circuit board*, a board prepared from the printing of a chemically resistive ink.

pc board control point—A contact area on a circuit board to make it easier to reconfigure the circuitry or conduct tests.

pc board test language—A language used in automatic pc board testing which is specifically designed for the requirements of testing complex boards containing microprocessors and other LSI components. A typical test language is capable of:

(1) Loading registers
(2) Data transfer between registers
(3) Generating repetitive routines
(4) Performing limited tests

pc board test point—An area on a pc board used as a probe contact point during testing.

p-channel—A p-type semiconductor region that functions as the conducting channel in n-gate FETs.

p-channel enhancement-mode MOS FET—A metal-oxide field-effect transistor whose conducting channel between source and drain is doped with p-channel impurities.

p-channel MOS—Metal-oxide semiconductor devices that use a p-channel conduction mode. P-channel devices tend to be slower than n-channel units and also exhibit a lower gain.

PCM—Abbreviation for *pulse-code modulation*, the modulation of a pulse train using a specified code or code system.

PDM—Abbreviation for *pulse-duration modulation*, the modulation of pulse data using varying widths of pulses to convey information.

peak—The maximum instantaneous value of a quantity.

peak amplitude—Refers to the maximum deviation of a wave from its average position.

peak clipper—A device that passes signals and cuts off peaks above a predetermined level without otherwise altering the waveform.

peak data transfer rate—The maximum rate at which data is transmitted through a channel. The peak data transfer rate is usually measured in characters per second, discounting gaps between blocks and words.

peaking network—A circuit used to increase the amplification at the upper end of the frequency range for a system.

peak limiter—A device that passes signals of average amplitude, but which compresses or otherwise restricts signal peaks to some established preset value. Compare *peak clipper*.

peak load—The maximum instantaneous rate of power consumption for a circuit, load, or system.

peak transfer rate—Peak data transfer rate.

peek-a-boo system—An information retrieval system which uses small cards with drilled or punched holes. Also called *batten system* and *cordonnier system*.

pen light—A pen-like device with light and a photosensor on one end for communicating with a computer through a CRT device.

perforated tape—A tape usually made of paper in which data is stored in the form of punched holes. The hole locations are arranged in columns across the width of the tape, and there are usually 5 to 8 positions or channels per column. Also called *paper tape* or *punched tape*.

performance requirements—The set of values, conditions, and operating criteria that define the acceptable operation for a computer system and its subsystems. The computer system must fulfill minimum requirements for online response time, operating time, and record or file size.

period—1. The time required for one complete cycle. 2. A specified time duration during which newly installed or modified equipment is evaluated. 3. The reciprocal of frequency.

periodic—Repeating a cycle regularly in time and form.

periodic pulse train—A group of pulses which repeat at regular intervals in time sequence.

periodic rating—The electrical load which can be handled for alternate periods of load and rest without exceeding the specified heating limits for the equipment, or without significant degradation of circuit or system performance.

peripheral—An equipment item distinct from the CPU, but which connects to the computing system usually by means of a bus.

peripheral disk file—A file management system for use with floppy-disk peripherals. The systems can be accessed by macro language programs and include complete sets of utility programs for the updating, copying, purging, or addition of files.

peripheral equipment—Equipment distinct from the CPU which work in conjunction with it. Peripheral equipment includes all the auxiliary units that may be placed under the control of the computer such as card readers, card punches, magnetic tape units, printers, tape readers, analog-to-digital converters, and typewriters. Peripheral equipment may be used online or offline, depending upon the system job requirements and economic considerations.

peripheral interface adapter—A device (abbreviated *PIA*) for matching the input/output channels of a microprocessor with peripheral equipment. A PIA is designed to simplify the task of the user by providing the necessary buses for interfacing the peripherals, and the control logic signals for synchronizing the I/O devices with the microprocessor.

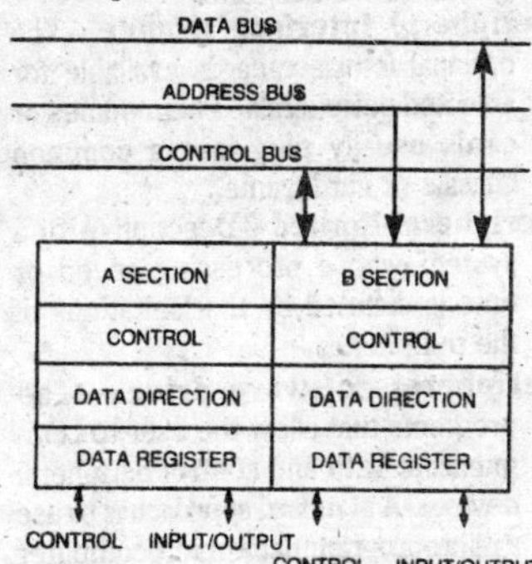

Peripheral Interface Adapter

A typical PIA uses a data bus line for data flow between the microprocessor and the PIA. The direction of data flow is controlled by the microprocessor using the control bus. When more than one PIA is used, chip select lines allow the selection of the desired PIA. The microprocessor can read or write into the data registers by addressing the unit over the address and control buses. The 8-bit outputs are bidirectional and the control input/output lines can be used for interrupts.

Each half of the two symmetrical sections has a control register, a data direction register, and a data register. The *data direction register* is used to establish the lines to the peripheral units as inputs or outputs. The *data registers* store the data which is on the data bus during a write command; during a read operation, data is transfer red directly to the data bus from the peripherals. The *control registers* establish and control the operating modes of control lines to the peripherals.

The functional configuration of the PIA is programmed by the microprocessor during system initialization. Each of the peripheral lines is programmed as an input or an output, and the control lines are also programmed at this time.

peripheral interface module—The optional interface cards available for selected peripherals. The modules or cards usually plug into a common chassis or card frame.

peripheral-limited—Descriptive of a system whose processing speed or time is dictated by the limitations of the peripherals.

peripheral software driver—The programs that allow the user to communicate with and control peripheral devices. A standard approach is to use a microprogrammable microcomputer to emulate a standard minicomputer CPU for which there exists compatible peripheral software.

peripheral subsystem—A group of one or more peripheral units of the same type which are connected to an available input/output channel. A channel synchronizer-control unit interprets the control signals and instructions issued by the central processor and effects the transfer of data to and from the selected unit and the processor. It also indicates status of the peripheral units and informs the central processor when errors or faults occur.

peripheral support computer—A computer used for auxiliary operations in support of a large processing complex and compatible with the host computer only to the extent that data interchange is not required for auxiliary conversion. The peripheral support computer is used primarily for card-to-tape, tape-to-card, and tape-to-printer conversions, along with peripheral control operations.

peripheral transfer—The process of transmitting data between two or more peripheral units.

permanent dynamic storage—A form of dynamic storage in which the maintenance of the data stored does not depend on a flow of energy into the storage medium. Examples include magnetic disks and drums.

permanent error—An error which is not eliminated by reprocessing.

permanent memory—Stored data that remains intact when power is removed.

permanent storage—Storage that is not altered by computer instructions, such as magnetic core with a lockout feature. Also called *nonerasable storage, fixed storage,* and *read-only storage.*

permeability—The ratio of magnetic field flux density to the magnetizing force.

permeability constant—Symbol, μ_0. The inductance per unit area in a near-perfect vacuum or in free space. In the International System of Units, the value is 12.566 370 614 × 10^{-7} henrys per meter.

permittivity—The ratio of electric displacement to the electric field intensity in a material.

permittivity constant—Symbol, ϵ_0. The capacitance per unit area in a near-perfect vacuum or in free space. In the International System of Units, the value is 8.854 187 818 × 10^{-12} farads per meter. ϵ_0 is the reciprocal of the product of free-space permeability and the speed of light squared.

permutation—Any one of the total number of changes in position or form that are possible in a group.

permuted cyclic code—A code in which words are represented by a fixed number of bits and arranged in sequence such that the signal distance between consecutive words is always one or unity.

permuted index—An index developed by producing an entry for each word of interest, including those within the context of meaning. A permuted index is most often used only for title words.

personality card—A PROM programmer card which contains the specialized instructions for interfacing and programming that are unique for that particular PROM or family of PROMs being programmed. Personality cards may provide the proper timing patterns, voltage levels, and other requirements for the PROM.

personality module—A module used for PROM interlacing and programming; a personality card.

PERT—Acronym for *program evaluation and review technique*, a program or project management technique which uses critical path analysis for program and system performance evaluation.

phase—The angular relationship between waveforms in AC circuits.

phase-by-phase—Refers to a modular buildup or growth of a system according to scheduled "milestones."

phase library—An ordered set of program phases processed and entered by a linkage editor for execution.

phase-locked loop—A control circuit (abbreviated *PLL*), usually integrated, which locks the phase of the controlled frequency with a reference frequency.

phase-locked-loop motor control—A motor control system using PLL techniques. With the combination of PLL control and a microprocessor, a single reference or clock can be used to provide high accuracy, and the microprocessor can be programmed to provide flexible counting and to compare functions for tracking.

phase logic—The general instructions which transfer the machine from one operational phase to another, such as *fetch* and *interrupt*. Combinatorial logic can be used to establish the current phase and the next phase. In some systems, a phase may be a microcoded subroutine.

phase modulation—A modulation system (abbreviated *PM*) in which the carrier angle is varied by an amount proportional to the modulating signal. PM is used in most so-called FM two-way communications systems.

phase-modulation recording—A recording method in which each cell is divided into two parts and magnetized in opposite senses with the sequence of the senses, indicating if the bit represented is a one or a zero.

phase shift—The change in the phase of a periodic waveform with respect to a reference point, usually occurring as a direct result of a connection of a component or circuit to the waveform-producing circuit or device.

phasing—Causing two systems or circuits to operate in phase, or at some established phase difference.

photocell—1. A device that converts light into electricity. 2. A device whose resistance changes with relative linearity according to the amount of light impinging on its surface.

photodiode—A junction diode constructed to provide an electrical output under the influence of light. Photodiodes are widely used as optical sensing devices in data processing equipment.

photographic storage—Storage methods that use photographic processes, such as high-density storage on photographic disks, photographic data shown on CRT screens, or computer-output microfilm and facsimile systems.

photo-optic memory—A memory or storage system that uses an optical medium such as a light beam to record on photographic film.

photoresist—A substance that resists the erosion properties of an etchant when exposed to intense light. It is used in fabrication of printed circuits.

photoresist process—The process used to remove, in a selective manner, portions of a light-exposed surface of a semiconductor chip or a circuit board. The photoresist is usually an organic material that polymerizes on exposure to intense light, which allows it to resist the etchant solution used to eat away nonconductive areas of the board or substrate.

physical simulation system—An operating computer system designed to represent or simulate physical systems for research and study.

PIA—Abbreviation for *peripheral interface adapter*, a hardware unit for matching the input/output channels of a microprocessor with peripheral equipment. A typical PIA provides 8 or 16 bits of external interface and four or more control lines at addressable locations in memory. Each interface bit is individually programmable to act as either an input or an output.

PIA read-write—A signal generated by the microprocessor unit to control data transfers on the data bus of the PIA.

pico—Prefix meaning 10^{-12}.

picoprocessor—A self-contained high-speed miniature digital processor used in intelligent cable systems to provide controller functions for data transfer, control signaling, status monitoring, and interrupt generation. The picoprocessor is usually microprogrammed; because of its small size, it can be attached almost anywhere in the system.

picofarad—A capacitance value equal to 10^{-12} farad (abbreviated *pF*).

picosecond—A time period equal to 10^{-12} second (abbreviated *ps*).

piezoelectric—A property of certain crystals which produce a voltage when under mechanical stress, and produce a mechanical vibration at a specific frequency when subjected to a voltage.

piezoelectric crystal—A crystal transducer which converts mechanical pressure into an electrical signal, or converts an electrical signal into mechanical pressure.

piezoelectric device—A device which uses the conversion properties of a piezoelectric substance, such as an oscillator crystal used as a frequency reference, or a crystal microphone that produces an electrical analog of the vibrations of a modulated diaphragm.

piezoelectric transducer—A transducer that depends upon a material with piezoelectric properties for its operation. Also called ceramic or crystal transducer. See also *piezoelectric crystal* and *piezoelectric device*.

piezoelectricity—The electrical signal produced by a stressed piezoelectric crystal.

pilot system—A collection of file records and data obtained from a business over a period of time and used for simulation purposes.

pinboard—A type of control panel that uses pins rather than wires to control the operation of the computer. Some such systems allow the operator to change programs by removing one pinboard and inserting another.

pinchoff—The cessation of channel (source-to-drain) current in field-effect transistors as a result of increased gate bias. This state is comparable to *cutoff* in bipolar-transistor and vacuum-tube operation.

pin-connect crystal—A clock crystal which is connected to a microprocessor system with two separate external pins.

pin diode—A semiconductor diode with an intrinsic layer between the p and n junctions. The term "pin" is an acronym for *positive, intrinsic, negative*.

pip—A spot of light on a CRT screen for display pointing, calibration, or—in radar—for target indicating.

pipeline—An executed serial program using a register at the output of the microprogram memory. Pipelining can produce a faster configuration than a normal series mode of operation. Since only conditional instructions can test the results of previous instructions, the pipelined machine may require more memory. For example, a serial machine may execute as a single microinstruction.

ADD AND BRANCH IF ZERO

The pipeline machine may require two microinstructions for the same operation.

PLA—Abbreviation for *programmed logic array*, an arrangement of logical AND and OR functions programmed for specific operations. PLAs are used for code conversion, instruction decoding, and command decoding. The output of a PLA is the sum of the products of the input addresses programmed by a masking step during manufacture. PLAs offer some advantages over random logic, but generally require more interconnections and board space. Compared to random logic, they are also slow and may cost more than random logic equivalents. PLAs have been used for correct sequencing of instructions in CPUs and to translate codes in microprogramming functions.

planar—Refers to a semiconductor processing technology where monolithic components extend below the

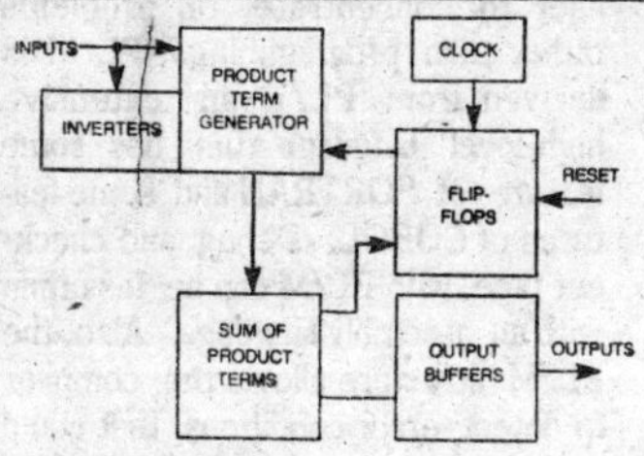

PLA Block Diagram

the surface of the substrate, but the plane surface remains relatively flat during fabrication.

planar integrated circuit—An integrated circuit produced using the planar process.

planar transistor—A transistor constructed by etching a thin slice of semiconductor and characterized by a parallel plane protected by an oxidized surface.

PLA output latch—A latch available in some microcomputer systems which allows the PLA to be pipelined. The PLA output latch fetches the next control sequence while the CPU is executing the current sequence.

plasma—An ionized gaseous discharge within the display units which make use of this effect for segment illumination.

plasma display—A display panel with supporting electronics which uses the plasma or gas-discharge effect.

plastic package—An integrated circuit or transistor housed within an inexpensive plastic enclosure. The package is molded directly on the assembled lead frame and semiconductor die. Bonding wire is attached using a thermocompression technique. All materials are thermally matched for expansion.

PLL—Abbreviation for *phase-locked loop*.

PL/M—A high-level compiler language developed for microcomputer systems. PL/M is an assembly language replacement that can command the 8080 and other microprocessors to produce object code. It allows the user to concentrate on problems rather than programming. PL/M is derived from PL/1, an extensive high-level language that has some features of FORTRAN and some features of COBOL. Debug and checkout time with PL/M can be less than with an assembly language. Also, the PL/M structure allows the compiler to detect error conditions that could get past an assembler. The PL/M compiler is written in FORTRAN IV and will execute on most large machines without modification.

PL/M-plus—An extended version of PL/M which can compile programs on microcomputers rather than the larger machines. PL/M-plus allows the user direct access to all bits and fields for manipulation operations. This allows all standard compiler operations on bits, fields, and whole words. Also written *PL/M+*.

plotter—A peripheral unit in which a dependent variable is graphed by an automatically controlled pen or pencil as a function of one or more variables. Any position on a two-dimensional area can be referenced, accessed, or written onto by precise control of both vertical and horizontal axes.

plotting board—An output unit which graphs the curves of one or more variables as a function of its input variables.

plugboard—1. A board with removable connections for changing the wiring pattern. 2. A board that can be removed and replaced to change the program or wired connections for a machine.

plugboard computer—A computer which generally has a punched-card input and output with program instructions on a removable plugboard.

plugging chart—A diagram or chart which indicates where plugs, pins, or wires are to be placed on a plugboard.

plug-in—Descriptive of devices in which connections are completed using conductors with pins, plugs, sockets, jacks, or other connectors that are readily removed.

plug-in unit—A self-contained assembly which can be inserted or unplugged easily.

plug-PROM—A read-only-memory diode array that is programmed by inserting small plugs into edge connectors. After it is connected to the microcomputer system, programming consists of selecting the proper plugs (each representing a 4-bit hexadecimal value) and inserting them into the edge connector of the word being programmed. Changing a program requires only removing and replacing the plugs.

plug wire—A flexible wire with a metal pin at each end for connecting to the sockets of a plugboard.

plus zone—Those bit positions in a code which represent the algebraic plus sign.

PMOS—Abbreviation for ***p-channel metal-oxide semiconductor***, a field-effect-transistor technology based on use of p-type material for the source-and-drain channel.

PM—Abbreviation for ***phase modulation***, a method of modulation in which the amplitude of the carrier remains the same, while the phase is changed as a function of the amplitude of the modulating signal.

pn boundary—The surface where the donor and acceptor concentrations are equal in the transition region between n and p zones in a semiconductor.

pnip transistor—A transistor with a layer of intrinsic (undoped) material between the base and collector to extend the high-frequency range.

pn junction—A region of transition between p and n semiconductor materials which has the properties of a diode.

pnp—A transistor consisting of two p-type regions separated by an n-type region, and characterized by flow of holes as majority carriers (rather than the more mobile electrons).

pnpn—Refers to a semiconductor switching device with three junctions.

pnp transistor—See *pnp*.

pointer—1. The indicating needle of an analog meter. 2. The most recently stored word in a stack, which gives the address of another memory location; the word is taken temporarily from a register that is to be used for another purpose or from the program counter during subroutine jumps; it is replaced following the temporary operation or jump.

point-of-sale system—An electronic system for automating the various functions of retail sales operations. Point-of-sale systems include inventory control using electronic cash registers, crefit authorization via a reader terminal to a central computer, and electronic funds transfer using card activated systems.

point-of-sale terminal—A sale recorder or electronic cash register which may include a merchandise tag reader, keyboard for data entry, printer for sales slips and audit tapes, numeric display for keyboard input, plus supporting logic, control, and memory, and sometimes optional magnetic tape and modem units.

polar—1. A logic technique in which a binary one is represented by current flow in one direction and a zero by current flow in the opposite direction. 2. Having poles (as a magnet). 3. A type of plot showing coordinates over a two-dimensional plane, and used to depict signal distribution from an antenna, the pickup field of a microphone, etc.

polarity—1. The orientation of any device that has poles or signed electrodes. 2. The value established by the ungrounded electrode of any grounded direct-current electrical system; for example, the polarity of most modern vehicle electrical systems is +12 volts. 3. Electrical opposition.

polarized plug—A plug constructed in such a manner that it can only be inserted into a socket with proper polarity.

polarizing slot—A cutout in the edge of a circuit board to properly align certain types of connectors or to insure that proper pin polarity is maintained.

pole—1. An electrode of an electrical device such as a battery, switch, or relay. 2. Either of two opposite signs (as + or −). 3. One of the regions in a magnetized body where the magnetic flux density is concentrated.

Polish notation—A system of expressing logical and arithmetic statements without using parentheses. In Polish notation, the expression *A plus B multiplied by* C would be represented by *+ABC*. Also called *Lukaseiwicz notation, parentheses-free notation*, and *prefix notation*. (Compare *reverse-Polish notation*.)

poll—A systematic method for sampling the output of stations on a multipoint system. The computer contacts the stations according to an order specified by the user.

polling—A technique by which each of the terminals sharing a communications line is periodically sampled to determine if it requires servicing. Polling is also used to determine the source of multiple interrupt requests in multiprocessing systems. If several interrupts occur at the same time, the control program is used to make the decision as to the order of servicing.

polling characters—The characters which are used to identify a particular terminal during a polling operation. The characters also indicate to the computer whether or not the terminal has a message to send.

polling interval—The time between polling operations if no data is being transmitted from a polled station.

polling list—A list containing control information and the order in which terminals are to be polled.

polymorphic—Capable of existing in several different forms.

polymorphic system—A system which can take on various forms for the problem at hand by altering its interconnections or functions. A polymorphic system may change its logic construction or operation in order to handle a variety of tasks.

polyvalence—The property of being interrelated in several ways.

polyvalent notation—A method of describing characteristics in condensed form in which each character or group of characters represents one of the characteristics.

port—1. A place of access to a system or circuit. 2. An opening or connection that provides electrical or physical access to a system or circuit. The point at which an input or output is in contact with the CPU can be considered a port, along with any entrance or exit from a network or system. 3. An opening of critical but controllable dimensions in a tuned enclosure (such as a cavity or loudspeaker cabinet).

portable compiler—A device which edits, enters, and compiles programs in a high-level language and which is capable of being hand-carried from job to job. Portable compilers generate machine-language programs which are loaded into the process controller. They contain a keyboard to enter data and a display or printer for program listings.

portable data medium—A data medium intended to be easily transportable independently of the mechanism used in its interpretation.

POS—Abbreviation for *point-of-sale*.

positional operand—In assembler programming, an operand in a macroinstruction that assigns a value to the corresponding positional parameter which is declared in the prototype statement of the called macro definition.

position code—The established positions or sites in recording media in which data may be entered or recorded according to specific conventions adopted to standardize the locations for coding information.

positive electrode—The conductor node that serves as the anode terminal of a polarized device such as a battery, an electrolytic capacitor, or a self-contained two-pole circuit.

positive feedback—A system in which the amplification is increased at the cost of fidelity by returning a part of the output in phase with the input signal. An oscillator, for example, employs positive feedback to sustain self-amplification. Also called *regeneration*.

positive logic—A logic convention in which the positive voltage is defined as a 1 and the more negative voltage is defined as a 0.

postedit—To edit output data resulting from a previous computation.

postinstallation evaluation—An evaluation of a computer configuration to determine if it meets the objectives established at the time of acquisition.

post mortem—1. The analysis of a condition or malfunction after its completion. 2. Collectively, the routines and listings used to locate a malfunction or an error in the program or system. A post mortem routine can automatically print information on the contents of registers and storage locations at the time the routine is stopped in order to assist in the location of a mistake in coding.

post mortem routine—A service routine used in analyzing the cause of a malfunction. See *post mortem*, 2.

postprocessor—A set of instructions used to transform tool centerline data into machine-tool motion in a computer-controlled system. The postprocessor set typically includes rate feed calculations, spindle speed calculations, and function commands for auxiliary operations.

pot—1. A potentiometer or variable resistor. 2. To encapsulate a circuit or device into an inaccessible, usually epoxy, package. 3. Abbreviation for potential (as in *hi-pot*, for *high potential*).

potential—The voltage between two points in a circuit, device, or system; electromotive force; electrical pressure.

potential difference—The voltage existing between two points in a circuit or system.

potentiometer—A usually circular or disk-type resistor with two fixed terminals and a third terminal connected to a variable contact arm.

powered enclosure—A unit with a recessed frame and power supplies with connectors for specific microcomputers.

power-fail—A specific interrupt which occurs when a loss of primary power is detected.

power-fail detect module—A unit designed to provide an interrupt or flag at least 500 microseconds before a low-power condition is detected and program execution is halted. Such a device can be used to prevent loss of data in memory for critical applications.

power-fail recovery—A system (abbreviated *PFR*) with charging and automatic switching circuitry which provides for computer restart without operator intervention after a power failure. A PFR system can maintain solid-state memory integrity for several hours after a power failure.

power-fail/restart—An option on some computer systems which monitors power supply voltages and allows an orderly shutdown upon a power failure and automatic restart when power is restored.

power-fail/restart diagnostic—A test routine which checks for proper operation of the power-fail/restart option.

power failure—A usually temporary and inadvertent loss of power to an otherwise functioning machine.

power frequency—The frequency in hertz at which electric power is generated and distributed.

power gain—1. The ratio of output power to input power in an amplifier. 2. The relative level increase of a directional or omnidirectional antenna as compared with (usually) a reference dipole fed with the same signal and measured at a given reference distance from the radiators.

power level—The ratio of power at a point in the system to some arbitrary amount of power chosen as a reference. Power-level differences are usually expressed in decibels.

power loss—The ratio of the power absorbed by the input circuit to the power delivered to a specified load under specified operating conditions.

power-on reset—A signal used at power turnon in some systems to initialize the CPU to a known state; it allows the proper sequence of events to occur. The power-on reset signal is generated external to the CPU, which receives the signal and sets the internal logic states and produces a signal which can be used to initialize other circuits.

power pack—1. A unit for converting power from AC to DC or DC to AC for electronic devices. 2. A battery of cells for powering electronic equipment.

power supply—The system and circuitry for converting the AC line power into suitable DC voltages for the electronic equipment in a system.

power supply circuit—An arrangement of components that convert an AC input voltage into a DC output voltage. A basic power supply includes a transformer, rectifier, and filter. Regulators are often used to supply constant voltages or currents.

power switch—1. A mechanical switch used for high-current control applications or for application of operating voltages to equipment. 2. An electronic circuit that performs a switching action to deliver high-current voltages to equipment.

power-switch module—A module used to drive solenoids, motor starters, and other such high-current devices.

power transistor—A transistor capable of handling relatively heavy current loads.

pp junction—A region of transition between two regions having different properties in p-type semiconductor material.

PPM—Abbreviation for *pulse-position modulation*, a pulse modulation system in which the position of the pulse is a function of the modulating signal

PPS—1. Abbreviation for *parallel processing system*, a set of circuits which can be used to build equipment requiring digital data processing. The PPS system includes CPU, RAMs, ROMs, and clock circuits for equipment such as calculators, cash registers, credit terminals, process controllers, and general-purpose data processors. 2. In lowercase form, an abbreviation for *pulses per second*.

preanalysis—An initial review of a computer task, for the purpose of increasing the efficiency of the computer for that task.

preassembly time—The time used by an assembler to process macro definitions and perform conditional assembly operations.

precision—The degree of exactness with which a quantity is defined. Precision is related to the number of distinguishable alternatives from which a representation is selected, such as the number of digits or bits in a number or word. Double-length precision pertains to words or operations with twice the normal length of a unit of data in a computing system.

predictive control—A control system which uses a computer for real-time repetitive comparison of pertinent parameters.

preedit—A checking of application or operational programs before the test run. A preedit run can eliminate errors resulting from program segmentation and supervisory procedures.

prefix—An add-on designator for the scheduling and transferring of control between programs.

prefix multiplier—A scale or conversion factor for increasing a basic unit or quantity.

PREFIX	FACTOR	SYMBOL
exa	10^{18}	E
peta	10^{15}	P
tera	10^{12}	T
giga	10^{9}	G
mega	10^{6}	M
kilo	10^{3}	k
hecto	10^{2}	h
deka	10^{1}	da
deci	10^{-1}	d
centi	10^{-2}	c
milli	10^{-3}	m
micro	10^{-6}	μ
nano	10^{-9}	n
pico	10^{-12}	p
femto	10^{-15}	f
atto	10^{-18}	a

prefix notation—A method of forming mathematical expressions in which each operator precedes its operands. Also called *Polish notation*. (See *reverse-Polish notation.*)

preparatory function—A command for changing the mode of operation of a control system from positioning to contouring, or calling for a fixed cycle by the machine.

preprocessor—A program that converts data from the format of an emulated system to the format accepted by an emulator.

preset—An activity to set the contents of a storage location to an initial value or to establish the initial control value of a loop.

presettable I/O—A set of switches which allow the programmer to verify microinstructions that perform input/output data transfers before actual peripherals are connected to the system.

presumptive address—The address constant containing the absolute address of a memory location and a relative address; base address.

preventive maintenance—Precautionary measures designed to forestall system failures.

prewired external circuitry—Connectors and cable systems that are prewired to extend the input/output system.

prr—Abbreviation for *pulse repetition rate*, usually expressed in pulses per second.

primary store—The main storage method in a computer system (not necessarily the fastest).

primitive—Descriptive of the lowest level of a machine instruction, or the lowest unit of language translation.

printed circuit—A circuit in which interconnecting wires have been replaced by conductive strips bound onto an insulating board.

printed circuit board—An insulating board (also called *card*) onto which circuit paths have been printed or etched. Printed circuit boards may be single-sided, double-sided, or multilayer for high-density applications.

printed circuit switch—A rotary switch that can be soldered in place directly onto a printed circuit board.

printed element—An element such as a resistor formed on a circuit board by deposition or etching.

printed wiring—A conductive path formed on the surface of an insulating baseboard by plating or etching.

printer—A typewriter-like machine that produces human-sensible marks or impressions, usually on paper, and in the form of graphic characters. A typical desktop printer produces up to 100 characters per second and 70 lines per minute on 8½-inch roll paper.

printer controller—A device that contains the circuitry necessary to interface a printing unit to a microcomputer. Components are usually mounted on a card which plugs directly into the microcomputer chassis assembly.

priority circuits—Circuits which grant memory access to the various units of a system in a sequence that enables each input and output to be used most efficiently. The priority circuits receive, store, and grant requests for access to memory made by the various parts of the system. Proiority is usually established based upon the data transfer rate of the device requesting access.

priority indicators—Code signals which form a queue of data for processing in order of importance.

priority interrupt control unit—A unit (abbreviated *PICU*) with up to eight levels of priority which is designed to simplify the interrupt system for a microcomputer. A typical unit can

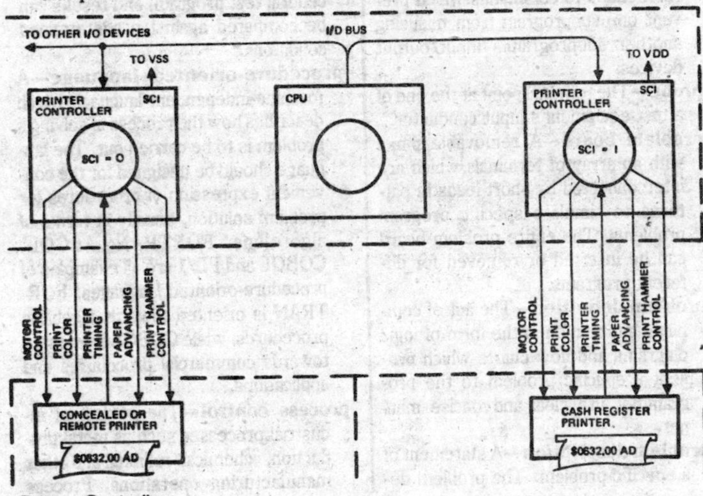

Printer Controllers

accept eight requesting levels, determine the highest priority, compare this priority with the current status register, and issue an interrupt along with vector data to identify the service routine.

priority interrupt module—A device which acts as the monitor for a number of field contacts and notifies the computer when an external priority request has been made.

priority interrupt table—A table that lists the priority sequence for handling and testing interrupts in systems without fully automatic interrupt capability.

private automatic branch exchange—A private automatic exchange (abbreviated *PABX*) that provides for the transmission of calls to and from a public telephone network.

private line—1. A channel furnished to a subscriber for exclusive use. Also called a *private wire* or *leased line*. 2. Trade name (when capitalized) for a selective calling system in two-way communications characterized by a continuously transmitted low-frequency tone during all station transmissions.

privileged instructions—Specialized restrictions to commands which prevent one subprogram from misusing another subprogram's input/output devices.

probe—The terminal point at the end of a test equipment's input conductor.

problem board—A removable panel with an array of terminals which are interconnected by short leads in patterns to simulate specific program problems. The entire problem board can be inserted or removed for different programs.

problem definition—The act of compiling information in the form of logic diagrams and flow charts which present a specific problem to the programmer in a clear and concise manner.

problem description—A statement of a specific problem. The problem description may include the method of solution, the solution, the transformations of data required, and the relationships of procedures, data, and constraints.

problem determination—The process of identifying a hardware or software failure and determining responsibility and cause.

problem diagnosis—The analysis used to identify the precise cause of a hardware or software failure.

problem language—The language used by a programmer in stating the definition of a problem.

problem-oriented language—A programming language designed for the convenient expression for a given class of problems, usually a source language suited to describe procedural steps. A problem-oriented language is designed for the convenience of program specification in a general problem area, rather than for easy conversion to machine code.

procedural test—A check of machine control and operation before processing. Procedural test data should cover all or most of the conditions that can occur during the run. A control panel can be used to insert a procedural test program, and results can be compared against predetermined conditions.

procedure-oriented language—A machine-independent language which describes how the process of solving a problem is to be carried out. The language should be designed for the convenient expression of procedures for problem solution, usually in terms of algorithms. FORTRAN, ALGOL, COBOL and PL/1 are all examples of procedure-oriented languages. FORTRAN is oriented towards algebraic procedures, while COBOL is oriented towards commercial procedures and applications.

process control—The control of industrial processes such as metal production, chemical refining, and other manufacturing operations. Process control usually implies on continuous operation or production.

process control analog modules—Refers to signal conversion, sample-and-hold, amplifiers, multiplexers, and signal conditioning units designed especially for process control applications.

process control compiler—A compiler used to program PROMs using a process control language or machine language. The compiler accepts keyboard entry of data, displays the data for verification and editing, compiles the program, and loads it into the PROM chips.

process control computer—A computer designed for process control applications. It is generally limited in software requirements, instruction capacity, word length, and accuracy.

process control language—A language (abbreviated *PCL*) which resembles beginning FORTRAN and is modeled after relay logic for arithmetic and logic commands. PCL allows a control program to be created in English, which is entered using a keyboard and converted into machine language for storage in a PROM. The following features should be a requirement for a powerful process control language:

(1) Compatibility with a major language
(2) Efficiency of overhead
(3) Simplicity for beginners
(4) Facility for running multiple tasks
(5) All common machine operations
(6) Interrupt capability
(7) Subroutine and compilation capability

process controller—A computer which controls the process to which it is connected and executes machine-language programs to accomplish this control.

process control loop—Refers to a complete process control system in which computers are used for the automatic control and regulation of industrial processes and operations.

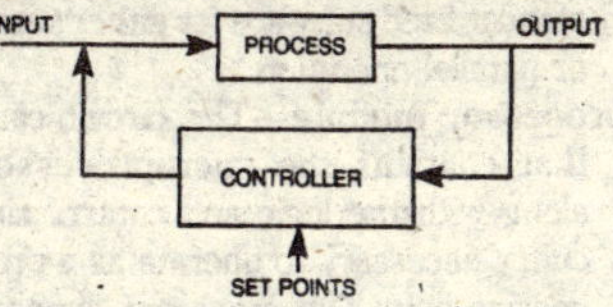

Process Control Loop

process control system—A system which uses a computer or digital logic to regulate and control industrial operations such as the production of chemicals. A typical process control system contains:

(1) CPU
(2) PROM
(3) RAM for data storage
(4) Input/output modules
(5) Communications cables

processing section—The portion of a computer that does the changing of input data into output data. The processing section usually includes the arithmetic and logic sections.

process loop test—A check made to determine the need for loop operations.

processor—A hardware data processor or a program that performs the functions of compiling, assembling, and translating for a specific language. Processor operations can involve registers, accumulators, program counters and stacks, input/output control, and internal instruction control.

processor evaluation module—A circuit card which contains all the necessary components of a microprocessor set. A processor evaluation module contains:

(1) CPU
(2) RAM
(3) Clock generator
(4) Input/output circuits
(5) Power-on circuits

processor interface module—A unit which connects the LSI processor to as many as eight input/output devices. It provides a common interface and standardized software for either serial or parallel operation.

processor module—The circuit card that contains the microprocessor along with the logic and control circuitry necessary to operate as a processing unit. The processor support circuits consist of clock circuits, multiplexer, bus control, input/output control, and interrupt logic.

processor status word—A word (abbreviated *PSW*) containing information on the current processor status. The PSW may include information on priority conditions of arithmetic or logic results.

processor transfer time—The time required for data transfer (before the processor acknowledges the data as input or output). Processor transfer time depends on the internal cycle time and channel transfer rate of the processor.

production automation—The automatic techniques used in such industrial applications as machine tool control, material handling, mixing of materials, inspection systems, and assembly operations.

production automation microcomputer—A rugged, compact microcomputer system designed for industrial control and automation applications. A typical production automation microcomputer system contains the microprocessor, RAM, input/output channels, DMA channel, interrupt facility, power-fail and automatic restart circuits, and an operating console.

productive sampling tests—Tests made on a portion of a production run or lot in order to determine the general performance level.

program—1. A set of instructions arranged in proper sequence for directing the computer in performing a desired operation, such as the solution of a mathematical problem or the sorting of data. 2. To prepare a set of ordered instructions for automatic computer operation.

A program includes plans for the transcription of data, coding for the computer, and plans for the absorption of results into the system. Programming consists of:

(1) Analysis of the problem
(2) Preparation of flow diagrams
(3) Preparation of subroutines
(4) Allocation of storage locations
(5) Specification of input/output formats
(6) All computer integration tasks

program address counter—A sequential counter (abbreviated *PAC*) which keeps track of the location of the next instruction to be executed from the program memory. The most significant bits may concern the page, while the other bits contain the word address of the instruction on the page. Also called *program counter* and *index address register.*

program address register—A register which holds the instruction location to be transmitted to the control ROM.

program analyzer—A development unit designed for the convenient field service of microcomputer systems. It can be used for software debugging and troubleshooting in the field. The analyzer connects to the CPU and displays the contents of bus lines along with the processor state, including instructions and data.

program control unit—A unit or section of the central processor for controlling the execution of computer instructions and their sequence of operation.

program counter—A counter which contains the address of the next instruction to be fetched from memory. The address is automatically incremented after an instruction fetch except when modified by branch instructions. During interrupts, the program counter saves the address of the instruction.

program development system—A development aid that allows users to make, simulate, and debug programs on a system that has a CRT display, keyboard, floppy disk, and printer.

program documentation—The hard-copy printout and coding sheets of a program, including program name and function, required hardware and software, interface details between the user and program, and program listing.

program error—A mistake made in the program code by the programmer, keypuncher, compiler, or assembler.

program generation system—A system (abbreviated *PGS*) that allows the user to output selected areas of memory in object-program format and load programs into memory. It will load programs produced by itself and those produced by the memory load builder or assembler.

program generator—A program that permits other programs to be written automatically. A character-controlled generator operates like a compiler that takes entries from a library tape. It also examines the control characters and alters the instructions according to directions found in the control characters. A pure generator is a program that writes another program. Most assemblers are also compilers and generators. The generator in an assembler is usually a section of program which is called by the assembler to write one or more entries in another program.

program instruction—The set of characters which may include one or more addresses that define an operation and cause the computer to operate on the indicated quantities.

program library—A collection of available computer programs and routines. A typical microcomputer library might include text editor, loader, assembler, RAM test program, decimal addition, PROM programmer, A/D conversion, logic subroutines, and BCD-to-binary conversion.

programmable calculating oscilloscope—A programmable instrument for the acquisition and manipulation of electronic data. This instrument combines an oscilloscope and a microprocessor in a single unit with the capability to calculate rise times, integrals, differentials, peak areas, averages, and many other values.

programmable calculator—A calculating device that is programmed by a keyboard or simple storage devices. High-level programmable calculators may use BASIC keywords and can be used as elements in data communication nets, instrumentation, and peripheral controllers, or to perform remote job-entry functions.

programmable clock—A system timing device that can be used to synchronize the CPU to external events, measure time intervals between events, and provide interrupts at preset intervals.

programmable communications interface—A chip designed for data communications and usually referred to as a USART (for *universal synchronous/asynchronous receiver/transmitter*). It is used as a peripheral device and can be programmed by the CPU to operate with any serial data transmission technique. Most USARTs are TTL-compatible, operate from a single 5V power supply, and have a single clock.

programmable controller—A control unit designed as a direct replacement for a relay panel in industrial control applications. Programmable controllers are usually programmed directly from ladder diagrams or English-like logic statements. In general, programmable controllers sacrifice many of their data-handling capabilities for programming simplicity. Programmable controllers can be configured to handle as few as eight outputs or as many as 256, with or without timing or counting. They can also be used for arithmetic and shift register operations.

programmable data mover—A custom configured modular data acquisition and transmission device. It can control the signal timing and conditioning for a wide variety of input and output signals. Typical programs can be written in about 20 minutes using a 16-pad keyboard and 32-character display.

programmable logic array—A mask-programmable chip which provides functions from arrays of AND and OR gates.

programmable logic—Devices and systems which provide logic functions that can be changed by the user. Programmable logic devices include FPLAs, PLAs, ROMs, EAROMs, RAMs, CAMs, and microprocessors. Programmable logic systems include microcomputers, programmable calculators, minicomputers, and large-scale computers.

programmable memory—A memory with locations that are addressable by the program counter. A program within this memory may directly control the operation of the arithmetic and control unit.

programmable peripheral interface—An input/output device with individually programmable pins. The pins can be programmed either as inputs or outputs.

programmable point-of-sale terminal—A terminal that has a read-only microprogram memory for retail sales applications.

programmable read-only memory—1. A ROM which is user-programmable, generally by electrical methods such as deliberately blowing selected diodes. 2. A circuit board that contains the sockets for PROM along with the necessary address decoding, control, and timing circuits. The sockets allow PROM chips to be added or deleted to satisfy the system requirements.

programmable read-only memory blaster—A device for changing the protected read-only memory section found in some PROMs. The blaster allows the entire PROM to be changed by the user.

program maintenance procedures—The checking and testing requirements designed to reduce machine malfunctions or human mistakes in programming.

programmed check—A check of machine functions performed by the machine in response to an instruction included in the program. The programmed check may be a sample problem with a known answer.

programmed learning—An instructional method which uses expository material along with questions coupled to branching logic for remedial purposes. Programmed learning has been applied in books called programmed texts, or in computers as computer-assisted instruction (CAI).

programmed logic—A logic system which is alterable in accordance with a program which controls the equivalent connections of all the gating elements. In programmed logic, the instruction repertoire can be changed to match the machine capability to the problem.

programmed logic array—See *PLA*.

programmer—1. A person involved in the writing and testing of programs. 2. A device designed for program generation. An EEROM programmer is a unit that provides a means of programming an electrically erasable ROM from paper tape or from a keyboard and display.

programmer check—A check procedure designed by the programmer and implemented specifically as a part of the program.

programmer control panel—A panel that is usually supplied with a microcomputer system to provide access to the CPU registers and memory. It may also include data switches, data and address indicators, and function switches. Through the panel, the operator can address, load, and examine the memory and CPU registers and thus control the operation of the microcomputer.

programmer's console diagnostic—A routine that tests most of the console logic using an automatic loop-back test. It will also test all lights and switches under control of the operator.

programmer tools—All hardware and software designed for generating a system's programs. Programmer tools include assemblers, simulators, editors, and assemblers. Some may run on time-sharing systems, while others may be run on the microcomputer system itself.

programming—The design, writing, and testing of programs. Programming may consist of:

(1) Definition of problem
(2) Preparation of flow chart
(3) Listing of computer instructions
(4) Selecting circuit patterns or control modes

programming control panel—A panel with indicator lights and switches that the programmer can use to enter or change the routines in the program.

programming flow chart—A flow chart used to represent the sequence of operations in a program.

programming language—A language used for the preparation of programs.

programming module—A discrete identifiable set of instructions which is handled as a unit by an assembler, compiler, linkage editor, or loader.

program parameter—An adjustable quantity which can be given different values each time the quantity appears in a different subroutine. The program parameters may be altered by the routine and may vary depending upon the point of entry into the routine.

program reference table—An area of memory (abbreviated *PRT*) for storage of operands or references to arrays, files, or segments of the program. The PRT permits programs to be independent of the actual memory locations occupied by data and parts of the program.

program register—The computer control register into which the program instruction being executed is stored. The program register controls the computer operation during the cycles required to execute that instruction. Also called *program counter* and *index address register*.

program run—1. The actual processing time period of a computer program. 2. Collectively, those steps performed by a computer as it executes all cycles of a program.

program scheduler—A facility that permits use of the central processing unit among programs based in storage, depending upon priority requirements.

program segments—The logically discrete units such as subprograms, which comprise a user's complete program. Program segments consist of sequences of program statements which make up the main program. Control and data can be passed between segments as desired.

program stack—A dedicated memory portion for providing multiple-level nesting capability. The stack nests subroutine addresses and program counter words for orderly return to the main program following subroutine calls. As new values are added to the stack, all previous values are pushed down with the top level being the most recent entry.

program statement—A basic unit used to construct programs. A typical assembly language statement begins in character position number one of a source line and is terminated with a carriage return or a semicolon. A semicolon allows multiple statements to be coded on the same physical source line:

LOC 1 ADI 2 ; (add 2 to accumulator)

program status word—A word (abbreviated *PSW*) containing information used during processing (such as interrupt status).

program step—A single operation or phase of one instruction or command in a sequence of instructions.

program stop instruction—An instruction that is used to automatically stop the machine under certain conditions, such as reaching the end of processing or completing the solution of a problem.

program storage—The section of internal memory reserved for the storage of programs, routines, and subroutines. Program storage areas are sometimes protected using various schemes to prevent the alteration of the contents.

program storage unit—An integrated circuit (abbreviated *PSU*) used for the storage of programmed instructions and nonvolatile data constants required for program execution. A PSU may interface directly with the CPU without the need for buffers; the chip may also include a program counter, stack register, plus interrupt control and timing circuits.

program tape—A specific tape which contains the sequence of instructions required for solving a problem and which is read into a computer before running a program.

program test—A check made before running a program in which a sample problem of the same general type is run in the program to furnish a known answer.

program testing time—The time expended for the testing of a machine or system program to insure that no malfunctions or faults are present. Program testing may include debugging and special diagnostic routines, or circuit and component testing to determine machine status.

program test system—A checking system in which a sample problem with a known answer is run before running the program to solve the actual problem.

PROM—Abbreviation for ***programmable read-only memory***, usually a semiconductor memory which is not programmed during fabrication and requires a physical or electrical operation to program it. A specific PROM consists of a diode array which is programmed by burning out diodes. Other types can be erased by ultraviolet light and reprogrammed electrically. Devices are also available for automatically copying master PROMs quickly and easily.

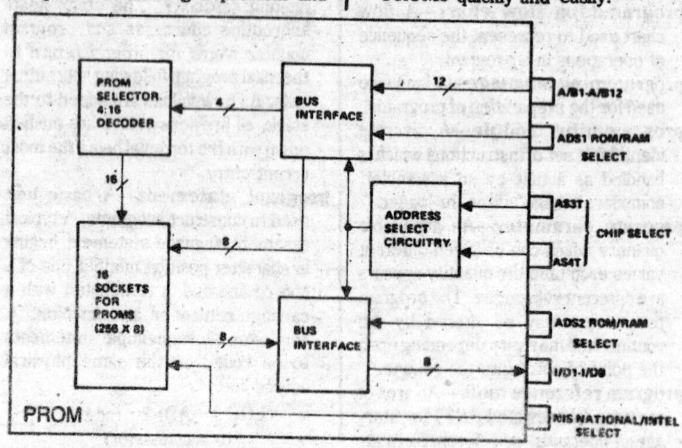

PROM monitor—A program stored in PROM which allows the microcomputer to be programmed using a simple keyboard. Functions of the monitor include:

(1) Addressing the memory at any location
(2) Reading memory contents
(3) Writing data into RAM
(4) Executing the user program in RAM

PROM programmer—A device or unit capable of programming PROMs, usually with a teletypewriter or keypad. One typical PROM programmer can copy PROMs in less than one minute using a control program.

PROM programmer card—A card that allows blocks of memory to be automatically programmed into PROM.

PROM programmer control program—A program used when programming PROMs on a PROM programmer. Data to be programmed is usually read from binary tapes using a teletypewriter or reader, other PROMs, or a keypad.

PROM programming system—A system for low-cost microcomputer programming which uses PROMs. The system has four basic parts:

(1) Prototype board
(2) Microprogram control programs
(3) Programmer for the PROM
(4) Keyboard

PROM simulator—A device which uses RAM for testing and debugging operations prior to PROM programming.

proof listing—A report (prepared by the processor) which shows the coding as originally written, with comments and the machine-language instructions.

propagated error—An error occurring in one operation and affecting data required for subsequent operations, so that the error is spread through much of the processed data.

propagation—The traveling of waves or pulses through or along a transmission medium.

propagation delay—The time required for a signal to travel from one point in a circuit or transmission path to another.

proportional control—A type of control in which there is a continuous linear relation between the output and the input.

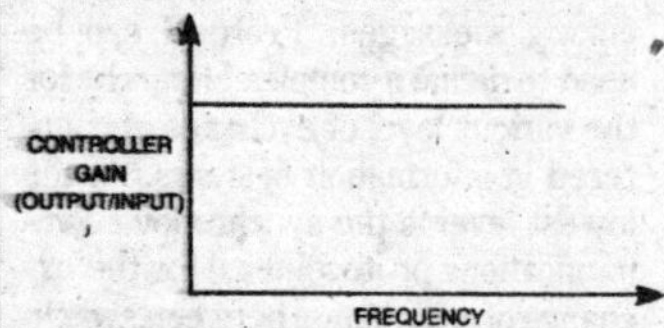

Proportional Control

proportional control system—A feedback control system that generates a correction signal that is a linear function of the error.

proportional gain—The ratio of the change in output due to a change in input in a proportional control system.

proportionality—Refers to that part of a linearity curve when it passes through a zero-error reference point or an origin.

proportional range—A band or set of values of a specific condition being controlled which causes the controller to operate over a linear range.

proprietary program—A program which is controlled by the owner through the legal right of possession and title.

protected check—A check prepared in such a manner as to prevent alterations.

protected key—A key on a keyboard that protects a character on the display screen from strikeover.

protected location—A storage location reserved for special purposes. Data to be stored in these locations is required to undergo a screening procedure. Protected locations may be block locations in main storage or in disk files where data may be read from, but not written into.

protection key—An indicator in the program status word which is associated with a task and which must match the storage keys of all storage blocks that it is to use.

protocol—The set of conventions between communication lines and links on the format and content of messages to be exchanged; especially those conventions which set the precedence among messages. Protocol can be used to define a complex hierarchy for the various level of exchange encountered in information systems. At the lowest level is the synchronous communications protocol used for the exchange of information between switching computers; next, a first level of protocol exists for the exchange of information between a host computer and its interface. The next level of protocol uses these two levels to control the flow of information between host computers. Level-three protocols are used to control the flow of information between processes, where a process may be a program or a terminal. Specific protocols are used to make initial connections in a link, for the transmittal of large files between computers, and for batch communication.

prototype—Refers to an initial design system or package which usually is a model for additional development.

prototype board—A circuit board used in development systems to evaluate new system concepts.

prototype development system—A collection of modules and equipment used for software development and PROM programming. A typical system includes the processor, control panel, teletypewriter interface, RAM, PROM programmer, and power supplies. Software includes an assembler, text editor, PROM programmer, plus debug and control programs.

prototype statement—An assembler statement that provides a name to a macro definition for a model, or for the macroinstruction that is to call the macro definition.

prototyping—The initial design and fabrication of a system on a trial basis for "shakedown."

proving time—The time used in running a test program to check if a particular fault has been corrected.

PRT—Abbreviation for *program reference table*, a table of the locations reserved for program variables, data descriptions, and other program information. When a program references a word in the PRT, the relative address is used rather than the absolute address. The relative address of any particular location is based upon its position relative to the start of the table.

ps—Abbreviation for picosecond (10^{-12} second).

pseudo code—A code that requires translation prior to execution. Pseudo codes are often used to link a subroutine into the main routine, and they usually express programs in terms of source language by referring to locations and operations using symbolic names and addresses.

pseudo instruction—A group of characters having the same general form as an instruction, but never executed as an actual instruction. Pseudo instructions are used as symbolic representations in compilers, interpreters, and assemblers to designate groups of instructions for performing a particular task. Also called *quasi instruction*.

pseudo random code—A digital code which has the appearance of a random sequence of finite length. Pseudo random codes repeat themselves and are not truly random, but they are useful for synchronization and sequence control.

pseudo random-number sequence—A sequence of numbers that is considered random for a given purpose. The sequence may be used to approximate a particular distribution of parameters.

PSW—Abbreviation for ***program status word***, a word in main storage used to control the order in which instructions are executed and to hold and indicate the order or status of the system in relation to a particular program.

p-type conductivity—The conductivity in a semiconductor as expressed by the movement of holes.

p-type semiconductor—A semiconductor in which the hole density exceeds the conduction electron density.

pull operation—An operation in which operands are taken from the top of a pushdown stack in memory and placed in general registers. The operand remains in the stack unchanged; a pointer value is changed to indicate the current top of the stack.

pulse—A variation in a quantity such as a voltage which is characterized by a rise and decay of finite duration.

pulse accumulator module—A module with counters for accumulating pulses from several sources for frequency measurements. Input pulses can be accumulated and then held for interrogation by the CPU on the basis of jumpered or preselected intervals ranging from 100 microseconds to ten seconds.

pulse amplifier—An amplifier with a wide bandwidth that can amplify pulses without excessive distortion.

pulse amplitude—The level of a pulse or waveform of pulses.

pulse-amplitude modulation—A form of modulation (abbreviated *PAM*) in which the amplitude of the pulse carrier is varied in accordance with the modulating signal.

pulse code—1. A code in which sets of pulses have been assigned particular meanings, such as in the Morse, Baudot, or binary codes. 2. Pulse code modulation.

pulse code modulation—A form of pulsed modulation in which the signal is sampled periodically and each sample is quantized and transmitted as a digital binary code.

pulse counter—A device which gives an indication of or actually records the total number of pulses that has been received during a given time interval.

pulse counting module—A device to count and store pulse information and transmit this information to a computer upon command.

pulse digit—A drive pulse corresponding to a logical 1 digit position in some or all of the words in a storage unit. The pulse digit may be an inhibit pulse or an enable pulse in specific applications.

pulse duration—The time interval between the leading and trailing edge of a pulse.

pulse duration modulation—A type of modulation (abbreviated *PDM*) in which the value of a sample of the modulating wave is used to modulate the duration of a pulse.

pulse frequency modulation—A modulation method (abbreviated *PFM*) in which the pulse repetition rate is varied in accordance with the amplitude and frequency of the modulating signal.

pulse generator—A device for generating a series of pulses of specific form, duration, and repetition rate.

pulse interleaving—A process in which pulses from two or more time-division multiplexers are systematically and alternately combined for transmission over a common path.

pulse length—The time interval between specified rise and fall points of a pulse.

pulse length modulation—Pulse duration modulation.

pulse mode—A coded group of pulses used to select a particular communication channel from a common carrier.

pulse modulation—The modulation of pulses by a carrier. Pulse modulation includes pulse amplitude modulation (PAM), pulse position modulation (PPM), and pulse duration modulation (PDM).

pulse position modulation—A form of modulation in which the positions in time of pulses are varied without modifying their duration.

pulse ratio—The ratio of the length of a pulse to its total period.

pulse repeater—A device that receives pulses from one circuit and transmits corresponding pulses at another frequency or wavelength into another circuit. Also called a *transponder*.

pulse repetition frequency—The rate at which pulses occur in a given unit of time. More correctly termed *pulse repetition rate*, since pulses are digital in character and "frequency" is generally applied to analog (AC) signals.

pulse repetition rate—The number of pulses per unit time experienced at a point in a device, circuit, or system, usually expressed in terms of pulses per second (pps).

pulse string—A sequential group of pulses; a pulse train.

pulse time modulation—Modulation in which the modulating wave is used to vary a time characteristic of the pulse carrier, such as in pulse duration modulation and pulse position modulation.

pulse train—A group or sequence of pulses with similar characteristics.

pulse train generator—A circuit or device which produces a fixed number of usually equally spaced pulses.

pulse-width modulation—Pulse duration modulation.

pulse-width recording—A method of recording in which each storage cell is made up of two regions magnetized in opposite senses with unmagnetized regions on each side. A zero bit is represented by a cell containing a negative region followed by a positive region.

punch—1. A perforation in a punched card or tape. 2. To make a paper-tape or card perforation. 3. The machine or device used to make coded paper perforations.

punch card—A card suitable for punched patterns of holes which are used to represent data.

punch-card check—A bank check which has perforations either in the body of the draft or along a portion of its border.

punched card—A precisely sized heavy paper material on which information can be coded in the form of holes. The holes can be of many shapes and may be punched either by machine or by hand.

punched card reader—A device which senses hole patterns in punched cards and performs some operation as a result of the content, such as translating them into machine language.

punched-card verifier—A machine which insures that data punched into cards is the same as the data on original documents from which it was punched. The process of punching from the initial documents is repeated, and the machine detects any differences between the holes and the key depressions.

punched paper tape—Paper tape on which information is or may be stored in the form of punched holes. Each character of information is punched in an established code across the width of the tape. There are usually 5 to 8 punch positions which represent channels or levels along the length of the tape. Also called *paper tape* and *punched tape*.

punched tape—Punched paper tape.

punch position—A defined location on a card or tape where a hole may be punched.

punch station—An area in a given facility where a punching unit is located for the coded perforation of punched cards or tape.

pure generator—A routine which is capable of writing another routine. The pure generator may be a section of a program in an assembler on a library tape. It can then be called by the assembler to perform.

pushdown list—A list that uses the last-in-first-out system. The item to be retrieved is the most recently stored item in the list, and the last item entered becomes the first item retrieved from the list.

pushdown queue—A last-in-first-out method of ordering data in which the last item attached to the queue is the first to be withdrawn.

pushdown stack—A segment of memory used to receive information from the program counter and store address locations of the instructions which have been pushed down during an interrupt. The pushdown stack can be used for subroutining; its size determines the level of subroutine nesting. When instructions are returned, they are "popped back" on a last-in-first-out basis. The stack tends to minimize register transfers, facilitate counting and sorting, and limit transfers to and from main memory.

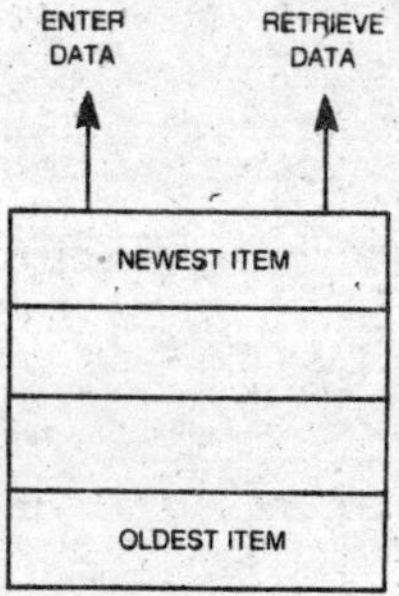

Pushdown Stack

push operation—The operation in which operands from a general register are stored in the top location of a pushdown stack in memory.

pushup list—A list that uses a first-in-first-out order. The next item to be retrieved and removed is the oldest item on the list. Each item is entered at the end of the list, and the previous items maintain their same relative position in the list.

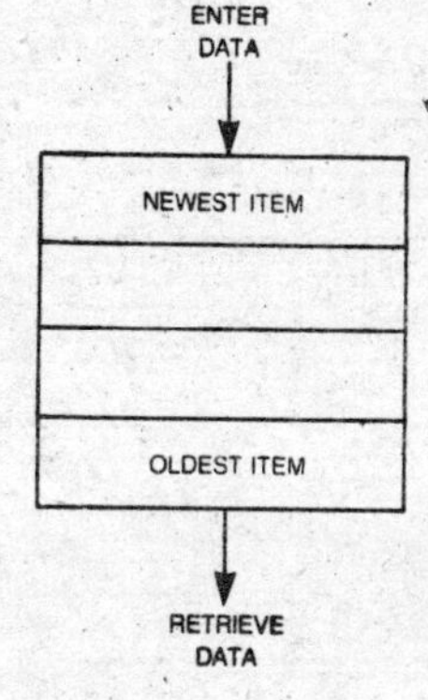

Pushup List

pushup storage—A method of storage in which the next item of data to be retrieved is the oldest and has been in the queue the longest.

PWM—Abbreviation for *pulse-width modulation*, a pulse modulation technique in which the modulating wave is used to vary the width of a pulse proportionally.

Q

Q—1. Symbol for *figure of merit* for a resonant circuit or device. 2. Symbol for *electric charge*. 3. Schematic designation of active solid-state devices (usually followed by a numeral).

QIL—Abbreviation for *quad-inline*, a dual-inline package (DIP) with four similar functional units or circuits.

Q output—The reference output of a flip-flop. The Q output corresponds to a one condition, and the $\overline{Q}$ output is the Q output inverted, or a zero in the normal state.

QTAM—Abbreviation for *queued teleprocessing access method.*

quad—1. A packaged integrated circuit containing four identical stages. 2. Four-channel stereophonic sound. 3. Containing four identical or nearly identical electrodes, terminals, or leads (as outputs).

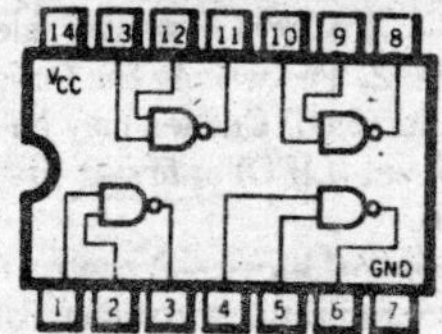

Positive logic: $Y = \overline{AB}$

Quad NAND Gate

quad clock driver—A driver circuit with four separate outputs. It is useful for driving the address, control, and supplementary timing circuits for various logic systems.

quadratic programming—A type of nonlinear programming used in operations research in which the function to be maximized or minimized is a quadratic function and the constraints are linear functions.

qualification—1. Testing of a program, equipment, or system prior to its delivery from the manufacturer to the user. 2. In COBOL, a technique used to make a name or situation unique by adding IN or OF.

qualification testing—The testing of programs, equipment, or systems prior to delivery to the user.

qualified name—A data name accompanied by the class to which it belongs in a given classification system.

qualifier tester—A benchtop system for testing DTL, TTL, and CMOS devices. This tester uses a microcomputer to control all internal test functions, and it can be used with RS-232C terminals.

quality assurance—The systematic methods that are used to provide suitable confidence that an item will perform satisfactory.

quality control—The process of monitoring, in an organized and formal manner, workmanship, processes, and materials to produce a consistent, uniform product. Quality control may involve the keeping of batch logs, error summary reports, and evaluation records.

quality diagnostic—Software that verifies the proper operation of the CPU, memories, and input/output functions. Quality diagnostics include routines to check instructions, memory, real-time clock, printer and associated keyboard, power-fail/restart, automatic loader, etc.

quality engineering—An engineering program used to establish quality tests and acceptance criteria along with interpreting quality data.

quantity—Any positive or negative number used to specify a value; it may be a whole number, a fraction, or a combination of both.

quantization—The subdivision of an element or parameter into a finite number of distinct values such as occurs in analog-to-digital conversion and some forms of multiplexing.

quantum—1. A unit of processing time in a time-sharing system that may be allocated for operating a program during its turn in the computer. 2. A subrange in a quantization operation. 3. The smallest indivisible element of a quantized signal. 4. An indeterminate quantity; an amount. 5. The smallest increment into which an energy form can be described.

quantize—To subdivide an element or parameter into a number of distinct values.

quantum clock—The timing of an interval of processing time according to developed priorities in a time-sharing system.

quantum efficiency—1. The number of electrons released in a photocell per unit of incident radiation. 2. The ratio of energy output to input in an energy conversion system.

quartz—A piezoelectric material used in the manufacture of crystals for oscillators. It may be natural or man-made. Quartz exhibits a variety of predictable characteristics which vary according to the axis from which it is cut.

quartz crystal—A frequency-determining crystal cut to oscillate at some precise fixed frequency over a specified temperature range. It exhibits the properties of a resonant RLC circuit and is used in close-tolerance oscillators as a source for clock signals.

quartz delay line—A delay line which uses quartz as the medium.

quartz oscillator—An oscillator that uses a quartz crystal for frequency control.

quartz plate—Refers to a quartz crystal finished for a generalized frequency range but not trimmed to a specific frequency within that range. Also called a ***blank***.

quartz thermometer—A transducer that determines temperature from the frequency difference between a temperature-dependent quartz oscillator and a temperature-independent one.

query station—A terminal or station which introduces requests for data or information while the system is computing or communicating.

queue—1. To form a waiting line for service. 2. The waiting line for items to be serviced. Queues may be last-in-first-out (LIFO) or first-in-first-out (FIFO).

queue control block—A control block used for regulating the sequential use of a set of competing tasks.

queued access—An access method

that synchronizes the transfer of data between the program and input/output devices with minimal delays.

queue discipline—Refers to the method used to determine the order of service in a queued system.

queued sequential access—A method of sequential access in which queues are formed of input data blocks that are awaiting processing, and output data blocks that have been processed and are awaiting storage or transfer to an output device.

queued telecommunications access method—A method (abbreviated *QTAM*) used to transfer data between main storage and remote terminals. A macroinstruction is used to request the transfer, which is performed by a message control program that synchronizes the transfer with minimum delays.

queuing—The patterns and methods used in studying delays and waiting lines for servicing devices or items.

queuing list—A list used for scheduling actions in real time on a time priority basis.

queuing theory—A form of probability theory used in the study of delays or lines at servicing points. Queuing theory is concerned with minimizing the delays due to waiting lines at servicing areas or junctions.

quick-disconnect—A type of connector which allows quick locking and unlocking of all contacts.

quiescence—1. At rest, waiting for an input signal or command. 2. In a class A amplifier, the condition in which the input electrode is biased to the midpoint of the linear range (between cutoff and saturation), but no input signal is applied.

quiescent current—The current in an amplifier or control device in the absence of a command or control signal.

quiescing—The process of bringing a device or system, including a multiprogrammed system, to a halt by the rejection of new jobs or new requests for work.

quinary—Sometimes used as a shortened form of *biquinary*.

quoted string—A character string used in assembler programming in which the string is enclosed by apostrophes to represent a value that can include blanks in a microinstruction operand.

R

race—In any multisignal logic system, a condition in which the timing between two coincident signals is unpredictable even though the system operation requires a specific timed sequence for proper operation.

rack—A free-standing metal frame or cabinet into which panels of equipment may be installed.

rack-mounting—Descriptive of a piece of equipment whose front panel is designed to fasten to a standard, usually 19-inch rack (cabinet) in such a way that the equipment is contained within the rack, but the controls are accessible from the front.

radiation—The propagation of energy through space or a medium.

radio circuit—A communication system consisting of a radio link with a transmitter and antenna, the radio transmission path, and a receiving antenna and receiver.

radio-frequency interference—The unwanted interference (abbreviated *rfi*) in a circuit or device caused by electromagnetic radiation from another circuit or device.

radix—The quantity of characters for use in each of the digital positions of a numbering system. Also called *base*.

SYSTEM	CHARACTERS	RADIX
binary	0, 1	2
octal	0, 1, 2, 3, 4, 5, 6, 7	8
decimal	0, 1, 2, 3, 4, 5, 6, 7, 8, 9	10

radix complement—A complement obtained by subtracting each digit from one less than its radix, then adding one to the least significant digit and executing all carries required. Examples include the tens' complement in decimal notation or the twos' complement in binary notation. Also called *true complement*.

radix-minus-one complement—A complement obtained by subtracting each digit from one less than the radix. Examples include the nines' complement in decimal notation and the ones' complement in binary notation. Also called *diminished-radix complement*.

radix notation—A positional representation in which the significance of any two adjacent positions has an integral ratio which is the radix of the least significant of the two positions. The permissible values of the digit in any position range from zero to one less than the radix of that position.

radix point—The real or implied character that separates the digits associated with the integral part of a numeral from those associated with the fractional part.

RALU—Abbreviation for *register and arithmetic logic unit*, a collection of logic elements such as accumulators, stack, and arithmetic logic unit, which provide data storage and processing functions. A typical RALU is designed so that up to 8 units can be combined in parallel to allow the implementation of processors from 4 to 32 bits wide. All elements in the unit are tied together by a set of buses, and data flow can be defined using microprogramming (usually with a CROM chip).

ARITHMETIC AND LOGIC UNIT
ACCUMULATOR
ACCUMULATOR
ACCUMULATOR
PROGRAM COUNTER
MEMORY ADDRESS REGISTER
MEMORY DATA REGISTER

RALU

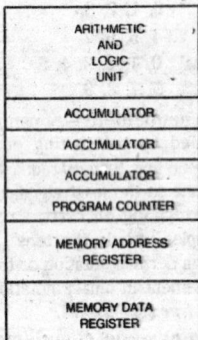

RAM—Abbreviation for *random-access memory*, a mass store that provides fast access to any storage location point by means of vertical and horizontal coordinates. Information is written in or read out using the same procedure. A RAM system can be divided into three main sections:

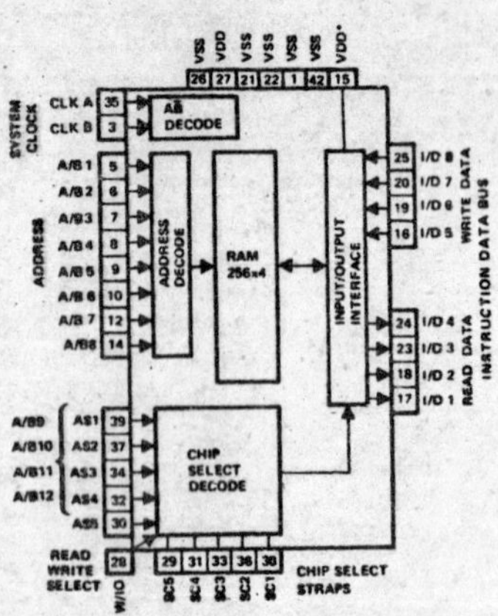

RAM

(1) Address buffers, read-write logic, and chip-select logic.

(2) Data bus buffers and memory array.

(3) Refresh and control logic.

During a cycle, a 1 on a write input/output line will be interpreted by the RAM as a write enable command, and data on the bus will be written in. Available RAMs have access times from 2 ns to 3 μs and range in size from 4 to 4096 bits per chip. RAMs provide the means for designers to program the logic of all programmable logic systems in use. They are also used as ROM and PROM emulators in many systems.

RAM address register—A register which contains the address location to be accessed in RAM.

RAM alarm—An alarm triggered when the data on a given channel in the memory system does not agree with alarm setpoint values. The microprocessor then prints out a complete data scan from memory, regardless of which channel is in alarm.

RAM card system—Refers to a complete RAM with control logic on a single circuit board or card. RAM cards may contain up to 16,000 words of 16 bits each and can be used to replace more costly core systems with only half the storage density.

RAM enable—A RAM control line that allows new data to be written into the address field.

RAM save—An option that prevents data in ROMs from being lost due to power outages. One type of system uses a custom initialization ROM that restores the full program to the ROMs, restarts the clock, and begins data scanning. Other types use battery banks or other units to provide power for 5 minutes, or until external power is returned.

RAM print-on-alarm—An operation mode in which continuous scanning takes place but data is read out only when an alarm is interpreted by the CPU.

RAM refresh—The periodic signals that must be applied to dynamic MOS RAMs to insure that stored data is retained. The refresh operation consists of a specified number of write cycles, and sometimes read cycles as well, on the least significant address bits within a given period of time. The number of cycles may vary from 16 to 64 within a 2 ms period. The refresh requirement tends to increase system costs and reduce the overall memory system performance due to the additional required timing logic circuitry.

RAM refresh clock—The source of the timing signals required for refreshing dynamic RAMs. A typical system uses a ripple counter to generate the sequential states and a multiplexer for gating these states with the CPU.

RAM refresh cycle—The period required for dynamic RAM refresh.

ramp—A signal that increases in level linearly with time. Usually, the ramp is repetitive, operating at a predetermined rate.

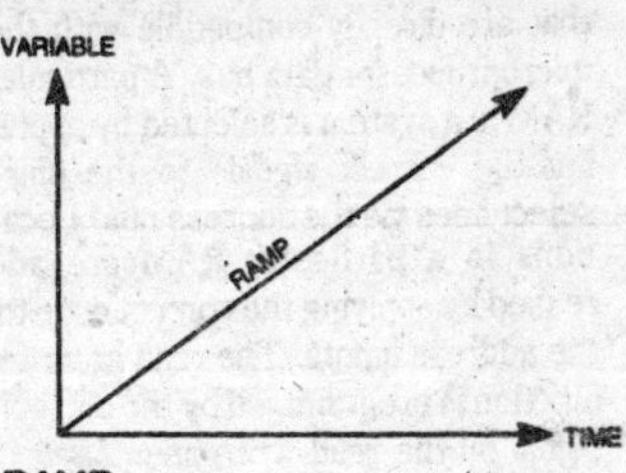

RAMP

RAM register simulator—A program that functionally simulates execution of microcomputer programs. Such simulators are interpretive and provide bit-for-bit duplication of instruction execution timing, register contents, and other functions.

RAM/ROM pattern processor—A test system which can be used to check RAM and ROM patterns.

RAM test program—A program that uses a PROM which plugs into prototyping boards for complete checkout.

random-access—1. The process of obtaining information from or placing information into a storage system where the time required for access is independent of the location of the information most recently obtained or placed in storage. 2. An access mode in COBOL in which specific logical records are obtained from or placed into a mass storage file in a nonsequential manner.

random-access device—A unit in which access time is independent of data location and system history.

random-access memory—A memory (abbreviated *RAM*) where information elements are organized into discrete sections with each location uniquely identified by an address. Data may be obtained from such a memory by specifying the data addresses.

A random-access memory may be implemented in many ways, such as core, drum, disk, or cards; however, popular usage of the abbreviation RAM usually refers to semiconductor types. A typical semiconductor RAM has bidirectional input/output lines that are directly compatible with the microprocessor data bus. A particular RAM in a system is selected by applying the correct signals to the chip-select lines via the address bus. Locations in a particular RAM are adressed by applying the correct code to the address inputs. The read or write function is programmed by the correct signal on the read-write line.

random-access storage—Storage in which the time required to obtain information is independent of the location of the information.

random-access time—The average time period between the end of readout of a word from storage at a randomly chosen address, and the end of readout of another word from any other randomly chosen address. The readout operations are performed as fast as the microcomputer can carry them out, so no waiting period for the arithmetic and logic unit is included in this time period. Minimum random access time is used to define the time period between the end of readout of a word at any given address and the end of readout of the word in the most favorable other address in the storage unit.

random failure—A failure whose occurrence at a particular time is unpredictable. Also called *chance failure*.

random logic—Logic circuits and collections of circuits that use discrete integrated circuits for individual functions. Random logic uses hardware gates to implement the logic equations. Design aids include Karnaugh maps, state diagrams, computer simulation, and breadboarding.

random logic devices—The SSI and MSI integrated circuits used to design random logic systems.

random noise—Refers to a large number of different overlapping transient disturbances. Also called fluctuation noise and white noise.

random number—A number in a series of numbers which is obtained completely by chance. Random numbers are considered to be free from bias and thus they are used for statistical testing.

random-number generator—A routine or device designed to produce a random number, or a series of random numbers according to specified limitations.

random variable—A variable which may assume any one of a number of values, each having the same probability of occurrence. Also called a *variate*.

random walk—A method used in problem analysis in which experiments with probabilistic variables are traced to determine if the results are significant.

range—1. The set of values between two limits that a quantity may assume. 2. The usable operating sphere of a communications system.

rapid-access loop—A section of storage which has a much faster access than the remainder of storage. Such loops are found in some disk, drum, and tape units. Sometimes called *revolver*.

raster—An illuminated gray cathode-ray screen without an image-forming video input.

raster count—The number of coordinate positions addressable on a cathode-ray screen.

rated output—The output power, voltage, or current at which a device is designed to operate under normal conditions.

rate test—A test in which problems are run with known solution times to determine if a computer is operating correctly.

rating—A value which determines the limiting capacity or limiting conditions for a device. Ratings are determined for specified values of environment and operation.

rating system—The set of principles upon which ratings are established and interpreted.

RC—1. Abbreviation for *resistance-capacitance*. 2. Abbreviation for *radio-controlled*. 3. Abbreviation for *resistance-coupled*.

RC amplifier—An amplifier that uses resistance-capacitance coupling.

RC circuit—A circuit which uses resistors and capacitors to form a time constant.

RC network—A circuit using resistors and capacitors to perform a particular function, such as filtering, timing, differentiation, integration, etc.

RC oscillator—An oscillator circuit in which the frequency of oscillation is determined by resistor and capacitor elements.

RCTL—Abbreviation for *resistor-capacitor-transistor logic,* a logic family that uses discrete transistors with RC coupling.

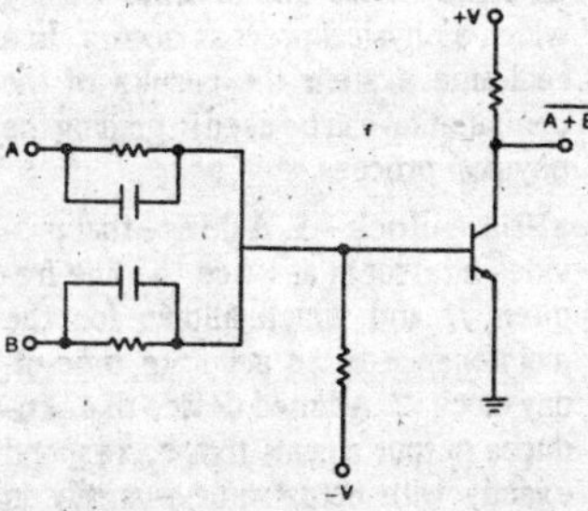

RCTL NOR Gate

reactance modulator—In FM communications, a circuit that modulates the capacitive reactance of a stage in accordance with the applied signal amplitude.

reactive mode—A condition of communications between remote terminals and a computer in which each entry causes an action by the computer, sometimes without an immediate reply.

read—1. To sense information contained in some storage medium. 2. To acquire and interpret information from a storage device.

read-after-write verify—A check for determining that information currently being written is correct as compared to the information source.

read-around ratio—The number of times a location in a storage medium may be consulted before deterioration results in the loss of data.

read-back check—A check in which the information that was transmitted to an output device is returned to the source and compared with the original information to insure accuracy.

reader—A device for sensing information stored in memory and for generating signals that represent such sensed data.

reader-interpreter —A service routine that reads an input stream, stores programs and data for later processing, identifies control information in the data stream, and stores this information in the proper control list.

reading rate—The number of characters, words, or items that can be sensed by an input unit in a given time.

read-only memory—A memory (abbreviated *ROM*) whose contents are not intended to be alterable by instructions. A typical semiconductor read-

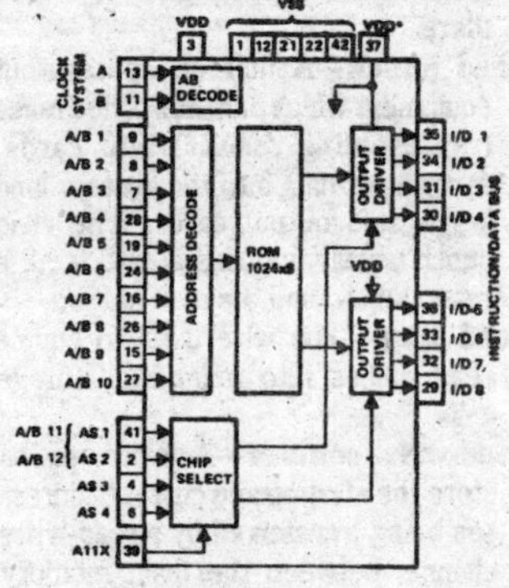

ROM Block Diagram

only memory is programmed by a mask pattern as part of the final manufacturing stage. ROMs are usually permanent, although some can be erased electrically or with the aid of ultraviolet radiation. ROMs are used to store microprograms or fixed programs in microcomputer systems.

The size of a ROM varies with system requirements, and the maximum size is usually dictated by the addressing capability of the miiroprocessor. A ROM does not need any store control circuitry; instructions can fetched from a ROM in half the time it would take with a RAM. But programs must be correct, since ROM gives no flexibility for changing the instruction sequence.

read-only storage—Read-only memory.

readout—An array of addressable display characters that collectively form numbers or words that are the result of a machine operation; thus, a display of alphabetical, numerical, or alphanumeric characters.

readout device—The collective addressable characters that indicate a computer or calculator output or result; thus, a display.

read pulse—A pulse applied to one or more binary storage cells to determine if a bit of information is stored there.

read punch—A unit of input/output equipment which punches coded holes (representing results) into cards, reads input data into the system, and segregates output cards. The read punch usually contains a card feed, a read station, and a punch station.

read wire—The wire used to couple read pulses into magnetic storage cells.

read-write counter—A device used to store the starting and current addresses being transferred by a read-write channel between the main memory and peripheral devices.

read-write head—The electromagnetic device that is used for recording or erasing information on magnetic tapes, drums, or disks.

read-write memory—A memory (abbreviated *RWM*) that can be altered at will. Read-write memories are used where it is desired to change the system application by the operator.

read - write memory module—A circuit board that contains a random-access memory along with all necessary timing, control, and decoding logic.

ready—The status or condition of being prepared to run. A program or device that is in a ready condition needs only a start signal to begin operation.

ready line—A line on some processors designed to interface the processor to a slow memory or to a slow input/output device.

ready status word—A status word used to indicate that the remote computing system is waiting for entry from the terminal.

real-time—The actual time during which a physical process occurs. In a real-time system the results of the computation can be used in guiding the physical process.

real-time clock—1. A device that provides interrupts at twice the line frequency, and which allows for the maintenance of an accurate time-of-day clock. 2. A timed device that produces output signals that correspond exactly with actual time—usually in hours, minutes, seconds, and tenths of seconds—and which may be used to indicate cumulative elapsed time, elapsed time, or time of day.

real-time clock diagnostic—A routine that tests for the proper functioning of a real-time clock.

real-time clock module—A circuit board or unit that provides programmable time bases for real-time clocking.

real-time debug routine—A program that allows the user to test, examine, and modify a program task while the real-time application program is running.

real-time executive—A multitasking program system that can handle all aspects of priority scheduling, interrupt servicing, input/output control, intertask communications, and all queuing functions. Executives are designed for operation with specific microcomputer systems. Tasks operating under executive supervision provide the mechanism to real-time events. The occurrence of an event typically results in the scheduling of a response task. This scheduling is performed using a priority structure which associates each task with a distinct priority level. A given task may be interrupted while in the process of execution and temporarily suspended while a higher priority task is executed.

real-time executive system—A multiprogramming foreground-background system with priority handling, interrupt capability, and program load-and-go capabilities.

real-time guard—A mode which results in an interrupt to an address in central store when any attempt is made to perform a restricted operation. The guard mode is terminated by the occurrence of an interrupt.

real-time information system—A system that provides information fast enough for the process to be controlled by the operator using this information.

real-time input—An input that goes to the computer as the activity occurs.

real-time input/output—Refers to signals that are accepted by the system as they occur, or output signals that are generated to control external devices in real time such as required in industrial process control.

real-time interface—An interface used for such tasks as controlling relays, solenoids, limit counters, and controllers.

real-time mode—A mode of operation in which data necessary for the control or execution of a transaction are affected by the results of the processing. Real-time modes eliminate slow information-gathering procedures along with lax reporting techniques and slow communications. It insures that facts within the system are as timely as the prevailing situation. The real-time mode provides answers when answers are needed and delivers data when the need for that data occurs.

real-time monitor—An operating and programming system designed to monitor the construction and execution of programs. An effective monitor will tend to optimize the utilization of hardware and to minimize programmer effort and operator intervention. The system is usually of a modular construction, tailored for a specific microcomputer and application.

real-time operating system—A comprehensive software operating system designed to support the microcomputer in dedicated real-time applications. The system usually includes a system generation program, input/output routines, and analog-to-digital conversion routines.

real-time operation—Data processing which allows the machine to use information as it becomes available. Real-time operation is opposed to *batch operation*, which processes information at a time unrelated to the time when the information was generated.

real-time option board—A circuit board that contains most of the interface circuits and other options that users need for real-time operation. A typical option board includes:

(1) Real-time clock
(2) Programmer console
(3) Input/output interface
(4) Time-share control
(5) Power-fail/restart circuits

real-time remote inquiry—Online inquiry stations that allow users to interrogate computer files and receive immediate answers.

real-time system—A system in which information is processed and responses are generated in a time interval directly related to the operational requirements of the system. Many real-time systems may also perform batch processing while concurrently processing inquiries. A typical microprocessor real-time system uses a compact memory-resident executive requiring in its simplest form less than 700 words of memory. It can be used in cost-sensitive applications such as controllers, which previously could not operate with the high overhead of real-time software. Some systems control 60 to 70 tasks on a fixed-priority basis.

reasonableness check—A test made on information in a computer system to insure that the data is within a desired range of values.

receiver—A device equipped for reception of incoming signals which are then transformed into a desired format.

receiver card—A circuit board that accepts incoming data and translates it into some other usable form. A typical receiver card accepts ASCII data and translates it into parallel digital data.

receiver register—A register used to input received data into the system at a clock rate determined by the control register.

receiver/transmitter communication controller—An asynchronous controller which can interface data sets to a microcomputer. The controller consists of timing and control interface circuits, a receiver, and a transmitter.

receiving perforator—A tape punch which converts coded electrical signals into perforations in tape.

recirculating loop memory—A section of magnetic memory in which stored information recirculates continuously to provide rapid access.

record—1. A collection of related items of data which can be treated as a unit. One line of an invoice may form a record, and a complete set of records may form a file. 2. A set or collection of related fields.

record blocking—The grouping of records into data blocks that can be read or written using magnetic tape in one operation. Record blocking allows for more efficient tape operation and reduces the time to read or write files.

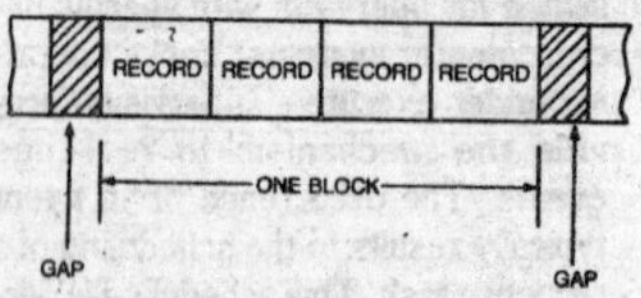

Record Blocking

record format—The design and organization of a record, usually a part of the program specification.

record gap—An area on a data medium which indicates the end of a block or record. Also called *interrecord gap.*

recording density—The number of bits in a single linear track measured per unit length of the recording medium.

record format—Record layout.

recording head—A transducer which accepts electrical variations and produces a corresponding field that selectively magnetizes a storage medium.

record layout—The arrangement and structure of a data record, including the sequence and size of components. Also called *record format*.

record length—A measure of the size of a record, usually specified in characters or words.

record separator—The information separator used to identify a logical boundary between the sets of items called records. Abbreviated *RS*.

recoverable error—An error condition which allows the continued execution of a program.

recoverable synchronization—An operational feature which allows synchronization to be recovered or reestablished when upset by disturbances.

recovery program—A program which allows a computer system to continue functioning when certain equipment fails.

rectifier—A device for converting alternating current into direct current by permitting the passage of signals in one direction only.

rectifier diode—A device intended for power rectification applications (as opposed to signal detection applications).

recursion—The continued repeating of the same operation or group of operations.

red-tape operation—An operation which is necessary to process data, but does not contribute to the final answer.

redundancy—1. That part of the information content which can be eliminated without loss of essential data. 2. The employment of several devices to perform the same function in order to improve the reliability of a particular portion of a system.

redundancy check—The systematic insertion of bits or characters in a message for error detection. The added bits are redundant, since they can be eliminated without the loss of message information. Parity checking is one form of redundancy checking.

redundancy-check character—A character used for checking the parity on a tape track. It is usually the last character recorded in each block.

redundant character—A character added to a group of characters to insure conformity with certain rules designed to detect errors.

redundant code—A self-checking code that uses an added check bit. Examples of redundant codes include the biquinary code and the two-out-of-five code.

reenterable—A routine which can be shared by several tasks concurrently by calling itself or a program which then calls it.

reenterable load module—A loading module which can be used repeatedly or concurrently by two or more jobs or tasks.

reference address—The common address or address portion for a group of relative addresses.

reference listing—A list printed by a compiler to indicate instructions as they appear in the final routine, and which usually includes details of storage allocation.

reference program table—A section of storage which is used as an index for operations, variables, and subroutines.

reference record—A compiler output that lists the operations and their positions in the routine, along with information on the segmentation and storage allocation of the routine.

reference voltage—A voltage used as a comparison standard for various circuit operations.

reflection loss—The loss in power from a source as a result of an impedance mismatch between source and load.

reformatting—The changing in the representation of data from one format to another. Reformatting may include the translation of data values from one character set to another, such as from ASCII to EBCDIC.

refresh—To restore signals or data states in a volatile storage system such as a dynamic MOS RAM.

regenerate—1. To restore information that is electrostatically stored, such as on a cathode-ray tube screen. 2. To produce a new pulse of proper shape when keyed by a degraded pulse.

regeneration—1. The process of restoring information or signals to specified requirements in amplitude or timing. 2. Positive feedback in usually a single amplifier stage.

regenerative feedback—A positive feedback of part of the output in a circuit or system to the input such that it causes an increase in the output. See *regeneration*.

regenerative memory—A memory or storage system that requires refreshing of the data to avoid loss of the contents.

regenerative read—A read operation which automatically refreshes or rewrites the data back to the positions from which it was extracted.

regenerative storage—Storage that requires periodic refreshing.

register—A set of flip-flops used as a storage device for usually one or two words. It is used for temporary storage of subsets of data to facilitate arithmetic, logical, and transfer operations. Typical registers in microcomputers include the accumulator, index address register, instruction counter, stack pointer, and others. These registers should have good accessibility to the CPU.

register address—An address where the operand lies in one of the general registers. In the 8080 system, an instruction such as:

ADDC ;(A = A + C)

will add the contents of C to the accumulator and then place the result in the accumulator.

register address field—The part of a computer instruction that contains a register address.

register and arithmetic logic unit—See *RALU*.

register transfer module—A functional register unit (abbreviated *RTM*) designed for the construction of register logic systems.

registration—The accuracy of the positioning of punched holes in a card.

relation—The comparison of two expressions in assembler programming to determine if the value of one is greater than, equal to, or less than the other.

relational operator—An operator used in assembler programming to indicate when a comparison is to be performed between different terms.

relative address—An address that is to be altered to an absolute address at the time the program is being run.

relative address label—A label used to identify the location of data by reference to its position with respect to some other location in the program.

relative addressing—A type of addressing which shortens the address part of an instruction by allowing a reference within some range relative to a register. In the 6800 system, a relative addressing instruction is formed by adding the second byte of the instruction to the op code plus two. Because the addition is in twos' complement arithmetic, the result is plus 127 or minus 128 of the original value, and the relative address lies between plus 129 and minus 126 of the current instruction. As an example:

BBC 12 ;(branch if carry clear)

transfers control to the current location plus 14 if the carry bit is cleared.

relative addressing mode—An addressing mode that specifies a memory location in the program counter or another register for reference. The relative addressing mode can be used for branch instructions, in which case an op code is added to the relative address to complete the instruction.

relative code—A code in which all addresses are specified or written with respect to an arbitrary position or represented symbolically in a computable form.

relating coding—To form or use a relative code.

relative time clock—A clock system (abbreviated *RTC*) used to allow the executive to keep track of time and service interrupts. At every relative time-clock interrupt, the program control is returned to the executive, which determines the priority of action.

relaxation oscillator—An oscillator that operates by being driven to a regenerative state rapidly and repetitively. Upon reaching the saturated regenerative state, the device "relaxes" to return to its original state and is immediately driven again to saturation.

relay—1. An electromechanical switching device usually composed of a solenoid, a movable armature containing at least one contact point, and a set of fixed contact points. Applying a voltage to the solenoid sets up a magnetic field that attracts the armature, thus causing it to make or break a circuit completed by the touching contact points. 2. A radio repeater system, usually automatically operated and controlled.

relay driver—A circuit that produces an output powerful enough to drive relay solenoids when a low-current logic signal is applied.

relay tree—A group of relays whose contacts are interconnected, but whose solenoids are independently driven; so called because each relay in the array has twice the contacts of the prior relay. Relay trees perform binary-to-decimal conversion (for driving 7-segment displays) and permit selection of a number of power-driving functions with only a few input signals.

release-guard signal—A signal sent in response to a clear-forward signal that indicates that the circuit is free at the incoming end.

reliability—The probability that a device will perform without failure for a specified time period under specified operating conditions.

reliability testing—Tests which are designed to determine the anticipated failure-free performance, or life expectancy of a product or system under specified conditions.

relocate—To move a routine from one part of storage to another and make the necessary adjustments to allow the routine to be executed.

relocatable assembler—An assembler which generates an object program with memory addresses entered as displacements from a relative program origin or as external references.

relocatable expression—An assembly expression whose value is affected by program relocation. A relocatable expression may represent a relocatable address.

relocatable program—A program designed so that it may be located and executed from many areas in memory.

relocatable term—A term in assembler programming whose value is affected by program relocation.

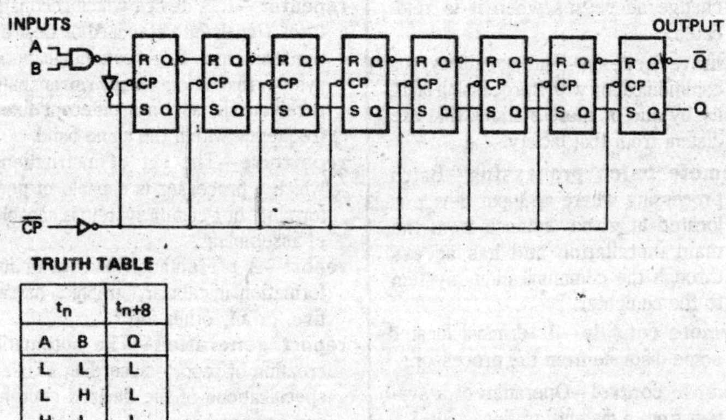

t_n		t_{n+8}
A	B	Q
L	L	L
L	H	L
H	L	L
H	H	H

Register

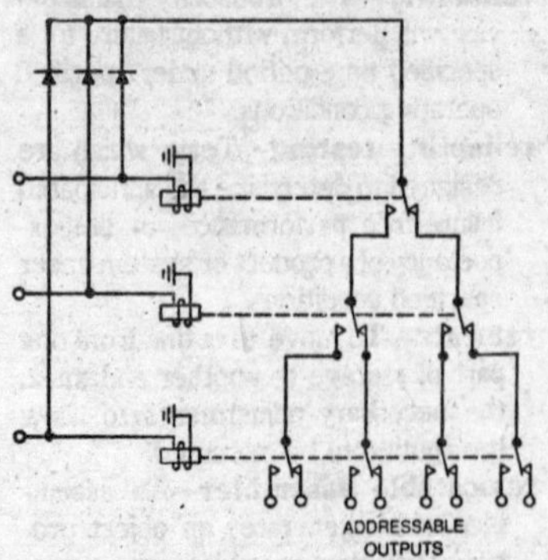

Relay Tree

relocatability—The ability to situate a program or data in an area of memory at different times without modification to the program.

relocating object loader—A program used to load and link object programs produced by assemblers. It satisfies external references between separate program segments, generates linkages as required, and loads only those segments required to satisfy external references.

relocation dictionary—The section of a program (abbreviated *RLD*) that contains the information required to change addresses when it is relocated.

remote access—The capability for communication with a processing facility by one or more stations that are distant from that facility.

remote batch processing—Batch processing where an input device is located at some distance from the main installation and has access through the communications system to the computer.

remote console—A terminal located some distance from the processor.

remote control—Operation of a system from a distant location.

remote control signals—Refers to signal lines that allow the microcomputer to be operated from a remote control panel. Remote control signals include REMOTE HALT, REMOTE LOAD, and REMOTE POWER-ON.

remote debugging—The use of remote terminals for the testing of programs.

remote inquiry—The interrogation of the contents of a data processing storage unit from a device displaced from the storage unit site. Remote inquiry stations allow the computer to be interrogated from various locations for immediate answers to inquiries.

remote job entry—The processing of stacked jobs over communication lines via terminals which are usually equipped with line printers. Small computers are also used to operate as RJE stations. A typical RJE station operates at 4800 baud for tasks such as data transmission, report transmission, file updating, and program compilation in FORTRAN or COBOL.

remote station—Terminal equipment for communicating with a processing system from a distant location.

remote terminal—An input or output terminal that can be located at some distance from the processor.

repeat counter—A counter used to control repeated operations, such as block transfer and search commands.

repeater—1. A device which reconstitutes signals into standard or desired requirements. 2. A communications system that automatically retransmits received signals on a different fixed frequency within the same band.

repertoire—The set of instructions which a processor is capable of performing or a coding system is capable of assembling.

report—A presentation of data or information in tabular, graphic, narrative, or any other form.

report generation—The automatic creation of reports according to user specifications of the desired content and arrangement.

report generator—A routine designed to produce an object routine which can then be run to produce a desired report. To use the report generator, the programmer prepares a set of parameters defining control fields and report lines. These parameters are used to produce a symbolic program. The assembled version of this program accepts the raw data as input, edits it, and generates the desired reports.

report program generator—1. A program (abbreviated *RPG*) used to generate object programs that produce reports from existing data. 2. The RPG language.

report program generator language—A problem-oriented language for commercial programming. Especially useful in smaller applications, RPG is like COBOL in having powerful and simple file manipulation capabilities, but lacks algorithmic facility.

reprogrammable associative ROM—A term sometimes used for a programmable logic array.

rerun point—One of a set of preselected points in a program which is used as a restarting point in the event of error detection.

rerun routine—A routine which uses rerun points for restarting.

rescue dump—A dump on magnetic tape of the entire memory, along with a starting point to allow the rerun from this point. Rescue dumps can prevent the rerunning of an entire program when the run is interrupted by an error or power shutdown.

reset—To return a device such as a register to zero or to an initial or selected condition.

reset key—A key or switch or the computer console used to reset the error-detection system and to restart the program after an error has been discovered.

reset pulse—A pulse used to set a flip-flop or a magnetic cell to its original state.

reset switch—A switch used for either an error reset or a master reset. For a master reset, all registers are set to zero, the interrupt system is disabled, the input/output interface is initialized, and the program counter is set.

resident compiler—A compiler that uses the computer itself to produce programs. A resident compiler may require several passes in a microcomputer system to reduce a source program to machine language.

resident program—A program that is permanently located in storage.

residue check—A check in which each operand is accompanied by the remainder obtained by dividing this number by *n*, the remainder then being used as a check digit or digits. Also called a ***modulo n*** check.

resist—The material used in printed circuit board manufacture to protect desired portions of the conductive material during additional processing steps. Also called ***photoresist***.

resistance—A property of conducting materials which determines the current produced by a given voltage. The unit of resistance is the ohm. The value of resistance of a given circuit component is equal to its voltage divided by its current.

resistance material—A material used for the construction of resistance elements. Typical materials are nichrome wire and carbon.

resistive coupling—The use of resistors to connect or link two circuits or gates.

resistor—A component with a specified resistance value designed to restrict the flow of current.

resistor-transistor logic—A logic family (abbreviated *RTL*) that uses resistors with discrete transistors.

resolution—1. The smallest incremental step in separating a value into constituent parts. 2. The smallest inseparable constituent part of a value.

resolver—1. A device which breaks up a quantity, such as a vector, into components or elements. 2. A small section of storage that has much faster access than the rest of the storage.

resolver differential—A device used to obtain zero shift or offset in control systems that use resolver feedback. It is connected between the reference and the feedback to furnish a signal to the position feedback unit.

resonant-gate transistor—A type of field-effect transistor with a mechanically tuned input.

response time—The time elapsed between generation of an inquiry at a terminal and receipt of a response at that same terminal.

restart—To reestablish the execution of a routine by using a checkpoint.

restart procedure—A procedure that allows processing to continue from the last checkpoint, rather than the beginning of the run. Restart procedures are used in machines with heavy scheduling, since complete reruns due to errors or interruptions cannot be tolerated.

restoration—Returning the DC component to an AC signal after passing the signal through a capacitive circuit.

restore—1. To return an index, address, word, or character to its initial state, sometimes by periodic recharge or regeneration. 2. To superimpose a DC level on an AC signal after loss of the original DC in a stage.

restorer generator—A device which generates the signals required to restore specific conditions in a system.

return address—Refers to that part of a subprogram that connects it with the main program or routine. A return address can be used to unite two or more separately written, compiled, or assembled programs or routines into a single operational unit.

return to bias—A mode of recording (abbreviated *RB*) in which the state of the medium changes from a bias state to another state, and then returns to record a binary one or zero.

reverse-Polish notation—A system for expressing mathematical statements wherein the operators follow the numbers, and the answer appears without an equal (=) sign. See *Polish notation*.

reverse scan—An editing operation used to suppress zeros by replacing them with blanks.

rewrite—The restoring of information in storage by repeated writing. Also called *regeneration*.

rf—Abbreviation for *radio frequency*.

rf amplifier—An amplifier capable of operation at radio frequencies.

RI—Abbreviation for *reliability index*.

right-justify—To adjust the printing positions on a page such that the right margin is flush.

right shift—An operation in which digits of a word are displaced to the right. A right shift has the effect of division if the word represents a binary number.

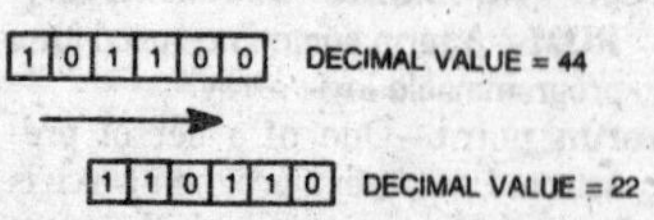

1	0	1	1	0	0	DECIMAL VALUE = 44

→

1	1	0	1	1	0	DECIMAL VALUE = 22

Right Shift

ring counter—A loop of connected bistable elements in which one and only one is in a specified state at any one time; as input signals are counted, the position of this state moves in an ordered sequence around the loop.

ripple counter—A counting circuit in which flip-flops are connected in series, with one flip-flop affecting the next in sequence until the last flip-flop is triggered.

ripple filter—A filter designed to reduce the ripple or AC variation produced by a rectifier circuit.

robot—1. A device or system that can detect input signals or environmental conditions and perform calculations for resultant actions of a control mechanism. Robots are being used for visual inspection and identity-and-attitude analysis. They have been used to determine the two-dimensional outline of an object, locate corners, find holes and grip points, separate multiple objects, and identify objects based on characteristics. 2. A mechanical simulation of a human and a human's movements; an automaton.

robotics—An area of artificial intelligence which deals with the development and use of robots.

rollback—A programmed return to a prior checkpoint.

robotics—An area of artificial intelligence which deals with the development and use of robots.

rollback—A programmed return to a prior checkpoint.

rollback snapshot—A recording of data taken at periodic intervals in a program to allow the program to restart at the last recording after a system failure.

roll-in—To restore to main storage the data which had previously been transferred from main storage to auxiliary storage.

rollout—To record the contents of main storage in auxiliary storage.

ROM—Abbreviation for *read-only* memory, a memory whose contents are not alterable by computer instructions. A semiconductor ROM is programmed by a mask pattern as a part of the final manufacturing process. The organization of the storage cells determines the number of input and output lines required for a given ROM. The address pins are the means by which a specific word is accessed or selected. If the ROM is organized as 32 words of 8 bits, then each word can be addressed using 5 input lines, since $32 = 2^5$ and:

WORD ONE ADDRESS = 00000

WORD TWO ADDRESS = 00001

The number of output lines is determined by the number of bits in the word. ROMs can be used to store microprograms or fixed programs, depending upon the application. A ROM can be used to implement in one package the functions that previously took up to 50 TTL packages.

ROM address lines—Refers to the lines or pins which are used to select a specific word in ROM.

ROM assimilator—A self-contained microcomputer system with assembly and utility programs which can develop, debug, and simulate proposed ROM programs. The system includes a debug console and terminal interface for input and output. Proposed ROM programs are stored in RAM and modified directly from the terminal.

ROM terminal—A terminal that uses a ROM for storing instructions.

ROM loader—A loader program that is implemented in ROM. A typical ROM loader is contained on a printed-circuit card for plugging into the microcomputer system.

ROM-oriented architecture—A system in which the microprocessor instruction set can be executed completely from ROM without the need for external RAM. This system requires an internal stack for subroutines and internal registers for indirect addressing operations. The instruction set needs logical instructions for bit manipulation.

ROM/RAM—A circuit containing a mask programmable MOS ROM as

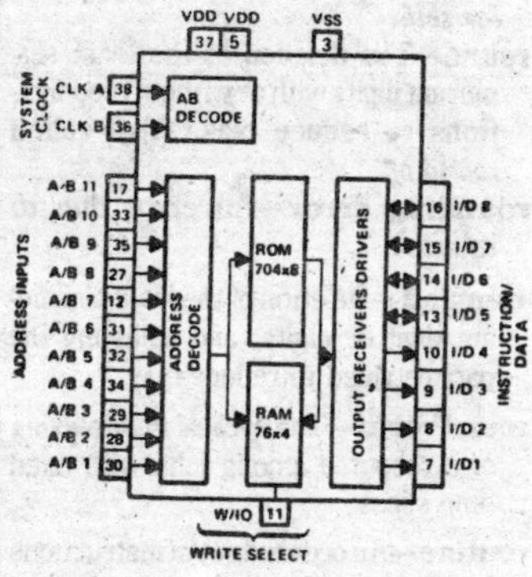

ROM/RAM

well as a RAM. The ROM/RAM is designed for applications requiring only a small amount of ROM and RAM. One specific unit has a ROM section of 704 words of 8 bits and a RAM of 76 words of 4 bits.

ROM/RAM/CPU—A chip for low cost applications that contains a processor along with RAM and ROM memories.

ROM simulator—An instrument designed to replace ROM or PROM during program development and debugging. The instrument can be used to simulate PROM or ROM configurations and provides an inexpensive means of altering microprograms. The memory modules are loaded and verified through the ROM simulator or front-panel address and data switches. Simulation is achieved by extending control of the read-only function to the user's equipment using simulation cables.

root segment—The master or controlling segment of an overlay structure which resides in the main memory. The root segment is usually the first segment within the program, and it is always the first to be loaded at program initiation time.

rotate—The process of moving each bit in a register in a circular manner, either to the right or the left. Each bit which leaves one end of the register enters the other end. Also called *circular shift*.

round—The deletion of the least significant digits with or without modifications to reduce bias. Also called *round off*.

rounding error—An error due to roundoff.

roundoff—Deletion of the least significant digit or digits, and adjusting the part retained to reduce bias.

round robin—The cyclical multiplexing of a resource among jobs with fixed time slices.

routine—An ordered set of instructions used to direct the computer to perform one or more specific tasks or operations. A closed routine is one that is not entered as a block of instructions within the main routine, but entered by a linkage from the main routine. A routine may be considered as a subdivision of a program with two or more instructions that are functionally related.

row binary—A method of representing binary numbers on a card where bits are represented by punches in a row as opposed to a series of columns. Row binary is useful in systems with words of 40 bits or less where the card can be used to store 12 words on each half of the card.

row pitch—The distance measured along paper tape between the centers of adjacent holes.

RPG—Abbreviation for ***report program generator***.

R-S flip-flop—A flip-flop consisting of two cross-coupled NAND gates and having two inputs, a ***set*** and a ***reset***.

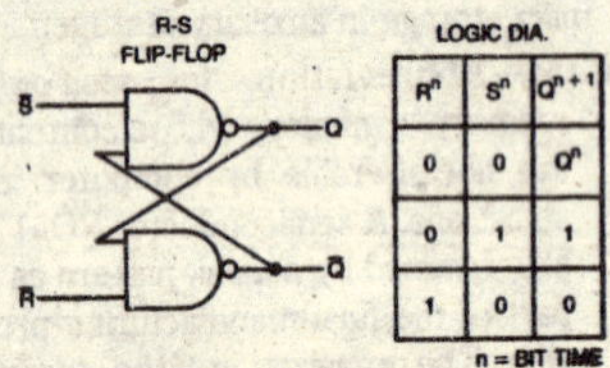

R-S
FLIP-FLOP
S
Q
R
Q̄
LOGIC DIA.
Rⁿ Sⁿ Qⁿ⁺¹
0 0 Qⁿ
0 1 1
1 0 0
n = BIT TIME

R-S Flip-Flop

R- S-T flip-flop—A flip-flop which operates like an R-S flip-flop with an additional input (the trigger), which is used to cause the flip-flop to change states.

RS-232—An interface standard designated by EIA and spelled out in *Standard RS-232*.

RS-232 compatible controller—A module designed to interface a microcomputer system to most asynchronous modems. Baud rates include 110, 300, 1200, 2400, 4800 and 9600, with selectable words lengths from 5 to 8 bits and either odd or even parity.

RS-232 interface—An interface used to connect a modem with associated data terminal equipment which is standardized by EIA Standard RS-232.

RTE—Abbreviation for *real-time executive*, a program which provides a multiprogramming foreground-background system with priority scheduling, interrupt handling, and load-and-go capabilities.

RTL—Abbreviation for *resistor-transistor logic*, a logic family that uses discrete transistors with resistive coupling.

ruly English—A language based on English in which every word has one and only one meaning, and each concept has one and only one word to describe it.

run—The performance of one program on a computer, or several routines linked together so that they form an operating unit. Usually during a run, manual operations are minimal; a typical run may involve loading, reading, processing, and writing.

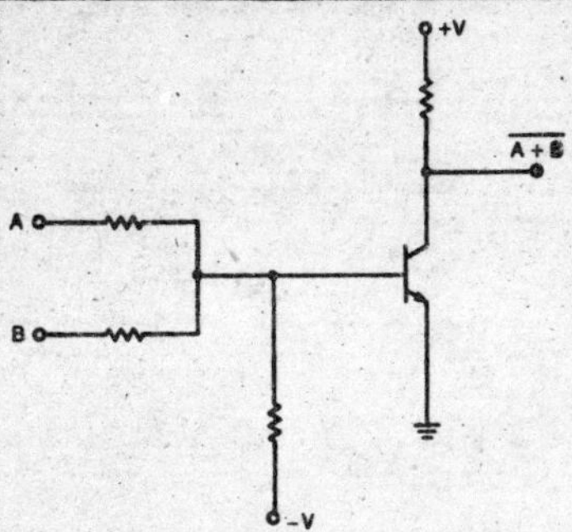

RTL NOR Gate

run book—The material needed to document a computer application, including problem statement, flow charts, and coding and operating instructions.

run indicator—An indicator used to indicate that the processor is in a run mode.

run switch—A switch which allows the processor to begin instruction execution, beginning at the address contained in the program counter.

S

sampling—1. Obtaining the values of a usually analog function by making automatic measurements of the function at periodic intervals. Each sample thus obtained becomes a digital value and is processed with digital circuitry. 2. A representative value of a population of values.

sampling gate—A device activated by a selector pulse usually to extract instantaneous-value information for a system.

sampling oscilloscope—An oscilloscope in which the input waveform is sampled at successive points along the waveform instead of being monitored continuously.

sampling period—The time between observations in a periodic sampling system.

sapphire—A material used as a substrate for some types of integrated-circuit chips.

sapphire substrate—The substrate used in silicon-on-sapphire (SOS) MOS chips. Silicon-on-sapphire chips have reduced parasitics and permit tighter geometries for high-speed applications.

satellite—1. A computer used to relieve a larger computer of simple but time-consuming tasks, such as editing and compiling. 2. An earth-orbiting usually electronic system for scientific, defense, or communications operations, observations, or measurements.

satellite computer—1. A computer connected to a larger computer and performing simple tasks or time-consuming operations. A satellite computer is usually subordinate to the central processor and sometimes independent. 2. An earth-orbiting system consisting principally of a usually dedicated computer or processor.

saturating integrator—An integrator modified to provide an output that is maximum negative, zero, or maximum positive.

saturation—1. In an amplifier, a condition in which an increase in the input signal no longer produces a significant change in the output. 2. The condition of maximum signal-carrying ability in any medium.

saturation limiting—Limiting the maximum output of an active device

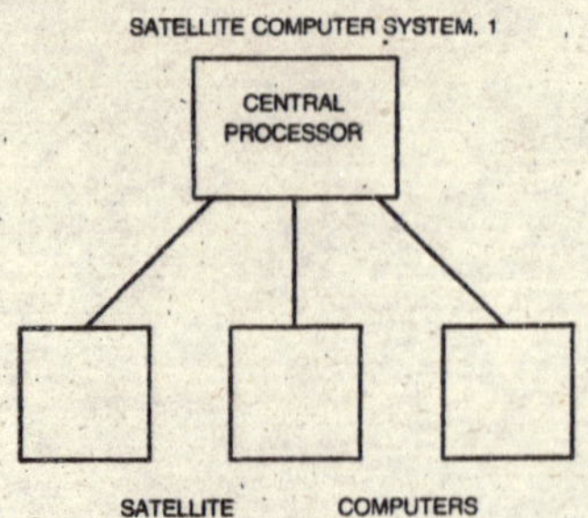

Satellite Computer System, 1

by operating the device in the region of saturation. When the input signal increases, saturation occurs immediately and the output is held at approximately the value of saturation.

saturation noise—1. Extra bits or words that can be removed or ignored before the data is used without affecting the data represented. 2. Errors introduced into a system due to disturbances occurring when the signal-carrying medium is at saturation.

saturation point—The point (in an amplifier) beyond which an increase in input signal magnitude produces no further increases in output signal magnitude. This is in contrast to the *cutoff point*, where usually negative-going signal inputs in excess of the cutoff-point value cause the amplifier to shut off momentarily. Linear amplifiers are operated in the relatively linear region between the two extremes.

sawtooth—A triangular waveform consisting of a fairly linear voltage or current ramp of ascending value that returns abruptly to the original value.

sawtooth generator—An oscillator-type circuit used to produce a sawtooth waveform, usually at some specific frequency or within a specific frequency range.

sawtooth wave—A signal composed entirely of a recurring sawtooth. Also called *sawtooth waveform*.

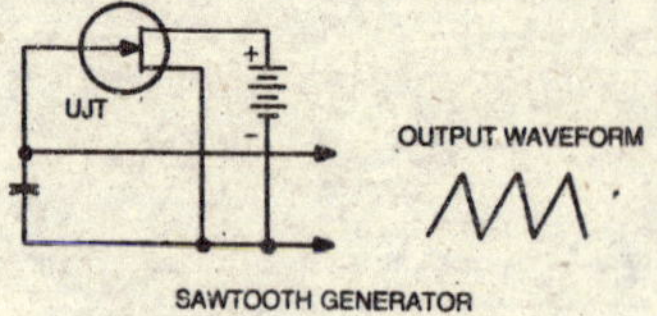

Sawtooth Generator

sawtooth waveform—Sawtooth wave such as the type used to establish the timebase in a cathode-ray oscilloscope.

scalar—Having a value that may be plotted on a graduated scale.

scalar product—The product of two quantities which itself has magnitude but no direction. In the example:

FORCE × DISTANCE = WORK

two vector quantities produce the scalar product, work.

scalar quantity—A quantity which has magnitude without direction, such as a real number.

scale—1. A range of values usually dictated by the computer word length or the routine being processed. 2. To change the units of a variable so that the quantity may be measured by a system whose limits are in a different range. Scaling can bring the values of a variable within the bounds required by register size or other factors. 3. Any value range which permits identification of any incremental value within that range, as a *temperature scale*.

scale factor—A value used to convert the magnitude of a variable to a usable value in another range, or to convert from one notation to another. Scale factors are often used to adjust the radix point so that the significant digits occupy specified positions in a word or register.

scaler—1. A unit that produces an output equal to the input multiplied by a constant. 2. A converter used at the input of a device (such as a frequency meter) to bring the quantity being measured to within the range of measurement of the instrument (a *frequency scaler*, for example).

scaling—The changing of a quantity from one notation to another, or from one value range to another, using scale factors.

scamp—Loose acronym for a small cost-effective microprocessor. Addresses are generated by four 16-bit pointer registers with processor timing generated on the chip.

scan—1. To examine sequentially using a part-by-part technique. 2. The successive trace-and-flyback operation required to produce a raster or image on a TV screen.

scanner—A device which samples or interrogates the state of a process or processes, including files and physical conditions. It then may initiate action or cause another device to initiate action based upon the information obtained. A typical scanner might connect a specified sensor to measuring or monitoring equipment for transmission to the processor.

scanning rate—The speed per unit time at which a scanner operates. Also called *scan rate*.

scan rate—The rate or speed at which a scanner operates.

scatter load—A method of loading a program into main memory such that each section occupies a single connected memory area without the sections being adjacent to one another. The sections are usually a page, and the system is usually implemented with a virtual memory structure.

scatter loading—The process of loading a program into main memory using pages which are not adjacent.

scatter read—The ability to distribute data into several memory areas as it is being entered into the system from magnetic tape.

scheduled maintenance—Maintenance which is carried out in accordance with an established plan.

schematic—A diagram that uses symbols to show components and their interconnections for a system or circuit.

schematic diagram—A diagram that shows the scheme of a circuit or system using graphic symbols. A schematic diagram permits tracing of circuit and flow paths for continuity; a *schematic*.

Schmitt trigger—A monostable circuit which has a sensitive, accurate, and stable trigger level.

Schmitt trigger circuit—A circuit which acts as a one-shot multivibrator with an accurate and stable trigger level. It is often used to restore pulses and pulse information.

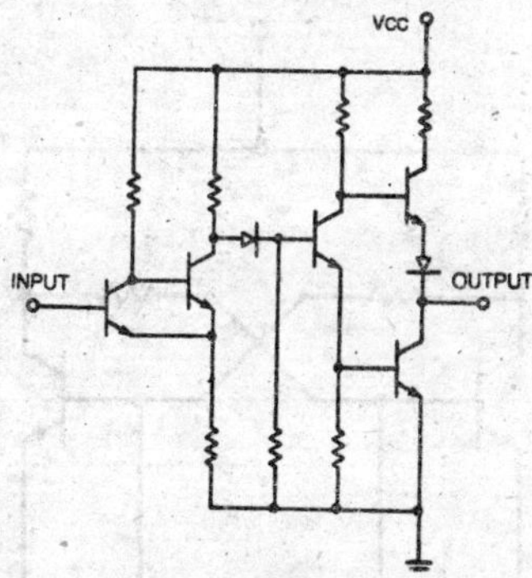

Schmitt Trigger Circuit

Schottky barrier—1. In a hot-carrier diode, the metal-semiconductor junction. 2. Hot-carrier diode junctions incorporated into some TTL devices to increase switching speed (transit times) and reduce system noise.

Schottky bipolar—TTL devices that use a Schottky clamping diode to prevent transistor saturation and improve switching speeds. With the use of integrated Schottky diodes, the saturation delay normally encountered is avoided. The process is simple and does not have a significant effect upon manufacturing costs.

Schottky bipolar latch—A latch circuit designed with the Schottky TTL process. It is used where high speed is important.

Schottky bipolar look-ahead carry—A high-speed circuit capable of anticipating a carry across the central processing array. In systems with multiple arrays, the carry circuit can provide high-speed look-ahead capability for any word length.

Schottky bipolar memory—A memory that uses Schottky barrier diodes to obtain fast switching speeds. Their high speed makes them ideal for scratchpad applications.

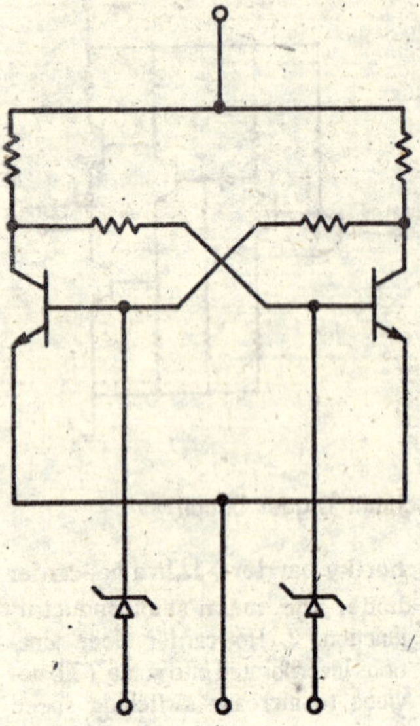

Schottky Bipolar Memory

Schottky bipolar microcomputer—A set of bipolar chips designed with the Schottky bipolar process for high speed. A typical microcomputer set of this variety includes:

(1) Central processing elements
(2) Bipolar PROM
(3) Microprogram control units

Schottky bipolar microcomputer chips can be much faster than available MOS chips. The chips allow a design that is fast, but smaller and less expensive than equivalent designs using SSI or MSI integration.

Schottky-clamped transistor—A bipolar transistor that is limited by a Schottky diode to prevent saturation and improve switching speeds.

Schottky diode—A hot-carrier diode that has a short recovery time and a low forward-voltage drop. It is formed by the metal-to-semiconductor contact at the surface of the crystal.

Schottky process—The manufacturing process used to produce Schottky diodes in bipolar circuits. The process is simple and does not have significant effects upon manufacturing costs.

Schottky TTL—TTL devices that use Schottky diodes for improved speed performance.

Schottky II—A TTL process that uses ion-implanted techniques and minimum geometry to extend the performance of Schottky devices into the 1 ns range. A Schottky II microprocessor chip set with a cycle time of 50 ns is available.

scratchpad—A memory used to hold temporary results in a computer system. It is usually the fastest memory in the system.

screen—1. The face of a TV tube (video monitor) on which graphic or other visual material is displayed. 2. To sift or cull a collection of data or data elements for the purpose of extracting only those of use in a subsequent process or operation. 3. In a vacuum tube, a shielding grid positioned adjacent to the control grid (between control grid and anode) to reduce interelectrode capacitance.

screen current—The electron current existing in the screen circuit of a vacuum tube.

screen grid—See *screen, 3*.

screen voltage—The voltage applied to the screen of a vacuum tube; it is usually of lower value than, but obtained from, the anode supply.

second—The international unit of time and equal to the duration of 9,192,631,770 periods of the radiation corresponding to the transition between the two hyperfine levels of the ground state of the cesium-133 atom.

secondary—1. Any output winding of any transformer that contains multiple windings. 2. Relating to the second order in a string of ordinally identified functions or values.

secondary emission—The phenomenon in which electrons bombarding the anode of a vacuum tube cause electrons to be dislodged from that electrode; the dislodged electrons comprise secondary emission.

secondary memory—A memory used to transfer large blocks of data into main storage; it usually has a large capacity, but a long access time.

secondary winding—See *secondary,*

secondary-level address—That portion of an instruction which indicates a location where the address of the referenced operand is to be found. Multiple levels of addressing can be terminated by control or by a termination symbol.

second-level addressing—A type of addressing in which instructions use a referenced location for the address of the operand.

second-source—To manufacture a product designed, developed, and also produced by another manufacturer. Second-sourcing results from the reluctance of the government to purchase devices available from only one maker, and it had its birth when government specifications for devices and systems were written after prototype development.

seek—1. The process of locating specific data in a random-access store. A seek refers to each memory location searched and the number of seeks determines the total search time. 2. To search a memory array.

seek time—The time required to locate data in a direct-access storage device, including the time needed to position the access mechanism.

segment—1. To divide a routine into parts with each one capable of being completely stored in internal storage and containing the necessary instructions to jump to other segments. 2. A part of a routine short enough to be sorted entirely in the internal storage of a computer, yet containing the coding necessary to call in and jump to other segments. A segment can be placed anywhere in memory and addressed relative to a common origin. 3. One of the components of a single-character numeric or alphanumeric display. (See also *seven-segment display.*)

selection check—A check that verifies the choice of devices in the execution of an instruction.

selective dump—A dump of one or more desired storage locations. A selective dump is usually a library subroutine that is called when other programs are running and a dump is desired.

selectivity—The degree of "narrowness" of a circuit's frequency response bandwidth. High selectivity implies high Q, narrow bandwidth, and single-frequency sensitivity. Low selectivity implies low Q, broadband response, and relatively uniform sensitivity over the response frequency range.

selector—1. A switching operation based on previous processing which allows a logical choice to be made in the program or system. 2. A mechanical multiposition switch. 3. Cursor.

self-adapting—The ability of a system to change its performance characteristics in response to environmental changes.

self-defining—Refers to terms in assembler programming with a value that is absolute and implicit in the specification of the term itself.

self-instructed carry—A carry process in which information is allowed to propagate to succeeding places as soon as it is generated, without requiring an external signal.

self-organizing machine—A machine (abbreviated *SOM*) in which the internal organization is conducted by the machine itself, without external intervention.

self-oscillation—Usually unwanted oscillation that is generated in a circuit as a result of inadvertent positive feedback, as through the interelectrode capacitance of an active device.

self-powered—Containing an independent power source, as a special voltaic cell or group of cells.

self-pulse modulation—A modulation which uses an internally generated pulse.

self-relocating program—A program that can be loaded into any area of main storage which uses an initialization routine to adjust its address constants so that it can be executed at that location.

self-resetting loop—A loop which contains instructions for restoring all locations affecting the operation of the loop to their initial condition upon entry of the loop.

semantic error—An error which results from an ambiguous meaning in a program statement. Semantic errors are the responsibility of the programmer and can be removed by debugging prior to use of the program.

semantics—The relationship between symbols and their intended meanings.

semicompiled—Descriptive of a program converted from source language to object language, but not called by the source program.

semiconducting material—Intrinsic or extrinsic material, such as germanium and silicon, used in the manufacture of active solid-state devices.

semiconductor—1. A material with a conductivity between a metal and an insulator. 2. Any member of the class of devices constructed from a semiconductor. Semiconductors include diodes, transistors, and the complex integrated circuits which are fabricated from wafers of semiconducting material.

semiconductor contact—Refers to the section of a semiconductor device where the interconnects for the leads are made.

semiconductor device—See *semiconductor, 2.*

semiconductor diode—A two-terminal semiconductor device with a pn junction possessing a nonlinear voltage-current characteristic.

semiconductor doping—Refers to the adding of impurities to semiconductor materials to produce desired conducting characteristics.

semiconductor integrated circuits—Complex single-package circuits fabricated from semiconductor wafers.

semiconductor junction—The region between *p* and *n* areas in a semiconducting material.

semiconductor memory—A memory that uses semiconductors for data storage. A typical semiconductor memory is contained on a single circuit card and contains all refresh, control, and interface logic required to operate as a memory unit.

sense—The action required to examine or determine the arrangement of coded items, as in reading the holes in punched cards or tape; read.

sense wire—A wire which carries the output signal in a magnetic core unit.

sensing—The process of determining the state or condition of an item.

sensitivity—The relative response of a device to an incoming signal or stimulus. The sensitivity of a receiver is the minimum input signal required to produce a specified output signal.

sensitivity analysis—A test or trial of a range of values at the input to determine the response and interdependence of the output values. Sensitivity analysis can be conducted using parametric programming in which parameters are allowed to vary in order to determine the solution of a problem.

sensitivity ratio—The measured ratio of the change in output to the change in input which causes it.

sensor—A transducer or other device which can be used to provide a quantity whose value is a measure of some physical phenomenon.

sensor-based—Refers to systems whose primary function is to monitor physical processes using transducers or sensors.

sensor-based computer—A computer designed to be used to receive real-time data from transducers or sensors that monitor a physical process. In a typical application, the computer might receive data from a pressure transducer or a flow meter, compare the data to required conditions, and then produce a signal to operate a control device.

sensor-based system—A system whose primary source of data is from sensors and whose output can be used to control a physical process.

sentinel—A character or indicator used to mark some condition, such as the beginning or end of a word.

separator—A specific character used for the demarcation of the logical boundary between items that can be considered as separate and distinct units.

sequence—An orderly progression of items and the act of putting items into such a progression.

sequence checking—A routine which checks every instruction executed and prints desired data. The printout may include coded instructions, the contents of registers, or transferred data.

sequence counter—A hardware register used by the computer to remember the location of the next instruction to be processed.

sequencer—A device or circuit used to trigger a predetermined series of events as a result of a specific action. The circuit selects the order of occurrence in accordance with the action to which it responds.

sequencer register—A counter which is reset following the execution of an instruction to form a new memory address for locating the next instruction.

sequential access—A type of access in which items of information are available in an ordered progression regardless of the amount of information required.

sequential-access storage—A form of storage in which the items of stored information are available in sequence regardless of the information desired.

sequential alarm—A device which monitors a group of alarm contacts and signals a priority interrupt to the computer when an alarm condition occurs. The computer can then establish an alarm sequence based on current and previous information.

sequential computer—A computer with built-in logic that executes instructions in a fixed sequence which can usually be overridden or changed by another instruction.

sequential control—A control mode in which instructions are set up in an ordered progression and fed into the machine consecutively during the solution of the problem.

sequential logic—A logic methodology in which the output state is determined by the previous state of the input.

sequential sampling—A type of sampling inspection in which the decision to accept, reject, or inspect another unit is made following the sampling of each unit.

serial—The time-sequential handling of individual items, such as the processing of a sequence of instructions one at a time. Serial transmission uses a time sequence for words with the same facilities required for successive parts.

serial access—The sequential or consecutive transmission of data to or from storage.

serial adder—A device which adds two binary words one bit-pair at a time. The least significant digit is performed first, and the more significant digits are added in succession with carries until the sum is formed. Serial adders require less hardware but are slower than parallel units.

serial-parallel converter—A unit designed for changing data in serial format to parallel format. A typical unit allows full-duplex operation between a CPU and a remote location. The modules are used in pairs, with one at the central processor and the other at the remote location.

serial-parallel register—A shift register that can be used to perform serial-to-parallel data conversion.

serial programming—Programming in such a way that only one arithmetic or logical operation can be executed at one time.

serial storage—Storage in which one of the storage parameters is in time sequence. Storage in which words appear one after another is *serial by word.* Bits which must appear in time sequence are found in serial-by-bit systems. Devices such as magnetic drums may be part serial and part parallel.

serial transfer—Data transfer in which the characters of information flow in sequence over a single path.

serial transmission—A sequential transmission of characters or items of data over a single path.

serial work flow—A system of operations in which each operation is performed singly, and not at the same time when other tasks are being operated on. The work moves along a single line or path where each operation is performed at a station, with none being performed at the same time.

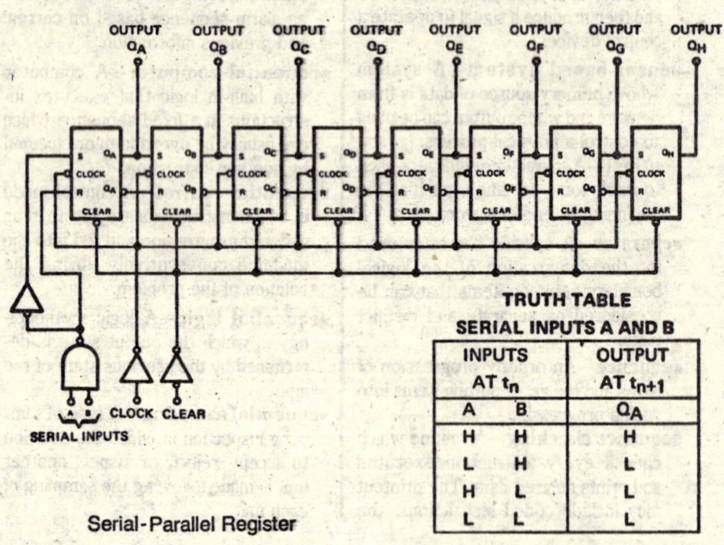

INPUTS AT t_n		OUTPUT AT t_{n+1}
A	B	Q_A
H	H	H
L	H	L
H	L	L
L	L	L

Serial-Parallel Register

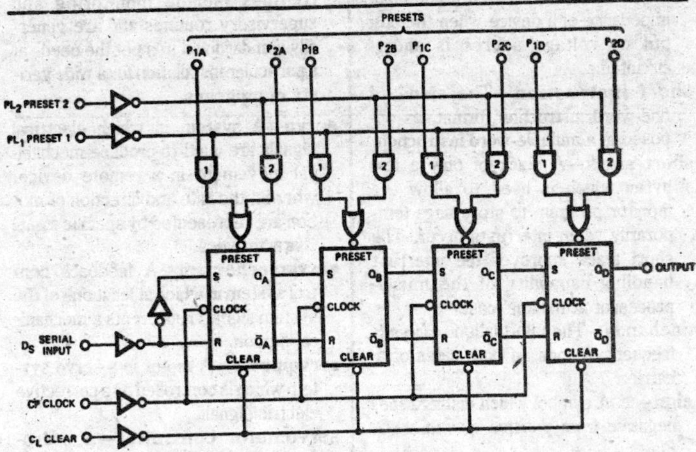

Shift Register (4 Bits)

serial-access system—A computer system in which the access time is dependent upon the location of the data most recently obtained or placed into storage.

serial computer—A computer that manipulates all bits of a word serially. It usually has a single arithmetic and logic unit.

serial data controller—A unit for providing the interface for full-duplex, synchronous, or asynchronous serial data communications. A typical device operates at 250,000 bps in the synchronous mode, or 16,000 bps in the asynchronous mode. Data formatting for bits per character, character framing, and parity is programmed by the CPU.

serially reusable—Descriptive of a reusable program which is not necessarily reenterable. The same copy of the routine or program can be used by another task after the current use has been concluded in main memory.

serial memory—A memory in which items are stored and obtained sequence, one at a time. Serial memories are used in large-volume applications that require low cost and high reliability, such as CRT storage. A typical serial memory contains 20,000 words of ten bits each on a memory card. The system is expandable in capacity and word length by stacking memory cards.

serial operation—1. Computer operation where numbers are processed one character at a time. 2. The flow of information in time sequence.

serial-parellel—The property of being partially serial and partially parallel, such as serial by character and parallel by bits that make up the character.

shift register—A register for the short or long-term storage of serial or parallel data in which data may be shifted to the right or left, and shifted out and shifted in. A typical shift register operates at speeds of 5 MHz from standard TTL voltage levels. It is composed of a series of flip-flops connected in tandem. Registers may be connected together to form larger memory units.

short circuit—1. A direct resistance-free connection between two points in a circuit or system that normally are not connected or are not intended to be connected. 2. To cause a short circuit.

short-circuit impedance—The input impedance of a device when the output or voltage source is short-circuited.

short instruction—The standard one-word instruction format, as opposed to a multiple-word instruction.

short stack—A stack of only a few bytes which is used to allow the monitor program to store flags temporarily when interrupts occur. The short stack improves the interrupt handling capability of the microprocessor at minimal cost.

sidebands—The information-carrying frequency bands on both sides of a carrier.

sign—1. A symbol which distinguishes negative from positive quantities. 2. Flag.

signal—The intelligence, message, or effect to be conveyed over a transferral system; it may be electrical, visual, or audible, and it is the event or phenomenon for conveying the data from one point to another.

series—1. The condition of being wired so that a single current flows through several devices. 2. A set of related terms in a mathematical expression. 3. A group. 4. Appearing in a string of individual but related items or values.

series circuit—A circuit in which a single current value flows through all elements sequentially.

series interface board—A circuit board designed to allow custom interfaces to be used with different types of series memory systems.

series-parallel circuit—A circuit that contains branches that are connected in both series and parallel configurations.

service organization—A company that offers contract maintenance and operation of computers.

service routine—A routine in general support of the operation of a computer. Service routines are designed to assist in the maintenance and operation of the computer as well as for the preparation of programs. Service routines include monitoring and supervisory routines and are generally standardized to meet the needs at a particular installation for a wide variety of programs.

servo—A system in which electrical signals are used to produce mechanical movement in a remote device, wherein the rate and direction of motion are represented by specific signal characteristics.

servomechanism—A feedback control system in which at least one of the system signals represents a mechanical motion.

servomotor—A motor in a servo system which is controlled by a corrective electric signal.

servomotor controller—A microcomputer-based unit capable of running multiaxis DC servomotor-controlled machines. It is usually controlled by a tape reader which accepts commands in ASCII format. The microcomputer reads an encoder on the motor and calculates motor speeds and positions, allowing precise control with programmable variables.

servo multiplier—An analog device capable of multiplying several different variables by a single variable or constant.

servo system—An automatic control system that compares an actual mechanical position with a desired position and generates an error signal to adjust the control element in accordance with this difference.

set— To place a storage device into a desired state. 2. A collection of values or items, such as all even numbers or positive integers. 3. An equipment system.

set breakpoint—A command which causes a breakpoint to be set in a specified location.

set point—Refers to the value of a variable to which specific control actions, such as alarms or process changes, are desired.

set-point control—A control system that operates from commands or information from variable set points in the system or process.

set symbol—A variable symbol used in assembler programming to communicate values during conditional assembly processing.

set theory—The mathematical study of groups, sets, and elements.

seven-segment display—A single-character readout with seven individually addressable segments which are illuminated selectively to form numerals and other symbols.

sexadecimal digit—A digit that is a member of the following group when used as a radix-16 system:

0, 1, 2, 3, 4, 5, 6, 7, 8, 9, A, B, C, D, E, F

Also called *hexadecimal digit*.

sexadecimal notation—A notation using the base of sixteen. Also called *hexidecimal notation*.

shared storage—The ability to share main storage between two processors. In shared storage, either machine can insert information into storage, and either machine can access the data and use it.

sharing—1. The use of a device for two or more purposes during the same time interval. 2. The apportionment of time intervals for different tasks by interlacing or interleaving.

shielded line—A transmission line which is enclosed in a conducting material to protect it from inadvertent signal pickup from stray radiation, or to protect adjacent circuits from radiation of the line.

shielded transmission line—An unbalanced line used for the transmission of information. It possesses a known characteristic impedance and exhibits predictable properties of inductance, capacitance, and resistance.

shielding—1. The protection of circuits, components, and conductors from radiated interference by enclosing them with conducting material. 2. The physical barriers placed within the confines of a chassis to minimize interaction between separated stages or circuits.

shift—To move digits or characters in a register to the right or left, either transferring the information or performing an arithmetical operation. If a register holds 8 digits:

23456789

a shift to the right produces

12345678

shifting register—A register which is designed or adapted to perform shifts.

shift instruction—A computer instruction which causes the contents of an accumulator register to shift to the right or the left. A right shift instruction is equivalent to dividing by two; a left shift instruction is equivalent to multiplying by two, or adding the contents of the register to itself.

shift-in character—A code extension character (abbreviated *SI*) used to return a register to its prior state before shifting operations.

shift out—To move information within a register towards one end so as to clear the register.

shift-out character—A code extension character (abbreviated *SO*) which can be used to replace one set of characters in a register with another set, or the null set.

shift pulse—A pulse which initiates the shifting of characters in a register.

SI—1. The shift-in character. 2. Abbreviation for *International System of Units*.

signal distance—The number of digit positions in which the corresponding digits of two words are different. Also called *Hamming distance.*

signal converter—A transducer which converts from one type of transmission signal to another.

signal element—The part of a signal which occupies the shortest interval of the signaling code.

signal generator—An oscillator used to provide a test voltage over a wide range of frequencies.

signal level—The magnitude of a waveform's or pulse train's voltage amplitude, either absolute or with respect to a reference value. Often expressed in decibels.

signal processor—A device which performs complex processing of waveforms for analysis and transmission. A typical signal processor is used with a host computer to provide the functions of a fast Fourier transform processor, array processor, display processor, and voice processor.

signal-to-noise ratio—The ratio of the magnitude of the signal to the magnitude of the noise at the same point when the signal is removed, and usually expressed in decibels.

signal tracing—The methodological following of a signal path in hardware or on diagrams in order to locate faults.

sign bit—A binary digit occupying the sign position in a word to give the value direction.

sign digit—A character used to designate the algebraic sign of a number.

significance—The weighting factor in positional representations which is dependent on the digit place and by which a digit is multiplied to obtain its additive contribution in the representation of a number.

sign position—In an array of binary digits, the position which contains an indication of the algebraic sign of a number.

silicon—A nonmetallic element having semiconducting properties and which is widely used in the manufacture of active electronic devices.

silicon controlled rectifier—A three-junction rectifying device (abbreviated *SCR*) which is triggered by means of a voltage applied to a gate terminal. The SCR is a member of the *thyristor* family of devices, which includes diacs, triacs, and a variety of 4-layer diodes.

silicon diode—A rectifying device that uses silicon as the semiconducting material.

silicon dioxide—In MOS device manufacturing, the layer used to insulate the metal gate from the *p* or *n* regions.

silicon-gate CMOS—A complementary MOS technology that allows high packing density with good speed performance and noise immunity along with low power dissipation. The internal logic structure for a microprocessor using this technology is fully static, which allows the clock to be stopped between instructions, cycles, and minor cycles. It requires only a single supply, and all signals are TTL compatible.

silicon nitride passivation—A semiconductor manufacturing process which involves use of a layer of silicon nitride to protect the surface of devices from ionic contamination. The silicon nitride layer is covered with a layer of phosphorous silicon dioxide. The double layer prevents both mechanical and ionic damage and enhances device reliability.

silicon-on-sapphire—A semiconductor technology (abbreviated *SOS*) in which a thin layer is grown on a sapphire substrate; sections of it are then removed, leaving small silicon pads or islands that are made into MOS transistors. All standard MOS techniques can be used with SOS; and because the sapphire substrate is a nearly ideal insulator, parasitic capacitance and leakage are greatly reduced.

silicon PROM fuse—In PROM programming, a fuse made of polycrystalline silicon which is deposited in a thick layer during the manufacturing process. The fuse is used to selectively blow gating elements of the device to program it for a specific application.

silicon solar cell—A photovoltaic cell which consists of a thin wafer of specially processed silicon designed to convert light energy into electrical energy.

silicon transistor—A transistor formed from a silicon crystal, as opposed to a germanium transistor.

simplex—A communications system or channel that is not capable of simultaneous transmission and reception.

simulate—To employ one system to duplicate the principal operational characteristics of another, using software to effect the simulation so that the imitating system accepts the same data, executes the same instructions, and performs the same operations.

simulation—1. The representation of physical systems by computers and models. 2. The technique of setting up a routine or program in one computer to make it simulate as nearly as possible the operational characteristics of another computer.

simulation language—A language designed for the simulation of systems using computers. Simulation languages include *Simscript* and *GPSS* (general-purpose simulation system). They tend to have more comprehensive diagnostics than general-purpose languages such as FORTRAN or PL/1. Both Simscript and GPSS have an event monitor that tracks events and can be used for clocking.

simulator—A program that can be used to emulate or imitate the operation of a given microprocessor. They are designed to execute object programs generated by a cross assembler on a machine other than the one being worked on. A simulator offers a powerful and flexible design support system which can reduce development time and allow products to get to market sooner.

A hardware simulator is a program which is usually stored in RAM which is used to simulate the execution of a test program, tracing its progress and detecting errors. It allows the user to interact with and modify the program in order to simplify the debugging process. A typical hardware simulator for a microprocessor comes complete with all timing details, breakpoints, and debug commands. Direct user control over RAM and register contents, interrupts, and input/output data is usually provided.

simultaneity—The facility of a machine to allow input/output operations on peripherals to continue in parallel with operations in the central processor.

simultaneous access—1. Immediate access. 2. Parallel access.

simultaneous computer—A computer that contains a separate unit to perform each portion of the computation concurrently. The units can be interconnected in a manner determined by the run.

sine wave—A wave which is the sine of a linear function of time or space; a sinusoidal waveform.

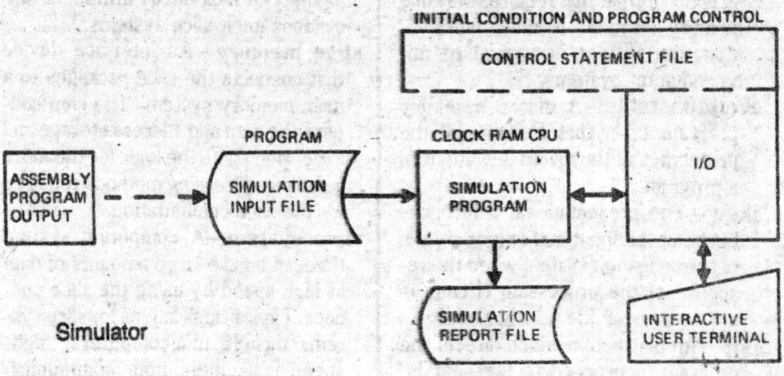

INITIAL CONDITION AND PROGRAM CONTROL
CONTROL STATEMENT FILE
PROGRAM
CLOCK RAM CPU
I/O
ASSEMBLY PROGRAM OUTPUT
SIMULATION INPUT FILE
SIMULATION PROGRAM
SIMULATION REPORT FILE
INTERACTIVE USER TERMINAL

Simulator

single pass—Refers to a program that generates the desired end result in one computer run.

single-bus operation—A microcomputer system that uses a single path or bus for all data transfers. Any device transmitting data can become bus master, while any device receiving data becomes a bus slave. Any master can transmit data to any slave without CPU intervention.

single-sideband—A method of amplitude-modulated communications in which either the lower or upper sideband-frequency signals produced as a result of modulation are retained and transmitted, and the carrier itself is suppressed. The signals are detected at the receiver by heterodyning them with an oscillator whose output is a modulated beat-frequency tone.

single-step—A method of operating a computer in which each step is performed under manual control.

single-step debug—A debugging method which uses short routines to set up system states for checking the response of the microprocessor.

single-step operation—A method of operating a computer manually in which a single instruction or part of an instruction is performed in response to a single operation of the manual control. Single-step operation is usually initiated to detect mistakes in programming.

single-word instruction—An instruction format that requires only one memory location. A single-word instruction format is typical of microcomputer systems.

skeleton table—A macro assembly program table that contains all the prototypes of the macro definitions in a program.

skew—The presentational differences between the input and output signals of a propagation system when the response of the processing circuits is not linear over the full signal range.

skip—An instruction which directs the program to proceed to the next instruction. Also called a *blank* instruction or a NO OP.

skip flag—A flag produced by a 1-bit register to represent the true or false condition with respect to the instruction being executed by the processor.

skip test—A microinstruction designed for conditional operations based on the state of readiness of devices or conditions in a register.

slave—A unit or device which is under the control of another unit or device. At any point in time, there is one device that has control of the communication bus—the *bus master*. The bus master may in turn communicate with any other device, which is called the *slave*.

slewing rate—1. The rate at which a device can be driven from limit to limit over the dynamic output range. 2. The maximum rate at which a circuit, device, or system can be cycled through its operational states.

slice—Refers to the type of microcomputer architecture which permits the cascading or stacking of devices to increase word length.

slice architecture—A microcomputer architecture which uses a section of the register file and ALU in one package. Each end of each 2- or 4-bit register is accessible through the chip's edge to allow registers (slices) to be cascaded together to form larger word lengths.

slice look-ahead—A circuit that allows high-speed look-ahead arithmetic operations in bit-slice systems.

slice memory—An interface device that connects the slice packages to a main memory system. The chip contains the data and address storage and logic along with the logic for the more complex addressing methods required for the slice configuration.

slice system—A computing system that can handle large amounts of data at high speed by using the slice concept. Typical applications for slice systems include minicomputers, high-speed instrumentation, communications processors, real-time analysis, scientific computers,and time-sharing systems.

slow death—A term used to describe the gradual deterioration of semiconductor devices, usually due to contamination of surfaces.

smart terminal—A terminal in which part of the processing is done using a microcomputer in the terminal itself. Sometimes called an intelligent terminal, the unit allows the user to program the terminal for his application. A typical smart terminal contains a CRT, keyboard, serial input/output device, and microcomputer. The microcomputer controls editing, formatting, and the protocol of communication with the central computer. Editing may include character, line, field, and page deleting and inserting as well as line, page, and memory clearing.

snapshot jump—A dynamic partial printout during computing at breakpoints and checkpoints, or selected areas of storage.

SO—The *shift-out* character.

soft limited—Refers to a limiting action with an appreciable tolerance in the limiting value.

software—The programs, routines, languages, and procedures used in a computer system. Software items include assemblers, generators, subroutines, compilers, and operating systems.

software cross assembler—A software system for translating a symbolic representation of instructions and data into a form which can be loaded and executed by the microcomputer. The cross assembler acts like an assembler executing on a machine other than the one to be used, which generates the code for the desired unit.

software development process—Refers to the cycle or systematic method used to develop the software for a system. A typical development process includes:

(1) Problem statement
(2) Design of algorithms
(3) Flow chart construction
(4) Program coding
(5) Preparation of source code
(6) Translation to object code
(7) Loading of object code
(8) Checkout and debugging
(9) Documentation

software development system—Hardware to be used for the rapid development of software. A typical system includes an editing CRT, a hard-copy device, mass storage (such as magnetic tape or disk), and a paper-tape unit.

The CRT terminal is used to construct and edit source programs. A hard-copy device such as a printer is required to create the hard-copy listings for debugging and documentation. A cassette or floppy disk unit is used to obtain rapid access to assemblers, editors, and debug programs, and a high-speed paper-tape unit is needed to handle the programs that come with many microcomputer development system packages.

software documents—Written or printed material associated with the microcomputer, including manuals, diagrams, and listings.

software evaluation and development modules—Refers to a software system of modules which allow a means of building up and testing a proposed microcomputer system before committing the design to hardware. First the functional specifications and programs are established, then the ROM program is assembled and simulated on a time-shared system, using the software modules.

software house—A company which offers software support services to users. This support usually includes consulting services along with programming support.

software kit—A collection of programming aids for a microprocessor system, usually provided in paper-tape format. A typical software kit includes:

(1) Language editor for source tapes
(2) An assembler for source tapes
(3) PROM programmer
(4) Debug program
(5) Paper-tape loader

software library—The collection of programs used by an operating system. A microcomputer software library may include a machine-language assembler, Teletype operating system, tape editor, simulator, cross assembler, map generator, and utility and diagnostic programs.

software network components—The software components available through a time-sharing service. These include cross assemblers, interactive simulators, and other software packages to aid software development.

software package—The programs or sets of programs used in a particular application or function. Many software packages include diagnostic programs for verifying processor and memory operation along with cross assemblers.

software system—The entire set of programs and software development aids used in a microcomputer system.

software test set—A set of programs used to support the development of custom programs and to verify the design under actual operating conditions prior to release of the ROM pattern to manufacturing. The software set usually consists of a cross assembler, simulator, and test-program generator.

software tools—Programs which assist the programmer during the development cycle. S ftware tools include editors, assemblers, compilers, loaders, linkage editors, debuggers, and simulators.

SOH—The *start-of-heading* character; in ASCII it is designated as a seven-bit binary 1.

solder—A tin-lead alloy used for making electrical connections. In use, molten solder is applied to conductor joints. When the solder cools, it solidifies to hold the conductors permanently in place.

solderless breadboard—A circuit breadboard that contains sockets and socket pins to allow temporary solder-free connections during test or debugging operations.

solderless connector—A device for clamping two wires together without the use of solder.

solderless wrap—A method of connection in which a solid wire is wrapped around a metal terminal using a special hand or power tool. Also called *wire wrap*.

solenoid—A current-carrying iron-core coil of wire typically used as a controllable magnet for opening or closing mechanical contacts or valves.

solid—Matter which has the definite shape and volume of a crystal structure, as opposed to a liquid or a gas.

solid-state—Descriptive of circuits or systems constructed with active devices other than vacuum tubes; or the active devices themselves.

solid-state component—A component which depends upon the control of electrical or electromagnetic phenomena in a solid material; thus, a transistor, diode, or integrated circuit.

solid-state memory—A memory constructed entirely of circuits employing semiconductor devices.

solid-state physics—The branch of physics that deals with the properties of solid materials, especially conduction in semiconductors and metals.

SOM—Abbreviation for *self-organizing machine*.

sonic delay line—A device for simulating the acoustical delay of a long transmission line and used to emulate the effect of reverberation, or for providing phase changes to input signals under controlled conditions.

sort—To rearrange or segregate usually listed items into groups according to a specified order. For example, a list of subjects in a book can be entered into a computer in order of page number, and a sort operation can cause the list to be printed out in alphabetical order.

sorter—A device or routine used as the basis for determining the sequential order of the items in a set and for producing the list in that order.

sort key—A key used as the basis for determining the sequential arrangement of items in a set.

SOS—Abbreviation for *silicon-on-sapphire*, a semiconductor process which uses a sapphire base to "grow" silicon for the production of MOS transistors. SOS devices achieve bipolar speeds, provide radiation protection for military applications, and are well suited for CMOS designs. SOS technology can be applied in memories, microprocessors, high-speed counters, and multiplexers.

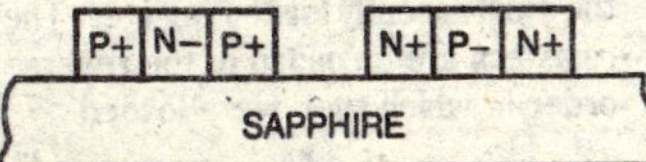

SOS Structure

SOS CMOS—Abbreviation for *silicon-on sapphire complementary metal-oxide semiconductor*, a low-power, high-speed MOS device.

SOS RAM—Abbreviation for a type of RAM that uses the silicon-on-sapphire technology. A typical unit uses the SOS MOS technology for a 1024-bit memory that operates with +4.5 to 6V and consumes only 4 mW of power. The unit is static with no requirement for refreshing, clocking, or pulsing circuitry.

SOS transistor—Abbreviation for *silicon-on-sapphire* transistor, an active device on a sapphire substrate that is electrically isolated from all others on the substrate.

source—1. A circuit or device which serves as a distributor (of voltage, data, timing pulses, etc.) to other devices. 2. An element in a circuit which serves as the starting point for an energy pulse of a given polarity (as a charged capacitor, for example). 3. Originator.

source code—Program statements, arguments, and codes generated by keyboard inputs to a system.

source-code instruction—An instruction used as a pointer in microprogrammed systems to emulate a particular instruction set being executed.

source data—Data generated in the course of research, design, and development.

source data automation—The recording of information in coded form on punch cards, paper tape, tags, and other media which may be used again and again without rewriting to produce other records of the data. Abbreviated *SDA*.

source deck—A stack of coded cards that contain a source program.

source editor—A program that allows the entry and modification of source code into the system for later translation or storage. Without a source editor, a program would have to be built up on a medium such as punched cards or paper tape.

source file editor—A line-oriented editor that operates on programs in a sequence determined by their assembler-produced statement line numbers. The editor produces an updated file while preserving the original master file.

source language—1. The language from which a statement is translated. 2. The original form in which a program is prepared prior to processing by the machine.

source language translation—The translation of a program to a target program, as from FORTRAN to machine language.

source library—A collection of programs (compiler or assembler) for a specific machine.

source module—A set of statements in a source language recorded in machine-readable form and suitable for input to an assembler or compiler.

source program—A program that can translated automatically into machine language to become an object program. Source programs are usually written in a language designed for ease of expression. A generator, assembler, translator, or compiler routine is used for translation into the object program in machine code.

source statement—A statement written in other than machine language. Source statements are written in symbolic terms for translation to machine code.

source tape—Refers to the tape that contains the source program.

source tape preparation—A program used to prepare and edit symbolic source tapes. The program allows the tape to be edited by typing commands on the keyboard to perform corrections and produce a new source tape.

source utility—A program that aids in the preparation and modification of symbolic assembly-language tapes.

space—1. A site intended for the storage of data, such as a specific position on a page in memory. 2. A unit of area for a single character on a line. 3. To advance a reading or display position in order to create a desired format.

space character—1. A nonprinting character used to separate words. 2. A format effector which controls the printing or display position in a system. Abbreviated *SP*.

special character—A graphic symbol which is neither a letter, a numeral, nor a space character.

special-purpose computer—A computer designed to handle a restricted class of problems.

specific address—Absolute address.

specific code—Absolute code.

specific routine—A routine used to solve a particular arithmetic, logic, or data-handling problem in which each address refers to explicitly stated registers and locations.

spooling—A procedure of temporarily storing data on disk or tape files until the CPU is ready for additional processing of the information.

sporadic—Intermittent.

stable trigger—A circuit with two binary states, each state requiring a trigger signal for transition from one state to another. Also known as *binary pair, trigger pair* and *R-S-T flip-flop*.

stack—A block of successive memory locations that are accessible from one end and coordinated with a stack pointer that keeps track of storage and retrieval of each word in the stack. A *pushdown* stack operates as a last-in-first-out (LIFO) buffer; as data is added, the stack moves down with the last item occupying the top position. The stack hardware is a collection of registers with a counter that indicates the most recently loaded register. The registers are unloaded in the reverse order in which they were loaded.

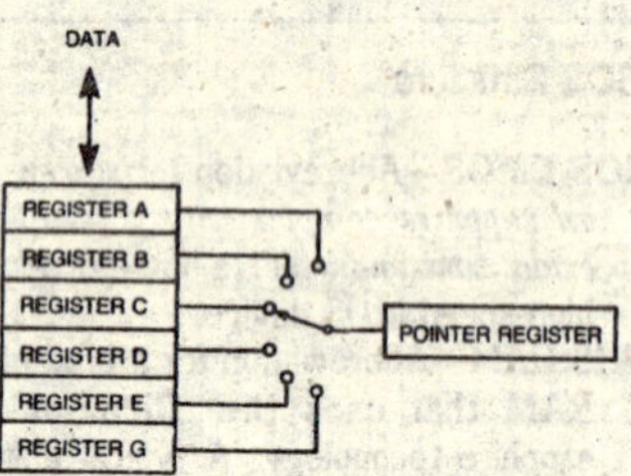

Stack

stack architecture—Descriptive of a microcomputer that uses a stack for part of its internal memory. Stack architecture reduces the number of registers required for temporary storage and can decrease the number of steps required in a program. Multiple-level interrupts can easily be handled with a stacked system, since system status can be saved when an interrupt occurs and restored after the interrupt.

stack manipulation—Refers to a system that has instruction addressing modes that allow temporary data storage structures for the convenient handling of data which is frequently processed. The register used to keep track of stack manipulation is called the ***stack pointer***. Stack manipulation is often used in microcomputers to offset the shortcomings of their smaller instruction sets.

stack pointer—The register used to keep track of the most recent register data stored in a stack.

standard component—A component that is regularly produced by one or more manufacturers and carried by one or more distributors.

standard deviation—The square root of the mean of the squares of a set of numbers representing statistical variations from an average value.

standard interface—An interface which allows several units or systems to be easily interconnected.

standard subroutine—A subroutine which is applicable to a specific class or set of problems.

standby—1. A nonoperating-but-ready condition of equipment which allows resumption of operation when permitted. 2. A duplicate set of equipment which is used when the primary equipment malfunctions.

standby application—An application where two or more machines are tied together as a part of the system design and stand ready for activation and processing of system inquiries.

standby register—A register in which information is stored for a rerun in the event of a mistake in the program or a malfunction in the machine.

standby time—The time between inquiries in a system, or the time two or more computers are connected for a standby application.

standing-on-nines carry—A high-speed carry in which a carry input to a given digit place is bypassed to the next digit place if the current sum in the given digit place is nine.

start-of-heading character—A communications control character (abbreviated *SOH*) used as the first character of a heading in a message.

start-of-text character—A control character (abbreviated *STX*) which indicates the beginning of text and the end of the heading.

statement—A meaningful expression or generalized instruction in a program.

static dump—A dump which is performed at a specific time in a machine run, usually at the end of the run.

static error—An error that is independent of time.

static gain—Refers to the gain of a device under steady-state conditions.

staticizer—A storage device for converting serial or time-sequential information into parallel static data.

static magnetic cell—A storage cell in which the two values are represented by different patterns of magnetization.

static magnetic storage—Storage of information bits on a medium that holds the data in place so that it is available at any time, such as in a core cell.

static memory—A semiconductor (usually) memory that holds data indefinitely as long as power is applied.

static memory card—A circuit board that contains a semiconductor memory.

static MOS—MOS memory circuits which are cross-coupled bistable units for storing information in one of two stable states.

static MOS RAM—A read-write memory that stores data in integrated flip-flops.

static MOS ROM—A static read-only memory based on MOS technology. Static MOS ROMs offer low-cost, simple interfacing and high performance for applications requiring large capacity. Applications include microprogramming, table lookup, code conversion, and character generation. In-

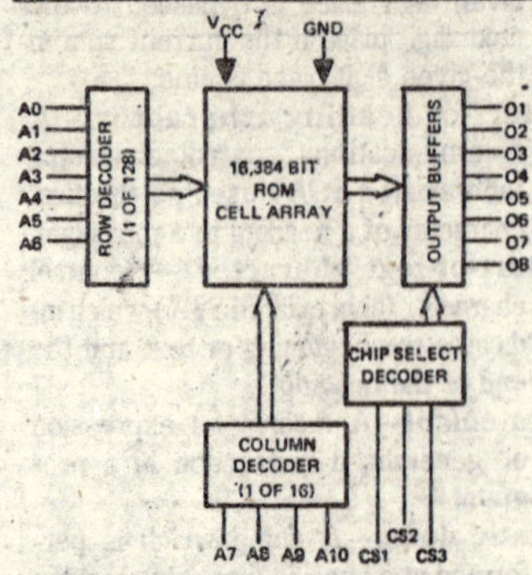

Static MOS ROM

puts and outputs are usually TTL compatible.

static storage—A memory that requires no refresh logic since data does not degenerate or leak away as long as power is applied to the memory elements. Compare *dynamic storage.*

static subroutine—A subroutine involving no parameters other than the addresses of the operands.

statistical universe—A complete set of items which are similar or related in certain respects.

status bit—A bit used in many systems to designate interrupt conditions. The status bit is tested by the program to check for the presence of an internal interrupt condition. The status bit can be used to check for console interrupts, DMA termination, clock interrupt, power-fail/restart interrupt, and others. Microprograms can be shortened with the use of status bits. Branches can be made after the status bits are set to eliminate premature branching and reduce the number of microinstructions required.

status register—A register used to hold information on communication errors, data register status, and communication device status. Some systems use several status registers and exchange data between the registers to allow limited nesting capability.

status word—1. A word used to resume processing after the servicing of an interrupt. 2. A word used to indicate the status of an internal or external device. The status word may provide information on the sign of a number, overflow conditions, carry bits, accumulator conditions, and interrupts.

steady-state—A condition in which all values remain essentially constant or recurring in a cyclic manner.

step-by-step switch—A stepper switch.

step counter—A counter used in the arithmetic unit to count the steps in a process such as multiplication, division or shift operations.

step function—A function which is zero preceding time zero, and then has a constant value after time zero.

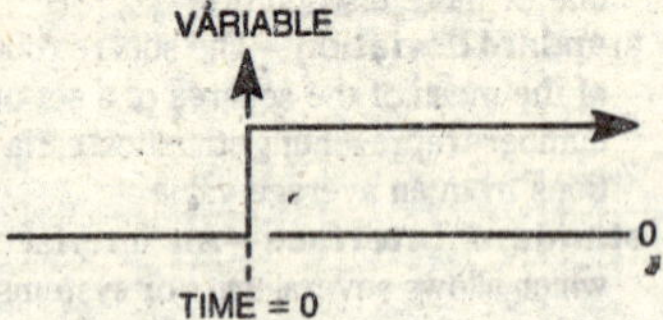

Step Function

stepper—A stepper switch.

stepper motor—A motor in which rotation occurs in a series of discrete steps which can be controlled by pulses.

stepper switch—An electromechanical relay with a number of contact positions. The wiper arms are rotated from contact to contact by applications of driving pulses to the relay coil.

stepping motor—A motor which can be stepped to rotate in a series of partial rotations using pulses.

stepping-motor controller—A module used to provide an interface between the microcomputer and the stepping-motor power amplifier. In a typical system the CPU uses a 16-bit word, with 12 bits for the number of pulses and 4 bits for direction and channel control.

stepping switch—A type of relay which advances its position each time it receives a pulse; a stepper switch.

step response—The response of a device to an instantaneous change in the input.

stochastic—An operation in which the element of chance cannot be avoided or excluded from consideration.

stochastic simulation—Refers to a simulation of the random variables and the properties of the system, rather than the system itself.

stop bit—The last element of a character in start-stop asynchronous serial transmission. The stop bit is used to insure recognition of the next start element. Also called *stop element*.

stop element—The last element or bit of a character in asynchronous serial transmission. Also called *stop bit*.

storage—A device or medium on or into which data can be entered, held, and retrieved later; a memory. Storage may use electrostatic, magnetic, acoustic, optical, electronic, or mechanical methods.

storage allocation—1. A specific cell or group of cells in memory. 2. The assignment of sections of data to specified sections of storage.

storage area—The section or space in memory used for specific data.

storage capacity—The amount of information that can be retained in a storage device, usually expressed in bits or words. Also called *memory capacity*.

storage cell—The elemental unit of storage in a storage system.

storage cycle—The sequence of events required when information is transferred to or from the storage device of a computer. The storage cycle may include storing, sensing, and regeneration.

storage cycle time—The time required for a complete storage cycle.

storage device—The medium or device in which data can be inserted, retained, and retrieved. Mass-storage devices are used to collect, organize, and retrieve large volumes of data.

storage element—A unit of memory capable of storing a single bit of information.

storage fragmentation—The sectionalizing of memory required as a result of the inability to assign actual storage locations to virtual addresses when the available spaces are smaller than the page size.

storage key—A special set of bits associated with every word or character in some block of storage, and which allows tasks with matching sets of key bits to use that block of storage.

storage module—A usually add-on circuit card or package which functions as an auxiliary memory for the storage and retrieval of data. A typical module uses a 4096-word RAM with two stack pointers. The processor accesses the memory using transfer instructions which reference the addresses assigned to the stack pointers.

storage oscilloscope—An oscilloscope in which the displayed trace of an extremely short-duration phenomenon is retained as long as desired. It is used for observation of nonrecurring pulses, aperiodic repetitive pulses, and transients.

storage protection—An arrangement for preventing access to storage for reading, writing, or both. Storage protection usually operates with a programmed protection key that prevents one program from destroying or covering another by protecting a specific area of storage.

storage switch—A switch provided on the console to allow the operator to read the contents of selected registers.

storage tube—A CRT-type tube capable of retaining a trace resulting from a nonrecurring phenomenon.

storage volatility—The inability of a storage device to retain data when power is removed.

store—1. Memory. 2. To enter or retain information in a storage device for later retrieval.

stored program—A set of instructions in a computer memory which specify the operations to be performed and the location of the data on which the operations are to be performed.

stored-program computer—A computer controlled by internally stored instructions which are used to synthesize, store, or alter data or other instructions.

straight-line code—To code using repetitions of sequences of instructions by explicitly writing the instructions for each repetition, with or without address modifications.

straight-line coding—Coding in which loops are avoided by explicitly writing the instructions for repetition of parts of the coding when required. Straight-line coding can require less execution time and more space than loop coding. A generator is usually required if the number of repetitions is large, since the coding is limited by the variable number of instructions required as well as the space available.

strain—The dimensional change in a medium when subjected to a stress.

strain gage—A transducer that detects changes in pressure of mechanical stress and delivers a corresponding electrical analog of that pressure.

STRESS—Acronym for *structural engineering system solver*, a language used in civil engineering for solving structural analysis problems.

string—A linear sequence of items which are grouped in series according to certain rules. A string may be a set of records grouped in ascending or descending sequence according to a key contained in the records.

string manipulation—The process of creating strings for the control of groups of items.

stripe recording—A magnetic recording in which a stripe of magnetic material is deposited on a document or card.

strobe pulse—A pulse used to gate the output of a circuit or device.

stroke—A straight line or arc used as a segment of a graphic character in character recognition.

stroke centerline—A line midway between the two stroke edges.

stroke edge—The line of discontinuity between the side of a stroke and the background, obtained by averaging the irregularities between the printing and detecting processes.

stroke width—The distance between the two stroke edges.

STRUDL—Acronym for *structural design language*, an extension of the STRESS language for the analysis and design of structures.

stunt box—A term for the unit which controls the nonprinting functions of a printing terminal or the response of stations to selective calling signals in a communications terminal.

STX—The *start-of-text* character; in ASCII it is designated as a seven-bit binary 2.

subaddress—An order code that allows access to an input/output device. In a disk system, the subaddress might be the module number.

subminiaturization—The technique of packaging miniaturized parts using methods to obtain increased densities.

subprogram—A segment of a program which can perform a specific function. Subprograms can reduce programming time when a specific function is required at more than one point in a program. If the required function is handled as a subprogram, the statements for that function can be coded once and executed at the different points in the program. Subroutines, functions, and macroinstructions may be used to provide subprograms, and they may be linked in one of two ways:

(1) The subprogram reference is replaced by a jump to the desired procedure.

(2) The subprogram reference is replaced with the actual statements for the desired procedure.

subroutine—A routine that can be part of another routine. A subroutine can be a portion of another routine which allows the computer to carry out a defined mathematical or logical operation. A subroutine may be used to

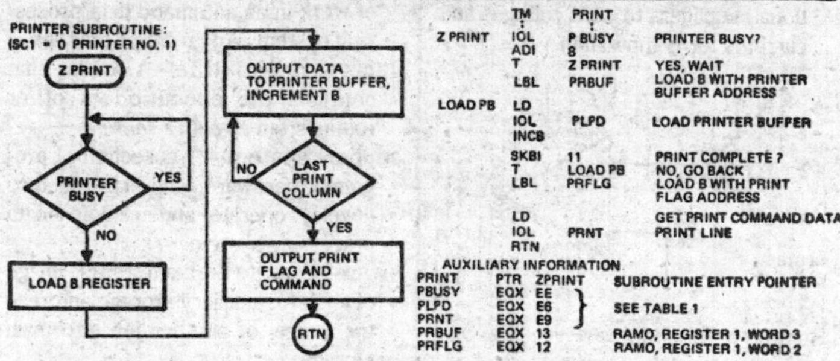

PRINTER SUBROUTINE:
(SC1 = 0 PRINTER NO. 1)
Z PRINT
PRINTER BUSY
YES
NO
LOAD B REGISTER
OUTPUT DATA TO PRINTER BUFFER, INCREMENT B
LAST PRINT COLUMN
NO
YES
OUTPUT PRINT FLAG AND COMMAND
RTN
TM PRINT
Z PRINT IOL P BUSY PRINTER BUSY?
ADI 8
T Z PRINT YES, WAIT
LBL PRBUF LOAD B WITH PRINTER BUFFER ADDRESS
LOAD PB LD
IOL PLPD LOAD PRINTER BUFFER
INCB
SKBI 11 PRINT COMPLETE ?
T LOAD PB NO, GO BACK
LBL PRFLG LOAD B WITH PRINT FLAG ADDRESS
LD GET PRINT COMMAND DATA
IOL PRNT PRINT LINE
RTN
AUXILIARY INFORMATION
PRINT PTR ZPRINT SUBROUTINE ENTRY POINTER
PBUSY EQX EE
PLPD EQX E6
PRNT EQX E9
SEE TABLE 1
PRBUF EQX 13 RAMO, REGISTER 1, WORD 3
PRFLG EQX 12 RAMO, REGISTER 1, WORD 2

Subroutine

perform a specific task for many other routines and may be distinguished from a main routine in that it requires a location specifying where to return to the main program after its function has been accomplished.

A *closed* subroutine may obtain control from a master routine and then return control to the master routine upon concluding its function by branching or jumping.

subroutine address stack—A stack register used to save the program return address for subroutines.

subroutine library—A set of standard, proven subroutines which are kept on file for use at any time in various programs. A subroutine library for floating-point operations might include decimal-to-floating-point conversion, addition, subtraction, multiplication, division, fixed-point-to-floating-point conversion, and floating-point-to-fixed-point conversion.

subsequent counter—An instruction counter designed to step through or count micro operations or parts of larger programs.

substitute character—An accuracy control character (*SUB*) used to replace a character that has been determined to be invalid or in error.

substrate—The physical material (such as silicon) on which an integrated circuit is fabricated.

subsystem—A secondary or subordinate system, which may be a self-contained portion of a major system. A subsystem may be used to provide one of the major system functions, with only minimal interaction with other portions of the system.

subtract—To find the difference between two quantities.

subtraction—The process of finding the difference between two quantities.

subtracter—A device used to perform the subtraction operation. Subtracters may use parallel or serial configurations.

subtracter-adder—An element designed to act as adder or subtracter, depending on the control signal or command issued to it.

subtrahend—The number or quantity subtracted from another number (the minuend).

sudden death—A term used to define an abrupt failure of a working device or system.

sum check—A check developed when groups of digits are summed. The check is usually made without regard to overflow, and this sum is compared with a previously computed sum to verify that no digits have changed since the last summation.

summation check—Sum check.

summing junction—A junction used in computing amplifiers and operational amplifiers to sum voltages and currents for computation.

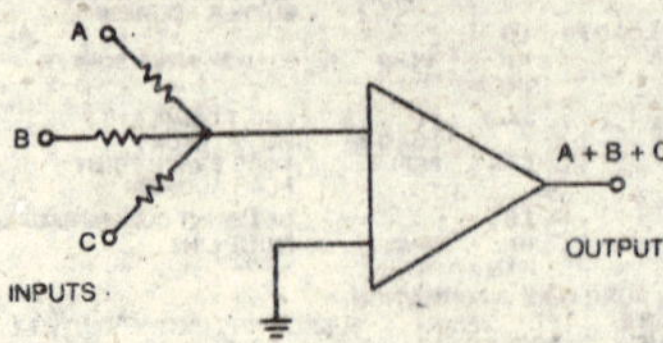

Summing Junction

supervising system—A set of coded instructions designed to process and control other sets of instructions. Supervising systems provide a master set of instructions to control the loading and relocation of routines and may also be used for automatic coding. Also called *supervisory routine, supervisory program* and *monitor routine*.

supervisor—A monitor or executive routine that controls the proper sequencing and positioning of segments of the program during execution.

supervisor mode—A mode of operation in which certain operations, such as memory protection instructions and input/output operations, are permitted.

supervisor overlay—A routine that controls fetching of overlay segments using information recorded in the overlay module by the linkage editor.

supervisory console—A system console that contains the operator control panel and operator input/output devices for system control.

supervisory control action—A mode in which control loops operate independently, subject to intermittent corrective action.

supply voltage—1. The steady-state DC potential required to operate an electronic system. 2. The AC line voltage required to power the circuits which produce system operating potentials.

supervisory program—A program used to organize and control the flow of work in an automatic data processing system. An *executive program*.

supervisory routine—A routine that controls the execution of other routines; an *executive routine*.

support system—A collection of programs, hardware, and skills used to develop, operate, and maintain a data processing system.

swap—To write the main storage image of a job to auxiliary storage and read the image of another job into main storage.

swapping—A type of memory multiplexing in which jobs are transferred between auxiliary and main storage. Swapping is usually found in timesharing applications.

sweep circuit—A circuit used to guide the movement of the electron beam in a cathode-ray tube.

switch—1. To make or break a connection between two stations or points. 2. The mechanical or electronic device that makes or breaks the circuit between two points. 3. A multivibrator (bistable, astable, or monostable).

switchboard loop panel—A patch panel with rows of jacks for access to local loops.

switched message network—A communications service which allows customers to communicate among themselves. Switches message networks include TELEX and TWX systems.

switching—Refers to the making and breaking of connections in a circuit or network. In message switching applications, the computer can be used to accept messages from terminals and route the messages over trunk lines to remote switching devices, while providing an audit trail along with the error control.

switching circuit—A circuit that can be used to perform a switching function, such as the connection of two or more inputs. Switching circuits include gates and the logic devices made from them.

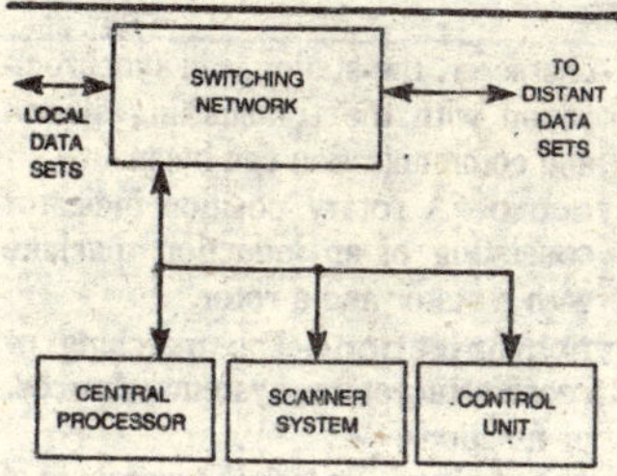

Switching System

switching device—A device or mechanism which can be electrically placed in a desired state or condition.

switching diode—A diode designed for high-speed switching applications.

switching module—A module used to provide isolated output voltages for driving solenoids and other high-power devices.

switching time—The time required for switching action to be completed from reference level to a final level, usually a fraction or percentage of the peak value.

switch matrix—An array of circuit elements interconnected to perform a specific function. The array elements may be transistors, diodes, or gates for functions, such as encoding, decoding, transformation, code conversion, or word translation.

switch register—An array of data entry switches that can be used to manually alter the contents of the accumulator, program counter, or memory data register. The switch register can also be read under program control.

symbol—A graphic representation of a concept or item, such as a letter representing a quantity in a formula. Although a symbol usually consists of a single character, in some computer systems a symbol may consist of up to eight letters. Symbols may be used as statement labels or equality symbols in these systems. The value of the symbol, when defined as a label, is the value of the location counter at the time the symbol is encountered. When used as an equality, the symbol is defined by the value of the expression.

symbolic address—An address expressed in symbols convenient to the programmer. Also called a *floating address*, the symbolic address is used as a label to identify a particular word, function, or other item which is independent of the location of the information within the routine. If the programmer can refer to memory locations by symbolic name rather than numeric addresses, the assembler can translate these as well as the instructions. The assembler requires less time than manual translation, so fewer coding errors result.

SYMBOLIC ADDRESSES

LABEL	MNEMONIC	OPERAND
XO	PTR	LXO
CLRX	LB	XO

Symbolic Addresses

symbolic assembler—A programming system which translates mnemonic instructions into binary machine-readable form.

symbolic assembly system—The use of an assembler to translate mnemonic instruction into machine format. A symbolic assembly system provides the means of entering linkages, mapping common data, and using address modifiers.

symbolic code—A code used to express programs in source language. The symbolic code allows the programmer to refer to storage locations and machine operations by symbolic names and addresses which are independent of their hardware-determined labels and addresses.

symbolic coding—A coding system that uses symbols rather than actual machine addresses and instructions.

symbolic concordance—A program used to produce a cross-referenced list of all the symbolic names in a program. Symbolic concordance programs are used for debuggin and modification of larger programs.

symbolic language—A language which expresses addresses and codes in terms convenient to humans (rather than in machine form). A program prepared in any coding other than a machine language uses a symbolic language which requires assembly or compiling.

symbolic logic—The study and discipline of formal logic using expressions which seek to avoid the ambiguity and inadequacy of ordinary language and expressions.

symbolic name—A label used in programs written in source language to reference data elements, peripherals, or instructions.

symbolic parameter—A variable symbol used in assembler programming to call a macro definition. The symbolic parameter is usually assigned a value from the corresponding operand in the macroinstruction that calls the definition.

symbolic programming—The use of symbols to represent addresses in order to facilitate programming. An assembly program is used to translate the symbolic program and assign instruction locations.

symbol string—A string of characters consisting entirely of symbols.

symbolic unit—A designation used to refer to an external storage area or input/output device during coding. The actual location or device to be used is determined at a later time.

symbol variable—A symbol used in macro assembly processing that can assume any of a given set of values.

sync—1. Synchronous operation. 2. To synchronize.

sync character—A character used to establish character synchronization in communications systems. When the receiving station recognizes the sync character, the station is in synchronization with the transmitting station and communication can begin.

synchro—A rotary position indicator consisting of an induction machine with a stator and a rotor.

synchronization—The matching or coordinating of two systems, devices, or functions.

synchronize—To lock the elements of a system into step with one another, such as synchronizing the operations of a computer to clock pulses.

synchronizer—A device or unit used to maintain synchronism between two devices or systems. Synchronizers include buffers or storage devices which are used to compensate for differences in the rate of flow of data or occurrence of events between devices or systems.

synchronous—Refers to a constant time interval between bits, characters, and events in a circuit or system.

synchronous clock—A system in which events are controlled by signals from a clock generator at a desired rate or frequency.

synchronous communications interface—An interface for providing two-way communications between devices in a synchronous mode. A specific interface for data-set applications operates at up to 9600 baud in half- or full-duplex modes. Programmable functions include parity checking, special character recognition, and synchronization modes.

synchronous computer—A computer in which each event is constrained by signals from a clock.

synchronous data line control—A type of protocol (abbreviated *SDLC*) used in data transmission.

synchronous data transmission—A system in which timing is derived by synchronizing characters at the beginning of each message.

synchronous gate—A gate which is controlled by time pulses and which in turn may be used to synchronize other operations in the computer system.

synchronous idle character—A communication control character (abbreviated *SYN*) used in synchronous transmission to provide a signal so that synchronism can be achieved between devices.

synchronous input—An input which allows data to be entered only when a clock pulse is present.

synchronous mode comparator—A comparator that is used in the synchronous mode to compare the assembled contents of registers. The comparator output allows character synchronization following successive matches of data.

synchronous operation—A mode of operation in which each event is timed by a signal generated by a clock.

synchronous preprocessor—A device used for interfacing synchronous lines to computers. It is designed to reduce the overhead for the computer by handling most of the interrupt processing and character manipulation.

synchronous receiver—A receiver that assembles characters from serial communications lines and asserts a flag as each character is received.

synchronous serial data adapter—A device that converts parallel data to serial or serial data to paralllel in a synchronous system. The adapter usually provides error detection and correction during transmission and reception.

synchronous time division multiplexer—A multiplexer (abbreviated *STDM*) which shares a synchronous data line by scanning and interleaving bits into frames of the incoming data stream.

synchronous transmission—A mode of transmission that uses a timed stream of bits or characters.

sync pulse—A pulse used by all system elements as a reference point for operational timing.

SYN register—A register used in some systems to hold the synchronous character code used for receiver character synchronization.

syntactic error—An error due to incorrect structure or symbols. Syntactic errors include typographic errors, incorrect punctuation, mixed-mode expressions, illegal statements, illegal transfers, references to nonexistent statement numbers, etc.

syntax—The relationship among characters and groups of characters and their structure in a language.

syntax error—Syntactic error.

syntax checker—A program that tests source statements in a programming language for violations of syntax.

synthesis—1. The act of combining parts to form a desired result based on the performance requirements, such as the formation of an analog signal by a rapid series of digital pulses. 2. The process of generating any one of a variety of fixed-frequency signals using special electronic techniques and devices.

synthetic language—A pseudo code or symbolic language; a fabricated language.

system—A collection of methods, devices, programs, equipment, or other items which are united by some form of regulated interaction to create an organized whole. A system could be a collection of routines for providing sequencing control or debugging operations, or it could be an overall relationship between hardware, programs, procedures, and management at a particular computer installation. An operating computer, for example, is a system.

system check—A performance check based on external program tests rather than built-in hardware circuits.

system check module—A device which monitors a system for power failure or deviations from desired performance, and when necessary, initiates emergency actions.

system command executive—An executive program which accepts and interprets commands by a user. Typical commands include:

(1) LOG IN, LOG OUT
(2) SAVE OR RESTORE PROGRAM
(3) COMPILE, EXECUTE
(4) INTERRUPT, TERMINATE
(5) EDIT, LIST
(6) REQUEST STATUS

system controller and bus driver—A single-chip unit that generates all signals required to interface RAM, ROM, and input/output devices to the microcomputer system.

system data bus—A bus designed for communications between all external units and the CPU. A typical bus transfers information between any two devices connected to the bus by granting access through a priority network for bus control.

system design—The specification of the working relationship between all parts of the system in terms of their characteristic actions.

system design aids—Hardware and software support items used in design of the various types of equipment encountered in microcomputer applications. Systems design aids include:

(1) Evaluation modules and support hardware
(2) Development and test equipment
(3) System design documentation and manual
(4) Support software

system diagnostic—A program used to detect overall system malfunctions rather than isolate errors or faults.

system engineering—An engineering approach where all aspects of the system are considered in arriving at a solution.

system handbook—A document that provides a concise reference of all the major characteristics of the microcomputer system. The system handbook will contain operation codes, addressing modes, device status details, interfaces, timing diagrams, and data flow.

system interface—Any device that connects support hardware to the microprocessor.

system interface module—A circuit board or card that provides the interface for external devices to the system. Modules are available for power switching, analog transducers, and communications in parallel or serial modes.

system loader—A supervisory routine used to retrieve program phases from an image library and load them into main storage.

system log—A set of records containing all job-related information, such as descriptions of unusual occurrences, and all commands and messages from or to the operator.

system monitor—A program which allows the user to load and execute programs stored on paper tape or other external devices. The system monitor usually has four sections which may be associated with a physical device or unit, and which controls the console, reader, punch, and list devices. The user controls the assignment of each physical device through a system command.

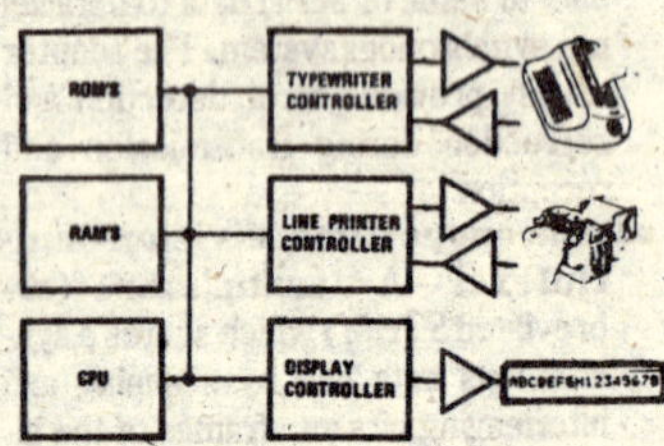

System-Oriented Application

system noise—1. The extra bits or words that must be removed from the data before it is used. 2. Any disturbance tending to interfere with the normal operation of the system by creating signals that can be read as pulses.

system-oriented—Descriptive of applications that use a common bus system for all data and communications within the microcomputer system itself.

system reliability—The probability that a system will perform its specified tasks under specific environmental conditions.

systems analysis—The examination and study of an activity, method, technique, procedure, or business operation to determine what operations must be accomplished and how they should be accomplished. The examination is usually aimed at achieving the maximum result at minimum cost and may include feasibility studies, identification of areas for study and correction, identification of requirements for information, assessment of costs and benefits, and definition of purpose and objectives.

system support—Generally refers to the support furnished by the manufacturer to simplify the application of the microprocessor and the design and development of the microcomputer system. System support may include manuals, literature, field and factory engineering specialists, prototyping hardware, and development software.

system-support program—A program that contributes directly to the use and control of the system and the production of end results. System-support programs include linkage editors, job control processors, and utility packages.

system test—A running or simulation of the total connected set of components of a system to obtain test data and check the adequacy of the design.

system tester—A test device used to check modules in modular industrial control systems. Some system testers use thumbwheel switches to select the test program desired.

T

table—A graphically arranged collection of data in which each item is uniquely identified by a label or position relative to other items. The items are usually laid out in rows and columns for reference or stored in memory as an array.

A *decision* table contains all contingencies that are to be considered in the solution of a problem, including all the actions to be taken. Decision tables can be used in place of flow charts for problem description.

A *lookup* table can be used to obtain a derived value of a variable which corresponds to an argument or table address.

table lookup—The procedure used to obtain the value of a function from a table of function values using the proper argument or address. Table lookup methods are used primarily to obtain a value for one variable when given another, where the relationship cannot be stated easily with a formula or algorithm (such as converting from one code to another).

table lookup instruction—An instruction which allows a reference to stored data arranged in tabular form. The instruction usually directs the computer to search for a named argument and to locate and retrieve a desired value. This operation is performed in place of a calculation.

tabulate—1. To form data into an array or table format. 2. To print out the totals of a section of storage.

tabulator—Mechanical calculating machine driven electrically or manually.

tactile keyboard—A pressure-sensitive keyboard with conductive sheets.

tag—One or more characters attached to an item for the purpose of identification, and sometimes used in place of a *flag*.

tape—1. Generally, paper or magnetic tape used as a medium for storage of data. 2. To record on tape.

tape cable—A type of cable which contains flat ribbon conductors imbedded side by side with an insulating material separating them.

tape cartridge—A self-contained continuous loop of magnetic tape in a plug-in package. A typical tape cartridge can store over two million 8-bit bytes.

tape cassette—A self-contained supply of magnetic tape and the reels (one for supply and one for takeup) for containing it. The cassette is a small plug-in package.

tape conversion program—A program (abbreviated *TCP*) for duplicating paper tapes and converting from one tape format to another. The program can be used to convert from hexadecimal to binary format, or binary to hexadecimal format. The conversion requires a minimum of 2000 bits of RAM.

tape deck—A device which contains a tape drive unit along with reading and writing heads and associated control circuitry. Also called *tape unit*.

tape drive—The mechanism used to move tape past read and write heads allowing tape rewinding.

tape-drive controller—A unit designed to interface one or more tape drive units to a microcomputer. The controller usually provides error checking and may provide buffering.

tape load point—The position on a magnetic tape where reading or writing can begin.

tape operating system—A software package (abbreviated *TOS*) designed for computers having at least 16,000 words of memory with no random-access storage, and at least four magnetic tape systems. It is used for smaller systems without disk drives.

tape perforator—A unit for creating paper tapes. Tape perforators are used for recording data in environments that demand rugged equipment. The cost is lower than magnetic tape and extreme cleanliness is not required. Recording density is lower, making it suitable for applications with smaller data requirements. Also called *tape punch*.

tape perforator interface—A circuit which provides the buffering and matching required to drive a tape perforator. It can be specified for connection to a desired microcomputer system.

tape reader-punch—A device designed to read and create paper tapes. Read operations are asynchronous at 300 characters per second. Punching is also asynchronous at 75 characters per second.

tape reader-punch controller—A device designed to interface paper tape equipment to a microprocessor system. The controller may also include tape handlers for folding and reel-to-reel operations.

tape recorder—A device containing a magnetic tape drive with read and write heads and associated controls. Magnetic tape recorders offer high recording speed and high density storage. Disadvantages include vulnerability to dust, temperature, and humidity.

tape recorder interface—A device designed for incremental recording of one multibit character. Each magnetic tape character describes a single printer character such as a letter, space, or punctuation mark.

tape transport—The mechanism which moves the magnetic tape past the sensing and recording heads. Also called *tape drive*.

tape unit—A device containing a tape transport with read and write heads and associated controls. Also called *tape recorder*.

target language—The language into which a program is to be translated.

target phase—The time when a number of target statements comprising a target program are run, usually during compiling operations.

target program—A fully compiled or assembled program which is to be loaded into the computer. Also called an *object program*.

tasking—A capability in a system which allows the handling of several tasks during the same time interval using task scheduling commands.

task management—A set of functions in the control program for allocating the hardware and software resources of the system by tasks.

task queue—A waiting line or list of all the task control blocks which are in the system at any one time.

TCAM—Abbreviation for *telecommunications access method.*

TCP—Abbreviation for *tape conversion program*.

TCS—Abbreviation for *terminal control system*.

TDR—1. Abbreviation for *time-domain reflectometry*. 2. Abbreviation for *transmit data register*.

telecommunications—The communication of information in written or coded verbal or pictorial form by electrical means using wire or radio waves.

telecommunications access method—A communication subsystem (abbreviated *TCAM*) designed to exchange information between a communications network and a set of message queues. The exchange is carried out according to information contained in the control blocks and headers. The control program is coded for each particular installation using a set of system macroinstructions.

teleconference—A conference between persons linked together by a telecommunications system.

telemeter—To transmit or cause the transmission of analog or digital data such as measurement results from a remote fixed or moving station to a control or recording station using radio waves.

telemeter service—A metered telegraph service between paired telegraph instruments over a time-shared circuit.

telemetry—The remote sensing of systems using transmitted electrical signals which are coded using a suitable modulation method.

telephone dialer—A circuit which converts pushbutton closures or stored information into dial pulses compatible with standard telephone systems. The circuit may store the last number dialed for automatic redialing.

teleprinter—A communications terminal that includes a printing device.

teleprinter interface—A serial interface that makes the computer system compatible with a teleprinter. In typical use, data is fed to the teletypewriter punch and stored for later transmission or fed to the computer and printed out at the same time. Standard output for the interface is a two-wire 20 mA current loop, with simplex operation at 110 baud, or 10 characters per second.

Teletype—Trade name for a terminal with a typewriter–printer which is used to send or receive messages by wire or radio.

Teletype controller—A device which contains parallel-to-serial and serial-to-parallel conversion circuitry to interface a Teletype terminal to a computer for asynchronous operation.

Teletype/CRT utility—A package of programs for performing the most common input/output functions for a Teletype or CRT terminal.

Teletype diagnostic—A diagnostic program for testing the keyboard, printer, and tape reader and punch, along with the motor operation. The program uses a lookback diagnostic mode.

Teletype exchange—The exchange services such as TELEX or TWX, which provide direct-dial point-to-point connections using Teletype equipment. Facilities are also available to allow computers to interface through these services.

Teletype microcomputer system—A system which includes a microcomputer with Teletype interface.

Teletype modification kit—A kit which contains the circuitry for converting TTL signals to 20 mA loop currents for Teletype units. It also contains incremental control circuits for the tape reader.

Teletype network—A system of points connected together by private telegraphic channels. Typically up to

20 channels time-share a single circuit.

Teletype utility—A software package for programming input/output functions through a Teletype.

teletypewriter—A teleprinter which is part of a communications terminal.

teletypewriter controller—A controller that allows the CPU to control the interface for full-duplex communication with a teletypewriter.

teletypewriter exchange service—A teletypewriter service (abbreviated *TWX*) for direct point-to-point communications for subscribers.

teletypewriter KSR—A keyboard send-receive unit that receives and prints incoming data. It also has a keyboard for manually sending out signals, but contains no paper tape.

teletypewriter KTR—A keyboard typing reperforator that receives, punches, and types on paper tape. It can punch and send simultaneously.

TELEX—The international network of teleprinter subscribers.

Telpak—A leasing service of wideband channels for communications.

temporary register—A register used as a latch to avoid race conditions. It can also be used as an internal register for microprogram control.

temporary storage—Storage that is reserved for intermediate results. Also called *working storage*.

temporary storage area—An area of memory reserved for data in process or in an intermediate state of computation. Also called *scratchpad memory*.

terminal—A point in a system or communications network at which data can be entered or retrieved. Some terminals have hard-copy and display capabilities. In systems where computers must communicate with each other, asynchronous and synchronous interfaces are used with modems for communications. A complete terminal facility may include a keyboard, display, microprocessor, memory, printer, modem, and adapters.

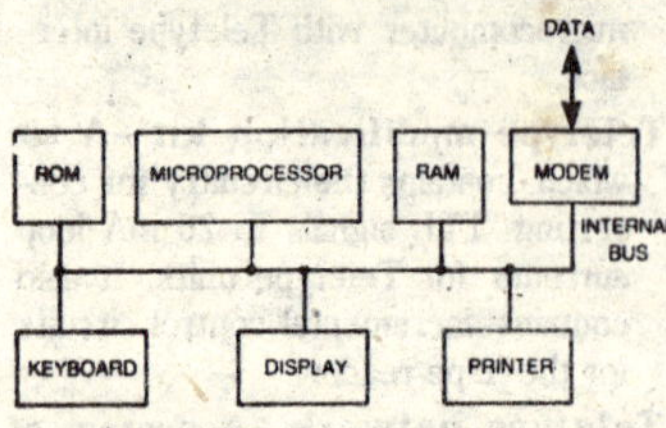

Terminal Block-Diagram

terminal controller—A unit that contains the circuitry to interface a teletypewriter or data terminal to a microcomputer. It contains a receiver which converts incoming serial data in parallel format with parity, framing, and overrun detection. The internal transmitter converts outgoing parallel data into serial format with start and stop bits.

terminal control system—A control program (abbreviated *TCS*) designed to handle multiterminal operations in a computer system. The program schedules the use of hardware and all input/output processing.

terminal display mode—The manner in which points are to be displayed on the CRT screen. Terminal display modes include vector, increment, characters, point, or vector continue.

terminal equipment—The equipment at the end of a communications channel used for the reception and transmission of messages. Terminal equipment may include telephone and teletypewriter switchboards in which communications circuits are terminated.

terminal fanout—The number of circuits designed to be supplied with input signals from an output terminal.

terminal interface—The connections, voltage levels, and impedance matching circuitry between data processing equipment and data communication equipment.

terminal keyboard—The keyboard which is part of a communications terminal and is normally used for manual input of data or control signals.

terminated line—A transmission line that has a fixed resistive load which is equal to the characteristic impedance of the line, thus minimizing reflected waves and increasing the likelihood of maintaining pulse integrity from one end of the line to the other.

termination—1. The connection or load at the end of a propagating medium. 2. The end of a program or program run.

ternary—1. The characteristic involving a selection or choice in which there are three possibilities. 2. A number system with a base of three.

ternary incremental representation—An incremental representation in which the value of the increment is rounded to one of three values.

tertiary—A separate output winding on a multiwinding transformer, but not the principal output for which the transformer is designed.

test card—A card which can be used to test all input/output functions and simulate regular and DMA controllers. The card includes special-purpose test logic for a complete test of every input/output bus signal. Connections typically are provided to check the power-failure restart system and to test automatic loaders.

test data—The data developed to check the adequacy of the run or computer system, and including data from previous runs or data created from simulated runs for test purposes.

testing nominative—A standard of performance established for quantitative and qualitative testing.

test macro—An ordered set of software and hardware designed for the testing of LSI devices. The total system includes a conditioning module, a memory, and a programmable clock generator with the associated software package.

test program package—A collection of test and diagnostic programs for microcomputers and peripheral devices. A typical package might consist of:

(1) Processor exerciser — 3 PROMs
(2) Interface test—1 PROM
(3) Interrupt test—paper tape
(4) RAM, reader, and punch tests—paper tape

test program system—A checking system sued before running the problem in which a sample problem of the same type with a known solution is run.

tetrad—A group of four pulses used to express a digit.

tetrode—A four-electrode active device, especially a vacuum tube, which contains cathode, control grid, screen grid, and anode.

tetrode transistor—A transistor with four electrodes.

text—A sequence of usually a great many characters treated as an entity.

text editing—An editing facility designed into the program to allow the keyboard entry of text or copy without regard to the final format. After the copy has been placed in storage, it can be edited and justified by specifying the desired format.

text editor—The software which provides the user with a source text generation system. The text editor permits the stored text statements to be altered at any time. The user can insert, delete, or replace lines in the text buffer. Some systems also allow editing on a word or character basis.

T flip-flop—A flip-flop that has only one input electrode that causes the device to be triggered (to change from one state to another). T flip-flops are used in ripple counter applications.

thermal noise—The electromagnetic noise due to thermal agitation in a material. Also called *Johnson noise.*

thermal runaway—A condition in semiconductor devices where an increased temperature results in increased power dissipation, which accordingly increases the temperature until ultimate destruction occurs.

thermal shock—An abrupt temperature change.

thermistor—A temperature-sensitive device whose resistance varies with temperature. Its temperature coefficient of resistance is usually high, typically nonlinear, and either positive or negative.

thermocouple—A junction of two dissimilar metals, which produces a voltage by virtue of the difference in the response of the atoms in the two metals to applied heat. The emf developed is typically very small and must be amplified or conditioned before use.

thermocouple linearization—A technique for correcting errors in a thermocouple measurement system and compensating for the known nonlinearity. Linearization can be accomplished using ROMs with a specific ROM for each calibrated thermocouple.

thermoelectric effect—The phenomenon whereby a small emf is produced by the difference in temperature between two junctions of dissimilar metals in a circuit.

thick-film circuit—A usually integrated circuit in which layers of appropriate conducting paths and components are deposited on an insulating substrate.

thin-film circuit—An integrated microelectronic circuit formed by means of a thin film, usually equal to the molecular thickness, deposited in a vacuum on a substrate.

thin-film magnetic module—A storage cell that uses thin films of magnetic alloys for switching action. The thin-film cells allow fast switching speeds and miniaturization of magnetic storage units.

thin-film memory—A memory made up of plates or disks of thin film magnetic layers deposited on a nonmagnetic base.

thin-film microelectronics—Circuits that use thin-film technology to achieve miniaturization.

third-generation computer—A computer utilizing solid-state electronic logic blocks in the form of integrated circuits.

three-address—An instruction format that contains three address parts.

three-D process—Refers to a triple-diffusion process for complementary integrated-circuit structures.

three-plus-one address—An instruction that contains three operand addresses and one control address.

threshold—1. The point at which an effect is first observed or measured. 2. A logic operator having the property: if P, Q, and R are statements, then the threshold of P, Q, R is true if at least *n* statements are true; it is false if less than *n* statements are true. In this context, *n* is a nonnegative integer called the ***threshold condition.***

threshold element—A device that performs the logic threshold operation in which the truth of each input statement contributes to the output determination.

throughput—The rate at which work can be handled by a system. Throughput is a measure of system efficiency, and it relates to the speed at which problems, programs, or routines are performed. Throughput can be measured as the total information processed in a specified time period, and includes input time, processing time, and output time.

tilt—Input-to-output waveform differences when the processing circuits are not fully linear; skew.

time constant—In an RC circuit, the product of *R* (ohms) and *C* (farads) expressed in seconds, which is the time required for an uncharged capacitor to charge to 63.2% of the applied voltage. After five such periods, the capacitor is considered to be fully charged (except in pulse circuits, where seven periods are considered necessary to completely charge the circuit).

When voltage is removed from an RC circuit, the time constant describes the complementary arrangement: the amount of time required for the capacitor to lose 63.2% of its charge (drop to the 36.8% voltage level). In an RL circuit, the time constant in seconds is equal to L/R (in henrys and ohms) and follows the same charge and discharge curves. See *time constant chart*.

time-constant chart—A chart showing universal charge and discharge curves for RC and RL circuits, where voltage or current is shown as a decimal fraction of 1.

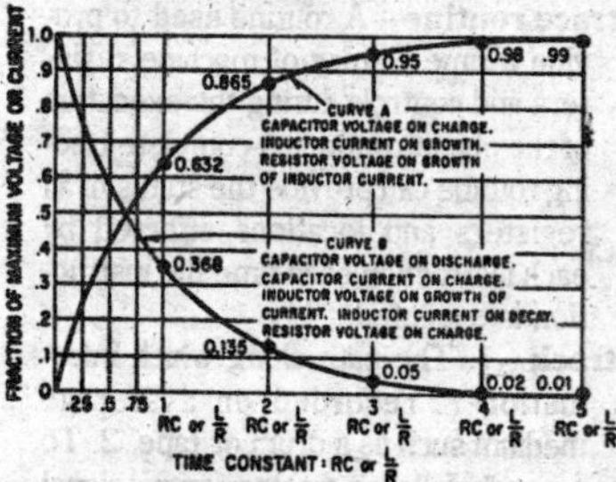

Time Constant Chart

time-delay circuit—A circuit or device that provides (1) electrical contact after a specified time, (2) the breaking of electrical contact after a specified time, or (3) the delayed transmission of input signals.

time-division multiplex—A multiplexing method (abbreviated *TDM*) which transmits two or more coincident signals over a common path using a sampling technique for sensing each signal alternately.

time-domain reflectometry—The study or measurement of phenomena associated with signal propagation along wires or other related media.

time pulse distributor—A device or circuit which allocates timing or clock pulses to one or more conducting paths in a specified sequence.

time schedule controller—A controller whose actions adhere automatically to a predetermined time schedule.

time-share—To use a device or system for two or more interleaved purposes.

time-shared BASIC—An enhancement of BASIC which is used as a conversational language to provide access to a computer system for a maximum number of users.

time-shared computer—A computer system that allows usage by a large number of subscribers, usually through data communication subsystems. Certain data and programs may be shared by all users, while other data and programs may only be provided and used by certain subscribers. Documentation for general programming on the system is available with the time-sharing service which provides system-dependent operating instructions. The programmer may be assigned a work area in the system for storing programs which can be edited using the system editor.

time-sharing—A computer technique in which a device or facility is shared by several other devices or users by allocation of separate time slots. Time-sharing programs are available for several microprocessors, and time-sharing services are available from a number of service organizations. Time-sharing allows a microcomputer system to be developed on a pay-as-you-go basis, since there is not normally a fixed overhead charge.

time slice—A designated interval of time during which a job or task uses a resource without being preempted.

time-slicing—1. The allocation of time slots to terminal jobs in time-sharing systems. 2. A feature in some systems which prevents a task from monopolizing CPU time in a system and delaying other jobs or tasks.

timing clock—The source of timing signals or clock pulses required for sequencing computer operation. This source usually consists of a clock generator and a cycling unit to derive the sets of pulses required at specific intervals. Sometimes called *timing master*.

timing master—The primary source of timing signals in a computer system; *timing clock*.

timing signals—The electrical pulses that are required at specific intervals to insure synchronization in processors. The synchronous logic used in most machines is based on a clock signal to trigger operations on pulses of a fixed period. Instruction times are based on the maximum clock frequency of the microprocessor, and other lower-frequency signals may be desired to optimize other functions, such as memory access time.

toggle—A bistable trigger circuit such as a flip-flop which switches between two stable states.

toggle switch—A circuit or switch that holds one of two states until changed.

token—A distinguishable unit in a sequence of characters.

TO package—A semiconductor package, usually metal, used to house discrete transistors.

totalizing—Registering a precise total count from a mechanical, electromagnetic, or electronic device.

trace—1. An interpretive diagnostic method which provides an analysis of each executed instruction and writes it on an output device as each instruction is executed. A selective trace may be used to trace instructions which satisfy certain specific criteria such as instruction type or data location. 2. The graphic representation of a waveform on a CRT screen. 3. To troubleshoot a circuit or system by monitoring signals at various points along the signal route.

trace program—A diagnostic program used to perform a check on another program. The trace program may include instructions as its output.

trace routine—A routine used to provide a time history of machine registers and controls during the execution of the object routine. A complete tracing routine can provide the status of all registers and locations affected by each instruction each time the instruction is executed.

track—1. The path along which information is recorded on a storage medium such as a drum or tape. 2. To properly follow a master control signal or control element.

trailer card—A card that contains information related to the data on preceding cards.

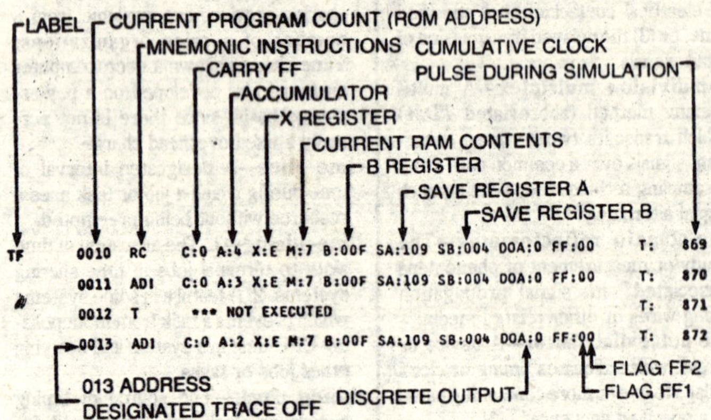

Trace, 1

transceiver—A terminal device that can be used to transmit and receive signals. A typical asynchronous transceiver provides a data communications interface for operation in full- or half-duplex modes. The unit accepts parallel data words from a computer or terminal and converts the data into asynchronous serial format. Received information is converted into parallel data for transmission to the computer or terminal. Baud rates, bits per character, parity mode, and number of stop and start bits are typically selectable by control signals or jumper leads.

transcribe—To copy, with or without translating, between storage media or between computers and storage media.

transcriber—The equipment ased for translating data recorded in one format to another format, and recording this data for later used elsewhere.

transducer—A device which converts one form of energy into another form. The energy may be electrical, mechanical, acoustical, thermal, etc.

transfer—1. To jump or cause to jump. 2. To transmit or copy information from one device to another.

transfer check—1. A check to determine if a transfer or jump operation was successfully completed. 2. A verification of data by temporarily storing, retransmitting, and comparing. The transfer check can be implemented by comparing each character with a copy of the same character transferred at a different time or by another route.

transfer circuit—A circuit which connects two or more communications networks to transfer the traffic between the networks.

transfer command—An instruction which changes control from one part of the program to another by indicating a remote instruction.

transfer function—The expression relating the output of a control system to its input.

transfer table—A table that contains a list of all transfer instructions of programs in main memory. The transfer table allows the transfer of control between programs.

transfer time—The time required to complete a transfer operation in a computer.

transform—To change the form of data according to specific procedure, usually leaving some feature of the data invariant. The structure or composition may be changed, but the meaning or value is not significantly altered.

transformer—An inductive electrical device which uses electromagnetic energy to transform voltage and current levels in a circuit.

transient—A sudden pulse in a signal; it is usually of extremely short duration and may be difficult to detect, but often it causes problems because it may be read by the system as a signal element. High-voltage transients can be destructive to unprotected components in a system.

transient analyzer—A device used for the study and observation of transient electrical phenomena in circuits and systems.

transient distortion—A distortion due to the inability of a system to reproduce transients linearly.

transient response—The fidelity with which a circuit responds to step voltages, pulses, or waveforms with extremely fast rise times.

transition card—A card used to signal the computer that the reading in of a program has ended and the execution of a program has begun.

transistor—A usually three-terminal active solid-state device which can be used for amplification and switching. Some two-terminal transistors have no input lead and are controlled by incident light.

transistor action—Refers to the physical mechanism of amplification in a transistor.

transistor amplifier—An amplifier that uses one or more transistors.

transistor and diode automatic test system—A computer-operated system for the testing of transistors and other semiconductor devices, including diodes, SCRs, and FETs.

transistor flip-flop—A flip-flop consisting of two cross-connected transistors.

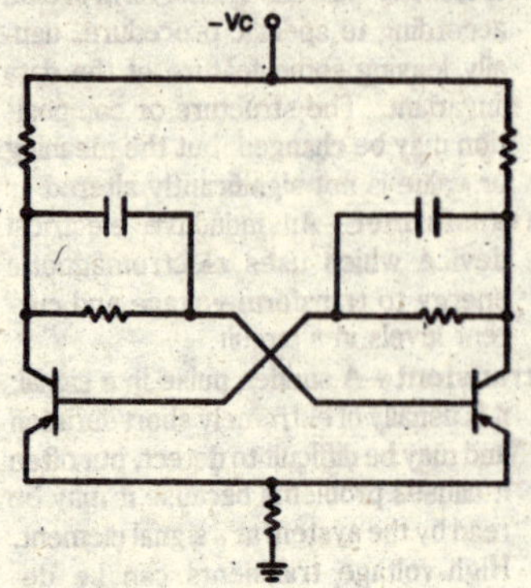

Transistor Flip-Flop

transistorized—Fabricated using transistors for active signal processing functions.

transistor logic—Circuits that use transistors with other components for performing logic functions.

transistor oscillator—An oscillator that uses at least one transistor to produce its output signal.

transistor seconds—Transistors in a production run that do not meet the primary manufacturing specifications, but which are functioning units suitable for less rigorous applications than specified.

transistor-transistor logic—A common logic family (abbreviated *TTL*) that uses integrated-circuit transistors in simple gate configurations. Also called *bipolar logic*.

translate—To change information from one form of representation to another without significantly affecting the meaning of the data. A translation may convert a source language program in FORTRAN or COBOL to a target program in machine language.

translator—1. A device or program which converts programs or data from one form to another. Translators include code converters, assemblers, compilers, and interpreters. Translators allow the user to express data or write programs using codes or languages that are convenient to humans. 2. An automatic radio relay station (repeater) that receives an entire frequency band and retransmits it in another frequency range.

translating program—A program designed to convert programs or data from one form to another.

transliterate—To convert the characters of one alphabet to the corresponding characters of another alphabet.

transmission—1. The sending or conveying of electrical energy or data along a path between locations of recipients. Transmission methods and systems include telemetering, telephony, broadcasting, facsimile, and television. 2. A message conveyed by wire or radio.

transmission preprocessor—A unit designed to remove a part of the processing overhead from the central processor in a system. A typical preprocessor handles protocol modes and performs block checks for redundancy.

transmission system—The collection of elements that are capable of functioning together for the transmission of signals and information.

transmit—To send signals or data from one location to another.

transmit data register—A register (abbreviated *TDR*) used in ACIA transmission systems to hold data ready to be transmitted out.

transmitter—The equipment used to generate and amplify carrier signals for the transmission of information.

transmitter card—A card which converts parallel digital data into asynchronous serial data in ASCII format. It contains a transmitter module, a clock module, and conditioning circuitry.

transmitter-distributor—A device used in a teletypewriter terminal to make and break the transmission line in timed sequence.

transmitter holding register—A register used to hold parallel transmitted data transferred from the data access lines by a write operation.

transmitter - receiver serial/parallel module—A unit used to convert (1) parallel data for serial transmission and (2) received serial data into a parallel format.

transmitter register—A register used to serialize data for the transmitted data output section. It may accept data from a holding register or the SYN register.

transponder—A type of transmitter-receiver which transmits signals automatically when it detects correct interrogation code.

transponder efficiency—For a given deployed transponder, the ratio of the number of replies to the number of interrogations.

transposition—An interchange of the positions of the conductors of a circuit, the characters in a printed word, or the data in a stream or block.

trap—1. A form of a conditional breakpoint activated by hardware or operating conditions. Traps are usually set by unexpected or unpredictable occurrences which cause an automatic transfer of control or jump to a known location. 2. A device to selectively filter a single frequency or a small frequency band.

trapped instruction—An instruction which is executed by a software routine when the hardware is unavailable.

trapping—A feature in which an unscheduled jump is made to a predetermined location in response to a machine condition. Trapping is used by monitor routines to provide automatic checking.

trapping mode—A method used for program diagnostic procedures. If the trapping mode flip-flop is set and the program includes a certain instruction of a set, the instruction is not performed, but the next instruction is taken from a specified location.

trap setting—Establishment of conditions to control interrupt signals when using trapping methods.

tree structure—A pyramid system such as a file or data addressing structure that selects an element by fan-in cascading, or all the members of a set by fan out cascading.

triac—A thyristor equivalent to a solid-state three-terminal AC relay; it is the structural equivalent to reverse-parallel connected SCRs, and can be gated by signals of either polarity.

triad—A group of three bits or three pulses, usually in sequence on one wire or simultaneously on three wires.

trigger—1. To start a circuit action. 2. The pulse used to start a circuit action. 3. The electrode on which a start pulse is applied. 4. The circuit which initiates an action as a result of a signal change, as a Schmitt trigger.

triggering—The starting of a circuit action which usually continues for a predetermined time under circuit control.

triggering circuits—The circuits used for triggering flip-flops or registers in a system.

trigger pair—A circuit which has two stable states and requires a trigger to cause a transition from one state to the other.

trigistor—A bistable pnpn semiconductor which acts as an R-S-T flip-flop, or bistable multivibrator.

trinistor—A three-terminal semiconductor device which operates like a thyratron for controlling large amounts of power.

triple diffusion—A semiconductor process in which three inpurity depositions are prepared on the substrate.

tripler—A circuit or device that multiplies an input frequency or voltage by three.

TROLL—A language for the implementation and testing of models using systems of linear and nonlinear equations. Capabilities include:

(1) Continuous simulation
(2) Regression methods
(3) Statistical analysis
(4) Vector transformations

trouble-location problem—A test problem which supplies information on the location of a fault. It is usually applied after a check problem has been used to show that a fault exists.

troubleshoot—To search for the cause of a failure for the purpose of isolating the responsible stage or device and correcting the problem.

truncate—1. To terminate a computational process in accordance with some procedure or rule. 2. To intentionally drop digits of a word or series. For example, 3.141 592 653 may be truncated to 3.1415, but 3.1416 would be the rounded-off value.

truncation—1. The ending of a computational procedure according to a specified rule. 2. The rejection of the final digits in a number, reducing precision.

truncation error—The error resulting from a truncation operation.

trunk—A single message circuit or a communications channel between two points or stations.

truth table—A table that describes a logic device or function by listing all possible logic-state combinations with the appropriate output values.

truth table generator—A technique that uses a microprocessor to develop the truth table from a diagnostic written in the microprocessor machine code or assembly language.

TSO—Abbreviation for *time-sharing option*.

TSO command language—The set of commands, subcommands, and operands recognized under the time-sharing option for a machine.

T-test—A comparison test of two units of quantitative data for the determination of which is greater.

TTL—Abbreviation for *transistor-transistor-logic*, a bipolar integrated-circuit logic that uses transistors with multiple emitters. The multiemitter transistors are easy to fabricate, requiring only a single isolated collector region upon which a single base region and then the several emitter regions are diffused. Operation is simple, but complex configurations require a lot of components or chip area with high power dissipation in comparison to other logic types. Noise immunity can also be a problem in some applications.

TTL character generator—A device which furnishes the correct drive to character displays from a coded set of inputs.

TTL compatibility—The capability of being directly interfaced with TTL circuits.

TTL parallel data controller—A unit (abbreviated *PDC*) which provides a flexible programmable interface between peripherals and the microcomputer. A typical PDC includes full handshaking under CPU control, and a direct memory-access function for data rates to 256,000 bps, along with four interrupt inputs.

TTTL—A modified TTL configuration in which a third transistor is added to the output of the TTL gate to increase drive and improve noise immunity.

TTY—Abbreviation for *teletypewriter*.

TTY controller—A unit that provides the 20 mA loop transfer currents, and the control between low- and medium-speed serial devices such as teletypewriters, CRT terminals, and microcomputers. Typical transmit and receive speeds range from 110 to 2400 baud.

Turing machine—A mathematical model of a machine that changes its internal state and reads from, writes on, and moves an infinite tape, providing a computer-like model. The behavior of the machine is specified by listing an alphabet of symbols for the control of tape motion and read-write operations.

turnkey system—A dedicated computer system whose hardware and software have been fully debugged before installation. The user's responsibility is then reduced to the task of learning the essential operational instructions only.

turnaround time—The total time between the submission of a job to a data processing facility and the return of the results.

tutorial light—An indicator which is used on a terminal to show the transaction history or provide indications of keyboard action.

twin check—A continuous computer check which uses a duplication of hardware and a comparison of results.

twelve-punch—A punch in the top row of a Hollerith punched card. Also called a *Y-punch*.

two-address—An instruction format that includes an operation and specifies the location of two registers, one for the operand and the other for the result of the operation.

two-chip microprocessor—A microprocessor whose complete architecture is developed using only two integrated-circuit chips.

two-level subroutine—A subroutine which contains another subroutine within its own structure.

two-out-of-five code—A positional notation in which decimal digits are represented by five binary digits are represented by five binary digits of which two are one kind (zeros or ones) and the others are another kind.

two-plus-one address—An instruction that contains two operand addresses and one control address.

twos' complement—The radix complement in binary notation. All positive numbers are the same as in standard binary, while negative numbers are the reverse of the negative standard binary number plus one.

two-valued variable—A variable which assumes values in a set of two elements, usually symbolized as one or zero. Also called *binary variable* or *two-state variable*.

TWX—Abbreviation for *teletypewriter exchange service*, a subscriber service for teletypewriter interconnections with communication rates of up to 100 words per minute.

U

UART—Acronym for ***universal asynchronous transmitter-receiver***, a device used to interface a parallel controller or data terminal to a bit-serial communications network. An asynchronous terminal can be connected to a UART which converts the parallel data inputs into a serial stream for communications, or converts received serial data input into parallel format. A typical UART is a single-chip MOS LSI device. It will transmit or receive words of 5, 6, 7 or 8 bits.

Options allow the generation and checking of odd or even parity, which is automatically added to the word for transmission. UARTs use double buffering, which allows one character to be read from a buffer as a shift register receives another. The UART has separate clock input pins for the receiver and transmitter sections so that receiving rates can be different from transmitting rates. This allows different rates to be used between terminals than from terminals to a microcomputer.

The receiver in the UART has priority on simultaneous interrupts. A typical communications section furnishes a 20 mA current loop interface for devices such as a TTY tape reader.

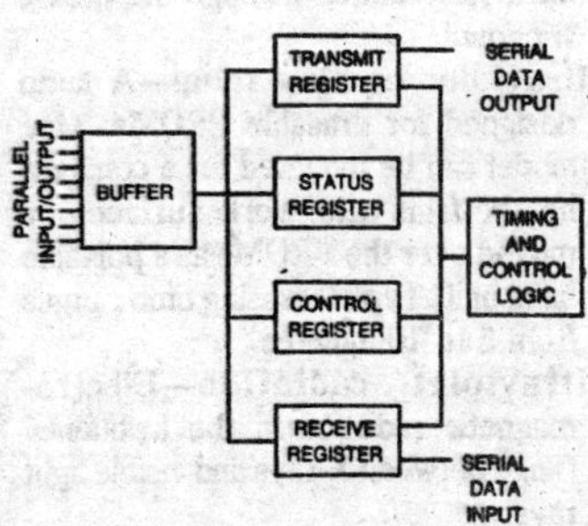

UART

UART simulator—A program which simulates UART operation in the microcomputer system. The UART has a complexity comparable to a 4-bit microprocessor and its functions can be transformed for execution in to an 8-bit microcomputer. The program passes characters to the UART simulator as if it were a hardware device.

U-contact—A type of contact and connector system that pierces the insulation of the conductors and compresses them in a firm connector grip.

UHF—Abbreviation for *ultrahigh frequency*, the range of frequencies from 300 to 3000 MHz.

ultrafiche—A sheet of film containing images or frames which have been reduced more than 100 times by photographic means.

ultrastrip—A film, usually 1.5 inches by 7 inches, containing images or frames which have been reduced 150 times by photographic methods.

ultraviolet—Electromagnetic radiation with frequencies higher than visible light and with wavelengths from about 200 to 4000 angstroms.

ultraviolet erasable PROM—A type of PROM that can be erased by concentrated ultraviolet light. The device package has a quartz top that is transparent to ultraviolet light. Unwanted bit patterns are erased by directing an ultraviolet source through the quartz window.

ultraviolet erasing lamp—A lamp designed for erasable PROMs. One model can be mounted for a constant height from the work surface, or moved over the PROMs as a portable hand unit. Typical erasing time ranges from 5 to 10 minutes.

ultraviolet radiation—Electromagnetic radiation in the frequency range between X-rays and visible light rays.

umbilical cord—A cable for interconnecting an equipment with a "mother" system which contains vital functions for system operation; because of this, it may be given special requirements or precautions.

unallowable digit—A character or digit combination that is not accepted as a valid representation by the program or computer.

unary operator—An arithmetic operator having only one term, such as the negation operator.

unary operation—An operation on one operand, such as negation.

unbundling—The separate pricing of software items from total equipment costs.

uncommitted storage list—A list of blocks of storage that are not allocated for any particular use.

unconditional branch—An instruction which switches the sequence of control to a specified location. Also called *unconditional jump* and *unconditional transfer of control.*

unconditional control transfer—An instruction which always causes a jump.

unconditional jump—An instruction which interrupts the normal process of obtaining instructions in ordered sequence and specifies the address from which the next instruction is taken.

unconditional transfer of control—An instruction which causes the instruction following it to be taken from an address that becomes the first one of a new sequence. Also called *unconditional branch* and *unconditional jump.*

uncorrectable error—An error where the intent of the programmer cannot be determined. The CPU usually rejects the statement and continues processing.

underdamped—Descriptive of a circuit in which the value of resistance is lower than the *critical resistance* and the response is oscillatory or the output level momentarily exceeds the input level.

underflow—A condition which occurs when a machine computation yields a result that is smaller than the smallest possible quantity capable of being stored.

undermodulation—In an AM system, a modulation percentage substantially below 100%. In an FM system, modulation insufficient to permit full carrier deviation to channel limits on amplitude peaks.

unichassis—A memory chassis designed for mounting memory and control cards in a rack panel.

unidirectional—Characterized by operation in one principal polarity or direction.

unidirectional bus—A bus over which signals are permitted to pass in one direction only.

unijunction transistor—A three-terminal semiconductor that exhibits stable negative-resistance characteristics. It is used in relaxation oscillators and trigger circuits.

union—A logical operator having the property: if P and Q are statements, then the union of P and Q is true if either P or Q is true; it is false if both P and Q are false.

unipolar—Refers to devices and signals having only one pole.

unipolar transistor—Obsolete term for *field-effect transistor*.

unit—1. A portion or subassembly of a system, usually one piece, which provides the means of accomplishing a specific operation or function. 2. The standard qualitative element by which a quantity is measured; for example, the ohm is the internationally accepted unit for measuring resistance, impedance, and reactance. 3. A whole, as *one*. 4. A digit in the least significant position of a whole number.

uniterm—A word, symbol, or number used as a descriptor for the retrieval of information from a collection, especially from one using a coordinate indexing system.

uniterm indexing—An indexing system that uses uniterm descriptors.

uniterm system—A data recording system which is based on classifying keywords in a coordinate indexing array.

uniterming—The selecting of words or parts of words that are considered descriptive of the contents of an item. The selected words or phrases are then included in a uniterm index.

unit record—A card containing a complete record.

unit record equipment—Typically, punched-card equipment such as collators and tabulating machines.

unit separator—The information separator (abbreviated *US*) intended to identify a boundary between units of information.

unit string—A string with only one entity.

unity—Contained as one.

unity-gain—Exhibiting a voltage amplification of 1 or less, as applied to follower circuits.

universal asynchronous receiver-transmitter—See *UART*.

universal PROM programmer—A device which allows users to program and verify PROMs using commands from the system console. The PROMs are programmed by plugging personality cards into the programmer card sockets.

universal synchronous-asynchronous transmitter-receiver—A chip (abbreviated *USART*) designed as a peripheral device for data communications. It is programmed by the PCU to operate in a desired serial data mode. The chip accepts data from the CPU in parallel and converts the data into a continuous serial stream for transmission. It also converts received serial data into parallel format for the PCU. The USART signals the CPU when it can accept new characters for transmission, or when it has new data for the CPU. The CPU can check the status of the USART at any time period. The USART may operate in the synchronous or asynchronous mode.

universal synchronous receiver-transmitter—A single-chip LSI device (abbreviated *USRT*) that provides serial-to-parallel and parallel-to-serial conversion to interface a parallel controller or terminal with a serial synchronous communication

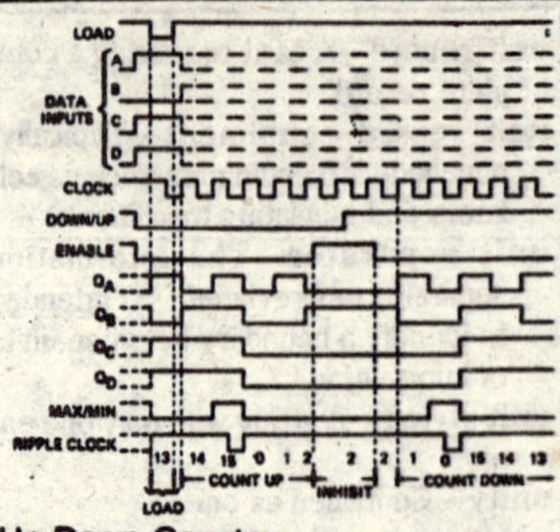

Up-Down Counter

network. The device consists of separate receiver and transmitter sections with independent clocks, status, and data lines. The transmitter and receiver have common word lengths and parity modes. Data is transmitted and received at a rate equal to the clock frequency. Data messages are transmitted in a data stream which is bit-synchronous with the clock and character-synchronous with respect to framing or sync characters which start and stop each message. The receiver compares the contents of the sync register with the incoming data, and when a match is made, the receiver becomes character-synchronous using a 5-, 6-, 7-, or 8-bit character.

universal Turing machine—A Turing machine that can simulate any other Turing machine.

unpack—To separate or decompose combined items or packed information into a sequence of items, words, or elements.

unwind—To code in full all the operations of a cycle in order to eliminate red-tape operations in the final coding. Unwinding is performed during assembly, generation, or compilation of programs.

update—1. To put into a master file changes required by current transactions. 2. To modify an instruction so that the address numbers it contains are increased by a desired amount each time the instruction is performed.

up-down counter—A binary counting unit that can change its counting mode from up to down or vice versa without disturbing the count stored up to that time.

up-down counter module—A module used to provide event counting for the microcomputer system. The module is capable of detecting count overflows and setting up flags for this condition. Count parameters are fully programmable along with reset conditions.

upward reference—A reference made in an overlay system from one segment to another segment higher in the same path which is closer to the root segment.

US—Abbreviation for ***unit separator.***

USART—Abbreviation for ***universal synchronous-asynchronous transmitter-receiver.***

USASCII—See *ASCII.*

user—Anyone who requires the use of services or products from a computing system or facility.

USRT—Abbreviation for ***universal synchronous receiver–transmitter.***

utility—A utility routine or program.

utility debug—A design-aid program for the testing and debugging of utility functions. The utility debug may allow memory and register changing, punching and loading of paper tapes, selecting breakpoints, and searching memory.

utility program—A program designed for such functions as changing or extending indexing structures or similar operations.

utility routine—A routine used to assist in the operation of the computer. Utility routines may include conversions, sorting, printout operations, tracing, mathematical functions, read and write for all peripherals, and text generation for Teletypes, CRTs, or other terminal devices. The utility routines may involve a large package for a variety of operations, but only those required for the application need to be loaded into memory.

V

VAB—Abbreviation for *voice answer-back*, an audio response unit which can link a computer system to a telephone network and provide voice responses to inquiries made from telephone terminals. The audio response is composed from a vocabulary prerecorded on a disk storage device.

valid—Legitimate; permissible; operationally acceptable.

validity—Correctness; especially the degree of closeness by which iterated results approach the correct result.

validity check—A check based on limits related to a specific problem; for example, in a validity check, a computed time of day would be rejected if greater than 24 hours.

validity checking—A screening procedure in which data records are checked for range, valid coding, illogical bit combinations or storage addresses, and similar factors.

valid memory address—An output line that indicates to peripheral devices that there is a valid address on the address bus.

variable—A quantity that can assume any of the numbers of some set of numbers, or a condition, transaction, or event which changes or may be changed as a result of processing data.

variable address—An address that is to be modified by an index register or similar device. Also called *indexed address*.

variable connector—1. The collective instructions that cause a logical chain to take one of several paths. 2. The device inserting such instructions. 3. A flow chart symbol representing a connection that is not fixed, but which can be varied by the program or procedure.

variable-cycle operation—Computer action in which any cycle or operation may be of a different time length. Variable-cycle operation is characteristic of asynchronous machines.

variable field—A field in which the vectors at any point can change during the time under consideration.

variable field length—A data field that can have a varying number of characters from record to record.

variable length record—A file that contains records that are not uniform in length.

variable master clock—A clock that provides frequencies from 100 kHz to 1 MHz for evaluation of microcomputer system components.

variable-point representation—A positional notation in which the position of the radix point is indicated by a character at that position.

variable-resistance transducer—A transducer that produces an electrical analog of the resistance value of its input device.

variable symbol—1. A symbol used in assembly programming that does not have to be declared since it is assigned a read-only value. 2. A symbol used to denote a variable quantity.

variable word length—Descriptive of a computer in which the number of characters addressed is not a fixed number but is varied by the data or instruction.

varistor—A silicon, carbon, or selenium device used for surge suppression or contact protection. Its resistance is a function of the applied voltage.

VDT—Abbreviation for *visual display terminal.*

vector—1. A symbol for a directed quantity. 2. A quantity that has direction, magnitude, and sense and which can be expressed graphically as a line segment referred to other coordinate line segments.

vectored priority interrupt—An interrupt that automatically determines priority.

vector instruction—An instruction that can accept an interrupt and branch to the correct routine or device.

vector quantity—A quantity with magnitude, sense, and direction.

vector transfer table—A transfer table used to communicate between two or more programs. The transfer vector provides the communication linkage between the programs.

Veitch diagram—A graphical technique used for the solution of problems arising in digital circuit design.

Venn diagram—A diagram in which each region represents an individual parameter. Sets are represented by the overlapping of regions. Basic logic relations, operations, and propositions are illustrated and defined by the inclusion, exclusion, and intersection of the regions.

C = A AND B

C = A AND NOT B

C = NOT A AND B

Venn Diagrams

verification—The process of checking the results of one data transcription against those of another.

verification mode—A mode of operation in time-sharing systems in which all edit subcommands are acknowledged and text changes are displayed as they are made.

verifier—A device on which a record or data can be compared or tested for identity, character by character, with a retranscription of copy as it is being prepared.

verify—To make a certain determination that a computer operation has been accomplished accurately.

vertical parity check—A check in which the binary digits of a character column are added and the sum is checked against a previously computed parity digit to test whether the number of ones is odd or even.

vertical tabulation character—A format effector (abbreviated *VT*) which causes the printing or display position to be moved up or down a predetermined number of lines.

vestigial sideband—The incomplete suppression of one sideband in an AM system to reduce the total signal bandwidth without degradation of information content.

vf band—Abbreviation for *voice-frequency* band, that frequency range between 600 and 3000 Hz that is adequate for transmission of speech with good intelligibility.

V format—A data record format with records of variable length. Each record begins with a record length indicator.

VHF—Abbreviation for *very high frequency*. The range of frequencies from 30 to 300 MHz.

vibrator—Multivibrator.

virtual—Conceptual rather than actual, but possessing the essential characteristics of a real function.

virtual address—A symbol or word that can be used as a valid address part, but does not necessarily refer to an actual memory location.

virtual address space—In a virtual storage system, the storage area assigned to a job, user, or task.

virtual circuit—A circuit or function that is established in a computer operation.

virtual image—The apparent spatial position of a reflection in a mirror.

virtual radiator—In an antenna system consisting of a quarter-wave vertical radiator over a ground plane, the label applied to the virtual image of the vertical element as "reflected" by the ground plane in the analysis of the antenna's propagation or radiation characteristics.

virtual machine—A system that uses multiple copies of another computer's hardware and software to create a machine environment which can be used to test software and hardware designs. The virtual machine allows a large memory capacity through the use of virtual memory, and provides simplified software and improved development reliability. The technique maps the memory plus the instructions; when instructions are executed, the machine traps and implements them directly.

virtual memory—A memory technique which transfers information one page at a time between primary and secondary memory, and adds only the page-swapping time to the operating time. The technique allows the programmer to address storage without regard to whether primary or secondary storage is being addressed. The technique has been used in large system development programs where an executive system allows the programmer to write programs as if memory capacity were unlimited. The executive keeps the programs on disks and out of use until required. Each disk is loaded into the system when called for by the program.

virtual memory pointer—A pointer used to keep track of the parts of programs and data that is scattered between main memory and auxiliary storage in a virtual memory system. The pointer system is usually transparent to the user.

virtual memory technique—A memory system (abbreviated *VMT*) which operates as if all instructions and data were on main memory when they may be actually segmented between main memory and secondary storage. The virtual memory technique locates the instruction and operands, and if not in main storage, transfers them from secondary storage sites which act as the virtual memory sites. The system permits a program to be larger than main memory, and with the use of a pointer arrangement, software can be much less that other types of segmentation systems.

virtual storage system—See *virtual memory*.

virtual terminal network—A network which allows the user to select the type of terminal to be used at each location independently. A user computer supporting the network has the capability to handle a wide range of terminal types without additional software.

visual display—A unit which can display characters of information, such as tables, graphs, charts, or the lines and curves of drawings as a series of connected points. Computer console displays may indicate the next instruction, parity, the contents of any memory location, or the status of interrupts in the system.

visual display interface—The circuitry required to connect the results of a measurement or computation to a display device for observing and recording.

visual display terminal—A device (abbreviated *VDT*) which permits inputs to a computer system through a keyboard or other manual input device such as a light pen, and whose primary output is visual through a CRT unit or other type of display. The terminals allow keyboarding, verification, editing, correction, and reformatting of material. They may be user programmable using parameter designations or data entry languages.

visual display station—An input/output unit which allows the interrogation of a CPU using a CRT or similar display.

visual terminal—A unit which allows the interrogation of a processor along with the input of data using a visual display technology. Visual terminals use cathode-ray tubes, magneto-optics, light-emitting diodes, and gas-discharge displays.

VMOS—A MOS transistor technology in which devices are formed using a vertical structure which permits high power dissipation capability.

VMT—Abbreviation for *virtual memory technique*.

vocoder—Voice encoder.

voice answer-back—See *VAB*.

voice channel—A circuit of sufficient bandwidth to allow a data transfer of 2400 bits per second.

voice grade—A classification for a communication line used in normal telephone service that is capable of handling speech data without significant degradation of signal regardless of path length.

voice-operated device—A device which allows the presence of an audio signal to actuate a desired operation or function. Also called *VOX box*.

volatile storage—A storage medium in which stored data is lost when power is removed.

volatile dynamic storage—A type of dynamic storage which depends upon the supply of power along with refresh circuitry to maintain stored information. Without such circuitry, stored data would be lost with the removal of power.

volt—The international unit of electromotive force (abbreviated *V*), equal to the product of current and resistance.

voltage comparator—A device which can compare two voltages and issues an output that is a function of the comparison.

voltage drop—The reduction of voltage along a conductor or through a device as a result of the conductor's (or device's) resistance.

voltage gain—The ratio of the output to input voltage in a circuit or device.

voltage regulation—A measure of the degree in which a power source maintains a stable output under varying load conditions, usually expressed as a percentage.

voltage regulator—A circuit or device used in conjunction with a power supply to maintain a stable voltage under different load and environmental conditions.

voltage regulator diode—A diode which is used as a stable reference source in a voltage regulator application.

voltage-to-frequency converter—A device for changing an input voltage into a proportional frequency which can then be counted by a digital device or processor.

voltmeter—An instrument for measuring voltage (potential difference), usually in any of a number of voltage ranges.

voltohmmeter—A portable instrument for measuring voltage and resistance. Abbreviated *VOM*.

voltohmmilliammeter—A generally portable instrument for measuring voltage, subampere current levels, and resistance.

voluntary interrupt—An interrupt caused by an object program's deliberate use of a function known to cause an interrupt.

VOM—Abbreviation for *voltohmmeter* (or *voltohmmilliammeter*).

VOX—Abbreviation for *voice-operated device*.

VOX box—A modular voice-operated device for interconnection to a tape recorder, radio transmitter, etc.

VT—The vertical tabulation character.

VTAM—Abbreviation for *vortex telecommunications access method*, a software package designed to simplify the data communications programming required to serve remote user stations with a host computer.

W

W—Symbol for *watt*.

waiting list—A queue of unprocessed data or operational programs.

waiting state—The state of an interrupt level that is armed and has received an interrupt signal, but has not yet been allowed to become active.

wait time—The time interval during which a processing unit is waiting for information. This time interval may occur while information is being retrieved from a serial access file or located by a search.

warmup time—The time required for a device to reach a stable state after application of power.

waste instruction—An instruction which specifically instructs the processor to do nothing but process the next instruction in sequence. Also called a *blank, skip,* or NO-OP.

WATS—Acronym for *wide-area telephone service*, a telephone-subscriber service which permits a customer to make calls to other telephones in distant zones on a flat-fee rather than a toll-call basis.

watt—The international unit of electric power (abbreviated *W*), equal to the product of voltage and current in DC circuits.

wave—1. A single cycle of a periodic propagated disturbance such as a radio wave, a sound wave, or a carrier wave for transmitting data signals. 2. A graphic representation of a recurring cyclic signal; a waveform.

wave analyzer—An instrument used to measure the amplitude and frequencies of the components of an electrical wave.

wave band—The band of frequencies assigned to a particular function or application.

waveform—The graphic representation of the shape of a wave, showing the variations in amplitude with time.

waveform analyzer—An instrument which measures or displays the components in an electrical waveform, usually with a variable-timebase capability.

waveform generator—A circuit used to produce a desired waveform in a system.

wavelength—1. The distance between two similar and successive points on a periodic wave. 2. The approximate length in meters (abbreviated λ) of any signal wave within a given band, used to express the approximate range of frequencies represented. The 6-meter band, for example, refers to frequencies between 50 and 54 MHz.

The formula for wavelength is $\lambda = c/f$ where c is the propagation speed of the wave (300 million meters per second) and f is the frequency of the wave in hertz.

waveshape—The graphic representation of one cycle of a wave, usually referenced against time. Principal waveshapes are sine, triangle, and square.

wearout failure—A failure that is due to normal deterioration or mechanical wear, the probability of which increases with use.

weighted average—An average adjusted to give a different significance to each item according to its importance to the problem being studied.

white noise—Noise which has equal energy at all frequencies, as opposed to *pink noise*, which has equal energies within a specified band and very little energy elsewhere.

wire printer—A high-speed printer that uses a character-like configuration of wire fingers from a matrix of wire ends, rather than from a selection of type faces.

wired-AND—The stringing together of a number of circuits or functions such that when all circuits are at a logic 1, a desired connection point is a logic 1.

wired-OR—The connecting of separate circuits or functions such that the combination represents an OR function or operation. The point at which the separate circuits are wired together will be a 1 if any of the wired-together circuits are a 1.

wired-program computer—A computer in which a majority of the instructions are determined by the placement of interconnecting patchcords or pins using a device such as a plug or patchboard. If the wires are permanently soldered, the computer is a *fixed-program machine*.

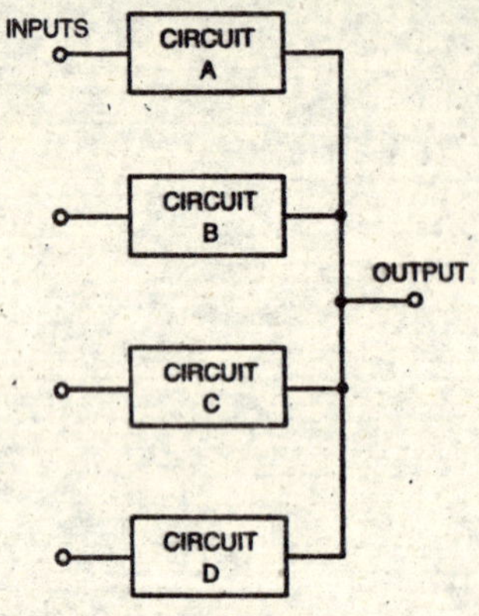

Wired-OR

wirewrap—An alternative to soldering connections in which a number of turns of a stripped solid conductor are wrapped around a metal post by special tools. With the proper technique, a good metal-to-metal contact results with enough corrosion resistance, mechanical stability, and conductivity to be used in military equipment. Wirewrap offers ease of design, freedom of layout, ease of design change, and good densities for logic designs.

wirewrap board—A board which allows users to adapt portions of a microcomputer system for special applications or changes during the development process.

wirewrap module—A module designed to fit into a microcomputer system that has wirewrap pins along with IC sockets for easy circuit modifications.

wirewrapped panel—A panel designed to accommodate a random-access memory system along with the read-only memory and microprocessor required for a microcomputer system. A typical panel has 200 to 300 input or output pins for wirewrap connections.

wirewrapped socket board—A board containing sockets and wirewrap pins for maximum flexibility of design of the microcomputer system. The sockets will accept components with 14 to 40 pins.

wirewrapping—The process in which a solid conductor is wrapped, using a special tool, around a metal post.

wirewrap tool—The hand or power tool used to accomplish prototype or production wirewrapping. Tools are available with electrical AC power, battery power, or air power.

wiring diagram—A circuit diagram which indicates the physical layout of equipment and the point-to-point distribution and interconnection of conductors.

wiring pencil—A prototype aid which contains a replaceable spool or wire and a pencil-like tip to guide and cut the wire. The wire is wrapped around the terminal and cut. Heat from a soldering iron melts the insulation and completes the connection as the solder bond is made.

word—1. An ordered set of characters which occupies one storage location and is treated as a unit. Usually a word is treated by the control unit as an instruction, and by the arithmetic unit as a quantity. Words lengths may be fixed or variable, depending on the system configuration. 2. A byte containing as many bits as the word-length capacity of the machine permits.

word address format—The order of appearance of the character information within a word.

word count—The number of words in a record or other data item.

word counter—A register that holds the transfer word count during block transfer operations. See also *word count register*.

word count register—A register used to keep track of input/output transfers. In a typical application, the word count register is loaded at the start of an operation with the number of data words to be transferred and then decremented after each transfer. When the register reaches zero, it signals the completion of the operation by generating an interrupt.

word generator—A circuit or device for providing words and sequences for testing and checkout. Many units are interactive and respond to levels or pulses from the device under test. Some word generators can perform program loops, generate serial or parallel data, generate data from selected locations in memory, and

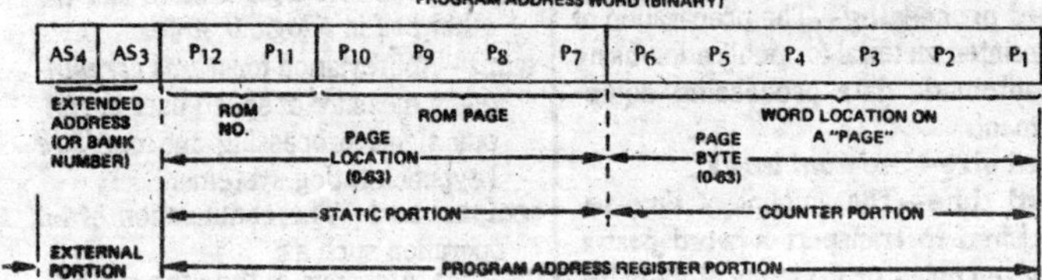

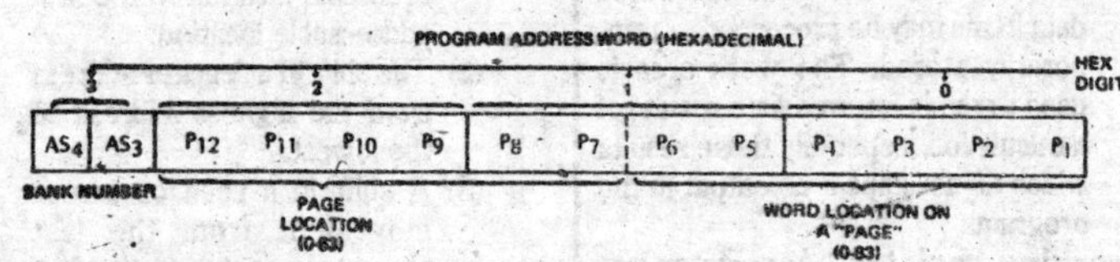

Word Address Format

generate data continuously or in single words.

A word generator can be used to test logic states in a system. With the generator supplying the desired signals, operation of the circuit or system is checked using an oscilloscope or logic state analyzer. It may also be used to test serial devices such as shift registers, disk memories, and terminal hardware.

word index—An index based on the selection of words as used in a document, without consideration to synonyms or generic concepts related to the term selected.

word length—A measure of the size of a word specified in characters or bits. Longer word lengths in a microcomputer system increase efficiency and accuracy but add to the system complexity and cost. For greater precision and memory access, multiple-word operands and instructions are used, although they increase execution time and complexity. In a fixed-point arithmetic system, a double-length word is stored in two registers.

word mark—An indicator used to signal the beginning or end of a word.

word-organized storage—A type of magnetic storage in which each word of storage has a winding common to all the magnetic cells of the word.

word processing—The preparation of printed material for publication using automatic data processing equipment.

word size—See *word length*.

word time—The amount of time required to transport a word past a given point, or from one storage device to another.

work area—A section of storage where data items may be processed or temporarily stored. The work area is used to retain intermediate results of a calculation, especially those results which do not appear as output in the program.

working register—A register reserved for data on which operations are being performed. Working registers can be specified using fewer bits than working-storage memory locations, and execution time can be faster.

working storage—A portion of storage reserved for data upon which operations are being performed. Working storage can be used in a microcomputer as buffer storage or for storage of intermediate program data.

work output queue—A list of data which is output, but is stored temporarily in an auxiliary medium until a printer or other output device is available.

worst-case—Refers to an analysis or design which considers the worst possible combination of possible parameter variations.

worst-case circuit analysis—A type of circuit analysis in which the worst possible effects are determined due to all possible combinations of circuit parameters.

worst-case design—A conservative design approach in which the circuit is designed to function assuming the worst possible combination of operating characteristics.

worst-case noise pattern—The noise appearing in a magnetic storage system when half of the selected cores are in a logic 1 state and the other half in a logic 0 state.

wpm—Abbreviation for ***words per minute***, a measure of speed user in various signal processing and operator keypunch rating systems.

wraparound—The continuation of an operation such as:

(1) A change in the storage location from the maximum addressable location to the first addressable location

(2) The shift of a register address from the highest address to the lowest.

(3) A shift in a read or cursor movement from the last character position to the first position.

writeable control storage—A read-write memory used in the control portion of a system. The read-write memory, or RAM, replaces a ROM and gives the designer additional capability to change the characteristics of the microcomputer system.

writeable control store—The control portion of a read-write memory which allows the user to microcode a specialized instruction set for the system application. This technique is especially suited for some communications and signal processing applications where a few well designed algorithms are required.

write—To transfer, record, or copy, usually from one storage device to another. The information may be recorded in a register or any other storage location or medium.

write addressing—To direct or control a write operation in a device, as with a binary counter, in which the first location address contains all zeros and each successive address is incremented by one bit, such as:

FIRST WRITE ADDRESS	00000000
SECOND WRITE ADDRESS	00000001
THIRD WRITE ADDRESS	00000010

write head—Magnetic-tape recording head.

write-read—1. An operation in which a block of data is read in while simultaneously processing the previous block and writing out the results of that block. 2. Possessing the capability of both read and write operations.

WRU—The who-are-you character.

WS—Abbreviation for *working storage*, an area of storage designed to hold dynamic or working data. The working storage area provides a user area for semipermanent data storage.

W-shaped plugboard—A plugboard with a W cut that allows easier insertion than conventional plugboards.

X

x-axis—1. The horizontal axis, as on a CRT screen, graph, printer, or plotter. 2. The reference axis of a quartz crystal.

xerographic printer—A device for printing an optical image on paper in which light and dark areas are represented by electrostatically charged areas on the paper. A powdered ink is dusted on the paper which adheres to the charged areas and is melted into the paper by heat.

xerography—A dry copying process in which light is used to discharge an electrostatically charged plate, which is then dusted with a dielectric powder to make the image visible. Fixing is usually done by heat directly after the dusting.

Xerox—Trade name for a particular line of xerographic equipment.

X-punch—A punch in the X or 11 row of an 80-column card. The X-punch is used to control, select, or indicate a negative number. Also called an 11-punch.

x-y plotter—A device used to plot coordinate points in the form of a graph.

x-y recorder—A recorder that traces the relationship between two variables on a chart or graph. The chart or graph may move such that one of the variables becomes time-dependent.

x-y switch—A type of switch in which the wipers are moved first in one direction, then in the other.

Y

y-axis—The vertical axis, as on a CRT screen, graph, printer, or plotter.

Y-circuit—A star connected three-phase power circuit, so called because of its resemblance to the letter Y. Also called *wye circuit* and *delta circuit*.

yig—Acronym for *yttrium-iron-garnet*, a crystal used in tuning devices in microwave circuits.

yig device—A device using a yig crystal with a magnetic field for functional applications in wideband circuits. Yig devices include filters, discriminators, and multiplexers.

yig filter—A filter that uses a yig crystal in a magnetic field provided by an electromagnetic coil.

yig oscillator—A microwave oscillator that uses a yig filter in a tunnel-diode oscillator circuit.

yoke—1. A piece of ferromagnetic material which connects two cores or heads for reading or writing operations. 2. A coil assembly used to provide electromagnetic deflection in a CRT.

Y-punch—A punch in the Y or 12 row of an 80-column card. A Y-punch is used to indicate a positive number. Also called a *12-punch*.

Y signal—In color TV, a luminance primary transmission signal.

Z

z-axis—The longitudinal or optical axis of a quartz crystal slab; it is perpendicular to both the x and y axes.

zener—A semiconductor diode with a high ratio of reverse to forward resistance until breakdown occurs. The voltage drop after breakdown remains essentially constant and the current is limited mainly by the circuit in which the device is connected. The zener is commonly used as a voltage regulator, reference, and AC clipper.

zener breakdown—The avalanche of a semiconductor device due to field emission of charge carriers in the depletion layer.

zener diode—A diode that exhibits a sharp increase of reverse current at a certain negative potential, which is called the zener, or breakdown voltage.

zener diode coupling—A method of coupling circuits using zener diodes to provide a high degree of noise rejection.

zener diode regulator—A power or voltage regulator that uses one or more zener diodes as the basic regulating element.

zener effect—A reverse-current breakdown due to the presence of a high electric field at the junction of a semiconductor or insulator.

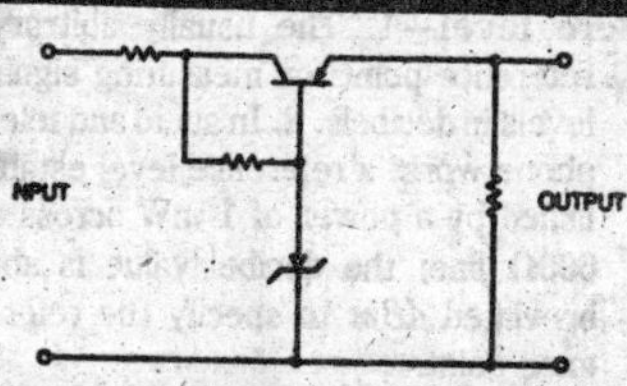

Zener Diode Regulator

zener voltage—The negative breakdown voltage of a zener diode, which remains essentially constant over a wide range of current values.

zero—1. A numeral denoting lack of magnitude. Some machines may have distinct representations for plus zero or minus zero. 2. The bit or state representing *false* or *off* in a two-state logic system.

zero access storage—A storage where waiting time is negligible and information is immediately available.

zero address instruction—An instruction consisting of an operation which does not require an address in the usual sense. For example:

SHIFT LEFT 0002

has in its address portion the amount of shift desired.

zero beat—The condition in which two signals, combined in a nonlinear element, are brought to the same frequency by nulling the element's output as a result of shifting the frequency of one of the two signals.

zero bit—A bit used in the program counter to indicate that the accumulator has been cleared.

zero compression—A method of data compression in which all nonsignificant leading zeros are eliminated.

zero fill—To fill in characters with the representation of zeros without changing the meaning or content.

zero level—1. The usually abitrary reference point for measuring signal levels in decibels. 2. In audio and telephone work, a reference level established by a power of 1 mW across a 600Ω line; the decibel value is abbreviated *dBm* to specify the reference point.

zero level address—An instruction address in which the address part of the instruction is the operand. Also called *immediate address*.

zero page addressing—A type of addressing which produces shorter code and execution times by fetching only the second byte of an instruction. Use of zero page addressing can result in a significant increase in code efficiency.

zero page addressing—A page-addressing method which uses only the second byte of an instruction and assumes a zero address byte. The technique is used in some systems with an index register in which the second byte is added to the contents of the register to produce an effective address.

zero suppression—The elimination of nonsignificant zeros, usually before printing or display.

zone—1. A portion of storage allocated for a particular purpose or function. 2. The top three of 12, 11, and 0 on certain punched cards. A second punch used with positions 1 to 9 can be used to represent alphabetic characters.

zone bit—1. A bit in a group of positions used to indicate a specific class of items. 2. A bit used as a key to a code.

zone digit—A digit used as a key to a section of code. Zone digits can be used independently of other markings for control significance in a system.

zone punch—A punch in the 11, 12, or 0 row of a punched card. Also called an *overpunch* when the card column already contains holes.